Study Guide for
BAUMOL AND BLINDER'S

ECONOMICS
PRINCIPLES AND POLICY

FIFTH EDITION

Study Guide for
BAUMOL AND BLINDER'S

ECONOMICS
PRINCIPLES AND POLICY

FIFTH EDITION

CRAIG SWAN
University of Minnesota

Harcourt Brace Jovanovich, Publishers
and its subsidiary, Academic Press

San Diego New York Chicago Austin
London Sydney Tokyo Toronto

ISBN: 0-15-518866-6

Library of Congress Catalog Number: 90-83733

Printed in the United States of America

Introduction

This study guide is designed to be used with *Economics: Principles and Policy*, Fifth Edition, by William J. Baumol and Alan S. Blinder. This guide is not a substitute for the basic textbook; rather, experience has shown that conscientious use of a supplement such as this guide can lead to greater learning and understanding of the course material. It might also improve your grade.

The chapters in this book parallel those in *Economics: Principles and Policy*, Fifth Edition. Each chapter here is a review of the material covered in the textbook chapters. You should first read and study each chapter in the textbook and then use the corresponding chapter in this book. "Use" is the correct verb, as chapters in this book are designed for your *active* participation.

The material with which you will be working is organized into the following elements.

LEARNING OBJECTIVES

Each chapter starts with a set of behavioral learning objectives. These indicate the things you should be able to do upon completing each chapter.

IMPORTANT TERMS AND CONCEPTS

As one of the learning objectives for each chapter states, you should be able to "define, understand, and use correctly" the terms and concepts that are listed in this section. They parallel the Concepts to Review listed at the end of the text chapter. Being able to *define* these terms is likely to be important for your grade. But to really *understand* what they mean, rather than to temporarily memorize their definition, is even better. The ultimate test of your understanding will be your ability to *use correctly* the terms and concepts in real-life situations.

CHAPTER REVIEW

Each review section has a summary discussion of the major points of each chapter. The reviews are designed to be used actively. Frequently, you will need to supply the appropriate missing term or to choose between pairs of alternative words. Some of the missing words are quite specific and can be found in the list of important terms and concepts. At other times, the answers are less clear-cut, as the following hypothetical example illustrates: "If people expect inflation at higher rates than before, nominal interest rates are

likely to _____." Any of the following would be correct answers: increase, rise, go up. In cases like this, do not get concerned if the answer you choose is different from the one in the back of the book.

DEFINITION QUIZ

Each chapter contains a definition quiz to help you review important terms and concepts. Match each term with the most appropriate definition.

BASIC EXERCISE

Most chapters have one or more exercises that are designed for you to use as a check on your understanding of a basic principle discussed in the chapter. Many of the exercises use simple arithmetic or geometry. While getting the correct answers is one measure of understanding, do not mistake the arithmetic manipulations for the economic content of the problems. A hand calculator may make the arithmetic less burdensome.

SELF-TEST FOR UNDERSTANDING

Each chapter has a set of multiple choice and true-false questions for you to use as a further check on your understanding. It is important to know not only what the correct answers are but also why other answers are wrong. Especially when considering the true-false questions, be sure you understand why the false statements are false. Answers for the Self-Tests are in the back of this guide and include page references back to the textbook to help you understand which choices are correct.

APPENDIX

Many of the chapters in the text contain an appendix, which generally is designed to supplement the chapter content with material that is either a bit more difficult or that offers further exposition of a particular economic concept. In some cases, the review material for the appendix parallels that for the chapter, including learning objectives, important terms and concepts, and so forth. In other cases, the appendix material is reviewed here in the form of an additional exercise designed to illustrate the principals discussed in the appendix.

SUPPLEMENTARY EXERCISE

Many chapters end with a supplementary exercise, which may be either an additional mathematical exercise or some suggestions that will allow you to use what you have learned in real-world situations. Some of the exercises use more advanced mathematics. Since many of these exercises review the material in the Basic Exercise, they illustrate how economists use mathematics and are included for those students with appropriate training. The most important thing is to understand the economic principles that underlie the Basic Exercise, something that does not depend upon advanced mathematics.

Being introduced to economics for the first time should be exciting and fun. For many of you, it is likely to be hard work, but hard work does not have to be dull and uninteresting. Do not look for a pat set of answers with universal applicability. Economics does not offer answers but rather a way of looking at the world and thinking systematically about issues. As the English economist John Maynard Keynes said:

The theory of economics does not furnish a body of settled conclusions immediately applicable to policy. It is a method rather than a doctrine, an apparatus of the mind, a technique of thinking, which helps its possessor to draw correct conclusions.

Bertrand Russell, the distinguished British philosopher and mathematician, had considered studying economics but decided it was too easy. The Nobel prize-winning physicist, Max Planck, also considered studying economics but decided it was too hard. Whether, like Russell, you find economics easy or, like Planck, you find it hard, I trust that with the use of this guide you will find it relevant and exciting!

The preparation of this guide would not have been possible without the help and contributions of others. I especially want to acknowledge the contributions of Peggy Berkowitz, Dr. Marianne Felton of Indiana University, Southeast, Sarah Knoblauch, Jack Stecher, my wife, Janet and my son, Andrew.

Craig Swan

Contents

Contents

PART

1

GETTING ACQUAINTED WITH ECONOMICS

1

What Is Economics?

LEARNING OBJECTIVES

After completing the material in this chapter you should be able to:

- define, understand, and use correctly the terms and concepts listed below.
- explain the role of abstraction, or simplification, in economic theory.
- explain the role of theory as a guide to understanding real-world phenomena.
- explain why imperfect information and value judgments will always mean that economics cannot provide definitive answers to all social problems.

IMPORTANT TERMS AND CONCEPTS

Voluntary exchange
Comparative advantage
Productivity
Externalities
Marginal analysis
Marginal costs
Abstraction and generalization
Theory
Correlation versus causation
Model
Opportunity Cost

CHAPTER REVIEW

Chapter 1 has two objectives: It introduces some of the types of problems economists concern themselves with, offering 12 important Ideas for Beyond the Final Exam; and it discusses the methods of economic analysis, in particular the role of theory in economics.

The problems discussed in the first part of the chapter have been chosen specifically to illustrate 12 basic economic issues to be remembered beyond the final exam. You should not only read this material now, but make sure to reexamine the list at the end of the course. Understanding the economic principles that underlie these 12 basic issues is the real final examination in economics as contrasted with the final examination for this course.

The methods of economic inquiry are perhaps best described as "eclectic," meaning that they are drawn from many sources and selected according to their usefulness to the subject matter. Economists borrow from all the social sciences in order to theorize about human behavior. They borrow from mathematics in order to express theories concisely. And, finally, they borrow from statistics in order to make inferences from real-world data about hypotheses suggested by economic theory.

Economists are interested in understanding human behavior not only for its own sake, but also because of the policy implications of this knowledge. How can we know what to expect from changes resulting from public policy or business decisions unless we understand why people behave the way they do? As an example of all this, consider the 12 ideas discussed in the first part of this chapter. Each idea derives from economic theory. As you will learn, each idea also offers important insights into actual historical experience and is an important guide to the evaluation of future changes.

As in other scientific disciplines, theory in economics is an abstraction, or simplification, of innumerable complex relationships in the real world. When thinking about some aspects of behavior, say a family's spending decisions or why the price of wheat fluctuates so much, economists will build a model that attempts to explain the behavior under examination. The elements of the model are derived from economic theory. Economists study the model to see what hypotheses, or predictions, are suggested by the model. These can then be checked against real-world data. An economist's model will typically be built not with hammer and nails, but with pencil, paper, and computers. The appropriate degree of abstraction for an economic model is, to a large extent, determined by the problem at hand and is not something that one can specify in advance for all problems.

Economists clearly believe that they can make a significant contribution to the discussion and resolution of many important social issues. It is hoped that by the time you finish this course you will agree with this belief. At the same time you should realize that the contribution of economics is that it offers a way of looking at questions rather than a comprehensive set of answers to all questions. Economists will always have

(1) differences of opinion when it comes to final policy recommendations because of incomplete _____ and different _____ judgments.

DEFINITION QUIZ

Choose the letter that is the most appropriate definition for each of the following terms.

1. _____ Voluntary exchange
2. _____ Comparative advantage
3. _____ Productivity
4. _____ Externalities
5. _____ Marginal analysis
6. _____ Marginal costs
7. _____ Abstraction
8. _____ Theory
9. _____ Correlation
10. _____ Model
11. _____ Opportunity cost

a. Additional cost incurred by a one unit increase in output.
b. Ability to produce a good less inefficiently than other goods.
c. Ignoring many details to focus on essential parts of a problem.
d. Situation in which the movements of two variables are linked, whether or not a causal relation exists.
e. Output produced by a unit of input.
f. Trade in which all parties are willing participants.
g. Evaluation of effects per unit.
h. Results of activities that affect others, without corresponding compensation.
i. Cost per unit produced.
j. Deliberate simplification of relationships to explain how those relationships work.
k. Value of what must be foregone to acquire an item.
l. Simplified version of some aspect of the economy.
m. Evaluation of the impact of changes.

SELF-TEST FOR UNDERSTANDING

Circle T or F for True or False as appropriate.

1. Economic models are no good unless they include all the detail that characterizes the real world.
T F

2. Material in this text will reveal to you the true answer to many important social problems.
T F

3. Opportunity cost is measured by considering the best alternative foregone.
T F

4. Economists' policy prescriptions will always differ because of incomplete information and different value judgments.
T F

5. Theory and practical policy have nothing to do with each other.
T F

6. If two variables are correlated, we can be certain that one causes the other.
T F

SUPPLEMENTARY EXERCISE

The following suggested readings offer an excellent introduction to the ideas and lives of economists past and present:

1. *The Worldly Philosophers*, Sixth Edition, by Robert L. Heilbroner, (Simon and Schuster/Touchstone Books), 1986.
2. In recent years the Banca Nazionale del Lavoro in Rome has been publishing a series of recollections and reflections by distinguished economists on their professional experience. If your college or university library receives the *Banca Nazionale del Lavoro Quarterly Review*, read what some of these authors have to say about their lives as economists. The December 1983 issue contains reflections by William J. Baumol.
3. *Lives of the Laureates: Seven Nobel Economists*, edited by William Breit and Roger W. Spencer (MIT Press), 1986. This is a collection of recollections by seven winners of the Nobel prize in Economics.

2

The Use and Misuse of Graphs

LEARNING OBJECTIVES

After completing the material in this chapter you should be able to:

- define, understand, and use correctly the terms and concepts listed below.
- interpret various graphs:
    use a two-variable graph to determine what combinations of variables go together.
    use a three-variable graph to determine what combinations of the X and Y variables are consistent with the same value for the Z variable.
    use a time series graph to determine how a variable of interest has changed over time.
- construct two-variable, three-variable, and time series graphs given appropriate data.
- compute the slope of a straight line and explain what it measures.
- explain how to compute the slope of a curved line.
- explain how a 45° line can divide a graph into two regions, one in which the Y variable exceeds the X variable, and another in which the X variable exceeds the Y variable.

- explain the implication of each of the following:
    failure to adjust variables for changes in prices and/or population
    the use of short time periods with unique features
    omitting the origin
    the use of different units to measure the same variables

IMPORTANT TERMS AND CONCEPTS

Variable
Two-variable diagram
Horizontal and vertical axes
Origin (of a graph)
Slope of a straight (or curved) line
Negative, positive, zero, and infinite slope
Tangent to a curve
Y-intercept
Ray through the origin, or ray
45° line
Contour map
Time series graph

CHAPTER REVIEW

Economists like to draw pictures, primarily various types of *graphs*. Your textbook and this study guide also make extensive use of graphs. There is nothing very difficult about graphs, but being sure you understand them from the beginning will help you avoid mistakes later on.

(1)   All the graphs we will be using start with two straight lines defining the edges of the graph, one on the bottom and one on the left side. These edges will usually have labels to indicate what is being measured in both the vertical and horizontal directions. The line on the bottom is called the (horizontal/vertical) axis, and

the line running up the side is called the _____ axis. The point at which the two

lines meet is called the _____. The variable measured along the horizontal axis is often called the X variable, while the term Y variable is often used to refer to the variable measured along the vertical axis.

Some graphs show the magnitude of something at different points in time, say gross national product, college enrollment, or grade point averages of college students. Such a graph will measure time along the horizontal axis and dollars, people, or grade point averages along the vertical axis. This sort of graph is called

(2)   a _____ _____ graph.

One does not always have to measure time along the horizontal axis. One could draw a picture plotting any two variables by measuring one variable on one axis and another variable on the other axis. Figure 2–1 is a two-variable diagram plotting expenditures on alcoholic beverages and ministers' salaries. Does this graph imply that wealthier clergymen are responsible for more drinking or does it imply that more drinking in general is increasing the demand for, and hence the salaries of, clergymen? Most likely neither interpretation is correct; just because you can plot two variables together does not mean that one caused the other.

Many of the two-variable diagrams that you will encounter in introductory economics use *straight lines*, primarily for simplicity. An important characteristic of a straight line is its *slope*, which is measured by comparing differences between any two points. Specifically one calculates the slope of a straight line by dividing

(3)   the (horizontal/vertical) change by the corresponding _____ change as we move to the right along the line. One can use the changes between any two points to compute the slope

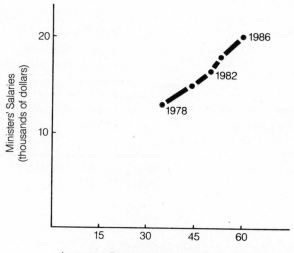

Aggregate Expenditures on Alcoholic Beverages
(billions of dollars)

FIGURE 2–1

MINISTERS' SALARIES AND
EXPENDITURES ON ALCOHOL
Source: U.S. Labor Department; U.S. Commerce Department

because the slope of a straight line is _____. If the straight line shows that both the horizontal and vertical variables increase together, then the line is said to have a (positive/negative) slope; that is, as we move to the right the line slopes (up/down). If one variable decreases as the other variable

increases, then the line is said to have a _____ slope. A line with a zero slope

shows _____ change in the Y variable as the X variable changes.

There is a special type of straight line that passes through the origin of a graph. This is called a

(4) _____ through the origin. Its slope is measured in exactly the same way as the slope of any other straight line. A special type of ray is one that connects all points where the vertical and horizontal variables are equal. If the vertical and horizontal variables are measured in the same units, then

this line has a slope of + 1 and is called the _____ line.

Like straight lines, curved lines also have slopes, but the slope of a curved line is not constant. We measure the slope of a curved line at any point by the slope of the one straight line that just touches, or is

(5) _____ to, the curved line at the point of interest.

A third type of graph is used by economists as well as cartographers. Such a graph can represent three

(6) dimensions on a diagram with only two axes by the use of _____ lines. A traditional application of such a graph in economics is a diagram that measures different inputs along the horizontal and vertical axes and then uses contour lines to show what different combinations of inputs can be used to produce the same amount of output.

DEFINITION QUIZ

Choose the letter that is the most appropriate definition for each of the following terms.

1. _____ Variable
2. _____ Two-variable diagram
3. _____ Horizontal axis
4. _____ Vertical axis
5. _____ Origin
6. _____ Slope
7. _____ Negative slope
8. _____ Positive slope
9. _____ Zero slope
10. _____ Infinite slope
11. _____ Tangent to a curve
12. _____ Y-intercept
13. _____ Ray
14. _____ 45-degree line
15. _____ Contour map
16. _____ Time series graph

a. Graph of how a variable changes over time.
b. Vertical line segment.
c. Straight line, touching a curve at a point without cutting the curve.
d. Scale along the bottom of a graph.
e. Straight line emanating from the origin.
f. Object whose magnitude is measured by a number.
g. Simultaneous representation of the magnitudes of two different variables.
h. Point where both axes meet and where both variables are zero.
i. Straight line through the origin with a slope of plus one.
j. Straight line through the origin with a slope of minus one.
k. Point at which a straight line cuts the vertical axis.
l. Line that goes down as one moves from left to right.
m. Line that neither rises nor falls as one moves from left to right.
n. Scale up the side of a graph.
o. Point at which a straight line cuts the horizontal axis.
p. Two-dimensional representation of three variables.
q. Ratio of vertical change to corresponding horizontal change.
r. Line that rises as one moves from left to right.

BASIC EXERCISES

These exercises are designed to give you practice working with graphs and economic data.

1. **Reading Graphs**
   The demand curve in Figure 2–2 represents the demand by colleges and universities for new Ph.D. economists.
   a. What quantity would colleges and universities have demanded if they had had to pay a salary of $45,000?

   _____

   b. What does the graph tell us would have happened to the quantity demanded if salaries had been $35,000? The quantity would have (increased/decreased) to

   _____

   c. What would have happened to the quantity demanded if salaries were $50,000? It would have (increased/decreased) to

   _____

   d. What is the slope of the demand curve?

   _____

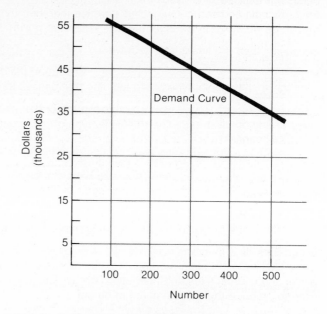

FIGURE 2–2

THE DEMAND FOR NEW Ph.D. ECONOMISTS

2. **Growth Trends**
   a. Look at Table 2–1, which has data on personal income after taxes, The data show that between 1945 and 1989 aggregate personal income after taxes increased over twenty-five fold (3,780.0 ÷ 149.2 = 25.3). Do you agree that individuals in 1989 were twenty-five times richer than individuals in 1945? Could they buy twenty-five times as many goods and services as they could in 1945?

TABLE 2–1

PERSONAL INCOME AFTER TAXES

Year	Aggregate Personal Income after Taxes (billions)	Population (millions)	Income per Capita	Price Index (1982 = 1.000)	Real Income per Capita (1982 prices)
1945	149.2	139.928	$_____	0.202	$_____
1955	278.8	165.275	$_____	0.295	$_____
1965	486.8	194.347	$_____	0.356	$_____
1975	1,142.8	215.981	$_____	0.592	$_____
1985	2,838.7	239.322	$_____	1.116	$_____
1989	3,780.0	248.830	$_____	1.300	$_____

Source: 1990 *Economic Report of the President*, Tables C–3, C–26, and C–27.

b. For each year in Table 2–1 divide aggregate income by the corresponding data for population to compute income per capita rather than aggregate income. Rather than a twenty-fivefold increase, per capita income in 1989

was only _____ times its 1945 level.

c. For each year divide income per capita by the corresponding price level to compute income per capita in constant prices. The figures in the last column of Table 2–1 will tell us how per capita purchasing power, or real income, has changed since 1945. (The appendix to Chapter 6 contains more information about how a price index is constructed and what can be done with it.) In 1989, per capita pur-

chasing power was _____ times its 1945 level.

3. Dangers of Omitting the Origin

Table 2–2 contains data on the number of housing units started each month during the first half of 1989. Plot this data in Figures 2–3a and 2–3b. Which figure gives the more accurate representation of the decline in housing starts and why?

TABLE 2–2

HOUSING UNITS STARTED: JANUARY 1989–JUNE 1989

Month	Units Started (thousands)
January	1,659
February	1,454
March	1,405
April	1,341
May	1,308
June	1,414

Source: U.S. Department of Commerce, *Housing Starts*, March 1990, Table 1.
Note: Monthly data is reported on a seasonally adjusted basis.

4. Choice of Time Periods

In 1960, John F. Kennedy campaigned on a promise to get the country moving, including more rapid economic expansion. When Kennedy was elected president the unemployment rate was rising as the economy was slipping into a recession. Many observers were claiming that for

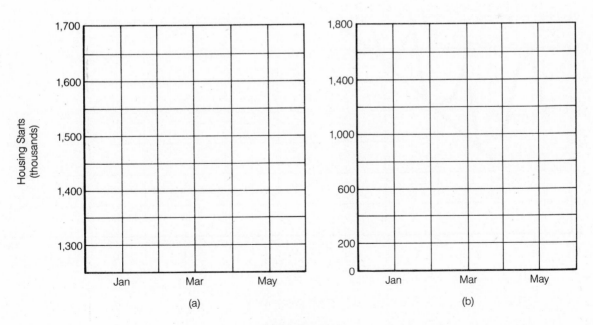

(a)   (b)

FIGURE 2–3

HOUSING STARTS: JANUARY–JUNE 1989

a variety of "structural" reasons the United States was entering a new era of permanently higher rates of unemployment. A major piece of evidence used to support this line of thinking was the rising succession of lowest unemployment rates in each postwar business expansion up to the early 1960s. The data are presented here, in Figure 2–4, together with a trend line connecting the succession of lowest unemployment rates. Use the data in Figure 2–4 to extend the time series graph and to check the accuracy of this argument. If the graph were restricted to data from 1968 to 1983, what would a similar trend line over this period show? What could one conclude from such a trend line?

SELF-TESTS FOR UNDERSTANDING

Test A

Circle the correct answer.

1. Referring to parts (1), (2), (3), and (4) of Figure 2–5, determine which line has a(n)
   a. positive slope _____.
   b. negative slope _____.
   c. zero slope _____.
   d. infinite slope _____.

2. Referring to Figure 2–6, determine at which points the curved line has a(n)
   a. positive slope _____ _____ _____.
   b. negative slope _____ _____ _____.
   c. zero slope _____ _____ _____.
   d. infinite slope _____ _____ _____.

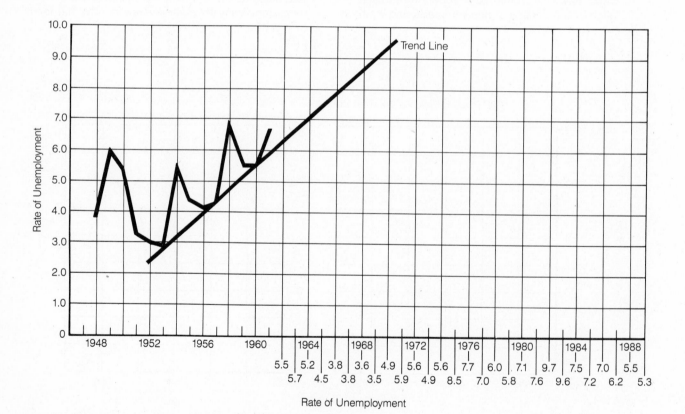

FIGURE 2-4

Source: 1990 *Economic Report of the President*, Table C–32.

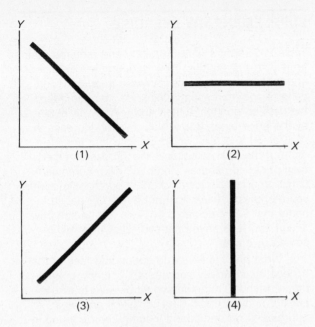

FIGURE 2–5

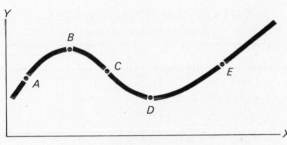

FIGURE 2–6

3. If when $X = 5$, $Y = 16$ and when $X = 8$, $Y = 10$, then the
   a. line connecting X and Y has a positive slope.
   b. line connecting X and Y is a ray through the origin.
   c. slope of the line connecting X and Y is $+6$.
   d. slope of the line connecting X and Y is -2.
4. The slope of a curved line is
   a. the same at all points on the line.
   b. found by dividing the value of the Y variable by the value of the X variable.
   c. found by determining the slope of a straight line tangent to the curved line at the point of interest.
   d. always positive.
5. A ray is
   a. any straight line with a slope of $+1$.
   b. any line, straight or curved, that passes through the origin of a graph.
   c. a straight line with a positive Y axis intercept.
   d. a straight line that passes through the origin.

6. If X and Y are measured in the same units, and we consider a point that lies below a 45° line, then we know that for the X and Y combination associated with this point,
   a. the X variable is greater than the Y variable.
   b. a line from the origin through this point will be a ray and will have a slope greater than $+1$.
   c. the Y variable is greater than the X variable.
   d. the slope of the point is less than 1.
7. Referring to parts (1), (2), (3), and (4) of Figure 2–7, determine which part(s) show a ray through the origin.
   a. (2)
   b. (1) and (3)
   c. (1) and (4)
   d. (3) and (4)

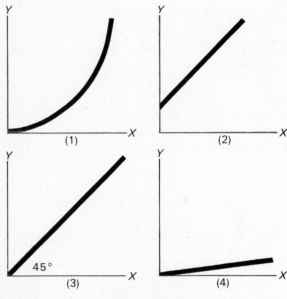

FIGURE 2–7

8. If in part (4) of Figure 2–7, the Y variable changes by 2 units when the X variable changes by 5 units, then the slope of the line is
   a. .4 (2/5).
   b. 2.5 (5/2).
   c. 10 (2 × 5).
   d. insufficient information to compute.

Test B

Circle T or F for True or False as appropriate.

1. The slope of a line measures the value of the Y variable when the X variable is equal to zero.

   T F

2. The slope of a straight line is the same at all points on the line. **T F**

3. A negative slope means that the *Y* variable decreases when the *X* variable increases. **T F**

4. A time series graph can be used to show what combinations of the *X* and *Y* variables are associated with a given value of a third variable. **T F**

5. Omitting the origin from a time series graph can exaggerate the magnitude of increases and decreases. **T F**

6. A straight line that has a *Y*-intercept of zero is also called a ray through the origin. **T F**

7. All rays through the origin have the same slope. **T F**

8. If *X* and *Y* are measured in the same units, then a 45° line is a ray through the origin with a slope of + 1. **T F**

9. If *X* and *Y* are measured in the same units, then any point above a 45° line is a point at which the *X* variable is greater than the *Y* variable. **T F**

10. The use of short periods for a time series graph may be misleading in that they record behavior that is unique to that particular period. **T F**

SUPPLEMENTARY EXERCISE

Table 2–3 reports data on tuition and required fees for 4 year universities. How do increases in tuition and fees compare to the increase in prices in general and increases in income? You can adjust the data on nominal tuition and fees by dividing it by the price index from Table 2–1. An increase in real tuition and fees would indicate that this element of the cost of college has increased faster than prices in general. Once you have computed tuition and fees in terms of 1982 purchasing power, you can divide these figures by real per capita income that you calculated in Table 2–1 to see how tuition and fees have changed relative to real income per capita.

What has happened to tuition and fees at the college or university you attend? The appropriate office at your institution should be able to provide current and historical data on tuition and fees. Information on prices and income can be found in the most recent *Economic Report of the President*.

TABLE 2–3

TUITION AND REQUIRED FEES
4-Year Universities

Year	Public	Private
1965–68	$ 327	$1,369
1975–76	$ 642	$2,881
1985–86	$1,536	$7,374

Source: *Digest of Higher Education Statistics*, 1989, Office of Educational Research and Improvement, U.S. Department of Education, Table 258.

3

Scarcity and Choice: *The* Economic Problem

LEARNING OBJECTIVES

After completing the material in this chapter you should be able to:

- define, understand, and use correctly the terms and concepts listed below.
- explain why the true cost of any decision is its opportunity cost.
- explain the link between market prices and opportunity costs.
- explain why the scarcity of goods and services (outputs) must be attributed to a scarcity of resources, or inputs, used in production processes.
- draw a production possibilities frontier for a firm or for the economy.
- explain how the production possibility frontier contains information about the opportunity cost of alternative output combinations.
- explain why specialized resources mean that a firm's or economy's production possibilities frontier is likely to bow outward.
- explain how an economy can shift its production possibilities frontier.
- explain why efficiency in production requires that an economy produce on, rather than inside, its production possibilities frontier.

- describe the three coordination tasks that every economy must confront.
- explain why specialization and division of labor is likely to require the use of markets.
- describe how a market economy solves the three coordination tasks.

IMPORTANT TERMS AND CONCEPTS

Resources
Scarcity
Choice
Rational Decision
Opportunity cost
Outputs
Inputs (means of production)
Production possibilities frontier
Allocation of resources
Principle of increasing costs
Consumption goods
Capital goods
Economic growth
Efficiency
Specialization
Division of labor
Exchange
Market system
Three coordination tasks

CHAPTER REVIEW

The issue of scarcity and the resulting necessity to make choices are fundamental concerns of economics. This chapter is an introduction to these issues. They have already been implicitly introduced in many of the 12 ideas for Beyond the Final Exam, and they will reappear many times throughout the text.

(1)   The importance of *choice* starts with the fact that virtually all resources are _____. No individual can do or buy everything in the world. Most people's desires exceed their incomes and, even for the very rich, there are only 24 hours in a day. Everyone makes choices all the time. Similarly, firms, educational institutions, and government agencies make choices between what kinds of outputs to produce and what combination of inputs to use. When an economist studies the use of inputs for the economy as a whole, she is studying the allocation of resources.

What is a good way to make choices? The obvious answer is to consider the available alternatives.

(2)   Economists call these forgone alternatives the _____ _____ of a decision. For example, imagine it is the night before the first midterm in Introductory Economics, an examination that will cover Chapters 1–6, and here you are only on Chapter 3. A friend suggests a night at the movies and even offers to buy your ticket so "it won't cost you anything." Do you agree that the evening out won't cost anything? (What will you be giving up?)

Economists often talk about the choices available to the economy as a whole. At first the idea of choices for the economy may sound a bit strange. It may be easiest to imagine such choices being made by the central planning bureau of an eastern European economy. Even though there is no central planning bureau for the U.S. economy, it is useful to think of opportunities available to the American economy. The opportunities selected result from the combined spending and production decisions of all citizens, firms, and governmental units, decisions coordinated by our reliance on markets.

The *production possibilities frontier* is a useful diagram for representing the choices available to a firm or an economy. The frontier will tend to slope downward to the right because resources are

(3)   (scarce/specialized). The frontier will tend to bow out because most resources are _____. For any one year the resources available to an economy—the number of workers, factories, and machines, and the state of technology—are essentially fixed. Over time, an economy can choose to increase its

resources if it chooses to produce (more/less) consumption goods and _____ capital goods. Similarly, technological advancements are more likely if an economy devotes (more/fewer) resources to research and development. In terms of a frontier showing possible combinations of consumption and capital goods, the true cost of faster economic growth is given by the forgone output of

_____ goods.

Opportunity cost is the best measure of the true cost of any decision. For an economy as a whole, with choices represented by a production possibilities frontier, the opportunity cost of changing the composition of

(4)   output can be measured by the _____ of the production possibilities frontier.

As an economy produces more and more of one good, say, missiles, the opportunity cost of further

(5)   increases is likely to (increase/decrease). This change in opportunity cost is an illustration of the principle

of _____ cost and is a result of the fact that most resources are (scarce/specialized).

For given amounts of all but one good, the production possibilities frontier for an economy measures the maximum amount of the remaining good that can be produced. Thus the production possibilities frontier defines maximum outputs. There is, of course, no guarantee that the economy will operate at a point that is

(6)   on the frontier. If there is unemployment, then the economy is operating (on/inside) the frontier. If a firm or

economy operates inside its production possibilities frontier, it is said to be _____; that is, with the same resources the firm or the economy could have produced more of some commodities.

All economies must answer three important questions:
1. How can we use resources efficiently to produce on the production possibilities frontier?
2. What combinations of output shall we produce; that is, where on the frontier shall we produce?
3. To whom shall we distribute what is produced?

The American economy answers these questions through the use of markets and prices. If markets are functioning well, then money prices (will/will not) be a good guide to opportunity costs. Problems arise when markets do not function well and when items do not have explicit price tags.

DEFINITION QUIZ

Choose the letter that is the most appropriate definition for each of the following terms.

1. _____ Resources
2. _____ Scarcity
3. _____ Choice
4. _____ Rational decision
5. _____ Opportunity cost
6. _____ Outputs
7. _____ Inputs
8. _____ Production possibilities frontier
9. _____ Allocation of resources
10. _____ Principle of increasing costs
11. _____ Consumption goods
12. _____ Capital goods
13. _____ Economic growth
14. _____ Efficiency
15. _____ Specialization
16. _____ Division of labor
17. _____ Exchange
18. _____ Market system
19. _____ Three coordination tasks

a. Resources used in production process.
b. Produced goods used to produce other goods in the future.
c. System in which decisions on allocation are made in accordance with centralized direction.
d. Breaking up tasks into smaller jobs.
e. Outward shift of the production possibilities frontier.
f. Decision on how to divide scarce resources among different uses.
g. Instruments used to create the goods and services people want.
h. Process whereby a worker becomes more adept at a particular job.
i. Situation in which the amount of an item available is less than people want.
j. Goods and services that firms produce.
k. System in which decisions on resource allocation come from independent decisions of consumers and producers.
l. Absence of waste.
m. Foregone value of the next best alternative.
n. Decision made from a set of alternatives.
o. System in which people can trade with others.
p. Item available for immediate use by households.
q. Tendency for the opportunity cost of an additional unit of output to rise as production increases.
r. Decision made from a set of alternatives which best serves one's objectives.
s. Graph of combinations of goods that can be produced with available inputs and technology.
t. Decisions on what goods to produce, how to produce them, and how to distribute them.

BASIC EXERCISE

1. This exercise is designed to explore more fully some of the implications of the production possibilities frontier for an economy. Figure 3–1 shows the production possibilities frontier for the economy of Adirondack, which produces only bread and automobiles.
   a. If all resources are devoted to the production of bread, Adirondack can produce

   _____ loaves of bread.

In order to produce 1000 cars, the opportunity cost in terms of bread is

_____ loaves. To produce another 1000 cars, the opportunity cost

(rises/falls) to _____ loaves. As long as the production possibilities frontier continues to curve downward, the opportunity costs of increased automobile output will (continue to rise/start to fall). These changes are the result, not of scarce

resources per se, but of _____
resources. (You might try drawing a production
possibilities frontier with constant opportunity
cost. Can you convince yourself that it should
be a straight line?)

b. Find the output combination of 2500 automobiles and 32,000 loaves on Figure 3–1.
Label this point A. Is it a feasible combination for Adirondack? Label the output combination 1500 automobiles and 40,000 loaves
B. Is this combination feasible? Finally, label
the output combination 1000 automobiles
and 52,000 loaves C. Is this combination
feasible? We can conclude that the feasible
output combinations for Adirondack are
(on/inside/outside) the production possibilities
frontier.

c. An output combination is inefficient if it is
possible to produce more of one or both
goods. Which, if any, of the output combinations identified in Question b is an inefficient

combination? _____. Show
that this point is inefficient by shading in all
the feasible points showing more of one or
both goods.

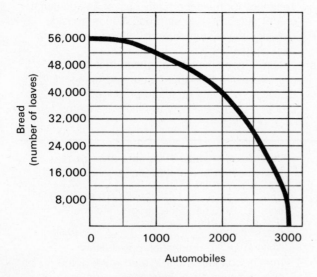

FIGURE 3–1

SELF-TESTS FOR UNDERSTANDING

Test A

Circle the correct answer.

1. Economists define opportunity cost as
   a. the dollar price of goods and services.
   b. the hidden cost imposed by inflation.
   c. the value of the next best alternative use that
      is not chosen.
   d. the *time* you must spend shopping.
2. Referring to Figure 3–1, determine which of the
   following output combinations would represent
   an efficient use of resources.
   a. 1000 automobiles and 30,000 loaves of
      bread.
   b. 1500 automobiles and 44,000 loaves of
      bread.
   c. 2000 automobiles and 44,000 loaves of
      bread.
   d. 2500 automobiles and 28,000 loaves of
      bread.
3. Consider the output combination 2000
   automobiles and 40,000 loaves of bread in
   Figure 3–1. The principle of increasing cost
   a. works only for increases in the output of
      automobiles (that is, movements along the
      frontier to the right).
   b. works only for increases in the output of
      bread (that is, movements along the frontier
      to the left).
   c. works for increases in the output of either
      bread or automobiles.
   d. refers to shifts in, not movements along, the
      frontier.
4. The fact that resources are scarce implies that
   the production possibility frontier will
   a. have a negative slope.
   b. be a straight line.
   c. shift out over time.
   d. bow out from the origin.
5. Which of the following statements imply that
   production possibilities frontiers are likely to be
   curved, rather than straight, lines?
   a. Ultimately all resources are scarce.
   b. Most resources are more productive in
      certain uses than in others.
   c. Unemployment is a more serious problem for
      some social groups than for others.
   d. Economists are notoriously poor at drawing
      straight lines.

6. Which of the following implies a shift in the production possibilities frontier for a shoe firm?
   a. Raising all prices by 10 percent.
   b. Borrowing money to hire more workers and buying more machines.
   c. Changing the composition of output toward more women's shoes and fewer men's shoes.
   d. Expanding the advertising budget.

7. Consider a production possibility frontier showing alternative combinations of corn and computers that can be produced in Cimonoce, a small island economy in the South Pacific. The opportunity cost of more computers can be measured by
   a. the slope of the production possibility frontier.
   b. the X-intercept of the production possibility frontier.
   c. the Y-intercept of the production possibility frontier.
   d. the area under the production possibility frontier.

8. Which one of the following situations reflects a shift of the economy's production possibilities frontier?
   a. The proportion of labor devoted to the production of agricultural products has declined from 21 percent in 1929 to less than 3 percent in 1990.
   b. Total real output for U.S. economy in 1990 was about six times greater than in 1929.
   c. Between 1981 and 1982 total real output of the U.S. economy declined by $28 billion as the unemployment rate rose from 7.6 to 9.7 percent.
   d. From 1979 to 1980 the rate of inflation was about 13.5 percent.

9. Which of the following would not shift an economy's production possibility frontier?
   a. A doubling of the labor force.
   b. A doubling of the number of machines.
   c. A doubling of the money supply.
   d. More advanced technology.

10. A rational decision is one that
    a. will win a majority if put to a vote.
    b. is supported unanimously.
    c. best serves the objectives of the decision maker.
    d. is supported by the *New York Times*.

Test B

Circle T or F for True or False as appropriate.

1. There can never be any real scarcity of manufactured goods as we can always produce more.　　　　T　F

2. Market prices are always a good measure of opportunity cost.　　　　T　F

3. The principle of increasing costs is a reflection of the fact that most productive resources tend to be best at producing a limited number of things.　　　　T　F

4. An economy can shift its production possibilities frontier outward by the process of economic growth.　　　　T　F

5. Because they have the power to tax, governments do not need to make choices.　　　　T　F

6. The existence of specialized resources means that a firm's production possibilities frontier will be a straight line.　　　　T　F

7 The existence of widespread unemployment means that an economy is operating inside its production possibilities frontier.　　　　T　F

8. When an economy is using its resources efficiently it will end up somewhere on its production possibilities frontier.　　　　T　F

9. Because they are nonprofit organizations, colleges and universities do not have to make choices.　　　　T　F

10. A sudden increase in the number of dollar bills will shift the economy's production possibilities frontier.　　　　T　F

SUPPLEMENTARY EXERCISES

1. The Cost of College

Those of you who are paying your own way through college may not need to be reminded that the opportunity cost of your lost wages is an important part of the cost of your education. You can estimate the cost of your education as follows: Estimate what you could earn if instead of attending classes and studying you used those hours to work. Add to this estimate your direct outlays on tuition, books, and any differential living expenses incurred because you go to school. (Why only differential living expenses?) (See also the Supplementary Exercise to Chapter 36.)

2. The Cost of Children

Bob and Jane both took Sociology 1 last year. As part of the course they were asked to compute the cost of raising a child. Bob estimated the cost as $150,000, an average of $4000 a year in increased family expenditures for the first 12 years, then $5000 a year for the next 6 years, and finally 4 years of college at $18,000 per year. Jane also was enrolled in Econ 1. She estimated the cost as $250,000. She started with all the same outlays that Bob did but also included $25,000 a year for four years as the opportunity cost of the parent who stayed at home to care for the child. Which calculation do you think is a more accurate reflection of the cost of raising a child? What would be the cost of a second child?

3. Consider an economy with a production possibilities frontier between cars (C) and tanks (T) given by

$$C = 6L^{.5}K^{.5} - 0.3T^2$$

where L is the size of the labor force (50,000 people) and K is the number of machines, also 50,000.

   a. What is the maximum number of cars that can be produced? Call this number of cars C^*. The maximum number of tanks? Call this number of tanks T^*.
   b. Draw a graph of the production possibilities frontier.
   c. Is this frontier consistent with the principle of increasing costs?
   d. Is the output combination ($\frac{1}{2}C^*$, $\frac{1}{2}T^*$) feasible? Is the output combination ($\frac{1}{2}C^*$, $\frac{1}{2}T^*$) efficient? Why or why not?
   e. What is the opportunity cost of more tanks when 10 tanks are produced? 50 tanks? 200 tanks?
   f. Find a mathematical expression for the opportunity cost of tanks in terms of cars. Is this mathematical expression consistent with the principle of increasing cost?
   g. Draw the new production possibilities frontier if the labor force and the number of machines both increase by 10 percent. Where does this frontier lie relative to the original frontier?

4. **The Cost of Economic Growth**
   If you have access to a microcomputer, you might try programming this small recursive model to investigate the cost of economic growth. You could either try writing your own program in BASIC or some other programming language, or you could use a spreadsheet program. Some programming hints are given at the end of the problem.
      Imagine an economy that produces bundles of consumption goods, C, and investment goods, I, with the help of labor, L, and machines, M, that exist at the beginning of the year. The pro-

duction of consumption and investment goods is described by equation (1)

(1) $C + I = (L)^{.75} \cdot (M)^{.25}$

Some machines wear out each year. The number of machines at the beginning of the next year, is equal to 92 percent of the machines at the beginning of the year plus investment during the year, or $.92 \cdot M + I$. The number of machines will be constant when investment is sufficient to replace the eight percent that wear out. If investment is greater, then the number of machines will increase, and the economy's production possibility frontier will shift out.
   This economy has 10,000 laborers, $L = 10,000$, and originally there are 20,000 machines, $M = 20,000$.

   a. Verify that if $I = 1600$ then total output and consumption will be constant.
   b. What happens to total output and consumption over time if I increases by 25 percent to 2000?
   c. In question b you should find that consumption initially declines as some output is diverted from consumption to investment. However, over time, the output of consumption goods should increase and surpass it's earlier value found in a. If an increase in investment from 1600 to 2000 is a good thing, what about an increase from 2000 to 2400? How does the eventual increase in consumption following this increase compare with what you found in b?
   d. Can there ever be too much investment? Try additional increases in investment and watch what happens to the eventual level of consumption. Can you explain what is going on?

Programming Hints   Columns in a spreadsheet would correspond to the following equations where subscripts refer to time periods. Note that equations for I and C are the same for all periods. Following the initial period you will need to be sure that your expression for the number of machines incorporates the subtraction of machines that have worn out and the addition of new machines from the production of investment goods. You will probably want to set your program or spreadsheet to run for about 100 periods.

$M_t = 20000$	$t = 1$
$I_t = 1600$	$t = 1, 2, \ldots$
$C_t = (10,000)^{.75} \cdot (M_t)^{.25} - I_t$	$t = 1, 2, \ldots$
$M_t = .92 \cdot M_{t-1} + I_t$	$t = 2, 3, \ldots$

4

Supply and Demand:
An Initial Look

LEARNING OBJECTIVES

After completing the material in this chapter you should be able to:

- define, understand, and use correctly the terms and concepts listed below.
- draw a demand curve, given appropriate information from a demand schedule on possible prices and the associated quantity demanded.
- draw a supply curve, given appropriate information from a supply schedule on possible prices and the associated quantity supplied.
- explain why demand curves usually slope downward and supply curves usually slope upward.
- determine the equilibrium price and quantity, given a demand and supply curve.
- explain what forces will tend to move market prices and quantities toward their equilibrium values.
- analyze the impacts on both prices and quantities of changes that shift either the demand curve or the supply curve or both.

- distinguish between a shift in and a movement along either the demand or supply curve.
- explain the likely consequences of government interference with market-determined prices.

IMPORTANT TERMS
AND CONCEPTS

Quantity supplied
Quantity demanded
Demand schedule
Demand curve
Supply schedule
Supply curve
Supply-demand diagram
Shortage
Surplus
Law of supply and demand
Equilibrium price and quantity
Equilibrium
Shifts in versus movements along supply and
    demand curves
Price ceiling
Price floor

CHAPTER REVIEW

Along with scarcity and the need for choice, *demand* and *supply analysis* is a fundamental idea that pervades all of economics. After studying this chapter, look back at the list of the 12 ideas for Beyond the Final Exam in Chapter 1 and see how many of these concern the "law" of supply and demand.

Economists use a *demand curve* as a useful summary of the factors influencing people's demand for different commodities. A demand curve shows how, during a specified period of time, the quantity

(1) demanded of some good changes as the _____ of that good changes, holding all other determinants of demand constant. A demand curve usually has a (negative/positive) slope, indicating that as the price of a good declines people will demand (more/less) of it. A particular quantity demanded is represented by a single point on the demand curve. The change in the quantity demanded as price changes is a (shift in/movement along) the demand curve. Quantity demanded is also influenced by other factors, such as consumer incomes and tastes, and the prices of related goods. Changes in any of these factors will result in a (shift in/movement along) the demand curve. Remember that a demand curve is defined for a particular period of time—a week, a month, or a year.

Economists use a *supply curve* as a useful summary of the factors influencing producers' decisions. Like the demand curve, the supply curve is a relationship between quantity and price. Supply curves usually

(2) have a (negative/positive) slope, indicating that at higher prices producers will be willing to supply (more/less) of the good in question. Like quantity demanded, quantity supplied is also influenced by factors other than price. The size of the industry, the state of technology, the prices of inputs, and the price of related outputs are important determinants of the quantity that producers are willing to supply. Changes in any of these factors will change the quantity supplied and can be represented by a (shift in/movement along) the supply curve.

Demand and supply curves are hypothetical constructs that answer what-if questions. For example, the supply curve answers the question "What quantity of milk would be supplied if its price were $10 a gallon?" At this point it is not fair to ask whether anyone would buy milk at that price. Information about the quantity

(3) demanded is given by the _____ curve, which answers the question "What quantity would be demanded if its price were $10 a gallon?" The viability of a price of $10 will be determined when we consider both curves simultaneously.

Figure 4–1 (on page 22) shows a demand and supply curve for stereo sets. The market outcome will

(4) be a price of $_____ and a quantity of _____. If for some reason the price is $300, then the quantity demanded will be (less/more) than the quantity supplied. In particular,

from Figure 4–1 we can see that at a price of $300, producers will supply _____ sets

while consumers will demand _____ sets. This imbalance is a (shortage/surplus) and will lead to a(n) (increase/reduction) in price as inventories start piling up and suppliers compete for sales. If, instead, the price of stereo sets is only $100, there will be a (shortage/surplus) as the quantity

(demanded/supplied) exceeds the quantity _____. Price is apt to (decrease/increase) as consumers scramble for a limited number of stereos at what appear to be bargain prices.

These forces working to raise or lower prices will continue until price and quantity settle down at values

(5) given by the _____ of the demand and supply curves. At this point, barring any outside changes that would shift either curve, there will be no further tendency for change. Because there is no futher tendency for change, the market-determined price and quantity are said to be in

_____. This price and quantity combination is the only one in which consumers demand exactly what suppliers produce. There are no frustrated consumers or producers. However, equilibrium price and quantity will change if anything happens to shift either the demand or supply curves. The Basic Exercise in this chapter asks you to examine a number of shifts in demand and supply curves.

Often one can identify factors that affect demand but not supply, and vice versa. For example,

(6) changes in consumer incomes and tastes will shift the (demand/supply) curve but will not shift the

_____ curve. Following a shift in the demand curve, price must change to reestablish equilibrium. The change in price will lead to a (shift in/movement along) the supply curve until equilibrium is reestablished at the intersection of the new demand curve and the original supply curve.

Similarly, a change in technology or the price of inputs will shift the _____ curve

but will not shift the _____ curve. Equilibrium will be reestablished as the

change in price induced by the shift in the supply curve leads to a movement along the _____
curve to the new intersection.

In many cases the government has intervened in the market mechanism in an attempt to control prices. Some price controls dictate a particular price; other controls set maximum or minimum prices. A *price ceiling*

(7) is a (maximum/minimum) legal price, typically below the market-determined equilibrium price. Examples of

price ceilings include rent controls and usury laws. A *price floor* sets a _____ legal price. To be effective, this price floor would have to be above the equilibrium price. Price floors are often used in various agricultural programs.

In general, economists argue that interferences with the market mechanism are likely to have a number

(8) of undesirable features. If there are a large number of suppliers, price controls will be (hard/easy) to monitor and evasion will be hard to police. In order to prevent the breakdown of price controls, governments are quite

likely to find it necessary to introduce a large number of _____ _____. The enforcement of price controls can provide opportunities for favoritism and corruption.

Firms are apt to try to get around effective price floors by offering nonprice inducements for consumers to buy from them rather than from someone else. (Remember that effective price floors result in excess supply.) These nonprice inducements are apt to be less preferred by consumers than would a general reduction in prices. Price floors will also result in inefficiencies as high-cost firms are protected from

(9) failing by artificially (high/low) prices. Another form of inefficiency involves the use of time and resources to evade effective controls.

DEFINITION QUIZ

Choose the letter that is the most appropriate definition for each of the following terms.

1. _____ Quantity supplied
2. _____ Quantity demanded
3. _____ Demand schedule
4. _____ Demand curve
5. _____ Supply schedule
6. _____ Supply curve
7. _____ Supply-demand diagram
8. _____ Shortage
9. _____ Surplus
10. _____ Equilibrium price and quantity
11. _____ Equilibrium
12. _____ Shifts in supply or demand curves
13. _____ Movement along a supply or demand curve
14. _____ Price ceiling
15. _____ Price floor
16. _____ Law of supply and demand

a. Observation that in a free market, price tends to level when quantity supplied equals quantity demanded.
b. Legal minimum price that may be charged.
c. Graph depicting how quantity demanded changes as price changes.
d. Change in price causing a change in quantity supplied or demanded.
e. Number of units consumers want to buy at a given price.
f. Price/Quantity pair at which quantity demanded equals quantity supplied.
g. Table depicting how the quantity demanded changes as price changes.
h. Situation in which there are no inherent forces producing change.
i. Table depicting how quantity supplied changes as price changes.
j. Legal maximum price that may be charged.
k. Number of units producers want to sell at a given price.
l. Table depicting the changes in both quantity demanded and quantity supplied as price changes.
m. Change in a variable other than price that affects quantity supplied or demanded.
n. Excess of quantity supplied over quantity demanded.
o. Graph depicting the changes in both quantity supplied and quantity demanded as price changes.
p. Excess of quantity demanded over quantity supplied.
q. Graph depicting how quantity supplied changes as price changes.

BASIC EXERCISES

These exercises ask you to analyze the impact of changes in factors that affect demand and supply.

1. a. Table 4–1 has data on the quantity of candy-bars that would be demanded and supplied at various prices. Use the data to draw the demand curve and the supply curve for candybars in Figure 4–2.

   b. From the information given in Table 4–1 and represented in Figure 4–2, the equilibrium

   price is _____ cents and the equilibrium quantity is

   _____.

TABLE 4–1

DEMAND AND SUPPLY SCHEDULES FOR CANDYBARS

Quantity Demanded (millions)	Price per Bar (cents)	Quantity Supplied (millions)
1200	35	1050
1100	40	1100
900	50	1200
800	55	1250
700	60	1300

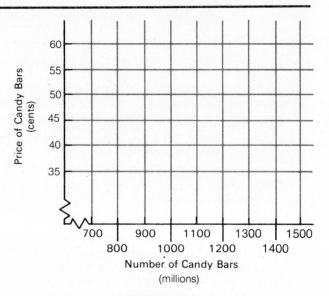

FIGURE 4–2

c. Now assume that increases in income and population mean that the demand curve has shifted. Assume that this shift is such that, at each price, the quantity demanded has increased by 300 candy bars. Draw the new demand curve. At the new equilibrium, price has (increased/decreased) to

_____cents, and quantity has (increased/decreased) to

_____ million candy bars.

d. Now assume that an increase in the price of sugar has caused a shift in the supply curve. Specifically, assume that, at each price, the quantity supplied has been reduced by 150 candy bars. Draw the new supply curve. The shift in the supply curve following the increase in the price of sugar will (increase/decrease)

equilibrium price and _____ the equilibrium quantity. Using the demand curve you drew in part c, above, the new equilibrium price following the increase in the

price of sugar will be _____ cents and the equilibrium quantity will be

_____ million candy bars.

2. Figure 4–3 shows the demand and supply of chicken. Fill in Table 4–2 to trace the effects of various events on the equilibrium price and quantity.

3. Figure 4–4 shows the demand and supply of bread. Complete Table 4–3 to examine the impact of price ceilings and price floors. What general conclusion can you draw about when ceilings and floors will affect market outcomes?

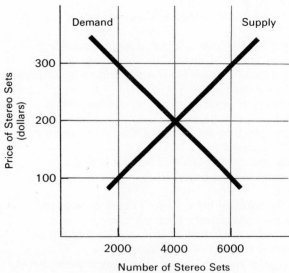

FIGURE 4–1

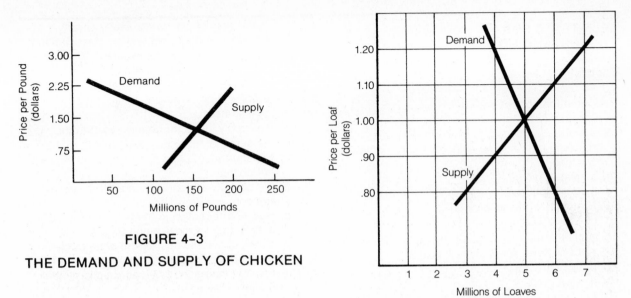

FIGURE 4-3

THE DEMAND AND SUPPLY OF CHICKEN

FIGURE 4-4

THE DEMAND AND SUPPLY OF BREAD

TABLE 4-2

Event	Which curve shifts?	Is the direction left or right?	Does the equilibrium price rise or fall?	Does the equilibrium quantity rise or fall?
a. A sharp increase in the price of beef leads many consumers to switch from beef to chicken.				
b. A bumper grain crop cuts the cost of chicken feed in half.				
c. An extraordinary period of cold weather destroys a significant number of chickens.				
d. A sudden interest in eastern religions converts many chicken eaters to vegetarians.				

TABLE 4-3

	Quantity Demanded	Quantity Supplied	Shortage or Surplus
a. Price ceiling = $1.20			
b. Price ceiling = $0.80			
c. Price floor = $1.10			
d. Price floor = $0.90			

SELF-TESTS FOR UNDERSTANDING

Test A

Circle the correct answer.

1. A shift in the demand curve for sailboats resulting from a general increase in incomes will lead to
   a. higher prices.
   b. lower prices.
   c. a shift in the supply curve.
   d. lower output.

2. A shift in the supply curve of bicycles resulting from higher steel prices will lead to
   a. higher prices.
   b. lower prices.
   c. a shift in the demand curve.
   d. larger output.

3. Which of the following is likely to result in a shift in the supply curve for dresses?
   a. An increase in consumer incomes.
   b. An increase in tariffs that forces manufacturers to import cotton cloth at higher prices than before.
   c. An increase in dress prices.
   d. Higher prices for skirts, pants, and blouses.

4. Which of the following is likely to result in a shift in the demand curve for dresses?
   a. An increase in consumer incomes.
   b. An increase in tariffs that forces manufacturers to import cotton cloth at higher prices than before.
   c. An increase in dress prices.
   d. The development of new machines that dramatically increase the productivity of dressmakers.

5. If for some reason the price of shoes is above its equilibrium value, which of the following is likely to occur?
   a. Shoe stores will find their inventories decreasing as consumers buy more shoes than shoe companies produce.
   b. The demand curve for shoes will shift in response to higher prices.
   c. Shoe stores and companies are likely to agree to reduce prices in order to increase sales, leading to a new lower equilibrium price.
   d. Equilibrium will be reestablished at the original price as the supply curve shifts to the left.

6. From an initial equilibrium, which of the following changes will lead to a shift in the supply curve for Chevrolets?
   a. Import restrictions on Japanese cars.
   b. New environmental protection measures that raise the cost of producing steel.
   c. A decrease in the price of Fords.
   d. Increases in the cost of gasoline.

7. If the price of oil, a close substitute for coal, increases, then
   a. the supply curve for coal will shift to the right.
   b. the demand curve for coal will shift to the right.
   c. the equilibrium price and quantity of coal will not change.
   d. the quantity of coal demanded will decline.

8. Price floors are likely to
   a. lead to a reduction in the volume of transactions, as we move along the demand curve, above the equilibrium price to the higher price floor.
   b. result in increased sales as suppliers react to higher prices.
   c. lead to shortages.
   d. be effective only if they are set at levels below the market equilibrium level.

9. Effective price ceilings are likely to
   a. result in the accumulation of surpluses.
   b. increase the volume of transactions as we move along the demand curve.
   c. increase production as producers respond to higher consumer demand at the low ceiling price.
   d. result in the development of black markets.

10. A surplus results when
   a. the quantity demanded exceeds the quantity supplied.
   b. the quantity supplied exceeds the quantity demanded.
   c. the demand curve shifts to the right.
   d. effective price ceilings are imposed.

Test B

Circle T or F for True or False as appropriate.

1. The Law of Supply and Demand was passed by Congress in 1776.   T F

2. The demand curve for hamburgers is a graph showing the quantity of hamburgers that would be demanded during a specified period of time at each possible price for hamburgers.   T F

3. The slope of the supply curve indicates the increase in price necessary to get producers to increase output.   T F

4. An increase in consumer income will shift both the supply and demand curves.   T F

5. Both demand and supply curves usually have positive slopes. **T F**

6. If at a particular price the quantity supplied exceeds the quantity demanded, then price is likely to fall as suppliers compete with one another. **T F**

7. Equilibrium price and quantity are determined by the intersection of the demand and supply curves. **T F**

8. Since equilibrium is defined as a situation with no inherent forces producing change, the equilibrium price and quantity will not change following an increase in consumer income. **T F**

9. A change in the price of important inputs will change the quantity supplied but will not shift the supply curve. **T F**

10. Price ceilings are likely to result in the development of black markets. **T F**

11. Price controls, whether floors or ceilings, are likely to increase the volume of transactions from what it would be without controls. **T F**

12. An effective price ceiling is normally accompanied by shortages. **T F**

13. An effective price floor is also normally accompanied by shortages. **T F**

14. An increase in both the market price and quantity of beef following an increase in consumer incomes proves that demand curves do not always have a negative slope. **T F**

SUPPLEMENTARY EXERCISES

1. Energy Policy—The Mix of Politics and Economics

The following quotation, written in the spring of 1977, is by Robert E. Hall and Robert S. Pindyck. As you read it, try to understand Hall's and Pindyck's argument in terms of simple demand and supply analysis.

National energy policy faces a deep conflict in objectives, which has been a major reason for the failure to adopt rational measures: Consumers want cheap energy, but producers need high prices to justify expanded production. So far the goal of low prices has dominated. Through a combination of measures, some longstanding and some thrown together quickly during the energy crisis of 1974, the price of energy to consumers in the United States has been held far below the world level. Domestic producers have been prohibited from taking advantage of the higher world price, and in the case of oil, a heavy tax has been imposed on domestic production to finance the subsidization of imports. These steps have caused demand to increase more rapidly than production, and energy imports have risen to fill the gap. If recent policies are continued, imports will continue to grow. Some painful choices regarding the objectives of energy policy will force themselves upon the United States in the next few years.

The economics of the nation's energy problem involves little more than the principle that higher prices result in less demand and more supply. The exact size and timing of the effects of price on demand and supply are still open to debate, but a summary of recent evidence indicates that demand falls by about one per cent for each four-per-cent increase in price, and supply rises by about one percent for each five-per-cent increase in price. Of course several years must pass before demand and supply fully respond to changes in price, and there is some uncertainty over the magnitude and speed of the supply response, but these numbers provide a reasonable basis for an initial description of the energy market in the United States. Policies in effect today have depressed the domestic price of energy, on the average, by about 30 per cent below the world price. Consumption, then, is about eight-per-cent higher than it would be otherwise, and supply is about six-per-cent lower. Stated in oil-equivalents, the total consumption of energy in the United States is about 38 million barrels per day: 31 million barrels are filled by domestically produced oil, natural gas, and coal, and the rest is imported. Eight per cent of consumption is just over three million barrels per day, and six per cent of domestic production is just under two million barrels, so the policy of depressing prices has the net effect of increasing imports by about five million barrels. But current imports are around seven million barrels per day, so a striking conclusion emerges from these simple calculations: *The problem of rising imports is largely of our own making.* Imports might well be much lower had our energy policy not been based on maintaining low prices.[1]

Table 4–3 presents data on U.S. demand for energy in oil equivalents and domestic U.S. supply, consistent with Hall's and Pindyck's argument.

a. From the data give in Table 4–3, plot the demand and domestic supply curves on a piece of graph paper. In 1977 the controlled U.S. price was $8.75 a barrel. What was the domestic demand for energy and what was the domestic supply? What was the demand for imports (the difference between demand and domestic supply)?

b. Hall and Pindyck indicate that the world price of energy in 1977 was $12.50 a barrel. What would have happened to demand, domestic supply, and imports if the price of energy in the United States had been permitted to rise to the world price?

c. What would have happened to energy prices and consumption if we had banned all imports and allowed domestic supply and demand to determine the equilibrium price and quantity?

d. Some people have argued that the demand and supply curves are actually much steeper. They contend that higher prices will not reduce demand by as much as Hall and Pindyck estimate and neither will higher prices increase supply by as much. Draw new, steeper demand and supply curves and examine the impacts of a market solution to the energy problem. (The new curves should intersect the original curves at a price of $8.75.)

e. You might enjoy reading the rest of the Hall and Pindyck paper and comparing their analysis and prescriptions with events since early 1977.

2. Imagine that the demand curve for tomatoes can be represented as

$$Q = 1000 - 250\,P.$$

[1]Robert E. Hall and Robert S. Pindyck, "The Conflicting Goals of National Energy Policy." Reprinted with the permission of the authors from: *The Public Interest*, No. 47 (Spring 1977), pages 3–4, © 1977 by National Affairs, Inc.

TABLE 4-3

Demand Quantity of Energy (millions of oil barrel equivalents)	Price per Barrel (dollars)	Domestic Supply Quantity of Energy (millions of oil barrel equivalents)
33.2	15	34.5
35.1	12	33.0
37.7	9	31.2
41.8	6	28.7

The supply curve is a bit trickier. Farmers must make planting decisions on the basis of what they expect prices to be. Once they have made these decisions, there is little room for increases or decreases in the quantity supplied. Except for disastrously low prices, it will almost certainly pay a farmer to harvest and market his tomatoes. Assuming that farmers forecast price on the basis of the price last period, we can represent the supply curve for tomatoes as

$$Q = 200 + 150\,P_{-1},$$

where P_{-1} refers to price in the previous period. Initial equilibrium price and quantity of tomatoes are $2 and 500, respectively. Verify that at this price the quantity supplied is equal to the quantity demanded. (Remember that equilibrium implies the same price in each period.)

Now assume that an increase in income has shifted the demand curve to

$$Q = 1400 - 250\,P.$$

Starting with the initial equilibrium price, trace the evolution of price and quantity over time. Do prices and quantities seem to be approaching some sort of equilibrium? If so, what? You might try programming this example on a microcomputer or simulating it with a spreadsheet program. What happens if the slope of the demand and/or supply curve changes?

Ask your instructor about cobweb models. Do you think that looking at last period's price is a good way to forecast future prices?

PART
2

THE MACRO-ECONOMY: AGGREGATE SUPPLY AND DEMAND

5

The Realm of Macroeconomics

LEARNING OBJECTIVES

After completing the material in this chapter you should be able to:

- define, understand, and use correctly the terms and concepts listed below.
- explain the difference between microeconomics and macroeconomics.
- determine whether particular problems are within the realm of microeconomics or macroeconomics.
- describe the role of economic aggregates in macroeconomics.
- explain how supply-demand analysis can be used to study inflation, recessions, and stabilization policy.
- distinguish between real and nominal GNP.
- explain how GNP is a measure of economic production, not economic well being.
- characterize, in general terms, the movement in prices and output over the last 100 years.

IMPORTANT TERMS AND CONCEPTS

Microeconomics
Macroeconomics
National product
Aggregation
Aggregate demand and aggregate supply curves
Inflation
Deflation
Recession
Gross national product (GNP)
Nominal versus real GNP
Final goods and services
Intermediate goods
Stagflation
Stabilization policy

CHAPTER REVIEW

Economic theory is traditionally split into two parts, microeconomics and macroeconomics. If one studies

(1) the behavior of individual decision-making units, one is studying _____. If one

studies the behavior of entire economies, one is studying _____. This chapter is
an introduction to macroeconomics.

The American economy is made up of tens of millions of firms, hundreds of millions of individuals, and
billions of different goods and services. Since it would be impossible to list each of these firms, individuals,
and commodities, economists have found it useful to use certain overall averages or aggregates. The concept of *national product* is an example. If we concentrate on macroeconomic aggregates, we ignore much of
the micro detail; whereas by concentrating on the micro detail, we may blind ourselves to the broad overall
picture. The two forms of analysis are not substitutes; rather, they can be usefully employed together.
(Remember the map example in Chapter 1 of the text.) It has been argued that only successful macroeconomic policy leads to a situation in which the study of microeconomics is important, and vice versa.

Supply and demand analysis is a fundamental tool of both micro and macro theory. In microeconomics
one looks at the supply and demand for individual commodities, while in macroeconomics one studies aggregate supply and aggregate demand. The intersection of the demand and supply curves in microeconomics

(2) determines equilibrium _____ and _____. In macro-
economics the intersection of the aggregate demand and supply curves determines the cost of living, or the

price level, and aggregate output, or the gross _____ _____.

(3) A sustained increase in the price level would be called _____, whereas a

sustained decrease would be called _____. National product in the U.S. economy
usually increases every year for reasons that will be discussed in Chapters 17 and 38. Periods when

national product declines are referred to as _____. With an unchanged aggregate
supply curve, an outward (rightward) shift of the aggregate demand curve would lead to (higher/lower)
prices and (higher/lower) output. Higher prices would also result if the aggregate supply curve shifted to
the (left/right), but, this time, higher prices would be associated with a(n) (increase/decrease) in output.

Such a combination of rising prices and declining output is called _____. If
both curves shift to the right at the same rate, then it is possible to have increased output with constant
prices.

(4) The gross national product is defined as the sum of the _____ values of all

_____ goods and services produced by the economy during a specified period
of time, usually one year. Economists and national income statisticians use prices to add up the billions of
different kinds of output. If one uses today's prices, the result is (nominal/real) GNP. If one values output by

prices from some base period, one gets _____ GNP. Which is the better measure of changes in output? (Nominal/Real) GNP. If all prices rise and all outputs are unchanged,

(nominal/real) GNP will increase while _____ GNP will not. It is important to
remember that GNP is a measure of production; it (is/is not) a measure of economic well being.

If you look at a long period of American history, you will see that there have been periods when both
(5) output and prices have risen and fallen. The long-term trend for output is (up/down). The overall trend for
prices (depends/does not depend) upon the period you are looking at. Up until World War II, prices

_____ and _____ whereas since 1945, prices

seem only to have _____.
The government would like to keep output growing, thus avoiding recession; at the same time, it would
(6) like to keep prices from rising, thus avoiding (inflation/deflation). Attempts to do just this are called

_____ policy. The American government has been formally committed to such
policies only since the end of World War II. A look at Figures 5–3 and 5–4 on text pages 83 and 84 sug-

gests that since 1945 stabilization policy has been pretty good at avoiding _____

but not so good at avoiding _____. Chapter 16 discusses why this result is not surprising; that is, why, if one concentrates on maintaining high levels of employment and output, the result is likely to be higher prices.

DEFINITION QUIZ

Choose the letter that is the most appropriate definition for each of the following terms.

1. _____ Microeconomics

2. _____ Macroeconomics

3. _____ National product

4. _____ Aggregation

5. _____ Aggregate demand curve

6. _____ Aggregate supply curve

7. _____ Inflation

8. _____ Deflation

9. _____ Recession

10. _____ Gross national product

11. _____ Nominal GNP

12. _____ Real GNP

13. _____ Final goods and services

14. _____ Intermediate goods

15. _____ Stagflation

16. _____ Stabilization policy

a. Period of expansion in an economy's total output.
b. Period of decline in an economy's total output.
c. Inflation occurring while the economy is growing slowly or in a recession.
d. Gross national product calculated at current price levels.
e. Total production of a nation's economy.
f. Government programs designed to prevent or shorten recessions and to counteract inflation.
g. Products purchased by their ultimate users.
h. Study of behavior of an entire economy.
i. Combining individual markets into a single, overall market.
j. Gross national product calculated using prices from some agreed-upon year.
k. Products purchased for resale or for their use in producing other products.
l. Sustained decrease in general price level.
m. Graph of quantity of national product demanded at each possible price level.
n. Gross national product net of depreciation.
o. Sum of money values of all final goods and services produced within a specified time period.
p. Graph of quantity of national product produced at each possible price level.
q. Study of behavior of individual decision-making units.
r. Sustained increase in general price level.

BASIC EXERCISES

These exercises use the aggregate demand—aggregate supply diagram to review a few basic concepts.

1. Figure 5–1 has four panels. The solid lines indicate the initial situation, and the dashed lines indicate a shift in one or both curves.
   a. Which diagram(s) suggests a period, or periods, of inflation? _____

   b. Which diagram(s) suggests a period, or periods, of deflation? _____

(Have prices in the U.S. economy ever declined in the twentieth century?

_____ If so, when?

_____)

c. Which diagram(s) illustrates growth in real output with stable prices?

_____

d. Which diagram(s) illustrates stagflation?

_____

2. Stabilization policy involves changes in government policies designed to shorten recessions and stabilize prices. For reasons explored in

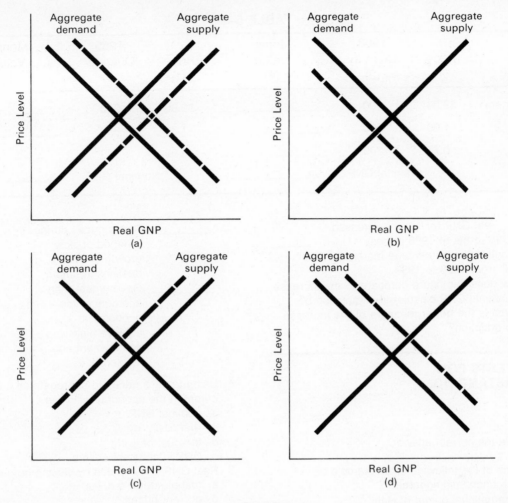

FIGURE 5-1

Chapters 11 through 16, stabilization policies have their primary effect on the aggregate demand curve. For the cases of inflation and recession, explain how stabilization policy can reestablish the initial levels of output and prices. Do this by indicating the appropriate shift in the aggregate demand curve. (The exact policies that will achieve these shifts will be described in detail in Chapters 11 through 16.)

a. Inflation [diagram (d)]

b. Recession [diagram (b)]

c. Consider diagram (c), the case of stagflation. If the government is restricted to policies that shift the aggregate demand curve, what will happen to output if the government adopts policies to combat inflation and restore the original price level? What happens to prices if the government is committed to maintaining the original level of output?

3. Table 5–1 contains data on output and prices in a hypothetical economy that produces only fast food.

a. Calculate the money value of the production of hamburgers, shakes, and fries by multiplying price and quantity. Sum these results to calculate nominal gross national product (GNP) for each year.

b. What is the percentage increase in nominal GNP from 1988 to 1989? _____

c. Use 1988 prices to compute real GNP for 1989 based on 1988 prices.

Value of 1989 hamburger
production using 1988 prices   _____

Value of 1989 shake production
using 1988 prices   _____

Value of 1989 fries production
using 1988 prices   _____

TABLE 5-1

	Price (1)	1988 Quantity (2)	Money Value (3)	Price (4)	1989 Quantity (5)	Money Value (6)
Hamburgers	$2.00	300	_____	$2.80	310	_____
Shakes	1.00	300	_____	1.30	320	_____
Fries	0.75	300	_____	0.90	330	_____
		Nominal GNP	_____		Nominal GNP	_____

Real GNP for 1989 (expressed in terms of 1988 prices) _____

d. Calculate the percentage increase in real GNP from 1988 to 1989.

e. How does this figure compare to the increase in nominal GNP calculated in question b? Which is the better measure of the increase in production?

SELF-TESTS FOR UNDERSTANDING

Test A

Circle the correct answer.

1. Which of the following is an example of a macroeconomic aggregate?
   a. The national output of Haiti.
   b. The total output of General Motors.
   c. Employment at Sears.
   d. The price Exxon charges for unleaded gas.

2. Which of the following would not be included in GNP for 1992?
   a. The production of microcomputers in 1992.
   b. The government's purchase of paper clips in 1992.
   c. Consumer expenditures on haircuts in 1992.
   d. General Motors' expenditures on steel for producing Cadillacs in 1992.

3. Match up each of the following definitions with the appropriate concept.

_____ A sustained decrease in price level.	a. Inflation
	b. Deflation
	c. Stagflation
_____ A decline in real GNP.	d. Recession
	e. Real GNP
_____ A sustained increase in the price level.	f. Stabilization policy

   _____ Rising prices during a period of slow growth or actual declines in output.

   _____ Government management of the economy to achieve high employment and stable prices.

4. Using today's prices to aggregate all final output in the economy will yield
   a. nominal GNP.
   b. real GNP.
   c. the cost of living.
   d. GNP in constant dollars.

5. Real GNP is computed by valuing output by
   a. manufacturer's costs.
   b. current prices.
   c. some fixed set of prices.
   d. last year's rate of inflation.

6. Which of the following will be measured as an increase in GNP but need not reflect an increase in economic well being?
   a. Expenditures to clean up a major oil spill in Prince William Sound.
   b. The value of the time Roland spends painting his own house.
   c. The cost of new medical care that reduces infant mortality.
   d. Earnings of numbers runners in Chicago.

7. Which of the following is measured by the GNP statisticians?
   a. Jerita's purchase of Boeing stock from Walter.
   b. Your spending on tuition and fees for this year.
   c. Durwood's winnings from his bookie.
   d. The value of Yvonne's volunteer time at her daughter's school.

8. Which of the following conditions will result in stagflation?
   a. The aggregate demand curve shifts to the right.
   b. The aggregate demand curve shifts to the left.
   c. The aggregate supply curve shifts to the right.
   d. The aggregate supply curve shifts to the left.
9. In the period following World War II, the historical record shows
   a. more frequent and more severe recessionary dips in real output than before World War II.
   b. an almost continuous increase in prices.
   c. little if any increase in real GNP.
   d. relatively little inflation.
10. In 1974 nominal GNP was $1.473 trillion. In 1975 nominal GNP increased to $1.598 trillion. On the basis of just this information, which of the following statements is true?
   a. Total output of the American economy was greater in 1975 than in 1974.
   b. The whole increase in nominal GNP was the result of inflation.
   c. Actual output increased by 8.5%
      ([(1.598 − 1.473) ÷ (1.473)] × 100).
   d. It is impossible to determine what happened to prices and output from data on nominal GNP alone.

Test B

Circle T or F for True or False as appropriate.

1. A study of the economy of Luxembourg would be an example of microeconomics.　　T F

2. Gross national product is an example of a macroeconomic aggregate.　　T F

3. A decrease in nominal GNP necessarily implies a recession.　　T F

4. Real GNP is a better measure of national output than is nominal GNP.　　T F

5. Deflation can occur only as a result of shifts in the aggregate supply curve.　　T F

6. Even during the Great Depression of the 1930s prices did not decline.　　T F

7. On the eve of World War II, national output, or real GNP, was not much greater than at the end of the Civil War.　　T F

8. Stagflation refers to the simultaneous occurrence of rising prices and little if any increase in output.　　T F

9. Stabilization policy refers to attempts by the government to influence both prices and output by shifting the aggregate demand curve.　　T F

10. Stabilization policy to combat a recession would call for policies that shift the aggregate demand curve to the left.　　T F

6

Unemployment and Inflation: The Twin Evils of Macroeconomics

LEARNING OBJECTIVES

After completing the material in this chapter you should be able to:

- define, understand, and use correctly the terms and concepts listed below.
- describe how the Bureau of Labor Statistics measures the number of unemployed and in what ways this number may be an overestimate or an underestimate of the unemployment level.
- explain the differences between frictional, structural, and cyclical unemployment.
- explain why unemployment insurance only spreads the financial burden of unemployment that individuals would otherwise face, but does not eliminate the economic cost of unemployment.
- summarize the debate over how much unemployment is consistent with full employment.
- distinguish between real and mythical costs of inflation.
- explain how the concept of real wages suggests that inflation has not systematically eroded the purchasing power of wages.

- distinguish between changes in prices that reflect a change in relative prices and changes that reflect general inflation.
- distinguish between real and nominal rates of interest.
- describe how the difference between real and nominal rates of interest is related to expectations about the rate of inflation.
- explain how the taxation of nominal interest income can mean that, during a period of inflation, savers will receive a reduced real return after taxes.
- explain why and how usury ceilings, based on nominal interest rates, can have undesirable impacts during periods of rapid inflation.
- distinguish between creeping and galloping inflation.
- explain why the variability of inflation is important to an understanding of the cost of inflation.

IMPORTANT TERMS AND CONCEPTS

Unemployment rate
Labor force
Discouraged workers
Frictional unemployment
Structural unemployment
Cyclical unemployment
Employment Act of 1946
Full employment
Unemployment insurance
Potential GNP

Purchasing power
Real wage
Relative prices
Redistribution by inflation
Real rate of interest
Nominal rate of interest
Expected rate of inflation
Inflation and the tax system
Usury laws
Creeping inflation
Galloping inflation

CHAPTER REVIEW

Ever since the Employment Act of 1946 committed the federal government to deliberate macroeconomic policy, policymakers have been facing the choice between the twin evils of macroeconomics. Attempts to
(1) lower unemployment have usually meant (more/less) inflation and attempts to fight inflation have usually

meant _____ unemployment. How is one to make the choice? Economics cannot provide a definitive answer to this question, but the material in this chapter will help you understand the issues and enable you to make a more informed choice.

Unemployment has two sorts of costs. The personal costs include not only the lost income for individuals out of work, but also the loss of work experience and the psychic costs of involuntary idleness. The economic costs for the nation as a whole can be measured by the output of goods and services that might have been produced by those who are unemployed.

Unemployment insurance can help ease the burden of unemployment for individual families, but it
(2) (can/cannot) protect society against the lost output that the unemployed might have produced. Employing these people in the future does not bring back the hours of employment that have already been missed. Unemployment compensation provides (complete/partial) protection for (all/some) unemployed workers.

Economists have attempted to measure part of the cost of unemployment by estimating how much
(3) output would have been produced at full employment. These figures are estimates of (potential/actual) GNP.

The economic cost of unemployment is the difference between potential GNP and _____.
(4) Full employment (is/is not) the same as zero unemployment. Some unemployment occurs naturally from the normal workings of labor markets, as people initially look for jobs, improve their own skills, look for better

jobs, move to new locations, and so forth. Such unemployment is called _____ unemployment and involves people who are temporarily without a job for more or less voluntary reasons. Full employment would not eliminate this kind of unemployment. Full employment would eliminate unemployment that is due to a decline in the economy's total production; that is, at full employment there would be no

_____ unemployment. Unemployment may also occur because people's skills are no longer in demand due to automation or massive changes in production. This type of unemployment is

called _____ unemployment.

Unemployment statistics come from a monthly survey by the Bureau of Labor Statistics. People are asked whether they have a job. If they answer no, they are asked if they are laid off from a job they expect to return to, are looking for work, or are not looking for work. From these answers government statisticians derive estimates of employment, unemployment, and the labor force. These numbers are not above criticism. When unemployment rates are high, some people give up looking for work because they believe that looking
(5) for work is not worth the effort. These people are called _____ workers. An increase in the number of people who have given up looking for work means a(n) (increase/decrease) in the amount of statistical unemployment and is an important reason why some observers feel that the official unemployment statistics (understate/overstate) the problem of unemployment.

(6)   Some argue that the increased importance of young workers in the labor force has increased the percentage of (cyclical/frictional/structural) unemployment. They have naturally higher rates of unemployment because they more frequently enter and leave the labor force, and because they change jobs more often. Another factor may be that more liberal unemployment compensation induces people to call themselves unemployed even if they have no intention of looking for work.

(7)   There are important and valid reasons why people are concerned about continuing inflation. Nevertheless, quite a few popular arguments against inflation turn out to be based on misunderstandings. Many people worry that a high rate of inflation reduces their standard of living, or their (real/nominal) income. But the facts show that periods of high inflation are usually accompanied by equally large if not larger increases in wages. For most workers, the real standard of living, or the change in wages adjusted for the change in prices, continues to increase, even during periods of rapid inflation. A worker whose wages double when prices double is able to consume (more/less/the same) goods and services (than/as) before the rise in prices and wages. In this case one would say that real wages (increased/were unchanged/decreased).

(8)   During inflationary periods most prices increase at (the same/different) rates. As a result, goods and services with smaller than average price increases become relatively (more/less) expensive than they were before. Analogously, goods and services with larger than average price increases become relatively

_____ expensive. Relative prices change all the time, during both inflationary and noninflationary periods. Changes in relative prices usually reflect shifts in demand and/or supply curves or various forms of government interventions. It is inaccurate to blame inflation for an increase in relative prices.

But inflation does have real impacts. An important effect is the redistribution of wealth between borrowers and lenders in inflationary periods. If lenders expect higher prices in the future they will demand (9) (higher/lower) interest rates to compensate them for the loss of purchasing power of the future dollars used to repay loans. Economists have thus found it useful to distinguish between nominal and real interest rates. If one looks at interest rates only in terms of the dollars that borrowers must pay lenders, one is looking at

_____ interest rates. If one looks at interest rates in terms of the expected purchasing power the borrower will pay the lender, one is looking at _____ interest rates. The difference between these two measures of interest rate is related to expectations of

_____ .

(10)   If a change in the rate of inflation is accurately foreseen, and if nominal interest rates are correctly adjusted to reflect the change in expected inflation, then nominal interest rates (will/will not) change while real interest rates will (also change/be unchanged). More typically, expectations of inflation are incorrect, in which case inflation will result in a redistribution of wealth between borrowers and lenders. Who gains and who loses will depend on whether the adjustment of nominal interest rates is too large or too small. The tax treatment of interest payments can have a substantial impact on the real after tax rate of return. Problems here reflect the fact that the tax system, originally designed for a world of no inflation, focuses on (nominal/real) interest rates.

(11)   Legal ceilings on interest charges for different types of loans are called _____ ceilings. These ceilings are almost universally written in terms of (nominal/real) interest rates rather than

_____ interest rates. During periods of rapid inflation, (nominal/real) interest rates may rise very high, bumping into usury ceilings, while _____ interest rates may show little if any change. The result will be frustrated borrowers and lenders and reduced levels of economic activity in the affected areas.

Over the long run, small unexpected differences in the rate of inflation can compound into large differences in profits and losses. And since most business investments depend on long-term contracts, this area of economic activity may suffer during periods of high inflation.

Long-term inflation that proceeds at a fairly moderate and steady pace is referred to as

(12)   _____ inflation. Inflation that progresses at exceptionally high and often, accelerating rates, if only for brief periods of time, is called _____ inflation. There is no simple borderline between the two. In different countries or in different periods of time, the dividing line will vary considerably.

DEFINITION QUIZ

Choose the letter that is the most appropriate definition for each of the following terms.

1. _____ Unemployment rate
2. _____ Labor force
3. _____ Discouraged workers
4. _____ Frictional unemployment
5. _____ Structural unemployment
6. _____ Cyclical unemployment
7. _____ Unemployment insurance
8. _____ Potential GNP
9. _____ Purchasing power
10. _____ Real wage
11. _____ Relative prices
12. _____ Real rate of interest
13. _____ Nominal rate of interest
14. _____ Usury laws
15. _____ Creeping inflation
16. _____ Galloping inflation

a. Government program providing transfer payments to some unemployed workers.
b. Percentage of labor force unemployed.
c. Percentage by which money repayment exceeds borrowed money amount.
d. Number of people holding or seeking jobs.
e. Prices increasing at exceptionally high rate.
f. Unemployed people who cease looking for work believing that no jobs are available.
g. Unemployment attributable to decline in economy's total production.
h. Unemployment due to normal workings of the labor market.
i. Legal maximum interest rate.
j. Percentage increase in purchasing power borrower pays to lender.
k. Volume of goods and services that money wage will buy.
l. Unemployment due to changes in nature of economy.
m. Congressional act declaring full employment a goal of national policy.
n. Price of an item in terms of some other item.
o. Prices rising for a long time at a moderate rate.
p. Volume of goods and services that a sum of money will buy.
q. Real level of output attainable if all resources were fully employed.

BASIC EXERCISE

Real and Nominal Interest Rates

This problem is designed to illustrate how the adjustment of nominal interest rates, when it is an accurate reflection of future inflation, can leave the real costs and returns to borrowers and lenders unchanged. For simplicity the exercise ignores taxes.

Angela Abbott has a manufacturing firm. After paying other costs she expects a cash flow of $10 million, out of which she must pay the principal and interest on a $5 million loan. If prices are unchanged and if the interest rate is 5 percent, Angela expects a nominal and real profit of $4,750,000. This result is shown in the first column of Table 6–1.

The next three columns reflect three possible alternatives. The second column shows the consequences of unexpected inflation of 10 percent. In the third column, nominal interest rates have adjusted in expectation of an inflation of 10 percent, which actually occurs. And in the last column, nominal interest rates reflect the consequences of expecting a higher rate of inflation than actually occurs.

1. Fill in the missing figures in the second column. Compare the real returns to both Angela and her lender with those of the noninflationary situation in column 1. Who gains and who loses when there is unexpected inflation?

2. Fill in the missing figures in the third column. This is the case in which nominal interest rates have adjusted appropriately. (The approximation is to add the rate of inflation, 10 percent, to the rate of interest in the noninflationary situation, 5 percent. The extra 0.5 percent comes from a more complex and complete adjustment.) Compare the real returns in rows 7 and 9 with the comparable figures in column 1. Who gains and who loses now?

TABLE 6-1

	(1)	(2)	(3)	(4)
1. Price level	1.00	1.10	1.10	1.10
2. Sales revenue minus labor and materials costs*	10,000,000	11,000,000	11,000,000	11,000,000
3. Principal repayment	5,000,000	5,000,000	5,000,000	5,000,000
4. Interest rate	0.05	0.05	0.155	0.20
5. Interest payment [(4) × (3)]	250,000	_____	_____	_____
6. Total nominal payment to lender [(3) + (5)]	5,250,000	_____	_____	_____
7. Real payment to lender [(6) ÷ (1)]	5,250,000	_____	_____	_____
8. Nominal profits [(2) − (6)]	4,750,000	_____	_____	_____
9. Real profits [(8) ÷ (1)]	4,750,000	_____	_____	_____

*Inflation of 10 percent is assumed to increase sales revenue labor costs, and materials costs by 10 percent each. As a result, the difference between sales revenue and labor and material costs also increases by 10 percent in column 2, 3, and 4.

3. Fill in the missing figures in column 4, where interest rates have adjusted in anticipation of an even higher rate of inflation than occurs. Who gains and who loses when inflation turns out to be less than expected?

SELF-TESTS FOR UNDERSTANDING

Test A

Circle the correct answer.

1. Which of the following factors implies that official statistics may overstate the magnitude of the problem of unemployment?
   a. Discouraged workers.
   b. The loss of expected overtime work.
   c. Liberalized unemployment benefits.
   d. Involuntary part-time work.
2. Indicate which examples go with which concepts.
   a. An older, unemployed telephone operator replaced by new, computerized switching machines.
   b. An unemployed college senior looking for her first job.
   c. An ex-construction worker who has given up looking for work because of a belief that no one is hiring.
   d. An unemployed retail clerk who is laid off because of declining sales associated with a general business recession.

   frictional unemployment _____
   structural unemployment _____
   cyclical unemployment _____
   discouraged worker _____
3. The difference between potential GNP and actual GNP is a reflection of
   a. frictional unemployment.
   b. cyclical unemployment.
   c. galloping inflation.
   d. nominal interest rates.
4. Which of the following people are eligible for unemployment compensation?
   a. A mechanic for Ford Motor Company laid off because of declining auto sales.
   b. A housewife seeking paid work after six years spent at home with two small children.
   c. A college senior looking for his first job.
   d. An engineer who quits to find a better job.
5. A nominal interest rate of 10 percent and inflationary expectations of 4 percent imply a real interest rate of about _____ percent.
   a. 4
   b. 6
   c. 10
   d. 14
6. If suddenly everyone expects a higher rate of inflation, economists would expect nominal interest rates to
   a. rise.
   b. fall.
   c. stay unchanged.
7. If inflation is unexpected, there is apt to be a redistribution of wealth from

a. borrowers to lenders.
b. lenders to borrowers.
c. rich to poor.
d. poor to rich.

8. In a world with no inflation and no taxes, nominal interest rates of 5 percent offer a real return of 5 percent. If suddenly it is expected that prices will rise by 6 percent, what increase in nominal interest rates is necessary if the expected real interest rate is to remain unchanged at 5 percent?
a. 1 percent.
b. 5 percent.
c. 6 percent.
d. 11 percent.

9. If your wages go up by 10 percent when prices go up by 7 percent, the increase in your real wage is about _____ percent.
a. 3
b. 7
c. 10
d. 17

10. The historical evidence suggests that in periods with high rates of inflation, nominal wages
a. increase at about the same rate as before.
b. increase at much lower rates than inflation.
c. also increase at high rates.
d. remain unchanged.

Test B

Circle T or F for True of False as appropriate.

1. In periods of high unemployment the only people whose incomes are reduced are those who are out of work. **T F**

2. The official unemployment statistics are adjusted to include those people with part-time jobs who are looking for full-time work. **T F**

3. All major social groupings, young–old, men–women, blacks–whites, have essentially the same rate of unemployment. **T F**

4. Unemployment insurance protects society against lost output from unemployment. **T F**

5. Anyone who is officially counted as unemployed can collect unemployment benefits. **T F**

6. Potential GNP is an estimate of the maximum possible output our economy could produce under conditions similar to wartime. **T F**

7. The definition of full employment is an unemployment rate of zero. **T F**

8. Inflation does not redistribute wealth between borrowers and lenders because nominal interest rates are automatically adjusted to reflect actual inflation. **T F**

9. The historical record shows that creeping inflation will always lead to galloping inflation. **T F**

10. Predictable inflation is likely to impose less cost than unpredictable inflation. **T F**

Appendix: How Statisticians Measure Inflation

LEARNING OBJECTIVES

After completing the material in this appendix you should be able to:

- define, understand, and use correctly the terms and concepts listed below.
- construct a price index from data on prices and the composition of the market basket in the base year.
- use a price index to compute real measures of economic activity by deflating the corresponding nominal measures.
- explain how the market baskets differ for the Consumer Price Index and the GNP deflator.

IMPORTANT TERMS AND CONCEPTS

Index number
Index number problem
Consumer Price Index
Deflating by a price index
GNP deflator

DEFINITION QUIZ

Choose the letter that is the most appropriate definition for each of the following terms.

1. _____ Index number

2. _____ Consumer Price Index

3. _____ Deflating

4. _____ GNP deflator

5. _____ Index number problem

a. Dividing a nominal magnitude by a price index to express the magnitude in constant purchasing power.
b. Indicator of a percentage change in some variable from a chosen base period.
c. Price index obtained by dividing nominal GNP by real GNP.
d. Measure of price level based on typical urban household's spending.
e. Average level of producer prices.
f. Differences between consumption patterns of actual families and price index market basket.

BASIC EXERCISE

The following exercise should help you review the material on price indexes presented in the appendix to Chapter 6.

Table 6–2 presents data on expenditures and prices for a hypothetical family that buys only food and clothing. We see that in 1990 this family spent $5000 on food at $2 per unit of food, and $10,000 on clothing at $25 per unit. Note that between 1990 and 1991, dollar expenditures by this family increased by almost 16 percent, actually 15.65 percent, rising from $15,000 to $17,348. Is this family able to consume 16 percent more of everything? Clearly not, since prices have risen. How much inflation has there been on average? What is the increase in real income for this family? These are the sorts of questions that a good price index can help you answer.

1. Use the data in Table 6–2 to construct a family price index (FPI) using 1990 as the base year.
   a. Divide expenditures by price to find the quantities of each good purchased in 1990. This is the base-period market basket.

   Quantity of food   _____

   Quantity of clothing _____

   b. Use 1991 prices to find out how much the base-period market basket would cost at 1991 prices.
      1991 cost of 1990 market basket

      _____

   c. Divide the 1991 cost of the base-period market basket by the 1990 cost of the same market basket and multiply by 100 to compute the value of the FPI for 1991.

      FPI for 1991 _____

   d. Convince yourself that if you repeat steps b and c using 1990 prices you will get an answer of 100 for the value of the FPI for 1990.
   e. Measure the increase in the cost of living by computing the percentage change in your price index from 1990 to 1991.
      Inflation between 1990 and 1991.

      _____

   f. Divide total dollar expenditures in 1991 by the 1991 FPI and multiply by 100 to get a measure of real expenditures for 1991.
      Real expenditures
      in 1991 (1990 prices) _____

      Percentage change in
      real expenditures
      1990 to 1991 _____

Remember the following points about price indexes:

- Most price indexes, like the Consumer Price Index, are computed by pricing a standard market basket of goods in subsequent periods.
- A price index can be used to measure inflation and to deflate nominal values to adjust for inflation.

- Different price indexes, such as the Consumer Price Index and the GNP deflator, will show slightly different measures of inflation because they use different market baskets.

2. (Optional) Compute a new FPI using 1991 as the base period rather than 1990. Now the value of your price index for 1991 will be 100 and the price index for 1990 will be something less than 100. Does this index give the same measure of inflation as the index with 1990 as the base period? Do not be surprised if it does not. Can you explain why they differ?

SUPPLEMENTARY EXERCISES

1. Table 6–3 contains data on consumer prices for seven countries. Try to answer each of the following questions or explain why the information in Table 6–3 is insufficient to answer the question.
   a. In 1970 which country had the lowest prices?
   b. In 1988 which country had the highest prices?
   c. Over the period 1970–1988, which country experienced the most inflation as measured by the percentage change in the consumer price index? Which country experienced the least inflation?

2. Go to the library to document the current unemployment situation of different workers. *Employment and Earnings* is published monthly by the Bureau of Labor Statistics. It contains detailed data on employment and unemployment by age, sex, and race of workers. The *Survey of Current Business* is another good source, although less detailed than *Employment and Earnings*. The *Economic Report of the President*, issued annually, is a good source for historic data.

3. Learn more about the composition of the market basket for the Consumer Price Index. A good place to start is "New basket of goods and services being priced in revised CPI," Charles Mason and Clifford Butler, *Monthly Labor Review*, January 1987, pages 3–22. Mason and Butler report on a survey of 1982–84 consumer buying patterns.

TABLE 6–2
HYPOTHETICAL PRICES AND EXPENDITURES

Year	Price	Food Expenditures	Price	Clothing Expenditures	Total Expenditures
1990	$2.00	$5,000	$25.00	$10,000	$15,000
1991	2.36	5,900	26.50	11,448	17,348

TABLE 6–3
INDEX OF CONSUMER PRICES (1982–1984 = 100)

	Canada	France	Italy	Japan	United Kingdom	United States	West Germany
1970	35.1	28.7	16.8	38.5	21.8	38.8	52.9
1975	50.1	43.9	28.8	66.0	40.2	53.8	71.2
1980	76.1	72.2	63.2	90.9	78.5	82.4	86.8
1985	108.9	114.3	121.1	104.2	111.1	107.6	104.8
1988	123.2	124.3	141.1	105.7	125.6	118.3	106.3

Source: *1990 Economic Report of the President*, Table C–107.

7

Income and Spending: The Powerful Consumer

LEARNING OBJECTIVES

After completing the material in this chapter you should be able to:

- define, understand, and use correctly the terms and concepts listed below.
- describe what spending categories make up aggregate demand.
- distinguish between investment spending as a part of aggregate demand and financial investment.
- explain why, except for some technical complications, national product and national income are necessarily equal.
- explain why disposable income differs from national income.
- derive a consumption function given data on consumption and disposable income and compute the marginal propensity to consume at various levels of income.
- explain why the marginal propensity to consume is equal to the slope of the consumption function.
- distinguish between factors that result in a *movement along* the consumption function and factors that result in a *shift of* the function.

- explain why consumption spending is affected by a change in the level of prices even if real income is unchanged.
- describe why permanent and temporary changes in taxes of the same magnitude would be expected to have different impacts on consumption spending.

IMPORTANT TERMS AND CONCEPTS

Aggregate demand
Consumer expenditure (C)
Investment spending (I)
Government purchases (G)
Net exports (X − IM)
C + I + G + X − IM
National income
Disposable income (DI)
Circular flow diagram
Transfer payments
Scatter diagram
Consumption function
Marginal propensity to consume (MPC)
Movements along versus shifts of the consumption function
Money fixed assets
Temporary versus permanent tax changes

CHAPTER REVIEW

This chapter introduces two key concepts that economists use when discussing the determination of an economy's output: *aggregate demand* and the *consumption function*. These basic concepts will be fundamental to the material in later chapters.

The total amount that all consumers, business firms, and government units are willing to spend on goods

(1) and services is called aggregate _____. Economists typically divide this sum into four components: consumption expenditures, investment spending, government purchases, and net exports. Food, clothing, movies, and hamburgers are examples of (consumption/investment/government)

expenditures. Factories, office buildings, machinery, and houses would be examples of _____ spending. Red tape, bombers, filing cabinets, and the services of bureaucrats are examples of

_____ purchases. American wheat and tractors sold abroad are examples of (exports/imports), and American purchases of French wines, Canadian paper, and Mexican oil are examples

of _____. The difference between exports and imports is called _____.

Aggregate demand is a schedule. As we saw in Chapter 5, the exact amount of aggregate demand for any year will depend on a number of factors, including the price level.

Two other concepts that are closely related to aggregate demand are *national product* and *national*

(2) *income*. National product is simply the output of the economy. National income is the (before/after)-tax

income of all the individuals in the economy. Disposable income is the _____-tax income of individuals. The circular flow diagram shows that national product and national income are two ways of measuring the same thing: Producing goods and selling them results in income for the owners and employees of firms.

Economists use the concept of a *consumption function* to organize the determinants of consumption expenditures. Specifically, the consumption function is the relation between aggregate real consumption expenditures and aggregate real disposable income, if all other determinants of consumer spending are held

(3) constant. Higher disposable income leads to (more/less) consumption spending. A change in disposable income leads to a (shift in/movement along) the consumption function. A change in one of the other factors that affect consumer spending, such as wealth, the level of prices, or the rate of inflation, leads to a

_____ _____ the consumption function. (Two, more technical, aspects of the consumption function, the *marginal propensity to consume* and the *average propensity to consume*, are considered more fully in the Basic Exercise section of this chapter.)

An increase in the price level affects consumption spending and is an important reason why aggregate

(4) demand, the sum of _____ + _____ + _____ + _____ − _____, is a schedule. If prices are higher we expect (more/less) consumption spending. Consumption spending changes because the value of many consumer assets is fixed in money terms, and an increase in the price level will (increase/decrease) the purchasing power of these assets. It is important to remember that higher prices will lead to lower real consumption expenditures even if real disposable income is constant. A doubling of *all* prices will also double wages—the price for an hour of labor services. If wages and prices both double, there is no change in the purchasing power of labor income, but there is a loss to consumers from the decline in the purchasing power of their money fixed assets. It is this latter decline that leads to a shift in the consumption function in response to a change in the price level.

Separately from the level of prices, the rate of inflation may also affect consumption spending. On the one hand, the notion that one should buy now, before prices increase still further, suggests that inflation stimulates consumption spending. On the other hand, the notion that one may have to save more in order to meet higher prices tomorrow, suggests that inflation depresses consumption spending. For rates of inflation experienced in the United States there is no clear evidence as to which tendency is greater.

A change in income taxes immediately changes disposable income. The consumption function, then, tells us how a change in disposable income will affect consumption spending. For example, a reduction in

(5) income taxes would (increase/decrease) disposable income. After computing the change in disposable income, one could estimate the initial impact on consumption spending by multiplying the change in disposable income by the (marginal/average) propensity to consume. A permanent increase in taxes would be

expected to have a (larger/smaller) effect on consumption expenditures than a temporary tax increase of the same magnitude because the permanent increase changes consumers' long-run income prospects by (more/less) than the temporary increase. The same argument works in reverse and implies that temporary tax changes have a (larger/smaller) impact on consumption expenditures than do permanent tax changes.

DEFINITION QUIZ

Choose the letter that is the most appropriate definition for each of the following terms.

1. _____ Aggregate demand

2. _____ Consumer expenditure

3. _____ Investment spending

4. _____ Government purchases

5. _____ Net exports

6. _____ National income

7. _____ Disposable income

8. _____ Transfer payments

9. _____ Consumption function

10. _____ Marginal propensity to consume

11. _____ Movement along the consumption function

12. _____ Shift of the consumption function

13. _____ Money fixed asset

a. Government grants to individuals.
b. Personal income minus personal income taxes.
c. Purchases of newly produced goods and services by all levels of government.
d. Total amount spent by consumers on newly produced goods.
e. Change in consumption due to a change in disposable income.
f. Gross national product divided by price level.
g. Total amount consumers, firms, and governments are willing to spend on final goods.
h. Total spending by firms on new plant and equipment and by consumers on new homes.
i. Change in consumption divided by change in disposable income.
j. Item whose value is fixed in terms of dollars.
k. Exports minus imports.
l. Total earnings of all individuals in economy.
m. Change in consumption due to a change in any factor affecting consumption other than disposable income.
n. Relation between aggregate real consumption expenditures and aggregate real disposable income.

BASIC EXERCISES

These exercises will give you practice using a consumption function.

1. Table 7–1 reports some data on disposable income and consumption.
   a. For each change in income compute the marginal propensity to consume. (You will first have to compute the change in consumption.)
   b. The average propensity to consume is defined as the ratio of consumption expenditures to disposable income or APC = $C \div DI$. For the income of $12,000 the average propensity to consume is $10,400 \div $12,000 = .87. Use the data on income and consumption to fill in the column for the average propensity to consume.
   c. Are the average and marginal propensities equal? Do the differences surprise you? Can you explain them? Perhaps steps d to f will help.

   d. Use the graph of Figure 7–1 to draw the consumption function consistent with the data in Table 7–1. (Locate each income–consumption data pair and then draw a line connecting the points.)
   e. The marginal propensity to consume is represented by what part of your graph?
   f. The average propensity to consume can be represented by the slope of a ray from the origin to a point on the consumption function.

   Remember the slope of any straight line, including a ray, is the vertical change over the horizontal change. When measured from the origin, the vertical change of a ray to a point on the consumption function is C and the horizontal change is DI. Thus the slope of the ray, ($C \div DI$), is the APC. Draw rays to represent the APC for incomes of $12,000 and $28,000. How does the slope of your rays change as income increases? Is this change

TABLE 7-1

DATA ON DISPOSABLE INCOME AND CONSUMPTION

Average Propensity to Consume	Disposable Income (dollars)	Consumption (dollars)	Change in Disposable Income (dollars)	Change in Consumption (dollars)	Marginal Propensity to Consume
_____	12,000	10,400			
			4,000	_____	_____
_____	16,000	12,800			
			4,000	_____	_____
_____	20,000	15,200			
			4,000	_____	_____
_____	24,000	17,600			
			4,000	_____	_____
_____	28,000	20,000			

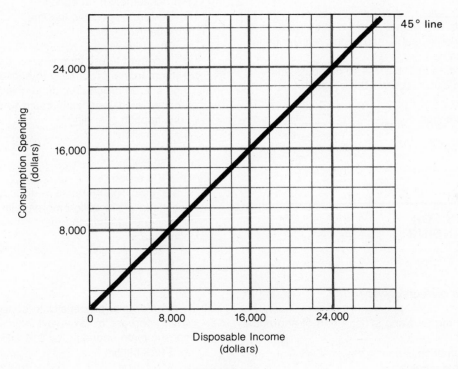

FIGURE 7-1

consistent with changes in the APC you calculated in step c?

2. Imagine an economy made up of 100 families, each earning $12,000 and 100 families each earning $28,000. Each family consumes according to the consumption function described in Table 7-1.

a. Fill in the following:

Consumption of a family earning $12,000

_____

Consumption of a family earning $28,000

_____

Aggregate consumption of all 200 families

_____

b. What is the average propensity to consume of

the richer families? _____

What is the average propensity to consume of

the poorer families? _____

c. Randy argues that since the lower-income families are spending a greater proportion of their income than the higher-income families, a redistribution of income from high- to low-income families will increase total consumption expenditures. Test Randy's assertion by assuming that the government takes $4,000 from each richer family and gives it to each poorer family, and that all families adjust their consumption in line with the consumption function described in Table 7–1. Then fill in the following:

Consumption of a family with $16,000 income

_____

Consumption of a family with $24,000 income

_____

Aggregate consumption of all 200 families

_____

d. Explain why in this example aggregate consumption is unaffected by the redistribution of income.

3. Use the data in Table 7–1 to compute an algebraic expression for the consumption function.

Consumption = _____ + 0._____ × (disposable income)

SELF-TESTS FOR UNDERSTANDING

Test A

Circle the correct answer.

1. Which of the following is not a part of aggregate demand?
   a. Consumption expenditures.
   b. National income.
   c. Net exports.
   d. Investment expenditures.
2. Which of the following would be an example of a government transfer payment?
   a. Wages paid to government bureaucrats.
   b. A tax refund for excess withholding.
   c. The purchase of paperclips by a government agency.
   d. Social security payments.
3. In a circular flow diagram all but which one of the following would be depicted as an injection into the stream of spending?

   a. The Defense Department's purchase of a new nuclear submarine.
   b. Joyce and Jim's purchase of an existing house.
   c. Alice's spending to rebuild her restaurant after the fire.
   d. The set of new micro-computers that Elaine's company bought for all its top management.
4. A graphical representation of how consumption spending varies with changes in disposable income is called the
   a. aggregate demand curve.
   b. income-expenditure schedule.
   c. consumption function.
   d. Phillips curve.
5. A change in which one of the following would be associated with a movement along the consumption function?
   a. Current disposable income.
   b. Wealth.
   c. The price level.
   d. Expected future incomes.
6. If the marginal propensity to consume is 0.7, then a $100 billion change in disposable income will be associated with what change in consumption spending?
   a. $20 billion.
   b. $30 billion.
   c. $70 billion.
   d. $100 billion.
7. If a $100 billion increase in disposable income results in a $75 billion increase in consumption spending, then the marginal propensity to consume is
   a. 0.25
   b. 0.50
   c. 0.75
   d. 1.0
8. If the marginal propensity to consume is 0.80, what decrease in taxes will initially increase consumption spending by $16 billion?
   a. $12.8 billion.
   b. $16 billion.
   c. $20 billion.
   d. $64 billion.
9. If consumption spending declines by $45 billion when disposable income declines by $50 billion, what is the marginal propensity to consume?
   a. 0.9
   b. 0.1
   c. −0.1
   d. −0.9
10. If the marginal propensity to consume is .8, a $100 billion change in the wealth of consumers will lead to

a. a $100 billion change in consumption spending.
b. an $80 billion change in consumption spending.
c. a movement along the consumption function.
d. a shift in the entire consumption function.

Test B

Circle T or F for True or False as appropriate.

1. Aggregate demand is the aggregate of individual household consumption decisions.　　T F

2. The consumption function reflects the close relationship between consumption spending and national output.　　T F

3. The U.S. government has often used changes in income tax rates as a way of influencing consumer spending.　　T F

4. A change in consumption divided by the change in disposable income that produced the change in consumption is called the marginal propensity to consume.　　T F

5. An increase in the level of prices is likely to reduce consumption expenditures.　　T F

6. The effect of a change in the level of prices on consumption would be viewed graphically as a shift in the consumption function.　　T F

7. By increasing household wealth, a big increase in the stock market is likely to lead to a movement along the consumption function.　　T F

8. The magnitude of the impact of a change in taxes on consumption expenditures is likely to depend on whether consumers view the change in taxes as permanent or temporary.　　T F

9. A temporary decrease in taxes is likely to have a smaller impact on consumption than will a permanent decrease.　　T F

10. The initial impact of a change in income taxes on consumption spending can be calculated by multiplying the change in disposable income by the marginal propensity to consume.　　T F

Appendix A: The Saving Function and the Marginal Propensity to Save

LEARNING OBJECTIVES

Working through the exercise below should help you understand the basic message of Appendix A to Chapter 7; that is: *We could just as easily have used the saving function instead of the consumption function.* When you have completed the exercise you should be able to:
- compute savings given data on disposable income and consumption.
- compute the marginal propensity to save.
- show that the MPC and the MPS sum to 1.0.

IMPORTANT TERMS AND CONCEPTS

Aggregate saving
Saving function
Marginal propensity to save

DEFINITION QUIZ

Choose the letter that is the most appropriate definition for each of the following terms.

1. _____ Aggregate saving

2. _____ Saving function

3. _____ Marginal propensity to save

a. Change in consumer savings divided by change in disposable income.
b. Consumer savings divided by disposable income.
c. Schedule relating consumer saving to disposable income.
d. Disposable income minus consumption.

BASIC EXERCISE

1. Table 7–2 reproduces the income and consumption data from Table 7–1. Use the data in Table 7–2 to compute the amount of saving at each level of income. Remember that saving is just the difference between disposable income and consumption, that is $S = DI - C$.
2. For each change in income, compute the marginal propensity to save. (You will first need to compute the change in savings.)
3. Using results from Tables 7–1 and 7–2, show that the sum of the marginal propensity to consume and the marginal propensity to save for each change in income is 1.0.
4. Use the data on income and saving to compute the average propensity to save.
5. Again, using results from Tables 7–1 and 7–2, show that the sum of the average propensity to consume and the average propensity to save at each level of income is 1.0.
6. It is because APC plus APS always equals 1.0 and MPC plus MPS always equals 1.0 that we can use the saving or consumption factor interchangeably.

    Some simple algebra also gives the same result. Start with the identity.

$$DI = C + S.$$

Now divide both sides of the equation by DI and interpret your results in terms of APC and APS.

We also know that since any change in income must be spent or saved

$$\Delta DI = \Delta C + \Delta S.$$

where Δ means change. Now divide both sides of the equation by ΔDI and interpret your results in terms of MPC and MPS.

Appendix B: National Income Accounting

LEARNING OBJECTIVES

After completing the material in this appendix you should be able to:

- define, understand, and use correctly the terms and concepts listed below.

- describe the three alternative ways of measuring GNP and explain why, except for bookkeeping or statistical errors, they give the same answer.

- explain why national income accounting treats government purchases of goods and services differently from government transfer payments.

- explain the difference in theory and practice between the following macro measurements: GNP, NNP, national income, personal income, and disposable income.

TABLE 7–2

DATA ON INCOME, CONSUMPTION, AND SAVING

Average Propensity to Save	Saving (billions of dollars)	Consumption (billions of dollars)	Disposable Income (billions of dollars)	Change in Disposable Income (billions of dollars)	Change in Saving (billions of dollars)	Marginal Propensity to Save
_____	_____	10,400	12,000			
				4,000	_____	_____
_____	_____	12,800	16,000			
				4,000	_____	_____
_____	_____	15,200	20,000			
				4,000	_____	_____
_____	_____	17,600	24,000			
				4,000	_____	_____
_____	_____	20,000	28,000			

IMPORTANT TERMS AND CONCEPTS

National income accounting
Gross National Product (GNP)
Gross private domestic investment
Government purchases

Transfer payments
Net exports
National Income
Net National Product (NNP)
Depreciation
Value added
Personal Income
Disposable Income (*DI*)

APPENDIX REVIEW

Although included in an appendix, this material on national income accounting deserves its own special treatment. When working through this material, do not lose sight of the forest for the trees. The forest has to do with broad income concepts, such as GNP, net national product, national income: what each of these concepts measures and how they relate to one another. This appendix is an introduction to the forest rather than to each individual tree.

The *national income accounts* measure economic activity: the production of goods and services and the incomes that are simultaneously generated. Accurate measurement of production and income is an important prerequisite to attempts to understand and control the economy. National income accounts are centered around measurement of the gross national product. Consumption (*C*), investment (*I*), government purchases of goods and services (*G*), and net exports (*X − IM*) are parts of GNP. Other concepts, such as *net national product (NNP)* and *national income*, are alternative measures of total economic activity.

(1) GNP is defined as the sum of the money values of all _____ goods and services that are (produced/sold) during a specified period of time. Economists use money values or market prices to add up the very different types of output that make up GNP. Two of the three exceptions mentioned in Appendix B—government output and inventories—arise because some production is not sold on markets.

The emphasis on *final* goods and services is important, because it avoids double counting of intermediate goods. (The need to avoid double counting is also the key to why the three alternative ways of measuring GNP are conceptually equivalent.) The third part of the definition says that GNP is a statement of production, not sales. It is only production that creates new goods available for consumption or investment. Thus GNP, as a measure of production, is the appropriate measure of how much new consumption or investment our economy can enjoy.

There are three ways to measure GNP. Perhaps the simplest, most straightforward way to measure GNP is to add up the purchases of newly produced final goods and services by private individuals and firms—for consumption and investment—and by the government. For the United States in 1989, this sum

(2) of *C + I + G + X − IM* was estimated to be $5,233 billion. Net exports? Net exports are (imports/exports) minus _____. We must add exports to *C + I + G* because, even though bought by foreigners, exports are American products and GNP is a measure of total U.S. production. We subtract imports because *C* and *I* and *G* are measures of total spending, including imports, and we want a measure that reflects only those goods and services (purchased/produced) in the United States.

All of a firm's sales receipts eventually end up as income for someone, directly in the case of workers, creditors, and firm owners, and indirectly in the case of payments to suppliers, who in turn use this money to pay their workers, creditors, and so forth. Thus, instead of measuring GNP as purchases of final goods and services, we could equivalently add up all incomes earned in the production of goods and services. This

(3) sum of factor incomes is also called national _____ and is the second way to measure GNP. It is conceptually similar to GNP but differs for U.S. national income accounts because of two items. Indirect business taxes are included in market prices paid by consumers but (do/do not) result in income for any factor of production as they are immediately collected by the government. National

income plus indirect business taxes is equal to NNP or _____ national product, which is almost, but not quite, equal to GNP. The difference between NNP and GNP is

_____ and, conceptually, refers to the portion of current total production that is used to replace those parts of the capital stock that have deteriorated as a result of current production. If GNP were all one edible good, we could eat NNP while maintaining our productive capacity. Eating GNP would reduce our productive capacity as we would not be replacing worn-out plants and machines.

To measure GNP as the money value of final goods and services, one would start by collecting sales data for final goods. The second way of measuring GNP, total factor incomes, would start by collecting income data from firms and individuals. The third way of measuring GNP looks at the difference between a firm's sales receipts and its purchases from other firms. This difference, also called a firm's

(4) _____ _____ , is the amount of money a firm has to pay the factors of production that it has employed, including the profits firm owners pay themselves. Thus, the sum of total value added in the economy is the third way to measure GNP.

DEFINITION QUIZ

Choose the letter that is the most appropriate definition for each of the following terms.

1. _____ National income accounting

2. _____ Net national product

3. _____ Depreciation

4. _____ Value added

a. Bookkeeping and measurement system for national economic data.
b. Value of an economy's capital used up during a year.
c. Revenue from sale of product minus amount paid for goods and services purchased from other firms.
d. Loss on value of business assets from inflation.
e. Gross national product minus depreciation.

BASIC EXERCISES

These problems are designed to give you practice in understanding alternative ways of measuring GNP.

1. Consider the following two-firm economy. Firm A is a mining company that does not make purchases from firm B. Firm A sells all its output to firm B, which in turn sells all its output to consumers.

	Firm A	Firm B
Total sales	$500	$1700
Wages	400	800
Profits	100	400
Purchases from other firms	0	500

1. What are the total sales for the economy?

$_____

2. What is the total value of sales for final uses?

$_____

3. What is the total of all factor incomes?

$_____

4. What is value added for firm A?

$_____

5. What is value added for firm B?

$_____

6. What is the total value added of both firms?

$_____

7. What is GNP? $_____

8. What is national income?

$_____

2. Table 7–3 contains information on a three-firm economy. Firm A sells only to other firms. Firm B has both an industrial and a household division. Firm C sells only to final consumers. Note also that production by firm C was greater than sales, thus the entry showing the addition to inventories. Simple addition shows that the sum of factor incomes, in this case wages and profits, is equal to $4,700. Answer the following questions to see if the two other ways of measuring GNP give the same answer. The tricky part of this question is the treatment of production that has not been sold, but added to inventories. You may want to review the discussion of inventories in Appendix B before answering the following questions.

TABLE 7–3

	Firm A	Firm B	Firm C
TOTAL SALES	$1,000	$2,500	$3,000
Sales to firm B	$400		
Sales to firm C	$600	$1,000	
Sales to consumers		$1,500	$3,000
Change in inventories			$200
Wages	$750	$1,800	$1,200
Profits	$250	$300	$400

a. Calculate value added for each firm and the sum of value added for all firms.

Value Added, firm A _____

Value Added, firm B _____

Value Added, firm C _____

Sum _____

b. GNP is defined as the production of newly produced final goods and services. It is typically calculated by summing sales of newly produced final goods and services. Calculate sales for final use for each firm and the sum for all firms.

Sales for final use, firm A

_____

Sales for final use, firm B

_____

Sales for final use, firm C

_____

Sum _____

SELF-TESTS FOR UNDERSTANDING

Test A

Circle the correct answers.

1. Which of the following would add to this year's GNP?
   a. Jim purchases a new copy of the Baumol-Blinder textbook for this course.
   b. Jill purchases a used copy of the Baumol-Blinder textbook for this course.
   c. Susan purchases 100 shares of GM stock.
   d. Steve sells last semester's textbooks.

2. Conceptually, GNP can be measured by all but which one of the following:
   a. Add up all factor payments by firms in the economy.
   b. Add up all purchases of final goods and services, $C + I + G + (X - IM)$.
   c. Add up total sales of all firms in the economy.
   d. Add up value added for all firms in the economy.

3. Which of the following events result in an addition to gross private domestic investment?
   a. Managers of the Good Earth, a newly formed food co-op, buy a used refrigerator case for their store.
   b. Roberta buys 100 shares of stock in Xerox.
   c. The U.S. Air Force purchases a new plane for the president.
   d. United Airlines purchases 20 new planes so it can expand its service.

4. Gross private domestic investment includes all but which one of the following?
   a. The new home purchased by Kimberly and Jason.
   b. The new Japanese computer purchased by Acme Manufacturing to automate their production line.
   c. The increase in the inventory of newly produced but unsold cars.
   d. The construction of a new plant to manufacture micro computers for IBM.

5. When measuring GNP as the production of final goods and services, $C + I + G + (X - IM)$, government purchases include all but which one of the following:
   a. Salaries paid to members of Congress.
   b. Newly produced red tape purchased by government agencies.
   c. Social security payments to older Americans.
   d. Concrete for new highway construction.

6. Which of the following transactions represents the sale of a final good as opposed to sale of an intermediate good?

a. Farmer Jones sells her peaches to the Good Food Packing and Canning Company.

b. Good Food sells a load of canned peaches to Smith Brothers Distributors.

c. Smith Brothers sells the load of canned peaches to Irving's Supermarket.

d. You buy a can of peaches at Irving's.

7. An increase in government transfer payments to individuals will lead to an initial increase in which one of the following?

a. GNP.

b. NNP.

c. Government purchases of goods and services.

d. Disposable income.

8. In measuring GNP, government outputs are

a. appropriately valued at zero.

b. valued by estimates of their market prices.

c. valued at the cost of inputs needed to produce them.

9. If net national product equals $5,000 billion and indirect business taxes are $300 billion, then national income would equal

a. $5,300 billion.

b. $5,000 billion.

c. $4,700 billion.

d. Insufficient information to determine national income.

10. Net national product is

a. always greater than GNP.

b. considered by many economists to be a more meaningful measure of the nation's economic output than is GNP.

c. conceptually superior to GNP because it excludes the output of environmental "bads."

d. measured by subtracting indirect business taxes from GNP.

Test B

Circle T or F for True or False as appropriate.

1. GNP is designed to be a measure of economic well-being, not a measure of economic production.　　　　　　　　　　　**T F**

2. If you measured GNP by adding up total sales in the economy, you would be double or triple counting many intermediate goods.　**T F**

3. Production that is not sold but is instead added to inventories is not counted in GNP.　**T F**

4. If GM started its own steel company rather than continuing to buy steel from independent steel companies, GNP would be lower because intrafirm transfers are not part of GNP but all interfirm sales are.　　　　　　　　**T F**

5. Since the output of government agencies is not sold on markets, it is not included in GNP.　　　　　　　　　　　　　　　**T F**

6. Value added is the difference between what a firm sells its output for and the cost of its own purchases from other firms.　　**T F**

7. The difference between GNP and NNP is net exports.　　　　　　　　　　　　**T F**

8. Disposable income is usually greater than net national product.　　　　　　　**T F**

9. Corporate profits are the largest component of national income.　　　　　　**T F**

10. The sum of value added for all firms in the economy is equal to the sum of all factor incomes—wages, interest, rents, and profits.　　　　　　　　　　　　　**T F**

SUPPLEMENTARY EXERCISES

1. The data in Table 7–4 come from a recent survey of consumer expenditures. (The survey was conducted in connection with revisions made in the consumer price index in 1978.) Use a piece of graph paper to plot these data. Measure consumption expenditures along the vertical axis, and measure income after taxes along the horizontal axis. Now use a ruler to fit a straight line to the data. How close are the points to your line? The slope of your line is the overall marginal propensity to consume. What is it? Next use these data to compute the marginal propensity to consume for each change in income. How similar is the marginal propensity to consume at different levels?

Notice that at low income levels consumption expenditures exceed income. How can this be?

2. Consider the following nonlinear, consumption function.

$$C = 100 \sqrt{DI}.$$

Restricting yourself to positive values for disposable income, graph this function. What happens to the marginal propensity to consume as income increases? Can you find an explicit expression for the marginal propensity to consume as a function of income? (A knowledge of simple calculus will be helpful.) Use this new consumption function to

TABLE 7–4

Income After Taxes (billions of dollars)	Current Consumption Expenses (billions of dollars)	Change in Income (billions of dollars)	Change in Consumption (billions of dollars)	MPC
3,347	4,000			
4,252	4,531	_____	_____	_____
5,084	5,100	_____	_____	_____
5,928	5,725	_____	_____	_____
6,715	6,148	_____	_____	_____
7,911	6,921	_____	_____	_____
9,491	7,889	_____	_____	_____
11,485	8,890	_____	_____	_____
14,541	10,639	_____	_____	_____
18,370	12,591	_____	_____	_____
		_____	_____	_____

The open-ended income categories, at the lowest and highest income levels, have been omitted.

Source: Table 1, *Consumer Expenditure Survey Series: Interview Series, 1972–73*, U.S. Department of Labor, Bureau of Labor Services, Report 454–4, 1977.

re-answer Basic Exercise question 2 about income redistribution. Does your answer change? If so, why?

What is the savings function that goes with this consumption function? Does MPC + MPS = 1? Does APC + APS = 1?

8

Demand-Side Equilibrium: Unemployment or Inflation?

LEARNING OBJECTIVES

After you complete the material in this chapter you should be able to:

- define, understand, and use correctly the terms and concepts listed below.
- describe some of the major determinants of investment spending by firms and explain which of these determinants can be directly affected by government actions.
- describe how income and prices, both American and foreign, affect exports and imports.
- draw an expenditure schedule, given information about consumption spending, investment spending, and net exports.
- determine the equilibrium level of income and explain why the level of income tends toward its equilibrium value.
- describe how a change in the price level affects the expenditure schedule and the equilibrium level of income.

- describe how the impact of a change in prices on the expenditure schedule and the equilibrium level of income can be used to derive the aggregate demand curve.
- explain why equilibrium GNP can be above or below the full employment level of GNP.

IMPORTANT TERMS AND CONCEPTS

Capital gains
Equilibrium level of GNP
Expenditure schedule
Induced investment
$Y = C + I + (X - IM)$
Income–expenditure (or 45° line) diagram
Aggregate demand curve
Full-employment level of GNP (or potential GNP)
Recessionary gap
Inflationary gap
Coordination of saving and investment

CHAPTER REVIEW

This chapter is the introduction to explicit models of income determination. The model discussed in this chapter is relatively simple and is not meant to be taken literally. Do not be put off by the simplicity of the model or its lack of realism. Careful study now will pay future dividends in terms of easier understanding of later chapters, in which both the mechanics and policy implications of more complicated models are described.

The central focus of this chapter is on the concept of the *equilibrium level of income and output.* (You may want to review the material in Chapter 7 on the equality of national income and national output.) The models discussed in this chapter show us how spending decisions are reconciled with production decisions of firms to determine the equilibrium level of GNP.

When considering the determination of the equilibrium level of GNP, it is important to distinguish between output and income on the one hand and total spending on the other hand. If total spending exceeds current production, firms will find that their inventories are decreasing. They are then likely to take steps to

(1) (decrease/increase) production and output. Analogously, if total spending is less than current output, firms are likely to find their inventories _____, and they are likely to take steps to _____ production.

The concept of equilibrium refers to a situation in which producers and consumers are satisfied with things the way they are and see no reason to change their behavior. Thus the equilibrium level of GNP must be a level of GNP at which firms have no reason to increase or decrease output; that is, at the equilibrium level of GNP, total spending and output will be equal. The determination of the equilibrium level of output thus reduces to

    1. describing how total spending changes as output (and income) changes, and
    2. finding the one level of output (and income) at which total spending equals output.

In the simplified model discussed in this chapter, there are three components to total spending: consumption, investment, and net exports. Chapter 7 discussed the important role that income plays as a determinant of consumption expenditures. There is no such central factor influencing investment expenditures. Instead, investment expenditures are influenced by a variety of factors, including business people's expectations about the future, the rate of growth of demand as measured against existing capacity, interest rates, and tax factors. If any of these factors change, investment spending is likely to change.

Net exports are the difference between exports and imports, specifically _____

(2) minus _____. Exports reflect foreign demand for American production and imports come from American demand for foreign goods and services. It should not be surprising that both are influenced by income and prices. The tricky part is keeping straight whose income influences which demand and how changes in American and foreign prices influence net exports.

The income-expenditure diagram is a useful tool for analyzing the determination of the equilibrium level of output. To find the equilibrium level of output and income we need to know how total spending changes as income and output change, and we need to know where total spending equals income. The relationship between total spending, $C + I + (X - IM)$, and income is given by the *expenditure schedule*. The 45° line shows all combinations of spending and income that are equal. The one place where spending is equal to

(3) income is given by the _____ of the expenditure schedule and the 45° line. This is the equilibrium level of output because it is the only level of output where total spending is equal to output. At any other level of output, total spending will not be equal to output. (You should be sure that you understand why the economy tends to move to the equilibrium level of output rather than getting stuck at a level of income and output at which total spending is either larger or smaller than output. Do not get confused between this automatic tendency to move to the equilibrium level of output and the lack, sometimes, of an automatic mechanism to ensure full employment.)

Any particular expenditure schedule relates total spending to income for a given level of prices. As prices change, total spending will change, even for the same level of real income. In particular, a higher

(4) price level is apt to mean (more/less) consumption spending because of the decline in the purchasing power of the money assets of consumers. This effect of prices on consumption will lead to a (downward/upward) shift in the expenditure schedule and a new equilibrium of income that is (higher/lower) than before. In the

opposite case, a lower price level would mean _____ consumption spending and a new, (higher/lower) equilibrium level of income. The relationship between the price level and the equilibrium level of income is called the *aggregate demand curve*. The aggregate demand curve is derived from the income–expenditure diagram and, from the viewpoint of demand, shows the relationship between the level of prices and the equilibrium level of income. The qualifier "from the viewpoint of demand" is important. Complete determination of the equilibrium level of income/output and the equilibrium price level comes from the interaction of the aggregate demand and aggregate supply curves.

Nothing that has been said so far implies that the equilibrium level of output will equal the full-employment level of output. The equilibrium level of output will be determined in part by the strength of aggregate demand and may be greater or less than the full-employment level of output. If the equilibrium

(5) level of output exceeds the full-employment level of output, the difference is called the _____ gap. In a case where the equilibrium level of output is less than the full-employment level of output, the difference is called the _____ gap.

DEFINITION QUIZ

Choose the letter that is the most appropriate definition for each of the following terms.

1. _____ Capital Gains

2. _____ Equilibrium level of GNP

3. _____ Expenditure schedule

4. _____ Induced investment

5. _____ Income-expenditure diagram

6. _____ Aggregate demand curve

7. _____ Recessionary gap

8. _____ Inflationary gap

9. _____ Saving schedule

a. Graph of quantity of national product demanded at each possible price level.

b. Line showing relationship between GNP and total spending.

c. Table or curve depicting how saving depends on GNP.

d. Increase in value of an asset between the time it is purchased and the time it is sold.

e. Amount by which real GNP exceeds full-employment GNP.

f. Level of output where aggregate demand equals total production.

g. Investment spending that changes with changes in GNP.

h. Table or graph showing how saving depends on consumption.

i. Amount by which full-employment GNP exceeds real GNP.

j. Graph that allows plotting of total real expenditures against real income.

BASIC EXERCISES

These exercises are designed to give you practice with manipulations on the income–expenditure diagram. They are based on data for income (output), consumption spending, investment spending, and net exports given in Table 8–1.

1. This exercise shows you how the expenditure schedule is derived and how it helps to determine the equilibrium level of income. For this exercise it is assumed that prices are constant with the consumer price index or price level having a value of 100.

   a. Use the data on consumption spending and income to draw the consumption function on the graph in Figure 8–1.

   b. Add investment spending to the line drawn in Figure 8–1 to show how consumption plus investment spending vary with income.

   c. Now draw the expenditure schedule, C + I + (X − IM) in Figure 8–1.

   d. Next draw a line representing all the points where total spending and income could be equal. (This is the 45° line. Do you know why?)

   e. The 45° line represents all the points that *could be* the equilibrium level of income. Now circle the one point that *is* the equilibrium

TABLE 8-1
(PRICE LEVEL = 100)

Real Income (Output)	Real Consumption Spending	Real Investment Spending	Real Net Exports	Total Spending
3600	3500	500	– 100	_____
3800	3600	500	– 100	_____
4000	3700	500	– 100	_____
4200	3800	500	– 100	_____
4400	3900	500	– 100	_____
4600	4000	500	– 100	_____

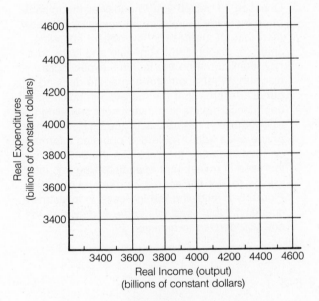

FIGURE 8-1

level of income. What is the equilibrium level of income on your graph?

f. Check your answer by filling in the Total Spending column in Table 8–1 to see where total spending equals income. You should get the same answer from Table 8–1 as you do from the graph.

g. Why isn't the equilibrium level of output $3800 billion? If for some reason national output and income started out at $3800 billion, what forces would tend to move the economy toward the equilibrium you determined in Questions e and f?

h. Using the data in Table 8–1 and assuming that the full-employment level of output

income is $4000 billion, is there an inflationary or recessionary gap? How large is the gap? If the full-employment level of income were $4500 billion, how large would the inflationary or recessionary gap be?

i. Assume now that an increase in business confidence leads to an increased level of investment spending. Specifically, assume that investment spending rises to $600 billion at all levels of national income. As a result of this shift, what happens to each of the following?

- The expenditure schedule.
- The equilibrium level of income.
- Consumption spending at the new equilibrium level of income.
- Net exports at the new equilibrium level of income.

2. This exercise explores the implications of changes in the price level. It is designed to show how a change in the price level implies a shift in the expenditure schedule and can be used to derive the aggregate demand curve.

a. The data in Table 8–1 assumed that prices were constant with the consumer price index, or the price level, at a value of 100. Mark the point in Figure 8–2 that shows the price level of 100 and the equilibrium level of income you found when answering Questions e and f of Exercise 1.

b. Economic research has determined that if prices rose to 110, consumption spending would decline by $100 billion at every level of real income. Table 8–2 shows the relevant information. Each entry in the column for a price level of 110 should be 100 less than the values you calculated for total spending in question 1.f. What is the new equilibrium level

TABLE 8-2

Real Income (Output)	Total Spending (Price Level = 90)	Total Spending (Price Level = 110)
3600	4000	3800
3800	4100	3900
4000	4200	4000
4200	4300	4100
4400	4400	4200
4600	4500	4300

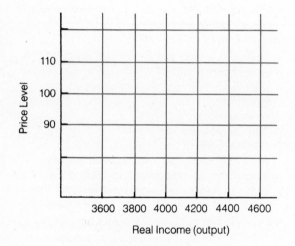

FIGURE 8-2

of income with this higher price level? Mark the point in Figure 8-2 that shows the price level of 110 and this new equilibrium level of income.

c. This same research determined that if prices fell to 90, real consumption spending would increase over amounts shown in Table 8-1 by $100 billion at every level of real income. What is the new equilibrium level of income on the income-expenditure diagram for this lower price level? Mark the point in Figure 8-2 that shows the price level of 90 and this new equilibrium level of income.

d. The points you have marked in Figure 8-2 help to trace out what curve?

e. Connect these points to verify that your curve has a (negative/positive) slope.

3. Question 1.i. asked you to consider the impact of an increase in investment spending. We saw then that an increase in investment spending shifts the expenditure schedule and leads to a new equilibrium on the income-expenditure diagram. What about the aggregate demand curve? Assume that the increase in business confidence means that investment spending rises to $600 billion regardless of the level of income or the price level. Table 8-3 contains information on total spending that includes the $100 billion increase in investment spending. Use this information to plot the aggregate demand curve in Figure 8-2 following the increase in investment spending. How does this curve compare to the one you derived in question 2?

TABLE 8-3

REAL INCOME AND TOTAL SPENDING WHEN I = 600

Real Income (Output)	Total Spending (Price Level = 90)	Total Spending (Price Level = 100)	Total Spending (Price Level = 110)
3600	4100	4000	3900
3800	4200	4100	4000
4000	4300	4200	4100
4200	4400	4300	4200
4400	4500	4400	4300
4600	4600	4500	4400

SELF-TESTS FOR UNDERSTANDING

Test A

Circle the correct answer.

1. The expenditure schedule is a relationship between
   a. the equilibrium level of income and prices.
   b. consumption spending and income.
   c. total spending and income.
   d. consumption spending and prices.
2. When total spending is less than output
   a. inventories are likely to be increasing.
   b. inventories are likely to be decreasing.
   c. there will be a shift in the expenditure schedule.
   d. firms are likely to raise prices.
3. In the income–expenditure diagram, the equilibrium level of output is given by the intersection of the expenditure schedule and the
   a. consumption function.
   b. aggregate demand curve.
   c. 45° line.
   d. level of full-employment output.
4. When total spending is equal to output,
   a. the resulting level of output is called the full-employment level of output.
   b. We know that consumers' savings plans and firms' investment plans are in balance.
   c. there is never an inflationary gap.
   d. the expenditure schedule and the aggregate demand curve coincide.
5. Government policies can directly affect all but which one of the following determinants of investment spending?
   a. Interest rates.
   b. The state of business confidence.
   c. Tax incentives.
   d. The overall state of aggregate demand.
6. If at the full-employment level of income, consumers' savings plans are equal to firms' investment plans, then
   a. the equilibrium level of income will be equal to the full-employment level of income.
   b. there will be an inflationary gap.
   c. firms will find their inventories increasing.
   d. the economy will be producing less than potential output.
7. The aggregate demand curve is a relationship between the price level and
   a. consumption spending.
   b. the equilibrium level of income on the income–expenditure diagram.
   c. full-employment GNP.
   d. the interest rate.
8. A lower price level will lead to a
   a. movement along the consumption function.
   b. shift in the consumption function.
   c. movement along the expenditure schedule.
   d. shift in the aggregate demand curve.
9. A shift in the investment function will lead to all but which one of the following?
   a. A shift in the expenditure function.
   b. A new equilibrium level of income.
   c. A movement along the aggregate demand curve.
   d. A change in consumption spending.
10. At the equilibrium level of income which one of the following is not necessarily true?
    a. The expenditure schedule will intersect the 45° line.
    b. The amount consumers want to save will equal the amount that businesses want to invest.
    c. There will be no unemployment.
    d. The equilibrium level of output and the price level will together determine one point on the aggregate demand curve.

Test B

Circle T or F for True or False as appropriate.

1. It is an easy task for government policymakers to influence the state of business confidence.   T F

2. The expenditure schedule refers to a relationship between total spending and the level of output (and income).   T F

3. The equilibrium level of GNP never equals the full-employment level of GNP.   T F

4. If total spending exceeds national output, the resulting decrease in inventories will lead firms to reduce the level of output and production.   T F

5. The intersection of the expenditure schedule and the 45° line determines one point on the aggregate demand curve.   T F

6. The vertical difference between the 45° line and the aggregate demand curve is called the inflationary gap.   T F

7. The term recessionary gap refers to a situation in which the equilibrium level of GNP is less than the full-employment level of GNP.   T F

8. Because consumers usually invest their savings at financial institutions, there can be no difference between desired savings and desired investment for the economy.   T   F

9. An increase in the level of prices, through its impact on consumption spending, will lead to a movement along the expenditure schedule.   T   F

10. The aggregate demand curve refers to a relationship between the equilibrium level of income and the price level.   T   F

Appendix A: The Saving and Investment Approach

LEARNING OBJECTIVE

The exercise below is intended to illustrate the basic content of Appendix A to Chapter 8; that is *The condition for the equilibrium level of income can be stated as $Y = C + I + (X - IM)$ or it can be stated as $S = I + (X - IM)$.* Both statements lead to the same result.

IMPORTANT TERMS AND CONCEPTS

$S = I + (X - IM)$
Saving schedule
Investment schedule
Induced investment

BASIC EXERCISE

Table 8–4 reproduces the data in Table 8–1.
1. Using the definition of saving, $S = Y - C$, determine the level of consumer saving at each level of income.
2. At what level of income is the sum of investment spending plus net exports equal to consumer saving? How does this level of income compare with the equilibrium level of income you computed in Question e of the first Basic Exercise to this chapter?
3. Construct a new version of Table 8–4 in which investment spending is $600 billion. Find the new equilibrium level of income where saving equals investment. How does your answer compare with your answer to Question i of the first Basic Exercise to the chapter?
4. In addition to working the same numerical example in different ways, we can also show the equivalence of the two conditions for the equilibrium level of income by using a little high school algebra. We know that in equilibrium

$$Y = C + I + (X - IM)$$

TABLE 8–4
(PRICE LEVEL = 100)

Real Income (Output)	Real Consumption Spending	Real Consumer Saving	Real Investment Spending	Real Net Exports	Investment plus Net Exports
3600	3500	_____	500	− 100	_____
3800	3600	_____	500	− 100	_____
4000	3700	_____	500	− 100	_____
4200	3800	_____	500	− 100	_____
4400	3900	_____	500	− 100	_____
4600	4000	_____	500	− 100	_____

We also know that at each level of income consumers either spend or save their income; that is, $Y = C + S$ at every level of income. We can thus substitute $C + S$ for Y in our equilibrium condition and get

$$C + S = C + I + (X - IM)$$

Subtracting C from both sides of this expression yields our alternative formulation of the equilibrium condition, or

$$\underline{\hspace{4cm}} = \underline{\hspace{4cm}}.$$

Appendix B: The Simple Algebra of Income Determination

BASIC EXERCISES

These exercises are meant to illustrate the material in Appendix B to Chapter 8. If we are willing to use algebra we can use equations rather than graphs or tables to determine the equilibrium level of output. If we have done all our work accurately, we should get the same answer regardless of whether we use graphs, tables, or algebra.

1. Determine the equilibrium level of income if the consumption function is given by

$$C = 1700 + .5Y$$

and investment expenditures are \$500 billion and net exports are − \$100 billion regardless of the level of income. Is your answer here the same as for Question e of the first Basic Exercise to this chapter? It should be.

2. Determine the equilibrium level of income, given the same consumption function as in Exercise 1 but the higher level of investment expenditure of \$600 billion. Is your answer here the same as for Question i of the first Basic Exercise to this chapter? It should be.

3. The equilibrium level of income will be affected by shifts in the consumption function as well as by changes in investment spending. Determine the equilibrium level of income if, following a decrease in the level of prices, the consumption function is

$$C = 1800 + .5Y$$

while investment spending and net exports are unchanged at \$500 billion and − \$100 billion.

9

Changes on the Demand Side: Multiplier Analysis

LEARNING OBJECTIVES

After completing the material in this chapter you should be able to:

- define, understand, and use correctly the terms and concepts listed below.
- explain why any autonomous increases in expenditures will have a multiplier effect on GNP.
- calculate the value of the multiplier in specific examples.
- explain how and why the value of the multiplier would change if the marginal propensity to consume changed.
- explain why the multiplier expression, 1/(1 – MPC), is oversimplified.
- explain the difference between an autonomous and an induced increase in consumption expenditures.

- explain how and why economic booms and recessions tend to be transmitted across national boundaries.
- explain why an increase in savings may be good for an individual but bad for the economy as a whole.
- describe how an autonomous increase in spending leads to a shift in the aggregate demand curve.

IMPORTANT TERMS AND CONCEPTS

The multiplier
Induced increase in consumption
Autonomous increase in consumption
Paradox of thrift

CHAPTER REVIEW

The main topic of this chapter is the *multiplier*. It is a fundamental concept in economics, which is why a whole chapter is devoted to explaining how it works. The multiplier has already played an important but unheralded role in Chapter 8, so those of you who paid close attention to the subject matter of Chapter 8 should have an easier time grasping the concept of multiplier analysis presented here.

(1)   The basic idea of the multiplier is that a change in autonomous spending by one sector of the economy will change the equilibrium level of income by (more than/the same as/less than) the change in autonomous spending. We have been studying the determination of the equilibrium level of income in the income–expenditure diagram. Multiplier analysis investigates changes in the equilibrium level of income when the expenditure schedule shifts. In this chapter we will be concerned with parallel shifts in the expenditure schedule which are represented graphically as a change in the vertical axis intercept of the expenditure schedule. A parallel shift in the expenditure schedule shows the same change in spending at all levels of income and is thus a change in (autonomous/induced) spending. Spending that changes when income changes, such as the response of consumption spending to a change in income, is called an _____ change.

    Multiplier analysis shows that the equilibrium level of GNP changes by a multiple of the change in autonomous spending, which is where the term "multiplier" comes from. The basic reason for this multiplier result is relatively simple: Increased spending by one sector of the economy means increased sales receipts for other sectors of the economy. Higher sales receipts will show up in bigger paychecks, or profits, or both; in short, higher income for some people. These higher incomes will then induce more consumer spending, which in turn will result in still higher incomes and more consumption spending by others, and so on and so on.

    You may be wondering at this point whether the multiplier is finite or whether income will increase without limit. Another way of looking at this question is to ask what determines the value of the multiplier. There are several alternative, but equally good, ways of answering this question. The discussion in the text approaches the question by summing the increments to spending and income that follow from the original autonomous change in spending. When increments to spending depend upon the marginal propensity to consume, the

(2) oversimplified multiplier expression is $1/(1 - $ _____).

    Here is an alternative derivation of the same result. We know that in equilibrium, national output, or income, will equal total spending. In symbols,

$$Y = C + I + (X - IM).$$

Now assume that there is an autonomous increase in investment spending which induces subsequent increases in consumption spending. At the new equilibrium we know that the change in the equilibrium level of national output will have to be equal to the change in total spending. If net exports are the same at all levels of income, the change in total spending will have two parts. One is the autonomous change in investment spending and the other is the induced change in consumption spending. In words, we know that

(3)
$$\begin{pmatrix} \text{Change in} \\ \text{equilibrium} \\ \text{level of} \\ \text{income} \end{pmatrix} = \begin{pmatrix} \text{Autonomous} \\ \text{change in} \\ \text{investment} \\ \text{spending} \end{pmatrix} + \begin{pmatrix} \text{Induced change in} \\ \underline{\hspace{3cm}} \\ \underline{\hspace{3cm}} \end{pmatrix}$$

    Let us use some symbols to say the same things. Let ΔY represent the change in the equilibrium level of income and ΔI represent the autonomous change in investment spending. What about the induced change in consumption spending? The discussion in Chapter 7 told us that consumption spending will change as

(4) _____ changes. Further, with the use of the concept of the marginal propensity to consume, we can represent the change in consumption spending as the product of the change in income times the _____. In symbols we could represent the induced change in consumption spending as $\Delta Y \times MPC$. If we substitute all these symbols for the words above, we see that

$$\Delta Y = \Delta I + (\Delta Y \times MPC).$$

We can now solve this equation for the change in income by moving all terms in ΔY to the left-hand side of the equation:

$$\Delta Y - (\Delta Y \times MPC) = \Delta I.$$

If we factor out the ΔY we can rewrite the expression as

$$\Delta Y (1 - MPC) = \Delta I.$$

We can now solve for ΔY by dividing both sides of the equation by $(1 - MPC)$.

$$\Delta Y = \left(\frac{1}{1 - MPC}\right)\Delta I.$$

Switching back to words, we find that

$$\begin{pmatrix}\text{Change in} \\ \text{equilibrium} \\ \text{level of} \\ \text{income}\end{pmatrix} = \text{Multiplier} \times \begin{pmatrix}\text{Autonomous} \\ \text{change in} \\ \text{investment} \\ \text{spending}\end{pmatrix}$$

Would our calculation of the multiplier be any different if we considered a change in net exports or an autonomous change in consumption spending? The Basic Exercises to this chapter are designed to help answer this question.

(5) The multiplier expression we just derived is the same as the one in Chapter 9 of the text and is subject to the same limitations. That is, this expression is oversimplified. There are four important reasons why an actual multiplier in the real world will be (smaller/larger) than our formula. These reasons are related to the

effects of higher _____, _____, the _____

system, and _____ _____.

(6) The simplified multiplier expression we derived above comes from shift in the expenditure schedule in the 45° line diagram. As such, this expression assumes that prices (do/do not) change. In Chapter 8 we saw that the income–expenditure diagram is only a building block on the way to the aggregate demand curve. (Remember from Chapter 5 that even the aggregate demand curve is only part of the story. For a

complete analysis we need both the aggregate demand and the aggregate _____ curves.) Thus, to complete our analysis on the demand side, we need to see how our multiplier analysis affects the aggregate demand curve. The multiplier analysis we have done by using the income–expenditure diagram shows us that if prices are constant, the equilibrium level of income will change following any change in (autonomous/induced) spending. This result is true at all price levels and implies that a shift in the expenditure schedule following a change in autonomous spending leads to a shift in the aggregate demand curve. In fact, it leads to a (horizontal/vertical) shift in the aggregate demand curve. The magnitude of the shift can be computed with the help of the multiplier, as shown in Figure 9–4 of the text and Figure 10–4 of the study guide.

DEFINITION QUIZ

Choose the letter that is the most appropriate definition for each of the following terms.

1. _____ Multiplier

2. _____ Induced increase in consumption

3. _____ Autonomous increase in consumption

4. _____ Paradox of thrift

a. Increase in consumer spending due to an increase in disposable income.
b. Attempts to increase savings that cause national income to fall with little net impact on savings.
c. Ratio of change in spending to change in equilibrium GNP.
d. Ratio of change in equilibrium GNP to change in autonomous spending that causes GNP to change.
e. Increase in consumer spending not due to increased incomes.

BASIC EXERCISES

These exercises are designed to illustrate the concepts of the multiplier and the paradox of thrift.

1. The Multiplier
   a. Using the data in Table 9–1, fill in the values for total spending and then find the equilibrium level of income.
   b. Table 9–2 has a similar set of data except that investment spending has risen by $100 billion. Find the equilibrium level of income after the rise in investment spending.
   c. What is the change in the equilibrium level of income following the increase in investment

   spending? _____
   d. What is the value of the multiplier for this increase in autonomous investment spending?

   Multiplier _____
   (Remember that the multiplier is defined as

   the ratio of the change in the _____

   _____ of _____

   divided by the change in _____

   _____ that produced the
   change in income.)
   e. Now let us verify that the value of the multiplier that you found in Question d is the same as the simplified formula 1/(1 − MPC). To do this we will first need to calculate the MPC. Write the value of the MPC here:

   _____. (If you do
   not remember how to calculate the MPC,

review the material in Chapter 7 of the textbook and in this study guide.)
   f. Now calculate the value of the multiplier from the oversimplified formula 1/(1 − MPC).

   Write your answer here: _____.
   (Check to see that it agrees with your answer to Question d.)

2. International Trade
   Assume that an increase in income abroad has increased the demand for American exports by $100 billion. Table 9–3 shows consumption spending, investment spending, and net exports following this increase in foreign demand.
   a. What is the new equilibrium level of domestic income following the increase in net exports?

   _____
   b. What is the change in the equilibrium level of income from its equilibrium in Table 9–2?

   _____
   c. What is the multiplier for the change in the equilibrium level of income following the $100 billion increase in net exports, and how does it compare to the multiplier computed above for a change in investment spending?

   _____

3. The Paradox of Thrift
   Assume that in the aggregate all consumers suddenly decided to save $50 billion more than they have been saving at every level of income. If people want to save more it means they must

   consume _____.

TABLE 9–1

($ billions)

National Income	Consumption Spending	Investment Spending	Net Exports	Total Spending $C + I + (X − IM)$
3800	3250	800	− 200	_____
4000	3400	800	− 200	_____
4200	3550	800	− 200	_____
4400	3700	800	− 200	_____
4600	3850	800	− 200	_____
4800	4000	800	− 200	_____
5000	4150	800	− 200	_____

TABLE 9-2

($ billions)

National Income	Consumption Spending	Investment Spending	Net Exports	Total Spending $C + I + (X - IM)$
3800	3250	900	− 200	_____
4000	3400	900	− 200	_____
4200	3550	900	− 200	_____
4400	3700	900	− 200	_____
4600	3850	900	− 200	_____
4800	4000	900	− 200	_____
5000	4150	900	− 200	_____

TABLE 9-3

($ billions)

National Income	Consumption Spending	Investment Spending	Net Exports	Total Spending $C + I + (X - IM)$
3800	3250	900	− 100	_____
4000	3400	900	− 100	_____
4200	3550	900	− 100	_____
4400	3700	900	− 100	_____
4600	3850	900	− 100	_____
4800	4000	900	− 100	_____
5000	4150	900	− 100	_____

TABLE 9-4

($ billions)

National Income	Consumption Spending	Investment Spending	Net Exports	Total Spending $C + I + (X - IM)$
3800	3200	900	− 100	_____
4000	3350	900	− 100	_____
4200	3500	900	− 100	_____
4400	3650	900	− 100	_____
4600	3800	900	− 100	_____
4800	3950	900	− 100	_____
5000	4100	900	− 100	_____

This change is an (autonomous/induced) change in savings and consumption. Table 9–4 shows the new values for consumption spending following the increased desire to save. Notice that the numbers for consumption spending in Table 9–4 are all $50 billion less than the numbers in the earlier tables, while investment spending and net exports are unchanged from Table 9–3.

a. Using the data in Table 9–4, find the new equilibrium level of income.

b. What is the change in the equilibrium level of income compared with Table 9–3?

_____

c. At this point we can conclude that if consumer saving shows an autonomous increase while investment spending and net exports are unchanged, then the equilibrium level of income will (rise/fall).

d. By how much does income change in response to this autonomous change in saving (and consumption)? We can use our multiplier analysis to find the answer. The equilibrium

level of income changed by $_____ billion in response to an autonomous decrease in consumption spending of $50 billion; thus the multiplier for this change is

_____.

e. How does this multiplier compare with the multiplier you computed for the increase in investment spending?

f. Why is the specific numerical value you have calculated likely to be an overstatement of the multiplier response of a real economy to a change in investment spending, net exports, or saving?

SELF-TESTS FOR UNDERSTANDING

Test A

Circle the correct answer.

1. The multiplier is defined as the ratio of the change in
   a. autonomous spending divided by the change in consumption expenditures.
   b. the equilibrium level of income divided by the increase in consumption spending.
   c. the equilibrium level of income divided by the change in autonomous spending that produced the change in income.
   d. consumption spending divided by the change in autonomous spending.

2. Which one of the following is not the beginning of a multiplier process?
   a. An autonomous increase in net exports.
   b. An induced increase in consumption spending.
   c. An autonomous increase in investment spending.
   d. An autonomous increase in savings.

3. If the marginal propensity to consume were 0.6 and prices did not change, the multiplier would be
   a. $\dfrac{1}{0.6} = 1.67$.
   b. 0.6
   c. $\dfrac{1}{1 - 0.6} = 2.5$.
   d. $\dfrac{1}{1 + 0.6} = 0.63$

4. If the marginal propensity to consume were 0.7 instead of 0.6, the textbook multiplier would be
   a. larger than in Question 3.
   b. smaller than in Question 3.
   c. the same as in Question 3.

5. Real-world multipliers will be less than textbook multipliers because of effects related to all but which one of the following?
   a. Income taxation.
   b. Accounting practices.
   c. International trade.
   d. The financial system.

6. The textbook multiplier would be largest if the marginal propensity to consume were
   a. 0.73
   b. 0.45
   c. 0.89
   d. 0.67

7. When compared with changes in investment spending, the multiplier associated with autonomous changes in consumption spending will be
   a. larger.
   b. smaller.
   c. about the same.

8. An autonomous increase in savings
   a. is necessarily accompanied by an increase in consumption spending.
   b. will shift the expenditure schedule down.
   c. will not affect the level of income as neither the aggregate demand nor the aggregate supply curve will shift.
   d. shifts the aggregate demand curve to the right.

9. The multiplier is useful in calculating
   a. the slope of the consumption function.

b. the horizontal shift in the aggregate demand curve following an increase in autonomous spending.

c. the slope of the expenditure curve.

d. the shift of the consumption function following an increase in autonomous spending.

10. When compared with increases in autonomous spending, multiplier responses for decreases in autonomous spending are likely to be
    a. smaller.
    b. larger.
    c. about the same.
    d. zero.

Test B

Circle T or F for True or False as appropriate.

1. The multiplier is defined as the ratio of a change in autonomous spending divided by the resulting change in the equilibrium level of income.   T F

2. Multiplier responses mean that the equilibrium level of national income is likely to change by less than any change in autonomous spending.   T F

3. Multiplier increases illustrated on the income–expenditure diagram are based on the assumption that prices do not change.   T F

4. In the actual world, multiplier responses to changes in autonomous spending are likely to be less than that suggested by the textbook formula 1/(1 − MPC).   T F

5. If income increases because of an autonomous increase in investment spending, the resulting increase in consumption spending is called an induced increase.   T F

6. An autonomous increase in savings by all consumers will immediately lead to a higher level of real GNP, as resources are freed for higher levels of investment.   T F

7. The multiplier for autonomous increases in investment spending is always greater than the multiplier for autonomous increases in consumption spending.   T F

8. An increase in European income that resulted in an increased demand for American exports would have no effect on the equilibrium level of American income.   T F

9. The multiplier works for increases in autonomous spending, but because of price and wage rigidities the multiplier is irrelevant when we examine decreases in autonomous spending.   T F

10. The impact of a shift in the aggregate demand curve on prices and real output will depend upon the slope of the aggregate supply curve.   T F

SUPPLEMENTARY EXERCISES

1. In 1963 the President's Council of Economic Advisers was considering how large a tax cut would be necessary to return the economy to full employment. These economists estimated that actual output was about $30 to $35 billion less than potential, or full-employment, output. That is, they wanted a tax cut that would increase output by $30 to $35 billion, yet they recommended a tax cut of only $13 billion, to be divided between consumers ($10 billion) and businesses ($3 billion). How could these economists expect that total spending could rise by $30 to $35 billion when taxes were only reduced by $13 billion? Even if consumers and businesses spent the whole reduction in taxes, spending would only rise by $13 billion, not nearly enough to return the economy to full employment.

    What is wrong with this line of reasoning?

2. Use the data in Table 9–1 and a piece of graph paper to draw the income–expenditure diagram.
    a. Show how the expenditure schedule shifts as a result of the increase in investment spending in Basic Exercise 1b. Does your graph give you the same result as Basic Exercise 1c?
    b. Show how the expenditure schedule shifts following the increase in net exports in Basic Exercise 2. How does the new equilibrium level of income, and hence the multiplier, on your graph, compare to your answers in the Basic Exercise?
    c. Show how the expenditure schedule shifts after the increase in savings described in Basic Exercise 3. How does your graph compare with your answer to 3c?

3. If you have access to a micro computer try programming or using a spread sheet to simulate the following model to investigate the dynamics of the multiplier.

    Assume that consumption spending responds to income with a one-period lag as follows

$$C = 400 + .75Y(-1)$$

where C is consumption and Y is national income. Remember that in the models of Chapters 8 and 9, disposable income is equal to national income.

a. If investment spending is always 800 and net exports are -200, then confirm that the equilibrium level of income is 4,000. That is, if income last period was 4,000, then $C + I + (X - IM)$ will equal 4,000 this period.

b. Now assume that investment spending increases by 100. Assuming that consumption responds with the one-period lag, simulate your model to investigate how the change in investment spending affects income over time. Does the level of income appear to converge to a new equilibrium value? What is that value? What is the multiplier for the change in investment spending? How does the multiplier from your simulation compare to the oversimplified formula of $1/(1 - MPC)$?

c. Investigate the impact of increases and decreases in net exports. Investigate the impact of autonomous changes in consumption spending. These latter changes can be modeled as a change in the constant term of the consumption function, that is, the 400 in the equation above. How would you model an autonomous change in savings?

d. What happens if the MPC changes? You will need first to determine the initial equilibrium level of income for given levels of investment spending, net exports, and autonomous consumption spending. Then simulate your model to see how the change in the MPC affects the multiplier.

10

Supply-Side Equilibrium: Unemployment *and* Inflation?

LEARNING OBJECTIVES

After completing the material in this chapter you should be able to:

- define, understand, and use correctly the terms and concepts listed below.
- describe how the aggregate supply curve is derived from an analysis of business costs and why it slopes upward.
- distinguish between factors that will lead to a movement along or a shift in the aggregate supply curve.
- explain why the aggregate supply curve normally gets steeper as output increases.
- use a graph depicting both the aggregate demand curve and the aggregate supply curve to determine the price level and the final equilibrium level of real GNP.
- use the same graph as above to analyze how factors that shift either the aggregate demand curve or the aggregate supply curve will affect the equilibrium level of prices and output.
- use the same graph to explain what kinds of shifts in the aggregate demand curve and the aggregate

supply curve can give rise to a period of stagflation.
- explain why an inflationary gap is apt to self-destruct.
- explain why a recessionary gap is not apt to self-destruct.
- use the aggregate demand/aggregate supply diagram to show how increases in prices reduce the value of the multiplier.

IMPORTANT TERMS AND CONCEPTS

Aggregate supply curve
Productivity
Equilibrium of real GNP and the price level
Inflationary gap
Self-correcting mechanism
Stagflation
Recessionary gap
Inflation and the multiplier

CHAPTER REVIEW

In Chapter 4 we learned that for individual commodities equilibrium price and quantity are determined by the intersection of the relevant demand and supply curves. The same logic holds when analyzing the economy as a whole. The level of prices and aggregate output is determined by the intersection of the aggregate demand and aggregate supply curves. In Chapter 8 we saw how the aggregate demand curve could be derived from the spending decisions of consumers and businesses. In this chapter we will derive the aggregate supply curve and use both curves to see how the price level and aggregate output are determined.

The aggregate supply curve is a schedule, showing for each possible price level, the total quantity of goods and services that all businesses are willing to supply. While a full discussion of supply decisions of individual business firms can be found in Chapter 24, you should note that the same logic applies here and there: Businesses will adjust supply in pursuit of profits.

(1) If prices rise while production costs per unit of output remain unchanged, we expect firms to (increase/decrease) the quantity of output supplied. In fact, if prices stayed higher and production costs did not increase at all, there would be no limit to the increase in profits firms could derive from increases in output. However, even if the prices of inputs do not increase production costs will eventually rise as firms try to expand output, putting a limit on the profitable increase in output. This increase in output induced by an increase in prices is a (movement along/shift in) the aggregate supply curve. Any change in production costs in the face of an otherwise unchanged price level—for example, an increase in energy prices imposed by a foreign supplier—will also affect profits and will lead to an adjustment in the quantity of goods and services that businesses are willing to supply. This time, however, the change in supply is a

_____ _____ the aggregate supply curve.

The increase in production costs associated with higher levels of output, the very increases that put a limit on the profitable increase in supply and helped to define the aggregate supply curve, are likely to be especially severe near full-employment levels of output and are an important reason why the slope of the aggregate supply curve depends upon the level of resource utilization. Near full employment, the aggregate
(2) supply curve is (steeper/flatter).

Now, having derived both the aggregate demand curve and the aggregate supply curve, we are in a position to use them to determine the final equilibrium level of prices and aggregate output, or GNP. See, for example, Figure 10–1, where the equilibrium price level of 100 and the equilibrium level of GNP of $4000
(3) billion are given by the (intersection/slope) of the aggregate demand and supply curves. A higher price level, say, 110, implies (1) a lower quantity of aggregate demand as consumers respond to the loss of purchasing power of their money assets and (2) a larger quantity of aggregate supply as firms respond to higher prices. Clearly, more supply and less demand cannot be a point of equilibrium, since firms would experience continual (increases/decreases) in inventories. The result is likely to be price reductions to stimulate sales and a movement toward equilibrium. Similarly, a lower price level, such as 90, would induce analogous, although opposite, reactions.

Nothing in the analysis so far guarantees that the intersection of the aggregate demand and aggregate supply curves will be at the level of output corresponding to full employment of labor. If the final equilibrium level of output is different from the full-employment level of output, the result is either a recessionary gap or

(4) an inflationary gap. Consider Figure 10-2, which shows a(n) _____ gap. The gap (is/is not) likely to self-destruct as continuing increases in the price of inputs lead to shifts in the aggregate supply curve. As unemployment falls below frictional levels and material inputs become scarce, higher input prices will shift the aggregate supply curve (inward/outward) leading to a (movement along/shift in) the aggregate demand curve, (higher/lower) prices, (higher/lower) output, and the elimination of the inflationary gap. Note that the simultaneous increase in prices and wages does not prove that increasing wages cause inflation. Both are best seen as a symptom of the original inflationary gap.

By contrast the rigidity of wages and other input prices in the face of unemployment means that a
(5) recessionary gap is (more/less) likely to self-destruct than an inflationary gap.

Stagflation refers to the simultaneous occurrence of increasing prices and increasing unemployment. The previous analysis suggests that stagflation is a natural result of the self-destruction of a(n)
(6) (inflationary/recessionary) gap. Stagflation can also occur as a result of adverse shifts in the aggregate

_____ curve.

DEFINITION QUIZ

Choose the letter that is the most appropriate definition for each of the following terms.

1. _____ Aggregate supply curve
2. _____ Productivity
3. _____ Self-correcting mechanism
4. _____ Stagflation

a. Economy's way of restoring equilibrium through inflation or deflation.
b. Amount of a given input required to produce a unit of output.
c. Graph of total quantity of goods and services produced at each possible price level.
d. Inflation that occurs while the economy is growing slowly or in recession.
e. Amount of output produced per unit of input.

BASIC EXERCISES

1. This exercise reviews the derivation of the aggregate demand curve and then uses both the aggregate demand and aggregate supply curves to determine the equilibrium level of income. Figure 10–3 shows an income–expenditure diagram in the top half and a price level–aggregate output diagram in the bottom half. The middle expenditure schedule in the top half duplicates the original situation described in Basic Exercise 1 of Chapter 9 and assumes that the price level associated with this expenditure schedule is 100. The dashed line extending into the bottom figure shows how this output level, together with its associated price level, can be plotted in the lower diagram. It is one point on the aggregate demand curve.

   a. A decrease in the price level to 90 would, because of its impact on the purchasing power of consumer money assets, increase real consumption expenditures. The shift in the consumption function shifts the expenditure schedule up. The new expenditure schedule, for a price level of 90, is shown in the top half of Figure 10–3. What is the equilibrium level of income in the income–expenditure diagram for a price level of 90?

   b. Plot the combination of prices and output from a in the lower diagram. This is a second point on the aggregate demand curve.

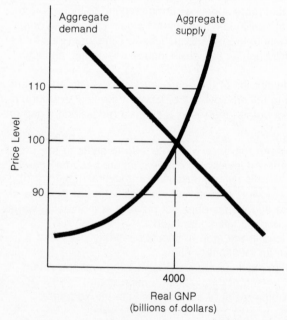

FIGURE 10–1

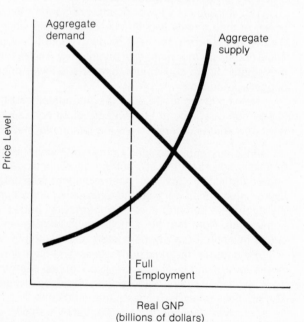

FIGURE 10–2

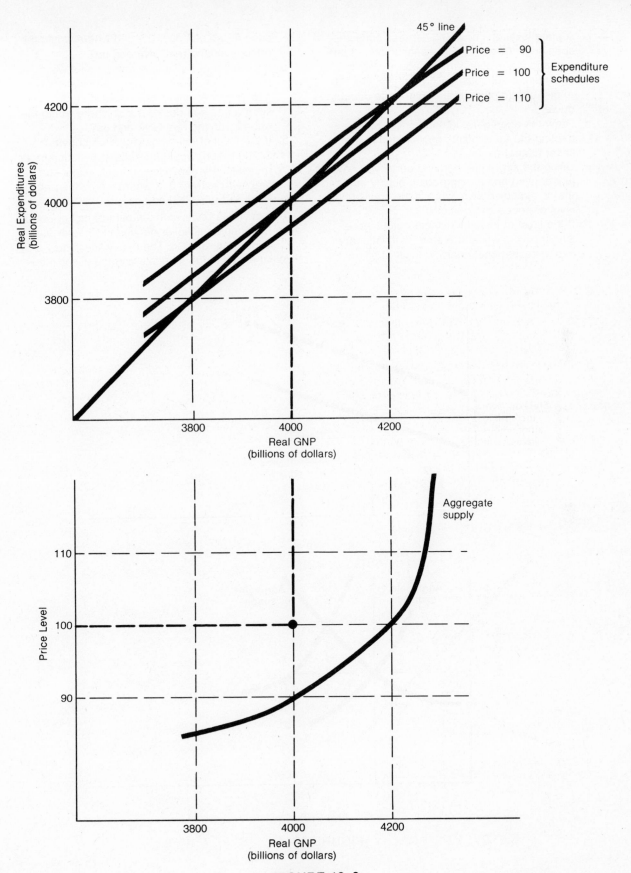

FIGURE 10-3

c. A price level of 110 would depress consumer spending, shifting both the consumption function and the expenditure schedule. Use the expenditure schedule for a price level of 110 to plot a third point on the aggregate demand curve.

d. Draw the aggregate demand curve by connecting the three points now plotted in the lower diagram.

e. Using the aggregate demand curve you have just derived and the aggregate supply curve that is already drawn, what is the equilibrium level of prices and real GNP?

f. If the level of full-employment output were $4000 billion, would there be an inflationary gap or recessionary gap? How, if at all, might

such a gap self-destruct and where would the price level and real GNP end up?

g. If the level of full-employment output were $4100 billion, would there be an inflationary gap or recessionary gap? How, if at all, might such a gap self-destruct and where would the price level and real GNP end up?

h. If the level of full-employment output were $4200 billion, would there be an inflationary or recessionary gap? How, if at all, might such a gap self-destruct and where would the price level and real GNP end up?

2. This exercise reviews the impact of higher prices on the simple multiplier derived in Chapter 9. Consider Figure 10–4. The heavy lines show an initial expenditure schedule and the associated

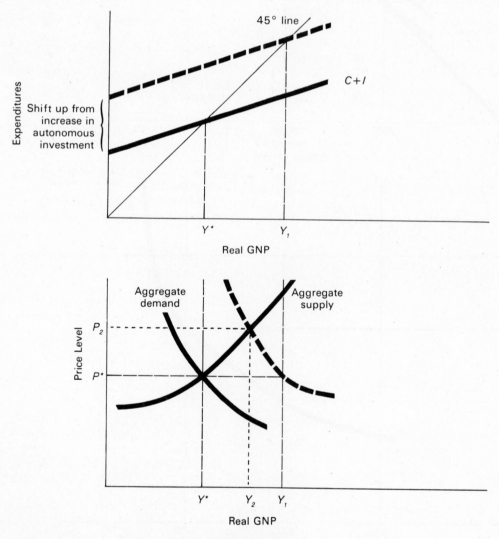

FIGURE 10-4

TABLE 10-1

	Aggregate demand curve	Aggregate supply curve	Equilibrium real GNP	Price level
A reduction in business investment spending				
An increase in the price of many basic commodities used as inputs in the production of final goods and services				
An increase in the demand for exports caused by an economic boom abroad				
An increase in labor productivity due to a technological breakthrough				
An upward shift in the consumption function due to a stock market boom				

aggregate demand curve. The initial equilibrium is at a level of income Y^*, and price level P^*. The dashed expenditure schedule comes from an increase in investment spending. Note that the shift in the expenditure schedule leads to a shift in the aggregate demand curve. In fact, the initial new equilibrium on the income-expenditure diagram, Y, is equal to the (horizontal/vertical) shift of the aggregate demand curve in the lower half of the diagram.

a. Is the combination Y_1, P^* the final equilibrium?
b. If Y_1, P^* is not the final equilibrium, describe what will happen during the transition to the final equilibrium.
3. In Table 10-1, fill in the blanks as indicated to analyze the response to each change. In the first two columns use S or M for "shift in" or "movement along." In the last two columns use + or −.

SELF-TESTS FOR UNDERSTANDING

Test A

Circle the correct answer.

1. The aggregate supply curve
   a. slopes down to the right.
   b. has a positive slope.
   c. slopes up to the left.
   d. has a negative slope.
2. The slope of the aggregate supply curve reflects the fact that
   a. inflation reduces the value of the oversimplified multiplier.
   b. the costs of important inputs, such as labor, are relatively fixed in the short run.
   c. the marginal propensity to consume is less than 1.0.

d. recessionary gaps take a long time to self-destruct.
3. The aggregate supply curve will shift following changes in all but which of the following?
   a. The price level.
   b. Wage rates.
   c. Technology and productivity.
   d. Available supplies of factories and machines.
4. The equilibrium price level and the equilibrium level of real GNP
   a. are determined by the intersection of the aggregate demand, and aggregate supply curves.
   b. will always occur at full employment.
   c. can be found in the income–expenditure diagram.
   d. do not change unless the aggregate demand curve shifts.
5. A change in the equilibrium price level
   a. will lead to a shift in the aggregate supply curve.

75

b. will lead to a shift in the aggregate demand curve.

c. reflects a shift in the aggregate demand curve and/or aggregate supply curve.

d. will always lead to stagflation.

6. Near full employment, the slope of the aggregate supply curve is likely to
   a. become negative.
   b. drop to zero.
   c. decrease, but still remain positive.
   d. increase.

7. From an initial position of full employment, which one of the following will not lead to a recessionary gap?
   a. A shift in the aggregate supply curve in response to an increase in energy prices.
   b. A reduction in investment spending due to an increase in business taxes.
   c. A reduction in consumer spending due to an adverse shift in consumer expectations.
   d. A shift in the aggregate supply curve in response to a dramatic technological breakthrough that reduces production costs.

8. Which of the following is not associated with the elimination of an inflationary gap?
   a. Rising prices.
   b. Falling output.
   c. Increased employment.
   d. Increased unemployment.

9. The economy's self-correcting mechanisms are likely to work better when
   a. there is an inflationary gap.
   b. there is a recessionary gap.
   c. there is a federal government deficit.
   d. the multiplier is working.

10. Prices rise following an increase in autonomous spending whenever the
    a. aggregate demand curve shifts.
    b. multiplier is greater than 1.0.
    c. aggregate demand curve has a negative slope.
    d. aggregate supply curve is not horizontal.

Test B

Circle T or F for True or False as appropriate.

1. The aggregate supply curve shows for each possible price the total quantity of goods and services that the nation's businesses are willing to supply.   T F

2. The aggregate supply curve slopes upward because businesses will expand output as long as higher prices make expansion profitable.   T F

3. The aggregate supply curve is likely to be steeper at low levels of unemployment.   T F

4. The impact of unemployment on wages and prices means that recessionary gaps are likely to quickly self-destruct.   T F

5. If the aggregate supply curve shifts inward, the result will be stagflation.   T F

6. The economy's self-correcting mechanisms insure that the aggregate demand and aggregate supply curves will always intersect at potential output.   T F

7. The final equilibrium level of prices and aggregate output is determined by the slope of the aggregate supply curve.   T F

8. A period of excessive aggregate demand is likely to be followed by a period of stagflation as the inflationary gap self-destructs.   T F

9. During the elimination of an inflationary gap, the real cause of inflation is excessive wage demands on the part of labor.   T F

10. Analysis of the aggregate supply curve shows that the multiplier derived from the income-expenditure diagram typically understates the final change in output.   T F

SUPPLEMENTARY EXERCISE

The following equations are consistent with Basic Exercise 1.

$$C = 900 + .75Y - 5P$$
$$I = 800$$
$$X - IM = -200$$
$$C + I = Y \text{ (45° line)}$$
$$Y = 2200 + 20P \text{ (aggregate supply curve)}$$
C = real consumption expenditures
I = real investment
Y = real GNP
P = price level
$X - IM$ = net exports

1. Use the consumption function along with the level of investment spending and net exports to determine an expression for the expenditure schedule. (Note that this expression will involve the variable P.)

2. Use the expenditure schedule and the equation for the 45° line to determine an expression for the aggregate demand curve.

3. Now use both the aggregate demand curve and the aggregate supply curve to determine the equilibrium level of prices and GNP.

4. Resolve the system on the assumption that investment expenditures decrease to $750 billion.

PART
3

FISCAL AND MONETARY POLICY

11

Fiscal Policy and Supply-Side Economics

LEARNING OBJECTIVES

After completing the material in this chapter you should be able to:

- define, understand, and use correctly the terms and concepts listed below.
- describe the process by which an increase in government purchases of goods and services will increase both prices and output.
- describe the process by which a reduction in taxes will increase both prices and output.
- explain why taxes that depend upon income reduce the value of the multiplier below the oversimplified expression in Chapter 9.
- explain why the multiplier for a change in income taxes will be less than the multiplier for a change in government purchases of goods and services.
- explain why economists treat government transfer payments like taxes, not like government purchases of goods and services.
- describe the process by which a change in government transfer payments affects both prices and output.

- explain why active stabilization policy need not imply that the size of government must get bigger and bigger.
- use the aggregate demand and supply diagram to show how supply-side tax cuts hope to reduce the impact on prices associated with the elimination of a recessionary gap.
- describe the kernel of truth in supply-side economics.
- discuss the reservations that most economists have in regard to supply-side economics.

IMPORTANT TERMS AND CONCEPTS

Fiscal policy
Government purchases of goods and services (G)
Government transfer payments
Effect of income taxes on the multiplier
Supply-side tax cuts
Depreciation allowances
Capital gains and losses
Productivity

CHAPTER REVIEW

This chapter reviews the models of income determination that were introduced in Chapters 8, 9, and 10, but this time for an economy that includes a government that both taxes and spends. With this expanded model we can then consider government fiscal policy. The only trick is to understand how government spending and taxes affect the curves we have already derived, that is, how government spending and taxes affect the expenditure schedule, the aggregate demand curve, and the aggregate supply curve. After this, the analysis proceeds exactly as before: For a given price level, the equilibrium level of income is determined by the inter-

(1) section of the (consumption/expenditure) schedule and the 45° line. A change in prices will affect consumption spending and thus shift the expenditure schedule, resulting in a different equilibrium level of income. The different price levels and their associated equilibrium levels of income can be combined to form the aggregate

_____ curve. This curve together with the aggregate _____ curve will help determine both income and prices, just as before. A change in the government's fiscal policy will shift one or more of the curves and lead to new equilibrium values for income and prices.

There are three important ways government fiscal policy influences total spending in the economy:

1. The government *purchases goods and services.*
2. The government *collects taxes,* thereby reducing the spending power of households and firms.
3. The government gives *transfer payments* to some individuals, thereby increasing their purchasing power.

Government purchases of goods and services are a direct addition to total spending in the economy;

(2) that is, they shift the expenditure schedule (up/down) by the full amount of the purchases. Thus, if govern-

ment spending increased by $1, the expenditure schedule would shift up by $_____. An increase in

autonomous investment spending or exports of $1 would also shift the expenditure schedule up by $_____. Thus, we see that changes in government spending shift the expenditure schedule in exactly the same way as do other changes in autonomous spending. Since the expenditure schedule shifts in an identical way, the oversimplified multiplier for a change in government spending is (less than/equal to/greater than) our earlier oversimplified multiplier for a change in autonomous spending.

(3) Government taxes (are/are not) a direct component of spending on currently produced goods and services. Personal income taxes affect spending through their impact on disposable income. Following a decrease in personal income taxes, consumers' disposable income will be (higher/lower). The change in disposable income is likely to (increase/decrease) consumption expenditures. A reduction in personal income

taxes of $1 will initially (increase/decrease) disposable income by $_____, but consumption spending is likely to change by (less/more) than $1. The initial effect on consumption spending will be given

by multiplying the change in disposable income by the marginal _____ to consume, which is (less/more) than 1. Thus, changes in personal income taxes affect spending, but indirectly through their effect on consumption expenditures. A change in corporate income taxes will change corporate profits after

taxes, and is likely to affect _____ expenditures. We saw earlier that a $1 increase in government purchases will shift the expenditure schedule up by $1. Now we see that a $1 reduction in personal income taxes will shift the expenditure schedule up, because of

(4) its effect on consumption; but the expenditure schedule will shift up by (more/less) than $1. Because the expenditure schedule shifts less in response to a change in personal income taxes as compared with an equal change in government purchases, the multiplier associated with changes in personal income taxes will be (less/more) than the multiplier associated with changes in government purchases.

The third important function of the government regarding total spending in the economy is the magnitude of government transfer payments. These payments, like taxes, are not a direct element of total spending on goods and services; and also like personal taxes, they affect total spending because they affect people's

(5) disposable _____ and thus their _____ expenditures.

An important feature of both taxes and transfer payments is that they vary with income. Typically taxes

(6) go (up/down) as aggregate income goes up, and transfer payments go _____ as aggregate income rises. These automatic, income-induced changes have an important implication for the

value of our oversimplified multiplier. In Chapter 9 we saw that the multiplier process arises from the fact that any autonomous increase in spending means higher income for those who supply the newly demanded goods. These higher incomes will lead to more consumption spending, and so on, and so on. This process continues to take place, but now we see that each round of spending results in an increase in income *before* taxes. Because some of the increase in before-tax income goes to pay higher taxes, after-tax income (or disposable income) will increase by (more/less). Thus, each induced round of consumption spending, responding to the increase in disposable income, will be (smaller/larger) than before.

(7) To summarize, in an economy with income taxes (and transfer payments) that vary with income, each round in the multiplier process will be smaller than before, and thus the multiplier effect on income, from any increase in automatic spending, will also be (smaller/larger) than before. The impact of income taxes on the multiplier is the second important reason why Chapter 9's formula for the multiplier was oversimplified.

(8) We have added government purchases of goods and services, taxes, and transfers to our model of income determination. Taken together, these variables are an important determinant of the equilibrium level of income. Changes in these variables, just like the autonomous changes we considered in earlier chapters, will have multiplier effects on the equilibrium level of GNP. Thus deliberate manipulation of these variables may help the government achieve its desired objectives for GNP and prices. Manipulation of government fiscal policy variables for GNP objectives is an example of active *stabilization policy*. For example, if the government wants to increase GNP, it could decide to (increase/decrease) government purchases of goods

and services, _____ personal taxes, _____ corporate taxes, or

_____ transfer payments to individuals.

One of the reasons it is so difficult to agree on fiscal policy is that there are so many choices, all of which could have the same impact on national income, but very different impacts on other issues, such as the size of the public versus private sector, the burden of taxes between individuals and corporations, the composition of output between consumption and investment spending, and the amount of income redistribution through transfers to low-income families.

One might believe that if we could decide upon the amounts of government purchases, taxes, and transfers, effective fiscal policy would be simply a technical matter of choosing the right numbers so that the expenditure schedule would intersect the 45° line, and the aggregate demand curve would intersect the aggregate supply curve at full employment. In actuality, uncertainties about (1) private components of aggregate demand, (2) the precise size of the multiplier, (3) exactly what level of GNP is associated with full employment, and (4) the slope of the aggregate supply curve all mean that fiscal policy will continue to be subject to much political give and take. One hopes that appropriate economic analysis will contribute to a more informed level of debate.

Changes in government spending or tax rates shift the aggregate demand curve directly, in the case of government purchases, and indirectly through impacts on private spending, in the case of taxes and transfer payments. Any shift in the aggregate demand curve, including government shifts, affects both prices and

(9) output as we move along the aggregate _____ curve. Thus, expansionary fiscal policy, designed to increase GNP, is also likely to (increase/decrease) prices. Supply-side policies attempt to minimize the impact on prices through changes in fiscal policy that shift the aggregate supply curve at the same time that they shift the aggregate demand curve. Recently there has been much attention given to supply-side tax cuts, including such measures as speeding up depreciation allowances, reducing taxes for increased research and development expenditures, reducing the corporate income tax, reducing taxes on income from savings, reducing taxes on capital gains, and reducing income taxes to encourage more work effort.

Most economists have a number of reservations about the exaggerated claims of ardent supporters of supply-side tax cuts: Specific effects will depend on exactly which taxes are reduced; increases in aggregate supply will take some time, while effects on aggregate demand will be much quicker; a realistic assessment suggests that by themselves supply-side tax cuts will have only a small effect on the rate of inflation; supply-side tax cuts are likely to lead to increased income inequality; and supply-side cuts are likely to lead to bigger, not smaller, government budget deficits. Do not let these serious objections to exaggerated claims blind you to the kernel of truth in supply-side economics: Marginal tax rates are important for decisions by individuals and firms. Reductions in marginal tax rates can improve economic incentives.

DEFINITION QUIZ

Choose the letter that is the most appropriate definition for each of the following terms.

1. _____ Fiscal policy
2. _____ Government purchases
3. _____ Government transfer payments
4. _____ Depreciation allowances
5. _____ Capital gains and losses
6. _____ Productivity

a. Amount of output produced per unit of input.
b. Cost per unit of output produced.
c. The government's plan for spending and taxation.
d. Tax deductions that businesses may claim when they invest.
e. Total goods and services bought by all levels of government.
f. Changes in the market value of an asset between the time it is bought and the time it is sold.
g. Money the government gives to individuals as outright grants.

BASIC EXERCISE

This exercise is designed to show how changes in government purchases and taxes will have multiplier effects on the equilibrium level of income and how these multipliers can be used to help determine appropriate fiscal policy. To simplify the numerical calculations, the exercise focuses on the shift in the expenditure schedule holding prices constant. Table 11–1 shows data on national income, taxes, disposable income, consumption spending, invest-ment spending, government purchases of goods and services, and net exports.

1. The equilibrium level of income is

   _____. (To determine the equilibrium level of income you will first need to compute total spending at each level of income. (Use Table 11–2 to record total spending.)

2. Assume now that government purchases decrease by $200 billion to $1,000 billion as shown in Table 11–3. Following the decrease in government purchases, the new equilibrium

   level of income is _____.

3. The multiplier for this decrease in government

   purchases is _____. (This multiplier can be computed by dividing the change in the equilibrium level of income by the change in government purchases.)

4. Now consider a subsequent across-the board reduction in income taxes of $250 billion. Table 11–4 shows the new relevant data for national income, taxes, disposable income, and consumption. The new equilibrium level of income after the reduction in taxes is

   _____.

5. The multiplier for this change in taxes is

   _____.

6. Why did it take a larger reduction in taxes to restore GNP to its initial level following the reduction in government purchases?

7. Question 4 asked you to analyze the impact of a reduction in income taxes. Was this reduction in taxes self-financing? That is, was the increase in GNP stimulated by the reduction in taxes large enough so that on balance there was no

TABLE 11-1

| | | | ($ billions) | | | |
National Income	Income Taxes	Disposable Income	Consumption Spending	Investment Spending	Government Purchases	Net Exports
4000	1000	3000	2500	800	1200	− 100
4500	1125	3375	2800	800	1200	− 100
5000	1250	3750	3100	800	1200	− 100
5500	1375	4125	3400	800	1200	− 100
6000	1500	4500	3700	800	1200	− 100

TABLE 11-2

National Income	($ billions) Total Expenditure (Table 11-1)	(Table 11-3)	(Table 11-4)
4000	_____	_____	_____
4500	_____	_____	_____
5000	_____	_____	_____
5500	_____	_____	_____
6000	_____	_____	_____

TABLE 11-3

National Income	Income Taxes	Disposable Income	($ billions) Consumption Spending	Investment Spending	Government Purchases	Net Exports
4000	1000	3000	2500	800	1000	− 100
4500	1125	3375	2800	800	1000	− 100
5000	1250	3750	3100	800	1000	− 100
5500	1375	4125	3400	800	1000	− 100
6000	1500	4500	3700	800	1000	− 100

TABLE 11-4

National Income	Income Taxes	Disposable Income	($ billions) Consumption Spending	Investment Spending	Government Purchases	Net Exports
4000	750	3250	2700	800	1000	− 100
4500	875	3625	3000	800	1000	− 100
5000	1000	4000	3300	800	1000	− 100
5500	1125	4375	3600	800	1000	− 100
6000	1250	4750	3900	800	1000	− 100

decrease in government tax revenues? (Be sure to compare tax receipts at the equilibrium level of income in Table 11-3 with those at the new equilibrium in Table 11-4.)

8. Now let us use the multipliers computed in Question 3 and 5 to figure out what changes in government purchases or taxes would be necessary to raise the equilibrium level of income from its initial value given in Question 1 to its full-employment level of $5250 billion. Assuming no change in tax rates, the necessary increase in government purchases is

$_____ billion.
Assuming no change in government purchases, the necessary reduction in taxes is

$_____ billion. (You can answer these questions by figuring out what appropriate change in government purchases or taxes, when multiplied by the relevant multiplier, will equal the desired change in income.)

9. What is the new equilibrium level of income if, from the initial equilibrium given in Question 1, investment expenditures rather than government purchases fall by $200 billion? (Now investment spending will be $600 billion while government purchases stay at $1,200 billion. Create a new version of Table 11-1 if necessary.) What can one say about multipliers for autonomous changes in public versus private purchases of goods and services?

10. (Optional) Use the data in Table 11-1 to com-

pute the tax rate and the marginal propensity to consume. Use these numbers to calculate the multipliers for a change in government purchases and across-the-board taxes as described in the Appendix to Chapter 11. Do these numbers agree with your answers to Questions 3 and 5?

11. (Optional) Construct a new version of Table 11–1 to analyze the effect on the multiplier when income taxes do not vary with income. When constructing this table, assume that income taxes are $1,250 billion for all levels of income. (Note that this will mean different levels of disposable income and consumption spending. Use the data in the original Table 11–1 to figure out the consumption function. then use this function to compute the amount of consumption spending consistent with the new values for disposable income.) Now find the equilibrium level of income. Next assume that government purchases fall by $200 billion. Find the new equilibrium level of income and compute the multiplier for a change in government purchases. How does this multiplier, computed for a case in which income taxes do not vary with income, compare with the multiplier you computed in Question 3? You might also use the data in the original Table 11–1 and from your new table to graph the two expenditure schedules for comparison.

SELF-TESTS FOR UNDERSTANDING

Test A

Circle the correct answer.

1. Fiscal policy involves decisions about all but which one of the following?
   a. Income tax rates.
   b. Eligibility rules for transfer payments.
   c. The money supply.
   d. Government purchases of goods and services.
2. A simultaneous reduction in income taxes and transfer payments of $15 billion will leave aggregate disposable income
   a. lower than before the change.
   b. unchanged.
   c. higher than before the change.
3. If the basic expenditure multiplier is 2.0 and if the government wishes to decrease the level of GNP by $80 billion, what decrease in govern-

ment purchases of goods and services would do the job?
   a. $20 billion.
   b. $40 billion.
   c. $80 billion.
   d. $160 billion.
4. Instead of decreasing government expenditures, the same objectives, in terms of reducing GNP, could also be achieved by
   a. reducing government transfer payments.
   b. reducing taxes.
   c. increasing both taxes and government transfer payments by equal amounts.
   d. reducing both taxes and government transfer payments by equal amounts.
5. If the basic expenditure multiplier is 2.0, a reduction in personal income taxes of $25 billion is likely to
   a. increase GNP by $50 billion.
   b. increase GNP by more than $50 billion.
   c. increase GNP by less than $50 billion.
6. A 10 percent reduction in income tax rates would
   a. lower the value of the basic expenditure multiplier.
   b. raise the value of the basic expenditure multiplier.
   c. not affect the value of the basic expenditure multiplier.
7. An increase in tax rates will lead to all but which one of the following?
   a. A decrease in the multiplier.
   b. A movement along the aggregate demand curve.
   c. A reduction in the equilibrium level of GNP.
   d. A shift of the expenditure schedule.
8. Assume that from a position of full employment the government wants to reduce defense spending by $50 billion in response to an easing of international tensions. To avoid a possible recession, the government simultaneously decides to reduce income taxes. In view of the different multipliers for changes in government purchases and taxes, the necessary change in taxes to keep the equilibrium level of income unchanged is
   a. less than $50 billion.
   b. $50 billion.
   c. more than $50 billion.
9. Which one of the following is *not* an example of supply-side policies?
   a. Lowering the corporate income tax rate.
   b. Establishing tax-free retirement savings accounts.
   c. Reducing tax rates on capital gains.
   d. Requiring firms to depreciate assets over a longer rather than a shorter period of time.

10. Critics of supply-side tax cuts would agree with all but which one of the following?
    a. Supply-side tax cuts are likely to increase inequality in the distribution of income.
    b. Supply-side tax cuts will substantially reduce the rate of inflation.
    c. Supply-side tax cuts are likely to mean bigger deficits for the federal government.
    d. Supply-side tax cuts will have a larger initial impact on aggregate demand than on aggregate supply.

Test B

Circle T or F for True or False as appropriate.

1. An increase in income tax rates will increase the multiplier.   **T F**

2. With income taxes, a $1 change in GNP will lead to a smaller change in consumption than would a $1 change in disposable income.   **T F**

3. Income taxation reduces the value of the multiplier for changes in government purchases but does not affect the multiplier for changes in investment.   **T F**

4. Since taxes are not a direct component of aggregate demand, changes in taxes do not have multiplier effects on income.   **T F**

5. Changes in government purchases of goods and services and in government transfer payments to individuals are both changes in government spending and thus have the same multiplier effects on the equilibrium level of income.   **T F**

6. A reduction in taxes matched by an equal reduction in government purchases of goods and services is likely to leave the expenditure schedule unchanged.   **T F**

7. Active stabilization policy implies that the government must get bigger and bigger.   **T F**

8. Since income taxes and transfer payments to individuals have their first impact on the disposable income of consumers, they should have similar multipliers.   **T F**

9. Only the aggregate supply curve will shift following a supply-side tax cut that increases investment spending by firms.   **T F**

10. There is general agreement among economists that supply-side tax cuts can increase output with little impact on prices.   **T F**

SUPPLEMENTARY EXERCISES

1. In his analysis of the impact of the 1964 tax cut, which reduced taxes on a permanent basis, Arthur Okun estimated that the marginal propensity to consume was 0.95.[1] At the same time, Okun estimated that the basic expenditure multiplier, applicable for any increase in autonomous spending, was only 2.73, not 20 which comes from the oversimplified formula of Chapter 9, $1/(1 - MPC)$. How can such a large marginal propensity to consume be consistent with such a small multiplier?

2. The 1964 reduction in personal taxes was about $10 billion. Okun estimated that this tax reduction raised GNP by $25.9 billion. The ratio of the change in GNP to the change in taxes was only 2.59, not 2.73, the value of the basic expenditure multiplier. How can you account for this discrepancy? (*Hint:* In his analysis, Okun assumed prices did not change, so price effects on consumption expenditures are not part of the answer. You should think about whether the basic expenditure multiplier—the multiplier for a shift in the expenditure schedule—is the appropriate multiplier to apply directly to the change in taxes.)

3. When analyzing the impact of the 1975 income tax rebate, Franco Modigliani and Charles Steindel concluded that it had very little impact on the economy.[2] Can you reconcile this finding of virtually no impact from the one-time 1975 income tax rebate with Okun's finding of a substantial impact from the permanent tax cut in 1964?

4. How has the distribution of income changed since 1980? Each year the Bureau of the Census reports information on "Money Income of Households, Families and Persons in the United States." A summary of this and related data can be found in the annual editions of the *Statistical Abstract of the United States*. More complete data is published annually by the Census Bureau in Current Population Reports, Series P-60. A copy of the latest data is likely to be available in your college or university library.

---

[1] Arthur M. Okun, "Measuring the Impact of the 1964 Tax Cut," in W. W. Heller, ed., *Perspectives on Economic Growth* (New York: Vintage Books, 1968), pages 25–49.

[2] Franco Modigliani and Charles Steindel, "Is a Tax Rebate an Effective Tool for Stabilization Policy," *Brookings Papers on Economic Activity*, 1977:1, pages 175–209.

Appendix: Algebraic Treatment of Fiscal Policy and Aggregate Demand

BASIC EXERCISE

This exercise is meant to illustrate the material in the Appendix to Chapter 11. Just as in the Appendix to Chapter 8, we can use equations rather than graphs or tables to determine the equilibrium level of output and relevant multipliers. If we have done our work accurately, we should get the same answer regardless of whether we use graphs, tables, or algebra.

The following equations underlie the numerical example in the Basic Exercise:

$$C = 100 + 0.8DI$$
$$T = (0.25)Y$$
$$DI = Y - T$$
$$Y = C + I + G + (X - IM)$$

1. What is the equilibrium level of income if investment spending is $800 billion, net exports are −$50 billion, and government purchases are $1,250 billion? Be sure that $C + I + G = Y$.

2. Assume that both across-the-board taxes and government purchases decline by $50 billion so that government purchases are $1,200 billion and the tax equation is

$$T = -50 + 0.25Y.$$

(I is still $800.) Is the equilibrium level of income unchanged following the balanced reduction in the size of the government? Why? What about the government deficit $(G - T)$?

3. What is the multiplier for the following:
   –change in investment spending
   –change in net exports
   –change in government purchases
   –change in taxes (that is, change in intercept of tax equation)

12

Money and the Banking System

LEARNING OBJECTIVES

After completing the material in this chapter you should be able to:

- define, understand, and use correctly the terms and concepts listed below.
- distinguish between various functions of money. Which are unique to money? Which are shared with other assets?
- distinguish between commodity money and fiat money.
- explain the differences between M1 and M2 as measures of money.
- describe the historical origins of fractional reserve banking and explain why the industry is so heavily regulated today.
- explain how the banking system as a whole can create deposits, given an initial injection of bank reserves.
- use the required reserve fraction to derive the oversimplified deposit creation multiplier.
- explain why the deposit creation multiplier, based on the required reserve fraction, is oversimplified.

IMPORTANT TERMS AND CONCEPTS

Run on a bank
Barter
Unit of account
Money
Medium of exchange
Store of value
Commodity money
Fiat money
M1 versus M2
Near moneys
Liquidity
Fractional reserve banking
Deposit insurance
Federal Deposit Insurance Corporation (FDIC)
Required reserves
Asset
Liability
Balance sheet
Net worth
Deposit creation
Excess reserves

CHAPTER REVIEW

Whether it is the root of all evil or not, there is no argument that money has an important influence on the way our economy operates. The right amount of money can help to keep employment up and prices stable. Too much money may lead to excessive inflation; too little money may lead to excessive unemployment. This chapter is an introduction to money. What is it? Where did it come from? and What role do banks play in the creation of money? Chapter 13 discusses how the government now regulates the amount of money in the economy, and Chapter 14 discusses the influence of money on economic activity.

It is possible that a society could be organized without money. If everyone were self-sufficient there would, by definition, be no trading between individuals and no need for money. Even if people concentrated their productive activities on what they did best and traded among each other to get goods they did not produce themselves, they might still be able to get along without money. Direct trading of goods for goods, or

(1) goods for services, is called _____. For it to be successful there must be a double coincidence of wants. As societies become more complicated and people become ever more specialized, it is clear that barter becomes increasingly (harder/easier).

When a society uses a standard object for exchanging goods and services, a seller will provide goods or services to a buyer and receive the standard object as payment. The efficiency of such a system should be obvious. You no longer have to find someone who not only has what you want but also wants what you have.

(2) Anyone who has what you want will now do. Economists would call the standard object _____. If the object serving as money has intrinsic value, such as gold or jewelry, it is called

_____ money. Today money has little intrinsic value and is called _____ money. Such money has value because everyone believes that everyone else will exchange goods and services for it. The bedrock for this foundation of faith is that the government will stand behind the money and limit its production.

When it comes to measuring the quantity of money, exactly where one draws the line is a bit unclear. We have defined money as a standard object used for exchanging goods and services. On this count, the sum of all coins and currency outside of banks plus checking accounts (including NOW accounts) surely

(3) belongs in any measure of money. The measure that includes only these items is known as _____. If one also includes savings accounts (because they can easily be transferred into checking accounts),

money market deposit accounts, and money market mutual funds, one is measuring _____.

Below are some data for 1989 from the *1990 Economic Report of the President*.

Currency (including traveler's checks)	$ 229.6 billion
Checking accounts at commercial banks	281.2 billion
Other checkable deposits	286.8 billion
Savings deposits	1,623.8 billion
Money market deposit accounts	486.5 billion
Money market mutual funds	309.1 billion

(4) How big is M1? $_____ billion.

M2? $_____ billion.

Given the importance of bank deposits in all measures of money, it is important to understand *how the banking system can create money.* Banks subject to deposit reserve requirements must hold reserves that are at least as great as some stated percentage of their deposits. Reserves can be either money in a bank's vaults or money that the bank has on deposit at its local Federal Reserve Bank. We will learn more about the Federal Reserve System in Chapter 13. The stated percentage is the required reserve ratio. Thus, only some of the money used to open or to add to a bank deposit must be kept by the bank to meet reserve requirements. The rest can be used to make loans in the search for more profits. This system is known as fractional reserve banking.

(5)   The multiple creation of deposits is the counterpart to bank (lending/borrowing). Consider an individual bank that is subject to a 15 percent reserve requirement. Following a new deposit of $1000, the maximum amount of the new deposit that this bank could lend out and still meet the reserve requirement is

$_____. As the proceeds of the loan are deposited in other banks, new deposits will be created. For the banking system as a whole, the maximum amount of loans that can be made, and thus the maximum amount of deposits that can be created following an increase in bank reserves, is

limited by the _____ _____. The precise sequence of the multiple deposit creation is illustrated in the Basic Exercise for this chapter.

        Mathematical formulas have been devised to determine the maximum increase in deposits that can be created by the banking system following an increase in bank reserves. In words,

(6)
$$\begin{pmatrix} \text{Maximum} \\ \text{increase} \\ \text{in} \\ \text{deposits} \end{pmatrix} = \begin{pmatrix} \text{Initial} \\ \text{increase} \\ \text{in bank} \\ \text{reserves} \end{pmatrix} \times \left(\underline{\hspace{4cm}} \right)$$

The increase in bank reserves may come from a deposit of cash. In this case, while deposits are up, cash outside banks is down, as some was deposited to start the process of multiple deposit creation. Thus, following a cash deposit, the maximum increase in the money supply will be (more/less) than the maximum increase in deposits.

        The deposit creation formula is oversimplified for two reasons:

1. The formula assumes that the proceeds of each loan will eventually be redeposited in the banking system. If some of the proceeds of a loan do not get redeposited, then the deposit creation multiplier will be
(7)   (larger/smaller).

2. The formula also assumes that every bank makes as large a loan as possible; that is, each bank is

    assumed to hold no _____ reserves. If banks do choose to hold such reserves, then the money creation formula would be (larger/smaller).

        The discussion of the deposit creation multiplier showed how deposits can be created following an increase in bank reserves. The emphasis was on how a change in reserves leads to a change in deposits. One should not be surprised to learn that *total* deposits in all banks are similarly limited by *total* reserves. The textbook discussion of a cash deposit at one bank implies an increase in total reserves of the banking system. Most increases in reserves at one bank are offset by a decrease in reserves at some other bank, with no increase in total reserves. Consider Lillian, who takes money out of her account at Bank A. Lillian uses the money to buy a home computer, and the dealer deposits this money in her bank, Bank B. At the same time reserves increase at Bank B, they decrease at Bank A. The process of multiple deposit creation initiated at

(8)   Bank B is offset by a process of multiple deposit _____ starting with Bank A, and the net effect is (some/no) increase in deposits. The important factor for expanding deposits is new reserves available to the banking system. We will learn in Chapter 13 how the Federal Reserve is able to influence the volume of reserves available to the banking system.

DEFINITION QUIZ

Choose the letter that is the most appropriate definition for each of the following terms.

1. _____ Run on a bank
2. _____ Barter
3. _____ Unit of account
4. _____ Money
5. _____ Store of value
6. _____ Commodity money
7. _____ Fiat money
8. _____ M1
9. _____ M2
10. _____ Near moneys
11. _____ Liquidity
12. _____ Fractional reserve banking
13. _____ Deposit insurance
14. _____ Required reserves
15. _____ Asset
16. _____ Liability
17. _____ Balance sheet
18. _____ Net worth
19. _____ Deposit creation
20. _____ Excess reserves

a. Reserves in excess of the legal minimum.
b. Item an individual or firm owns.
c. Many depositors concurrently withdrawing cash from their accounts.
d. Item used to hold wealth from one point in time to another.
e. Ease with which an asset can be converted into cash.
f. System where bankers keep reserves equal to only a portion of total deposits.
g. Standard unit for quoting prices.
h. Value of all assets minus the value of all liabilities.
i. Amount of money balances the public will hold at a given price level.
j. System of exchange where people trade one good for another without using money.
k. Sum of coins, paper money, checkable deposits, money market mutual funds, and most savings account balances.
l. Accounting statement listing values of assets on the left-hand side and those of liabilities and net worth on the right-hand side.
m. Standard object used in exchanging goods and services.
n. Object, without value as commodity, which serves as money by government decree.
o. Liquid assets which are close substitutes for money.
p. System which guarantees depositors against loss if bank goes bankrupt.
q. Process by which banking system turns one dollar of reserves into several dollars of deposits.
r. Item an individual or firm owes.
s. Sum of coins, paper money, and checkable deposits.
t. Object used as a medium of exchange that also has substantial nonmonetary uses.
u. Minimum amount of reserves a bank must hold.

BASIC EXERCISE

This exercise is designed to help you understand the multiple creation of bank deposits by working through a specific simplified example.

1. Column 1 of Table 12–1 is partly filled in for you to show the changes in the balance sheet of Bank A immediately following Janet's cash deposit of $10,000. At this point, bank deposits

   have increased by $_____ and the stock of money in the economy—that is, bank deposits plus currency outside banks—is (higher/lower/unchanged). Assuming the required reserve fraction is 10 percent, fill in the last two rows of column 1, showing the initial increase in required and excess reserves.

2. Assume that Bank A responds to Janet's deposit by making as large a loan as it can to Earl, given the required reserve ratio. Now fill in column 2 to represent the changes in Bank A's balance sheet after the loan has been made and Earl has taken the proceeds of the loan in cash.

TABLE 12–1
BALANCE SHEET CHANGES

	(1) Bank A	(2) Bank A	(3) Bank B	(4) Bank B	(5) Bank C
Assets					
Reserves	$10,000				
Loans	0				
Liabilities					
Deposits	$10,000				
Addendum					
Required reserves					
Excess reserves					

Note: Required reserve ratio is 10 percent.

3. Earl uses the money from the loan to buy a car and the car dealer deposits this cash in Bank B. Fill in column 3 to represent the changes in Bank B's balance sheet following this cash deposit. At this point, total bank deposits have increased by $_____ and the stock of money in the economy has increased by $_____.

4. Assume now that Bank B also makes as large a loan as possible. Fill in column 4 to represent changes in Bank B's balance sheet after it makes the loan and this latest borrower takes the proceeds in cash.

5. Assume that the proceeds of this loan eventually get deposited in Bank C. Fill in column 5 to represent the changes in the balance sheet of Bank C following the increase in deposits. At this point total bank deposits have increased by $_____ and the stock of money has increased by $_____.

6. Fill in the following sequence of increased deposits following the initial increase at Bank A assuming that each bank makes the largest possible loan.

Increased deposits at Bank A ____ $10,000
Increased deposits at Bank B _____
Increased deposits at Bank C _____
Increased deposits at Bank D _____
Increased deposits at Bank E _____

If you have not made any mistakes you will notice that each increase in deposit is less than the previous increase and can be expressed as

(1.0 − 0.1) × (the previous increase in deposits)

Mathematically this is an infinite geometric progression with decreasing increments. If we carried the sum out far enough it would approach a limit given by $10,000 ÷ _____, or $_____. (If you have a suitable electronic calculator or microcomputer you might try testing this result by actually calculating the sum for a very large number of terms.) This specific numerical example illustrates the more general principle that the multiplier for the maximum increase in deposits following an increase in bank reserves is 1 ÷

_____ _____

_____.

SELF-TESTS FOR UNDERSTANDING

Test A

Circle the correct answer.

1. Money serves all but which one of the following functions?
   a. Medium of exchange.
   b. Hedge against inflation.
   c. Unit of account.
   d. Store of value.
2. Which of the following is not an example of commodity money?
   a. Gold coins.
   b. Wampum.
   c. A $10 bill.
   d. Diamonds.

3. The most important government regulation of banks in terms of limiting the multiple creation of deposits is
   a. bank examinations and audits.
   b. limits on the kinds of assets that banks can buy.
   c. required reserve ratio.
   d. requirements to disclose the volume of loans to bank officials.

4. If the minimum reserve requirement for all bank deposits is 10 percent, then the maximum multiple creation of deposits by the banking system as a whole following a cash deposit of $1000 would be
   a. $(0.1) \times (\$1000) = \$100$.
   b. $(1 + 0.1) \times (\$1000) = \$1100$.
   c. $(\$1000) \div (1 - 0.1) = \$1111$.
   d. $(\$1000) \div (0.1) = \$10,000$.

5. The maximum increase in the money supply would be
   a. smaller than in Question 4.
   b. larger than in Question 4.
   c. the same as in Question 4.

   (In fact, it would be $_____.)

6. If the reserve requirement is 15 percent instead of 10 percent, then the maximum multiple creation of deposits would be
   a. smaller than in Question 4.
   b. larger than in Question 4.
   c. the same as in Question 4.

7. If banks hold some of every increase in deposits in the form of excess reserves, then the amount of deposits actually created following a cash deposit would be
   a. less than that indicated in Question 4.
   b. the same as that indicated in Question 4.
   c. more than that indicated in Question 4.

8. If the required reserve ratio is 20 percent and Rachel deposits $100 in cash in the First National Bank, the maximum increase in deposits by the banking system as a whole is
   a. 0
   b. $20
   c. $100
   d. $500

9. If the required reserve ratio is 20 percent and Rachel deposits $100 in the First National Bank by depositing a check from her mother written on the Second National Bank, the maximum increase in deposits by the banking system as a whole is
   a. 0

   b. $20
   c. $100
   d. $500

10. If a bank's total reserve holdings are $35 million and it has $12 million of excess reserves, then its required reserves are
    a. $12 million.
    b. $23 million.
    c. $35 million.
    d. $47 million.

Test B

Circle T or F for True or False as appropriate.

1. A major advantage of the use of money rather than barter is that money avoids the problem of finding a "double coincidence of wants."

   T F

2. Fiat money in the United States may be redeemed for gold from the U.S. Treasury.

   T F

3. Many assets serve as a store of value but only money is also a medium of exchange. T F

4. In periods with high rates of inflation, money is a good store of value. T F

5. Banks could increase their profitability by holding higher levels of cash reserves. T F

6. The existence of deposit insurance is an important reason for the dramatic decline in the number of bank failures. T F

7. The oversimplified deposit creation multiplier of 1 divided by the required reserve ratio is an underestimate of the more appropriate, but more complicated, deposit multiplier. T F

8. Multiple deposit creation applies to increases in the money supply, but reductions in the money supply can come about only through government taxation. T F

9. Required reserves are part of a bank's liabilities, whereas excess reserves are part of a bank's assets. T F

10. If a bank's liabilities exceed its assets, the bank is said to have negative net worth. T F

SUPPLEMENTARY EXERCISES

1. If the required reserve ratio is 20 percent and banks want to hold 10 percent of any increase in deposits in the form of excess reserves and people want to hold $1 more in currency for every $10 increase in deposits, what is the eventual increase in deposits following a $1000 cash deposit in the First National Bank? What is the eventual increase in the money supply?

2. If M is the required reserve fraction, E is the ratio of excess reserves to deposits, and C is the ratio of currency to deposits, what is the formula that relates the change in deposits to a change in reserves?

13

Monetary Policy and the National Economy

LEARNING OBJECTIVES

After completing the material in this chapter you should be able to:

- define, understand, and use correctly the terms and concepts listed below.
- distinguish between the concepts "money" and "income."
- analyze arguments in favor of and opposed to the independence of the Federal Reserve System.
- draw and explain the logic behind both the supply of money schedule and the demand for money schedule.
- analyze the impact of changes in the three major monetary policy instruments both in words and by using the demand for and supply of money schedules.
- explain how bond prices and interest rates are related.
- describe the impact of open market operations on bond prices and interest rates.
- explain why the Fed's control of the stock of money is not exact.
- explain how some suggested reforms might change the degree of control that the Fed has over the stock of money.

- describe how changes in monetary policy affect the expenditure schedule and the aggregate demand curve.
- use the expenditure schedule and aggregate demand curve to describe how changes in monetary policy affect the economy's macroeconomic equilibrium, that is, interest rates, investment spending, GNP, and prices.

IMPORTANT TERMS AND CONCEPTS

Central bank
Federal Reserve System
Federal Open Market Committee (FOMC)
Independence of the Fed
Reserve requirements
Open market operations
Bond prices and interest rates
Contraction and expansion of the money supply
Federal reserve lending to banks
Moral suasion
Supply of money
Demand for money
Opportunity cost
Equilibrium in the money market
Monetary policy
Why the aggregate demand curve slopes down

CHAPTER REVIEW

In Chapter 12 we learned how deposits are created by the actions of banks. In this chapter we will see how actions taken by the Federal Reserve System can influence the stock of money. Reserve requirements and the total amount of bank reserves are important keys to the Federal Reserve's control of bank deposits and the stock of money. We will also see how the equilibrium in the money market influences the economy's overall macroeconomic equilibrium. The emphasis in this chapter is on building models. In subsequent chapters we will use these models to understand policy issues.

(1)   The Federal Reserve System was established in _____ and is the nation's

_____ bank. There are _____ district banks throughout the country, with headquarters in Washington, D.C. The head honchos in Washington are the

seven members of the _____ of _____ of the Federal Reserve System. Major decisions about the stock of money are made by the FOMC, or the

_____ _____ _____ Committee. Government spending and taxes are the nation's (fiscal/monetary) policy. Policy actions by the Federal Reserve constitute

the nation's _____ policy.
    We saw in Chapter 12 that the multiple creation of bank deposits is limited by the required reserve ratio and by the volume of bank reserves. Reserve requirements are one policy instrument of the Federal Reserve. The other two major policy instruments—open market operations and lending to banks—directly affect total bank reserves. We also saw in Chapter 12 that controlling reserve requirements and the volume of bank reserves does not allow for the precise control of the stock of money because of possible changes in

(2) (excess/required) reserve holdings by banks and in currency holdings by the public. These slippages in the deposit creation formula are an important reason why the Federal Reserve's control over the stock of money, while strong and important, is not complete.
    A reduction in reserve requirements does not change total bank reserves, but it will initially result in a(n)

(3) (increase/decrease) in noninterest-earning excess reserves. Multiple deposit creation will take place as banks try to put these nonearning excess reserves to work. Thus, a reduction in minimum reserve requirements should be associated with a (larger/smaller) volume of deposits and is an example of a(n) (expansionary/contractionary) change in monetary policy. An increase in reserve requirements will typically force banks to curtail lending in order to meet new, higher holdings of (excess/required) reserves. Such an increase would

be an example of a _____ change in monetary policy.

(4)   Open market operations—the purchase and sale of government _____ —represent the most important and most commonly used instrument of monetary policy. Open market operations affect bank behavior by adding to or subtracting from the amount of bank reserves. The essence of an open market purchase is that the Fed creates bank reserves when it (buys/sells) a government security. The result is a(n) (increase/decrease) in noninterest-earning excess reserves, and the usual multiple deposit creation process is set in motion. An open market sale has exactly opposite effects. Payment to the Fed for government securities means a(n) (reduction/increase) in bank reserves and a process of multiple deposit (creation/destruction).
    Banks can add to their reserve holdings by borrowing directly from the Fed. Such borrowings might facilitate a multiple expansion of deposits or, more frequently, might forestall a multiple destruction of deposits. The Fed influences the volume of borrowing by changing the interest rate it charges banks and by

(5) _____ _____, which is the Fed's way of letting banks know that they are misusing their borrowing privileges. More banks borrowings would mean a (higher/lower) amount of bank reserves than otherwise, and eventually a (higher/lower) volume of bank deposits.
    Monetary policy decisions, affecting reserve requirements and the total volume of bank reserves, can be seen as putting an upper limit on the possible creation of bank deposits and hence on the stock of money. How much banks will want to exploit the potential to create deposits will be determined by the profitability of increased bank operations—more loans and more deposits. Higher interest rates on loans will induce banks

(6) to make (more/fewer) loans, hold (more/fewer) nonearning excess reserves, and borrow (more/less) from the Fed (if they can). All of these actions will expand the volume of deposits and hence the stock of

money. In brief, considering just banks, higher interest rates will be associated with a (larger/smaller) stock of money.

    This behavior by banks is summarized in Figure 13–1, which shows an upward-sloping supply of money schedule. Movements along the schedule are related to the decisions of commercial banks. Shifts in the schedule come from changes in monetary policy. For example, an open market purchase increases the

(7) amount of bank reserves and shifts the money supply schedule to the (left/right). Changes in other monetary policy variables will also shift the money supply schedule. To repeat, monetary policy decisions determine the position of the money supply schedule; they do not, by themselves, determine either the stock of money or the interest rate. The actual stock of money and the interest rate will be determined by

the intersection of the supply of money schedules and the _____ for money schedule.

    Figure 13–2 shows a demand schedule for money. The schedule has a negative slope, because as the

(8) interest rate rises, the demand for money (increases/decreases). The increase in interest rates means that the opportunity cost of holding money has (increased/decreased). If nominal GNP increases, that is, if real GNP or prices increase, the demand schedule will shift to the (right/left) as more transactions associated with a higher GNP will lead to a(n) (increased/decreased) demand for money at every interest rate. If nominal GNP decreases, the demand schedule will shift to the _____.

    Equilibrium values for the stock of money and the rate of interest will be determined by the forces of both supply and demand consistent with the process described in Chapter 4. Graphically, the equilibrium

(9) can be represented by the _____ of the demand and supply curves, as in Figure 13–3. Changes in monetary policy will change the equilibrium values for both the stock of money and the rate of interest. An expansionary change in monetary policy would be represented by a shift of the (demand/supply) schedule to the (left/right), a(n) (increase/decrease) in the stock of money, and a(n) (increase/decrease) in the interest rate. A contractionary change in monetary policy would be represented

by a shift of the supply schedule to the _____, a(n) _____

in the stock of money, and a(n) _____ in the interest rate.

    With an understanding of how the demand and supply for money work together to determine interest rates, we are in a position to see how changes in monetary policy affect aggregate demand. Policy shifts

(10) in the (supply/demand) of money schedule will change interest rates as we move along the _____ for money schedule. The change in interest rates will affect interest sensitive categories of demand, especially investment spending. Changes in investment spending lead to a (shift in/movement along) the expenditure schedule. The (shift in/movement along) the expenditure schedule will shift the aggregate (demand/supply) curve through the multiplier process described in Chapter 9. Overall macroeconomic equilibrium is reestablished at the new intersection of the aggregate demand curve and the aggregate supply curve. The division of effects, as between real output and prices, is determined by the slope of the

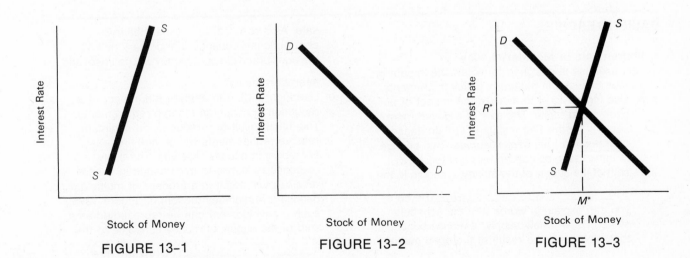

FIGURE 13–1   FIGURE 13–2   FIGURE 13–3

aggregate _____ curve. This sequence of events is diagrammed on page 262 of the text.

The same reasoning helps us to understand two other important points.

Why the aggregate demand curve has a negative slope
Higher prices not only reduce the purchasing power of money fixed assets, they also increase the transactions demand for money. With an unchanged supply of money schedule, the increase in the demand for money that comes with a higher price level will shift the demand for money schedule, leading to an increase in interest rates, lower investment spending, and a reduced equilibrium level of output.

Why the multiplier formula 1/(1 – MPC) is oversimplified
Increases in nominal GNP from the multiplier process increase the transactions demand for money. Interest rates rise as the demand for money schedule moves along an unchanged supply of money schedule. The reduction in investment spending induced by the rise in interest rates is the third important reason why the multiplier process of Chapter 9 was oversimplified.

DEFINITION QUIZ

Choose the letter that is the most appropriate definition for each of the following terms.

1. _____ Central bank

2. _____ Federal Reserve System

3. _____ Federal Open Market Committee

4. _____ Reserve requirement

5. _____ Open-market operations

6. _____ Moral suasion

7. _____ Discount rate

8. _____ Opportunity cost

9. _____ Equilibrium in the money market

10. _____ Monetary policy

a. Foregone value of next best alternative that is not chosen.
b. A bank for banks.
c. Branch of Treasury responsible for minting coins.
d. Quantity of money and level of interest rate where money demand equals money supply.
e. Minimum amount of reserves a bank must hold.
f. Fed's informal requests and warnings to persuade banks to limit their borrowings.
g. Actions Fed takes to affect money supply, interest rates, or both.
h. Central bank of the United States.
i. Interest rate Fed charges on loans to banks.
j. Fed's purchase or sale of government securities.
k. Chief policymaking committee of the Federal Reserve System.

BASIC EXERCISES

1. Instruments of Monetary Policy

This exercise is designed to review the impact of various changes in monetary policy instruments.

a. Use Figure 13–4 to analyze the impact of an open market sale. The sale of a government security by the Fed results in a(n) (increase/decrease) in total bank reserves. This change in bank reserves can be represented as a shift of the supply of the money schedule to the

_____. (Be sure you can explain in words why the schedule shifts.) Draw a new supply of money schedule that represents the result of the open market sale. As a result of this (expansionary/contractionary) change in monetary policy, the equilibrium stock of money will (fall/rise) and

interest rates will _____.

b. Use Figure 13–5 to analyze the impact of a reduction in minimum reserve requirements. The initial result of a reduction in minimum reserve requirements will be a(n) (increase/decrease) in excess reserves. The likely response by banks to this change in excess reserves will result in a process of multiple deposit (creation/destruction). In Figure 13–5 such a development can be represented as a shift of the supply of money schedule to the

_____. Draw the new

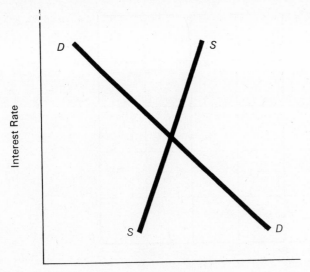

FIGURE 13-4

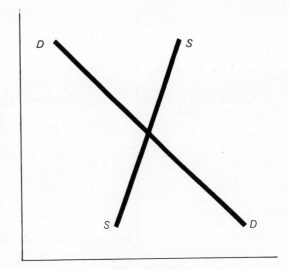

FIGURE 13-5

supply of money schedule. As a result of this

_____ change in monetary policy, the equilibrium stock of money will

_____ and interest rates

will _____.

c. Use Figure 13-6 to analyze the impact of an increase in the discount rate. An increase in this rate will make banks (more/less) willing to borrow from the Fed. One expects that the volume of member bank borrowing will

_____. The change in member bank borrowing is a direct change in bank reserves; so, as a result of the increase in the discount rate total bank reserves will

_____ and the supply of money schedule will shift to the

_____. Draw the new supply of money schedule in Figure 13-6.

As a result of this _____ change in monetary policy, the equilibrium stock

of money will _____ and interest rates will _____.

d. You should also be able to analyze the impact of each opposite change in monetary policy; that is, an open market purchase, an increase in minimum reserve requirements, and a decrease in the discount rate.

2. **Borrowing from the Fed**

Consider the data in Table 13-1 on interest rates and borrowings by depository institutions from the Federal Reserve. The federal funds rate is a market interest rate: it is the interest rate on most short term lending and borrowing between depository institutions. Follow the instructions below to explore the influence of market interest rates on bank borrowings from the Fed.

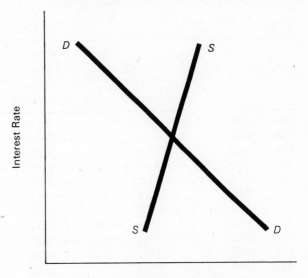

FIGURE 13-6

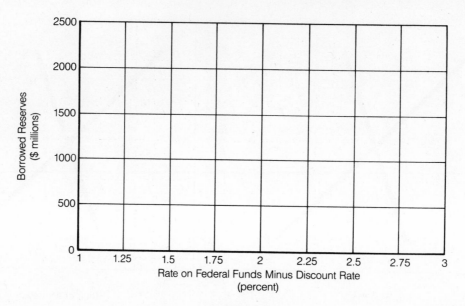

FIGURE 13-7

a. The financial incentive to borrow from the Fed can be represented by the difference between the discount rate and market interest rates, represented here by the federal funds rate. Plot the data from the last two columns of Table 13-1, one point for each month, in the two-variable diagram in Figure 13-7. What does your line suggest is likely to happen to bank borrowings from the Fed if market interest rates increase while the discount rate remains unchanged?

b. Whenever the federal funds rate exceeds the discount rate, some banks could make money by borrowing cheaply from the Fed and by lending at the higher federal funds rate. Why then wasn't there more borrowing in 1989?

3. The data in Table 13-2 is meant to help you explore the interest sensitivity of the demand for money, here measured as M2. As the text explains, the demand for money is likely to be affected by both nominal GNP and interest rates. One way to allow for the impact of nominal GNP

TABLE 13-1

		Discount Rate (percent)	Federal Funds Rate (percent)	Fed Funds Rate minus Discount Rate (percent)	Borrowings from the Federal Reserve ($ millions)
Jan	1989	6.50	9.12	2.62	1,662
Feb	1989	6.59	9.36	2.77	1,487
Mar	1989	7.00	9.85	2.85	1,813
Apr	1989	7.00	9.84	2.84	2,289
May	1989	7.00	9.81	2.81	1,720
Jun	1989	7.00	9.53	2.53	1,490
Jul	1989	7.00	9.24	2.24	694
Aug	1989	7.00	8.99	1.99	675
Sep	1989	7.00	9.02	2.02	693
Oct	1989	7.00	8.84	1.84	555
Nov	1989	7.00	8.55	1.55	349
Dec	1989	7.00	8.45	1.45	265

Source: *Economic Report of the President, 1990*, Tables C–69 and C–71.

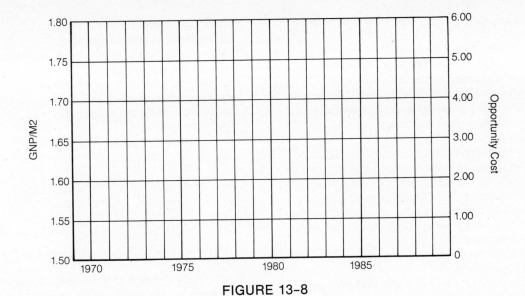

FIGURE 13-8

TABLE 13-2

Year	GNP divided by M2 Balances	Opportunity Cost of M2 Balances*
1970	1.68	3.26
1971	1.63	1.16
1972	1.59	0.83
1973	1.63	3.01
1974	1.66	3.34
1975	1.65	1.92
1976	1.63	1.04
1977	1.61	1.13
1978	1.68	2.48
1979	1.73	3.98
1980	1.74	4.13
1981	1.78	4.73
1982	1.69	2.41
1983	1.61	1.91
1984	1.65	1.96
1985	1.62	1.21
1986	1.57	0.75
1987	1.58	0.87
1988	1.62	1.29
1989	1.67	1.98

*Yield on three month Treasury bills minus weighted average yield on deposit components of M2.

Source: Federal Reserve Bank of Cleveland.

is to first calculate the ratio of GNP to money. If this ratio is constant as interest rates change, it would suggest that the demand for money was always proportional to nominal GNP and unaffected by interest rates.

Column 1 of Table 13-2 reports data on the ratio of GNP to the stock of money since 1970. Column 2 measures the opportunity cost of holding M2 as the difference between the yield on three-month Treasury bills, a measure of general market interest rates, and the weighted average yield on the deposit components of M2.

a. Plot the data in columns 1 and 2 in Figure 13-8. The left-hand axis measures the ratio of GNP to money and the right-hand axis measures the opportunity cost of holding money. What does your graph suggest about the interest sensitivity of the demand for M2 money balances?

SELF-TESTS FOR UNDERSTANDING

Test A

Circle the correct answer.

1. Which of the following is *not* an instrument of monetary policy?
   a. Open market operations.
   b. Lending to banks.
   c. Antitrust actions to promote competition in banking.
   d. Required reserve ratios.

2. Who has direct responsibility for open market operations?
   a. The Board of Governors.
   b. The Federal Open Market Committee.
   c. The President of the United States.
   d. The Banking Committee of the U.S. Senate.
3. Which of the following is *not* an example of expansionary monetary policy?
   a. An open market purchase.
   b. A reduction in reserve requirements.
   c. An increase in the interest rates charged on loans by the Fed to commercial banks.
   d. A reduction in the discount rate.
4. If the Fed wants to reduce the stock of money, which of the following policy actions would be inappropriate?
   a. An increase in minimum reserve requirements.
   b. The sale of a government bond from the Fed's portfolio.
   c. An increase in the discount rate.
   d. An open market purchase.
5. Important determinants of the demand for money include all but which one of the following?
   a. The discount rate.
   b. The level of real output.
   c. Interest rates.
   d. The price level.
6. A change in which of the following would lead to a shift in the demand for money schedule?
   a. Market interest rates.
   b. Reserve requirements.
   c. GNP.
   d. The discount rate.
7. The positive slope of the supply of money schedule indicates that
   a. at higher interest rates people will demand more money.
   b. banks are likely to respond to higher interest rates by holding fewer excess reserves.
   c. minimum reserve requirements increase directly with interest rates.
   d. the Fed is likely to engage in exansionary monetary policy actions as interest rates increase.
8. An open market purchase will lead to all but which one of the following?
   a. Supply of money schedule shifts to the right.
   b. Expenditure schedule shifts up.
   c. Multiplier increases.
   d. Aggregate demand curve shifts to the right.
9. An increase in reserve requirements will lead to all but which one of the following?
   a. An initial increase in required reserves.
   b. A reduction in the stock of money.

   c. An increase in interest rates.
   d. Higher investment spending.
10. An open market sale will result in all but which one of the following?
    a. decrease in the stock of money.
    b. increase in interest rates.
    c. lower investment spending.
    d. higher prices.

Test B

Circle T or F for True or False as appropriate.

1. The independence of the Federal Reserve System is now so well established that it is beyond debate.   **T F**

2. Most power in the Federal Reserve System is held by the 12 district Federal Reserve banks.   **T F**

3. Monetary policy decisions by the Federal Reserve are subject to review by the President of the United States before being implemented.   **T F**

4. An open market purchase by the Fed lowers interest rates without changing the stock of money.   **T F**

5. A reduction in minimum reserve requirements is likely to lead to an increase in both the stock of money and the interest rate.   **T F**

6. Changing the discount rate is the most frequently used instrument of monetary policy today.   **T F**

7. Since many forms of money do not earn interest, people's demand for money is unaffected by changes in interest rates.   **T F**

8. Higher interest rates would normally lead banks to reduce their holdings of excess reserves.   **T F**

9. The impact of changes in monetary policy on interest sensitive categories of demand affects GNP and prices as the economy moves along a given aggregate demand curve.   **T F**

10. The impact of the price level on the demand for money, and hence interest rates, helps to explain why the aggregate demand curve has a negative slope.   **T F**

SUPPLEMENTARY EXERCISES

1. Consider an economy where consumption and investment spending are given by

$$C = 325 + .6\,DI$$
$$I = 470 - 10\,r$$

where r is the interest rate. In this economy, taxes are one-sixth of income and net exports are 100.
   a. If government purchases are 425 and r is 12 (that is, 12 percent), what is the equilibrium level of income?
   b. If the Fed lowers the interest rate to 8, what happens to the equilibrium level of income?
   c. The Fed can lower the interest rate by an appropriate increase in bank reserves; that is, an appropriate shift in the money supply schedule. But what is appropriate? Assume the demand for money is

$$M^D = .25\,Y - 10\,r$$

   and the supply of money is

$$M^S = 5\,BR + 2.5r$$

   where BR is the amount of bank reserves. If $BR = 90$, what is the equilibrium level of income? r? and M?
   d. What increase in BR will reduce the interest rate to 8 and produce the increase in Y you found in Question 2? What happens to M? (You might start by trying an increase in BR of 10 and figuring out what happens to Y and r. Then use these results to figure out how to get r to drop to 8.)
2. Bond Prices and Interest Rates
   a. Consider a bond that pays $90 a year. If interest rates are 9 percent, such a bond should sell for $1000 as ($90 ÷ $1000) = .09. Assume now that interest rates fall to 6 percent. With bond payments of $90, what bond price offers investors a return of 6 percent? If interest rates rise to 15 percent, what must be the price of the bond paying $90 to offer investors a return of 15 percent?
   b. Bonds that pay only interest and never repay principal are called consols. Most bonds pay interest for a certain number of years and then repay the original borrowing or principal. Bond prices reflect the present value of those interest and principal payments as follows:

$$\text{Price} = \sum_{t=1}^{N} \frac{\text{INT}}{(1+r)^t} + \frac{\text{PRIN}}{(1+r)^N}$$

where INT = interest payments
   r = interest rate
   PRIN = principal
   N = number of years of interest payments (also number of years to principal payment)

It may be easier to answer the following questions if you have access to a microcomputer or sophisticated hand calculator.

Verify that if INT = $90, PRIN = $1,000, N = 10 and i = .09, the price of the bond = $1,000.
Calculate the price of the bond when i = .06 and when i = .15 while INT, PRIN, and N remain unchanged. These calculations show what would happen to the price of an existing bond if interest rates change. Do your results confirm the negative correlation between bond prices and interest rates discussed in the text?

14

The Debate over Monetary Policy

LEARNING OBJECTIVES

After completing the material in this chapter you should be able to:

- define, understand, and use correctly the terms and concepts listed below.
- compute velocity given data on nominal income and the stock of money.
- describe why the equation of exchange is not a theory of income determination and why monetarists' use of the same equation turns it into a theory of income determination.
- describe the determinants of velocity.
- explain the difference between the Quantity Theory and Monetarism.
- explain how investment spending and interest rates interact to help determine how monetary policy works in a Keynesian model of income determination.
- explain how expansionary fiscal policy, and related increases in the demand for money, interest rates, and velocity, interact to determine how fiscal policy works in a monetarist model.

- distinguish between lags affecting fiscal policy and those affecting monetary policy.
- explain why the Fed cannot control M and r.
- explain how and why the slope of the aggregate supply curve helps to determine the effectiveness of stabilization policy.
- explain how long lags might mean that efforts to stabilize the economy could end up destabilizing it.
- summarize the views of advocates and opponents of activist stabilization policy by the government.
- explain how automatic stabilizers help to reduce fluctuations in GNP.
- describe and distinguish between different types of economic forecasting: econometric models, leading indicators, survey data, and judgmental forecasts.

IMPORTANT TERMS AND CONCEPTS

Quantity theory of money
Velocity
Equation of exchange
Effect of interest rate on velocity
Monetarism

Effect of fiscal policy on interest rates
Lags in stabilization policy
Shape of the aggregate supply curve
Controlling *M* versus controlling *r*
Automatic stabilizers
Econometric models
Leading indicators
Judgmental forecasts
Rules versus discretionary policy

CHAPTER REVIEW

This is one of the most important and most difficult of the macroeconomic chapters. While not much new material is introduced, the chapter summarizes and synthesizes many of the concepts presented in preceding chapters concerning the theory of income determination as it discusses a number of issues that confront policymakers.

Earlier chapters presented an essentially Keynesian model of income determination. The monetarist viewpoint is a modern manifestation of an even older tradition known as the quantity theory of money. The concept of *velocity* is perhaps the most important tool associated with this theory. Velocity is the average number of times per year that a dollar changes hands to accomplish transactions associated with GNP.

(1) Velocity is measured as nominal _____ divided by the stock of

_____. Alternative measures of money, for example, M1 and M2, have given rise to alternative measures of velocity, V1 and V2.

Related to the concept of velocity is something called the equation of exchange, which is simply another way of stating the definition of velocity. In words, the equation of exchange says:

(2) Money supply × velocity = _____ _____.

In symbols, it is: _____ × _____ = _____ × _____.
Statisticians and national income accountants measure the stock of money and nominal GNP. Economists then calculate velocity by division. Different values of the stock of money could be consistent with the same

level of nominal GNP if_____ changes appropriately.

The quantity theory asserts that there is a close link between changes in nominal GNP and changes in

(3) the stock of _____. This link comes about because the quantity theory assumes that velocity (does/does not) change very much. If velocity is constant, then a change in the money stock

translates directly into a change in _____ _____.
If velocity is 5 and the money stock increases by $20 billion, then nominal GNP will rise by

$_____ billion.

Measures of velocity, as well as an analysis of the determinants of velocity, suggest that one
(4) (should/should not) expect velocity to be constant. Velocity reflects how much money people hold to make transactions, which in turn reflects such institutional factors as the frequency of paychecks and the efficiency of moving money between checking accounts and other assets, such as savings accounts. In Chapter 13 we saw that the amount of money people want to hold, and hence velocity, is also affected by the interest rate

as a measure of the _____ _____ of holding money.

Monetarism, like the quantity theory, starts with the equation of exchange. But rather than assuming that velocity does not change, monetarists try to predict *how* velocity will change. From a monetarist perspective, determinants of nominal GNP are broken down into implications for the stock of money and implications for

(5) _____. After accounting for appropriate changes, simple multiplication can be used to predict nominal GNP.

At first glance it appears that a Keynesian approach to income determination cannot analyze changes in monetary policy whereas a monetarist approach ignores fiscal policy. Such a conclusion would be oversimplified and misleading. In formal theory the two viewpoints are closer than is commonly recognized. Keynesian theory implies that monetary policy can have important impacts on aggregate demand through its impact on interest rates and investment spending. In Chapter 13 we saw that expansionary monetary policy will lead to

(6) a(n) (decline/increase) in interest rates. In Chapter 8 we saw that as a result of lower interest rates investment spending will (increase/decrease). In Chapter 8 we also saw that an increase in investment spending shifts both the expenditure schedule and the aggregate demand curve. Putting all the pieces together we can see that expansionary monetary policy will tend to (increase/decrease) GNP. Restrictive monetary policy would work in exactly the opposite way.

Monetarists are able to analyze the impact of changes in fiscal policy as follows. Expansionary fiscal policy will be associated with higher interest rates. As a result of higher interest rates, velocity will

(7) (increase/decrease) and a monetarist would forecast a (higher/lower) value for nominal GNP.

The impact of changes in fiscal policy on interest rates is not only important to a monetarist analysis of changes in fiscal policy, it is also vital to understanding the third reason why the multiplier formula for Chapter 9 is oversimplified; increases in autonomous spending will tend to increase interest rates which in turn induce partially offsetting changes in investment spending.

The choice between monetary and fiscal policy is often influenced by how quickly changes in policy can occur and how long it takes for changes, once made, to affect the behavior of firms and consumers. In

(8) general, lags in formulating policy are shorter for (fiscal/monetary) policy, whereas spending responses of

firms and households are typically shorter for _____ policy.

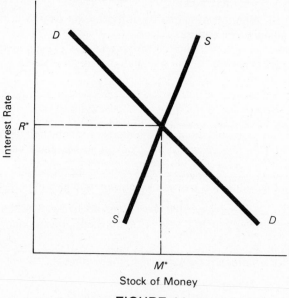

FIGURE 14-1

A major controversy in monetary policy is whether, when formulating monetary-policy decisions, the Federal Reserve should pay greater attention to the money supply or to the interest rates. Imagine, for instance, that the Fed is happy with the stock of money and the interest rate as given in Figure 14-1. Suddenly the demand for money schedule shifts to the right because of an increase in the demand for money from some factor other than interest rates. Draw in the new schedule. If the Fed did nothing, then

(9) as a result of this shift in the demand for money, the stock of money would be (higher/lower) and the interest rate would _____. To maintain the same original money supply, M^*,

the Fed should shift the supply of money schedule to the _____; while to maintain the same rate of interest, the Fed should shift the supply curve to the _____. It does not take any brilliant insight to see that the Fed cannot do both at the same time.

Decisions to stick to original monetary targets are likely to mean greater changes in interest rates, while decisions to stabilize interest rates will mean greater changes in the stock of money. An appropriate choice is likely to depend upon the state of the economy and the source of the original unexpected changes in interest rates and the stock of money.

Stabilization policy affects the economy primarily by shifting the aggregate demand curve. The final result, however, in terms of changes in output and prices, also depends upon the slope of the aggregate supply curve. A flat aggregate supply curve means that shifts in the aggregate demand curve will have

(10) large effects on (output/prices) with only a small change in _____. On the other hand, shifts of the aggregate demand curve will have big effects on prices without much change in output if the aggregate supply curve is (steep/flat). While some argue that the aggregate supply curve is flat and others that it is steep, an emerging consensus sees the slope of the aggregate supply curve as dependent upon the degree of resource utilization. When the economy is operating close to full employment, the aggregate supply curve is likely to be (flat/steep), while during periods in which there is significant slack in

the economy, the aggregate supply curve is likely to be _____.

Some economists favor an activist-oriented approach to stabilization policy. Others favor less activism

(11) and rely on _____ stabilizers to keep the economy on an even keel. Beyond views about the slope of the aggregate supply curve, these differences reflect differing political philosophies and judgments concerning the importance of such factors as the economy's self-correcting mechanisms, the length of various policy lags, the stability of the multiplier and velocity, and the accuracy of economic forecasting.

It takes time before someone notices that the economy is not operating as hoped for and before the appropriate part of the government can decide what policy measures should be adopted. Once a particular policy is decided upon, there may not be much effect on output and prices until the buying habits of households and firms adjust to the new policy. Because of lags, it is not enough to design policies just for today's problems. Economists must also try to predict the future. One way they attempt to do this is through the use of mathematical formulas called econometric models. Another method concentrates on historical timing relationships of some economic variables, called leading indicators.

In addition, the U.S. government and several private organizations periodically ask people and firms about their spending plans for the future. This survey data can also be a useful tool in forecasting. Forecasters who look at the results of all these techniques, as well as such things as sun spots, the length of

(12) women's skirts, and so forth, make what are called _____ forecasts. The more accurate the economic forecasts, the more demanding the standards we can set for stabilization policy. At the present time economic forecasts (are/are not) good enough for fine-tuning the economy.

Active use of fiscal policy to correct persistent and sustained deviations from potential output calls for changes in government spending or taxes. The fact that spending or taxes can be changed means that government spending need not take an ever larger proportion of the economic pie even if the government is committed to activist policy measures.

DEFINITION QUIZ

Choose the letter that is the most appropriate definition for each of the following terms.

1. _____ Quantity theory of money

2. _____ Velocity

3. _____ Equation of exchange

4. _____ Monetarism

5. _____ Automatic stabilizers

6. _____ Econometric models

7. _____ Leading indicators

a. Features of the economy that reduce its sensitivity to shifts in demand.

b. Mode of analysis that uses the equation of exchange to organize macroeconomic data.

c. Average number of times a dollar is spent in a year.

d. Variables that normally turn down prior to recessions and turn up prior to expansions.

e. Theory of aggregate demand stating that nominal GNP is proportional to the money stock.

f. Sets of mathematical equations that form a model of the economy.

g. Features of the economy that move opposite the business cycle.

h. Formula that states that nominal GNP equals the product of money stock times velocity.

BASIC EXERCISE

This exercise is designed to give you practice computing and using velocity.

Table 14–1 contains historical data for nominal GNP, M_1 and M_2

1. Use this data to compute V_1, velocity based on M_1, and V_2, velocity based on M_2.

2. Assume you are a monetarist working for the Federal Reserve and are supposed to estimate nominal GNP. Even if you knew the money supply, M, you would still need an estimate of V.

One way to estimate velocity is to use data from the previous year. The idea is that, since you can't know velocity for, say, 1982 until you know nominal GNP and M_1 or M_2 for 1982, you might use velocity for 1981 to predict GNP for 1982.

Table 14–2 assumes that the Federal Reserve can control the money supply exactly. Use your numbers for velocity to fill in the blank columns in Table 14–2 to predict income.

3. Which years show the largest prediction errors? Why?

SELF-TESTS FOR UNDERSTANDING

Test A

Circle the correct answer.

1. The equation of exchange says that
   a. for every buyer there is a seller.
   b. $M \times V$ = Nominal GNP.
   c. demand equals supply.
   d. P.T. Barnum was right when he said, "There is a sucker born every minute."

2. Velocity is measured by
   a. dividing the money stock by nominal GNP.
   b. computing the percentage change in nominal GNP from year to year.
   c. dividing nominal GNP by the stock of money.
   d. subtracting the rate of inflation from nominal interest rates.

3. Between 1956 and 1957 the money supply (M_1) was essentially constant and yet nominal GNP rose by slightly over 5 percent. It must be that
   a. velocity increased.
   b. velocity decreased.
   c. velocity was unchanged.

4. Initially the stock of money is $600 billion and velocity is 5. If one can be sure that velocity will not change, what increase in M will be required to increase real GNP by $25 billion?
   a. $5 billion.
   b. $10 billion.
   c. $25 billion.
   d. Insufficient information.

TABLE 14-1

	Nominal GNP ($ billions)	M$_1$ ($ billions)	M$_2$ ($ billions)	V$_1$	V$_2$
1980	2,732.0	399.2	1,566.8	_____	_____
1981	3,052.6	425.7	1,714.6	_____	_____
1982	3,116.0	457.8	1,875.2	_____	_____
1983	3,405.7	499.3	2,070.3	_____	_____
1984	3,772.2	537.0	2,276.6	_____	_____
1985	4,014.9	586.2	2,467.3	_____	_____
1986	4,231.6	673.2	2,689.3	_____	_____
1987	4,524.3	739.1	2,860.6	_____	_____
1988	4,880.6	771.3	2,989.8	_____	_____
1989	5,233.2	794.0	3,143.3	_____	_____

Source: *Economic Report of the President, 1990,* Tables C-1 and C-67.

TABLE 14-2

	Actual M$_1$ ($ billions)	V$_1$ from Previous Year	Estimated Income ($ billions)	Actual Income ($ billions)	Estimated Income ($ billions)	V$_2$ Previous Year	Actual M$_2$ ($ billions)
1981	425.7	_____	_____	3,052.6	_____	_____	1,714.6
1982	457.8	_____	_____	3,116.0	_____	_____	1,875.2
1983	499.3	_____	_____	3,405.7	_____	_____	2,070.3
1984	537.0	_____	_____	3,772.2	_____	_____	2,276.6
1985	586.2	_____	_____	4,014.9	_____	_____	2,467.3
1986	673.2	_____	_____	4,231.6	_____	_____	2,689.3
1987	739.1	_____	_____	4,524.3	_____	_____	2,860.6
1988	771.3	_____	_____	4,880.6	_____	_____	2,989.8
1989	794.0	_____	_____	5,233.2	_____	_____	3,143.3

5. Which of the following developments is *not* likely to lead to an increase in velocity?
   a. An increase in the expected rate of inflation.
   b. A reduction in the required reserve ratio for banks.
   c. An increase in interest rates as a result of an expansionary change in fiscal policy.
   d. A widespread trend toward more frequent pay periods.

6. Which of the following is *not* likely to increase nominal GNP according to a monetarist analysis of income determination?
   a. An open market purchase that increases the stock of money.
   b. An increase in government spending.
   c. A technological change in banking practices that increases velocity.
   d. An increase in income taxes.

7. Which of the following is an example of a lag in policymaking as opposed to a lag in spending by firms and households?
   a. The construction of a new plant, induced by lower interest rates, cannot start for nine months, because it takes that long to prepare architectural drawings and contractors' bids.
   b. Congress takes five months to consider a presidential tax proposal.
   c. Through multiplier impacts, a $3 billion increase in defense spending eventually raises GNP by $5 billion.
   d. Refrigerator sales rise in the month following a $300 tax rebate.

8. If the aggregate supply curve is relatively flat, then
   a. velocity will be constant.
   b. both monetary and fiscal policy will have relatively large effects on output without much effect on prices.
   c. a change in interest rates will have little impact on investment.
   d. monetary policy will be effective while fiscal policy will not.

9. Which of the following is *not* an example of an automatic stabilizer?
   a. Unemployment compensation.
   b. The corporate income tax.
   c. Increased highway building enacted during a recession.
   d. Personal income taxes.

10. Forecasting by extrapolating previous timing relationships between changes in the stock of money and GNP is an example of
    a. judgmental forecasts.
    b. econometric models.
    c. leading indicators.
    d. automatic stabilizers.

Test B

Circle T or F for True or False as appropriate.

1. If the stock of money is $800 billion and nominal GNP is $4800 billion, then velocity is 6.   T F

2. The quantity theory is not really a theory because velocity, by definition, is equal to the ratio of nominal GNP divided by the money stock.   T F

3. Monetarist and Keynesian theories are both incomplete in that they concentrate on demand and ignore the supply side of the economy.   T F

4. Expansionary monetary policy that increases the stock of money will only increase prices with no impact on real output.   T F

5. The lag between a change in fiscal policy and its effects on aggregate demand is probably shorter than the lag between a change in monetary policy and its effects on aggregate demand.   T F

6. The lag in adopting an appropriate policy is probably shorter for fiscal policy than for monetary policy.   T F

7. By simultaneously using open market operations and making changes in minimum reserve requirements, the Fed would be able to achieve any desired combination of the money stock and the interest rate.   T F

8. The shape of the aggregate supply curve is likely to be relatively steep when the economy is operating near full employment and relatively flat during periods of high unemployment and low rates of capacity utilization.   T F

9. Long lags will help make for better stabilization policy because there is more time for a complete analysis of possible actions.   T F

10. Automatic stabilizers reduce the sensitivity of the economy to shifts in aggregate demand.   T F

SUPPLEMENTARY EXERCISES

1. Leading Indicators

Is the stock market a good forecaster (leading indicator) of overall economic conditions? Figure 14-2 shows stock prices over the postwar period. Using just Figure 14-2, make an estimate of how many recessions there have been since the early 1950s. Try to date each one approximately. Now go to the library and find a recent copy of *Business Conditions Digest*, a monthly publication of the Commerce Department that publishes data on a large number of leading indicators and keeps track of recessions as identified by the National Bureau of Economic Research. How many recessions does the NBER identify? How many did you identify? How many false indications of recession were there? What about the forecasting record of other leading indicators? What are the stock market and other leading indicators saying about a possible recession in the next 6 to 12 months?

In addition to the problem of false indicators, there are two other limitations to a purely mechanical use of leading indicators that you should be aware of:

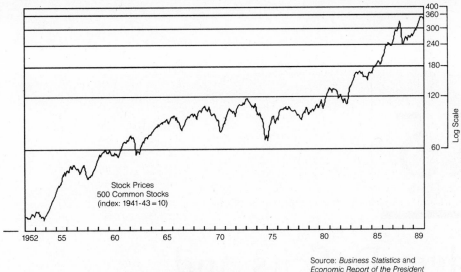

Source: *Business Statistics* and
Economic Report of the President

FIGURE 14-2

a. Most large declines in a leading indicator are the result of not one large decline, but rather a series of consecutive small declines. At the same time each series has so many random fluctuations that most small declines are followed by a small increase. One needs some way of separating those small declines that signal the start of a major slump from those that are quickly reversed.

b. A leading indicator that always changes direction a fixed time before the economy does would be an extremely useful variable. However, the length of time between movements in most leading indicators and the economy may be quite variable.

2. Judgmental Forecasts

Alan Greenspan's forecasting record came under public scrutiny in the summer of 1987 when President Reagan nominated Greenspan to be Chairman of the Board of Governors of the Federal Reserve System. Table 14-3 compares forecasts from Greenspan's consulting firm, Townsend-Greenspan & Company, made in November of the preceding year with the Blue Chip Consensus Forecast—the average of approximately fifty forecasters—made in October of the preceding year. How do you rate these forecasts? You might want to look at "Consensus Forecasting—A Ten-Year Report Card", Jim Eggert, *Challenge*, July/August 1987, pages 59–62.

TABLE 14-3

	Growth Rate of Real GNP (percent)				Percentage Change in GNP Implicit Deflator (percent)		
Year	Actual	Townsend-Greenspan	Blue Chip Consensus		Actual	Townsend-Greenspan	Blue Chip Consensus
1978	5.3	4.8	4.3		7.3	6.5	6.0
1979	2.5	2.5	2.7		8.9	7.6	7.3
1980	-0.2	-1.6	-0.2		9.0	8.4	8.5
1981	1.9	1.1	0.9		9.7	9.4	9.1
1982	-2.5	-1.0	2.2		6.4	8.4	7.8
1983	3.6	1.9	3.2		3.9	6.2	5.7
1984	6.8	5.8	5.1		3.7	4.9	5.0
1985	3.4	3.6	3.5		3.0	4.5	4.7
1986	2.7	2.9	3.1		2.6	4.4	3.8
1987	3.7	2.4			3.2	2.9	

Source: Actual: U.S. Department of Commerce.
   Townsend-Greenspan: "Forecasts: Greenspan's Grades", *The New York Times*, National Edition, July 24, 1987, page 25.
   Blue Chip Consensus: "Consensus Forecasting—A Ten-Year Report Card", Jim Eggert, *Challenge*, July/August 1987, pages 59–62.

15

Budget Deficits and the National Debt: Fact and Fiction

LEARNING OBJECTIVES

After completing the material in this chapter you should be able to:

- define, understand, and use correctly the terms and concepts listed below.

- explain how measures to balance the budget may unbalance the economy.

- explain how appropriate fiscal policy depends on the strength of private demand and the conduct of monetary policy.

- explain the difference between the government's budget deficit and the national debt.

- discuss some facts about budget deficits and the national debt: When have budget deficits been largest? When has the national debt grown fastest? What has happened to the national debt as a proportion of GNP?

- describe how the concept of structural deficits or surpluses differs from officially reported deficits or surpluses.

- describe how traditional accounting procedures will overstate the interest component of government expenditures during a period of inflation.

- distinguish between real and bogus arguments about the burden of the national debt.

- describe the inflationary consequences of a budget deficit and explain why deficits will be more inflationary if they are monetarized.

- explain how increased deficits can be associated with either higher or lower interest rates, higher or lower rates of inflation, and faster or slower growth in real output.

- evaluate arguments supporting the crowding-out and crowding-in properties of government deficit spending.

- explain how changing the mix of monetary and fiscal policy could change the budget deficit while leaving GNP and prices unchanged.

- explain why most economists measure the true burden of deficits by their impact on the capital stock.

**IMPORTANT TERMS
AND CONCEPTS**

Budget deficit
National debt
Real versus nominal interest rates
Inflation accounting

Structural deficit or surplus
Monetization of deficits
Crowding out
Crowding in
Burden of the national debt
Mix of monetary and fiscal policy

CHAPTER REVIEW

Ever since 1980 the federal government's budget deficits have been very much like the weather: everyone has been talking about them but no one seems able to do anything about them. By itself this chapter cannot make government deficits larger or smaller, but it can help to increase your understanding of the impacts of both government deficits and the national debt.

(1)   The government runs a deficit when its (spending/revenue) exceeds its_____.

There is a surplus when _____ is greater than _____. The national debt measures the government's total indebtedness. The national debt will increase if the government budget shows a (deficit/surplus). The national debt will decrease if the government budget shows a

_____.

What is appropriate deficit policy? Earlier chapters discussed the use of fiscal and monetary policy to strike an appropriate balance between aggregate demand and aggregate supply in order to choose between inflation and unemployment. Considerations of balanced budgets, per se, were absent from that discussion. The conclusion that budget policy should adapt to the requirements of the economy is widely shared by most economists.

Some have advocated a policy of strict budget balance. There is good reason to expect that such a policy would balance the budget at the cost of unbalancing the economy. Consider an economy in an initial equilibrium at full employment with a balanced budget. An autonomous decline in consumption spending

(2)   would shift the expenditure schedule (down/up), resulting in a shift of the aggregate demand schedule to the (right/left). In the absence of any further policy action the result would be a (decline/increase) in GNP. Since income taxes are a major component of government revenues, the change in GNP will also mean a(n) (decline/increase) in government tax revenues. The government's budget will move from its initial position of balance to one of (deficit/surplus). At this point, deliberate policy actions to reestablish budget balance would call for either a(n) (decrease/increase) in taxes or a(n) (decrease/increase) in government expenditures. In either case the result would be an additional shift in the expenditure schedule and aggregate demand curve that would (accentuate/counteract) the original shift that was due to the autonomous decline in consumption expenditures.

The fact that tax revenues depend on the state of the economy is important to understanding many complicated issues about the impact of deficits. As seen above, it helps to explain why a policy of budget balancing can unbalance the economy in the face of declines in private spending. It helps to explain why deficits can sometimes be associated with a booming economy and at other times with a sagging economy. It also helps to explain interest in alternative measures of the deficit. The concept of structural deficits or structural surpluses is an attempt to separate out the impact of the economy on the deficit. It does so by looking at spending and revenues at a specified high-employment level of income. Changes in tax revenues

(3)   due to changes in income (will/will not) affect the actual deficit but (will/will not) affect the structural deficit. For this reason many analysts prefer to use the structural deficit as a measure of the stance of fiscal policy.

Inflation and, especially, the impact of inflation on interest rates raise complicated measurement problems. As we learned in Chapter 6, during periods of inflation, increases in nominal interest rates that reflect expectations of future inflation may not imply any change in real interest rates. To the extent that nominal interest rates include such inflationary premiums, a proportion of interest payments is not interest in the sense of payment for the use of the purchasing power embodied in the original loan; rather it is a repayment of the purchasing power embodied in the original loan balance itself.

Are deficits inflationary? The short answer is yes and the more complete answer asks for more details. If the alternative to any deficit is more taxation or less spending, then any deficit, whether the result of deliberate policy or of a reduction in autonomous spending, will mean a higher price level, a higher level of output and less unemployment than the alternative of a balanced budget. This is so because the deficit keeps the aggregate demand curve farther to the right than would be the case with either a decrease in spending or an increase in taxes. The exact inflationary consequences of a budget deficit depend on where along the aggregate supply curve the economy finds itself and what monetary policy is doing. A government deficit during a period of recession may find the economy operating on a relatively flat portion of the

(4)   aggregate supply curve. If so, any reduction in the deficit will likely have a (large/small) impact on the price level but could have a relatively large impact on output and employment. In this situation, a deliberate increase in the deficit from expansionary fiscal policy could increase output and employment substantially (with/without) much impact on prices. On the other hand, substantial budget deficits at a time of full employment will find the economy on a relatively steep portion of the aggregate supply curve. In this case, a

reduction in the deficit is likely to have a (large/small) impact on output and a _____ impact on the price level.

A deficit that is associated with a deliberate reduction in taxes will increase output, prices, and interest rates as it shifts the aggregate demand curve to the right. Concerns about the impact of the deficit on interest rates may lead the Federal Reserve to increase the money supply. If the Federal Reserve acts to

(5)   increase the stock of money by buying government securities, one says it has _____ the deficit. As we learned in Chapter 13, expansion of the money supply will imply a further expansionary shift in the aggregate demand curve and will mean even higher prices.

Many feelings about the burden of the national debt may be as deeply ingrained and just as irrational as a Victorian's ideas about sex or a football coach's ideas about winning. Many bogus arguments about the burden of the debt do, however, contain some elements of truth. Arguments about the burden of future interest payments or the cost of repaying the national debt are not relevant when considering debts held by

(6)   domestic citizens but are relevant when considering debts held by _____. To the extent that debt is held by domestic citizens, interest payments and debt repayments impose little burden on the nation as a whole, they are only transfers from taxpayers to bondholders, who may even be the same individuals. However, the impact on incentives of higher taxes to service the debt should not be ignored.

A real burden of the debt would arise from a deficit in a high-employment economy that crowded out

(7)   private (consumption/investment) spending and left a smaller capital stock to future generations. There will continue to be arguments as to whether U.S. deficits have entailed such a burden. The federal government's

deficit has shown its largest increases during periods of _____ and

_____. Government deficits during periods of slack may actually result in a benefit rather than a burden if, as a result of increased demand, they lead to (crowding in/crowding out)

rather than _____. Major concerns about deficits during the late 1980s are that they occurred during a period of (high/low) employment and that they are thus likely to have led to crowding

_____.

DEFINITION QUIZ

Choose the letter that is the most appropriate definition for each of the following terms.

1. _____ Budget deficit
2. _____ National debt
3. _____ Structural deficit
4. _____ Inflation accounting
5. _____ Monetization of deficits
6. _____ Crowding out
7. _____ Crowding in

a. Amount by which revenue exceeds spending.
b. Deficit under current fiscal policies if the economy was near full employment.
c. Amount by which government spending exceeds revenue.
d. Increase in private investment spending induced by increase in government spending.
e. Adjusting standard accounting procedures for changes in purchasing power.
f. Contraction of private investment spending induced by deficit spending.
g. Federal government's total indebtedness.
h. Purchases of government bonds used to finance deficit by central bank.
i. Percentage by which money repayment exceeds money borrowed.

BASIC EXERCISE

This exercise is designed to show how a rigid policy of balanced budgets may unbalance the economy. To simplify the calculations, the exercise assumes that prices do not change and thus focuses on the horizontal shift in the aggregate demand curve.

1. Fill in the last column of Table 15–1 to determine the initial equilibrium level of income. The

   equilibrium level of income is _____.
2. What is the deficit at the initial equilibrium level

   of income? _____
3. The high employment level of income is $5200. Is the structural budget in surplus or deficit?

   _____

   What is the magnitude of the structural surplus

   or deficit? _____
4. Investment spending now declines by $80 billion. Use Table 15–2 to compute the new equilibrium level of income. What is the new equilibrium

   level of income? _____
   How has the deficit changed, if at all?

   _____

   How has the structural (deficit/surplus) changed, if at all?

   _____

   _____

5. If the government is committed to a balanced budget, would it raise or lower taxes to restore a

   balanced budget? _____ What would this change in taxes do to the equilibrium

   level of national income? _____

   _____

6. If the government decides to change government purchases to eliminate the deficit, would it raise

   or lower spending? _____
   What would this change do to the equilibrium

   level of national income? _____

   _____

7. (Optional) How large a lump-sum change in taxes, that is, the same change at every level of of income, would balance the budget?

   $_____ billion. The new equilibrium

   level of income would be $_____ billion.
8. (Optional) How large a change in government spending would balance the budget?

   $_____ billion. The new equilibrium level of income would be

   $_____ billion.

TABLE 15–1

(All figures are in billions of real dollars)

National Income	Taxes	Disposable Income	Consumption Spending	Investment Spending	Government Spending	Net Exports	$C + I + G + (X - IM)$
4400	1100	3300	2740	800	1250	− 150	_____
4600	1150	3450	2860	800	1250	− 150	_____
4800	1200	3600	2980	800	1250	− 150	_____
5000	1250	3750	3100	800	1250	− 150	_____
5200	1300	3900	3220	800	1250	− 150	_____

TABLE 15–2

(All figures are in billions of real dollars)

National Income	Taxes	Disposable Income	Consumption Spending	Investment Spending	Government Spending	Net Exports	$C + I + G + (X - IM)$
4400	1100	3300	2740	720	1250	− 150	_____
4600	1150	3450	2860	720	1250	− 150	_____
4800	1200	3600	2980	720	1250	− 150	_____
5000	1250	3750	3100	720	1250	− 150	_____
5200	1300	3900	3220	720	1250	− 150	_____

SELF-TESTS FOR UNDERSTANDING

Test A

Circle the correct answer.

1. The ratio of the national debt to GNP
   a. has declined continuously since WWII.
   b. has increased continuously since WWII.
   c. is about 3 to 1.
   d. has risen over the 1980s from its recent low point in the 1970s.
2. A comparison of the federal government's actual deficit and the structural deficit for the period 1980 to 1987 would show that the actual deficit was
   a. smaller than the structural deficit.
   b. about the same size as the structural deficit.
   c. larger than the structural deficit.
3. Rigid adherence to budget balancing will
   a. help the economy adjust to shifts in private spending.
   b. have little impact on business cycles.
   c. accentuate swings in GNP from autonomous changes in private spending.
   d. help maintain full employment.
4. A decline in private investment spending will lead to all but which one of the following?
   a. A downward shift in the expenditure schedule.
   b. A decline in the equilibrium level of GNP.
   c. An increase in the government deficit or a reduction in the surplus.
   d. A decline in the structural budget deficit or surplus.
5. If the Federal Reserve monetizes a budget deficit, there will be a(n)
   a. smaller inflationary impact.
   b. unchanged inflationary impact.
   c. larger inflationary impact.
6. The inflationary consequences of a budget deficit are likely to be greatest when
   a. the deficit is the result of a decline in private spending.
   b. the deficit is the result of a deliberate

decision to raise taxes and monetize the resulting deficit.

   c. the deficit is the result of a deliberate decision to increase government spending and to monetize the resulting deficit.

   d. the rate of unemployment is high.

7. Using real interest rates when measuring the deficit during a period of inflation would have what impact?

   a. It would make the deficit smaller.

   b. It would leave the deficit unchanged.

   c. It would make the deficit larger.

8. Which of the following is a valid argument about the burden of the national debt for an economy whose debt is held entirely by its own citizens?

   a. Future generations will find interest payments a heavy burden.

   b. When the debt is due, future generations will be burdened with an enormous repayment.

   c. The debt will bankrupt future generations.

   d. If the deficits causing the debt crowded out private investment spending, then future generations would be left with a smaller capital stock.

9. "Crowding out" refers to

   a. increased population pressures and arguments for zero population growth.

   b. the effects of government deficits on private investment spending.

   c. what happens at the start of the New York City marathon.

   d. the impact of higher prices on the multiplier.

10. Crowding in is more likely to occur when

   a. the economy is operating near full employment.

   b. prices are rising.

   c. the government lowers expenditures.

   d. there is substantial slack in the economy.

Test B

Circle T or F for True or False as appropriate.

1. A policy calling for continuous balance in the government's budget will help offset shifts in autonomous private demand.   **T F**

2. A balanced high employment budget is necessary if the equilibrium level of GNP is to equal the full employment level of GNP.   **T F**

3. Inflation accounting would increase the interest portion of government expenditures during periods of inflation.   **T F**

4. Increases in the government's deficit are always associated with increases in interest rates.   **T F**

5. The inflationary impact of any budget deficit depends on the conduct of monetary policy.   **T F**

6. Recent government deficits have meant that the ratio of national debt to GNP has never been higher than it is today.   **T F**

7. Interest payments on the national debt, whether to domestic citizens or foreigners, are not really a burden on future generations.   **T F**

8. A major limitation of the simple crowding-out argument is the assumption that the economy's total pool of savings is fixed.   **T F**

9. Crowding in is likely to occur when the economy is operating with lots of slack, whereas crowding out is likely to occur at full employment.   **T F**

10. Government deficits may impose a real burden on future generations if, as a result of crowding out, there is less private investment and a smaller capital stock in the future.   **T F**

SUPPLEMENTARY EXERCISES

1. Government Deficits and Interest Rates
Between 1957 and 1958, the federal government's budget shifted from a surplus of $2.3 billion to a deficit of $10.3 billion. At the time this was the largest deficit since World War II and was bigger than any deficit during the Great Depression. At the same time, interest rates declined dramatically. The rate on three-month Treasury bills declined from an average of 3.267 percent in 1957 to 1.839 percent in 1958. The rate on 3- to 5-year securities fell from 3.62 to 2.90 percent.

Between 1974 and 1975, the federal government's budget deficit increased from $11.6 billion to $69.4 billion. At the same time, interest rates again declined. The rate on three-month Treasury bills declined from 7.886 to 5.838 percent, while the rate on 3- to 5-year securities declined more modestly from 7.81 to 7.55 percent.

Between 1981 and 1982 the federal government deficit increased dramatically from $63.8 billion to $145.9 billion, the largest year-to-year increase on record. At the same time, interest rates declined. The rate on three-month Treasury bills declined from 14.029 percent to 10.686 percent. Interest rates on longer term government securities also declined.

How do you explain the seemingly contradictory results that larger deficits are associated with lower, not higher, interest rates? Do these observations prove that larger deficits will always be associated with lower interest rates?

2. Repudiate the National Debt?

If the national debt is so onerous, we could solve the problem by simply repudiating the debt; that is, we would make no more interest or principal payments on the outstanding debt.

Imagine that in keeping with democratic principles such a proposition were put to American voters. Who do you think would vote pro and who would vote con? Which side would win? Would the outcome of the vote be different if the debt were held entirely by foreigners? By banks and other financial institutions? (The Treasury publishes data on who holds the national debt in the *Treasury Bulletin*. This data is also published in the annual *Economic Report of the President*. You might want to look at these data and consider what would happen to depositors, shareholders, and pensioners, both current and prospective, if the national debt held by banks, corporations, and pension funds was suddenly worthless.)

Repudiating the national debt might well limit future budget flexibility. What would be the likely consequences during periods of recession? Inflation? War?

3. Continual Budget Deficits

What are the long run consequences of continual budget deficits? If you have access to a programmable hand calculator or to a microcomputer, experiment with the following simulation model to discover how results depend on particular coefficients.

a. Assume that nominal GNP grows at a constant rate, λ:

$$GNP_t = (1 + \lambda) \, GNP_{t-1}$$

b. Assume that tax receipts are proportional to nominal GNP.

$$T_t = \tau \, GNP_t$$

c. Assume that government purchases of goods and services plus all transfer payments except for interest on the national debt are also some constant percentage of nominal GNP:

$$G_t = g \, GNP_t; \, g > \tau$$

(This specification means that, not counting interest payments, the government deficit will always be a constant proportion $[g - \tau]$ of nominal GNP).

d. Assume that the government must pay interest on the national debt at a rate of interest R:

$$\text{Interest Payments} = IP_t = R \, (\text{Debt}_t)$$

e. The government's total deficit is:

$$\text{Deficit}_t = G_t + IP_t - T_t$$

f. The government debt grows as follows:

$$\text{Debt}_{t+1} = \text{Debt}_t + \text{Deficit}_t$$

g. Use these relationships to simulate your model economy and investigate what happens to the ratio of debt to GNP. To start your simulations you will need values for the four parameters, λ, τ, g, and R, and initial values for GNP and the national debt. Try starting with the following:

$\lambda = 0.10$	$R = 0.07$
$\tau = 0.20$	GNP = 5000
$g = 0.22$	Debt = 2100

What happens to the ratio of debt to GNP as your model economy evolves?

h. Try experimenting with some alternative parameters and initial values.

(i) Change the initial value of GNP, then change the initial value of the national debt. Do these changes affect what happens over time?

(ii) Now change τ and g. What happens? Do these changes affect the eventual ratio of debt to GNP? If so, how?

(iii) Finally, change λ and R, individually and then together. Remember that λ is the growth rate of nominal GNP and R is nominal interest rates. Higher inflation would be expected to change both λ and R, whereas a change in real growth or real interest rates would change them individually. Do these changes affect the eventual ratio of debt to GNP? If so, how?

16

The Trade-Off between Inflation and Unemployment

After completing the material in this chapter you should be able to:

- define, understand, and use correctly the terms and concepts listed below.
- explain how prices can rise following either the rapid growth of aggregate demand or the sluggish growth of aggregate supply.
- explain what the Phillips curve is and is not
- explain how the slope of the Phillips curve is related to the slope of the aggregate supply curve.
- explain how the source of fluctuations in economic activity—whether predominantly from shifts of the aggregate demand curve or from shifts of the aggregate supply curve—will affect the Phillips curve.
- explain why the economy's self-correcting mechanism means that the economy's true long-run choices lie along a vertical Phillips curve.
- use the long-run Phillips curve to show how the temporary impact of aggregate demand policy on unemployment can have a permanent impact on the rate of inflation.

- explain how and why one's views on appropriate aggregate demand policy are likely to depend upon one's views on
  — the social costs of inflation vs. unemployment.
  — the efficiency of the economy's self-correcting mechanism.
  — the current level of output vis-a-vis full-employment output.
  — how quickly inflationary expectations adjust.
- explain how the accuracy of expectations about inflation can affect the slope of both the aggregate supply curve and the Phillips curve.
- discuss the implications of and evidence for the doctrine of rational expectations.
- discuss measures that have been advocated to reduce the natural rate of unemployment.
- describe the various kinds of incomes policies and other plans that have been tried in the United States in an effort to improve the inflationary–unemployment trade-off.
- calculate how indexing would be applied to wages and interest rates, given the appropriate data on prices.
- discuss the advantages and disadvantages of universal indexing.

IMPORTANT TERMS AND CONCEPTS

Demand-side inflation
Vertical (long-run) Phillips curve
Rational expectations
Supply-side inflation
Trade-off between inflation and unemployment in the
   short run and in the long run
Phillips curve
Stagflation caused by supply shocks
Self-correcting mechanism

Natural rate of unemployment
Inflationary expectations
Incomes policy
Wage-price controls
Wage-price guideposts
Profit sharing
Indexing (escalator clauses)
Real versus nominal interest rates

CHAPTER REVIEW

This chapter discusses the hard choices that policymakers must make when deciding how to respond to inflation or unemployment. Chapters 11 through 14 discussed how changes in various tools of fiscal and monetary policy can be used to influence aggregate demand. Chapter 16 uses this material to study the policy implications for fighting unemployment and inflation. Here, as in many other areas of life, one cannot have one's cake and eat it too. Actions taken to reduce unemployment will often lead to higher rates of inflation, while actions to reduce inflation will often lead to higher rates of unemployment. Economists can help to define the nature of this trade-off, examine the factors that are responsible for it, and clarify the implications of different choices, but they cannot tell anyone which choice to make. In a democratic society, this decision is left to the political process.

(1)   Any shift in the aggregate demand or aggregate supply curve, whether induced by policy or not, is likely to affect both prices and output. The nature of the association between changes in prices and changes in output will depend upon which curve shifts. If fluctuations in economic activity are predominantly the result of shifts in the aggregate demand curve, higher prices will be associated with (higher/lower) levels of output. The transition to higher prices is a period of inflation. The associated higher level of output will require more employment, leading to a lower level of unemployment. Hence, shifts in the aggregate demand curve imply that inflation and unemployment are (negatively/positively) correlated. That is, if you plotted the rate of unemployment on the horizontal axis and the rate of inflation on the vertical axis, the resulting curve, called

the _____ curve, would have a (positive/negative) slope.

(2)   Data available through the end of the 1960s was consistent with the view sketched above and seemed to imply that policymakers could choose between inflation and unemployment. In particular, it used to be thought that the Phillips curve implied that policymakers could permanently increase output beyond the level of full employment or potential output at the cost of only a small increase in the rate of inflation. Subsequent experience and thought have shown that this view is (correct/incorrect). We saw earlier that output beyond the level of potential output results in a(n) (inflationary/recessionary) gap. The economy's self-correcting mechanism will shift the aggregate supply curve to reestablish long-run equilibrium at the

_____ rate of unemployment. Continual shifts of the aggregate demand curve would be necessary to maintain a lower rate of unemployment. These continual shifts of the aggregate demand curve will imply an ever-increasing rate of inflation. The only true long-run choices lie along a

_____ Phillips curve.

In the short run, shifts in the aggregate demand curve will move the economy up or down the short-run Phillips curve; but the economy's self-correcting mechanism implies that this trade-off is only temporary. How temporary depends upon the speed of the economy's self-correcting mechanism. Differing views about the speed of the mechanism are an important part of differences in Keynesian and monetarist policy prescriptions.

Changes in money wages are an important determinant of shifts in the aggregate supply curve that lead an inflationary gap to self-destruct. It is the original increase in prices above wages that induces firms to expand output. As workers recognize that the purchasing power of their money wages has declined, the subsequent increases in wages to restore real wages will lead to shifts in the aggregate supply curve. Rather than always being a step behind, workers can try to protect their real wages by anticipating the increase in prices. On this view the expectation of higher prices will lead to higher wages and a shift in the aggregate supply curve in anticipation of inflation. Compared with cases where the aggregate supply curve did not shift, a shift in the aggregate demand curve accompanied by an expectations-induced shift in the aggregate

(3) supply curve will have a (larger/smaller) impact on output and a _____ impact on prices. The result will be a (higher/lower) rate of inflation and the slope of the short-run Phillips curve will be (steeper/flatter).

Economists associated with the doctrine of rational expectations have focused attention on the formation of expectations. While much remains to be learned, these economists argue that errors in predicting inflation cannot be systematic. An implication of this view is that except for random elements, the short-run Phillips curve is vertical. Not only is there no long-run trade-off between inflation and unemployment, but, according to this view, there is also no systematic short-run trade-off.

Others are less convinced that expectations are rational in the sense of no systematic errors. These economists believe that people tend to underpredict inflation when it is rising and overpredict it when it is falling. Long-term contracts also make it difficult to adjust to changing expectations of inflation. These economists argue that policy measures to shift the aggregate demand curve can affect output and employment in the short run. But remember that these short-run impacts are constrained by the true long-run menu

(4) of choices which lie along a _____ Phillips curve.

Most economists believe that aggregate demand policy will affect employment and inflation in the short run and may also affect the place at which the economy ends up on the long-run Phillips curve. Thus, a policy to fight a recession rather than to wait for economy's self-correcting mechanism will mean more employment in the short run and is likely to mean more inflation in the long run as compared to a status quo policy that waits on the economy's self-correcting mechanisms. (See Figures 16–14 and 16–15 in the text.) Whether one wants to use aggregate demand policy or wait for natural processes depends on one's assessment of the costs of inflation and unemployment, the efficiency of the economy's self-correcting mechanisms, the current level of output vis-a-vis full employment, especially as it has implications for the slope of the aggregate supply curve, and the quickness with which inflationary expectations adjust.

A number of policies have been advocated in the hope that they will improve the inflation-unemployment trade-off. These policies run the gamut from presidential exhortations to elaborate wage-price monitoring bureaucracies to proposals for new forms of labor contracts that tie a portion of wages to profits.

Voluntary wage-price guideposts call for business and labor to set wages and prices in line with standards determined, in part, by increases in labor productivity. The logic of these guidelines is that competitive markets can allow wage increases in line with increases in productivity without inflation. Thus, if labor productivity is increasing at 2 percent a year and the government is aiming to hold inflation to 3 percent a year, the guidepost standard for wage increases would be 5 percent.

More drastic forms of incomes policies include wage-price controls or even a wage-price freeze. Neither policy is a desirable long-run option. If adhered to for a long time, either policy undermines the allocative role of prices and results in inefficient alternatives. Historically, the Nixon wage-price freeze was a tactical device in order to allow time for a program of controls. A wage-price freeze or a set of controls might work if it

(5) resulted in a significant lowering of inflationary _____. However, if there is no change in the underlying forces of aggregate demand and supply, there (is/is not) likely to be much change in expectations.

A number of individuals have argued that rather than trying to reduce the rate of inflation we should simply learn to live with it and rely on automatic adjustments of monetary payments to reflect changes in prices, also called indexing. The automatic adjustment of social security benefits, as well as other govern-

(6) ment transfer programs, and escalator clauses in wage contracts are examples of _____. A number of observers also advocate this mechanism for interest rates.

Indexing does seem to offer some relief from many of the social costs of inflation discussed in Chapter 6. As workers, firms, and lenders scramble to protect themselves against anticipated future increases in

(7) prices, current prices and interest rates will (increase/decrease) to reflect the expectation of inflation. If actual inflation turns out to be greater or less than expected, there will be a redistribution of wealth that many feel is essentially arbitrary. Legal prohibitions on nominal interest and profit rates can have extremely perverse effects in an inflationary world where inflationary expectations are reflected in (nominal/real) interest rates. Uncertainty over future prices may make individuals and businesses extremely reluctant to enter into long-term contracts.

Indexing offers relief from all these problems. Labor contracts and other agreements could be written in real rather than nominal terms, and arbitrary redistributions would be avoided because money payments would reflect actual, not expected, inflation. At the same time there is concern that learning to live with

(8)   inflation may make the economy (more/less) inflation prone.

DEFINITION QUIZ

Choose the letter that is the most appropriate definition for each of the following terms.

1. _____ Vertical Phillips curve

2. _____ Rational expectations

3. _____ Phillips curve

4. _____ Self-correcting mechanism

5. _____ Natural rate of unemployment

6. _____ Inflationary expectations

7. _____ Incomes policy

8. _____ Wage-price controls

9. _____ Wage-price guideposts

10. _____ Profit sharing

11. _____ Indexing

a. Graph depicting unemployment rate on horizontal axis and inflation rate on vertical axis.
b. Legal restrictions on the ability of industry and labor to raise wages and prices.
c. Unemployment rate at full employment.
d. Workers receive a base wage plus a fraction of the company's earnings.
e. Variety of measures to curb inflation without reducing aggregate demand.
f. Vertical line at natural rate of inflation.
g. Numerical standards for permissible wage or price increases.
h. Forecasts which make optimal use of available and relevant data.
i. Adjustments of monetary payments whenever a specified price index changes.
j. The economy's way of curing gaps via price level changes.
k. Vertical line at the natural rate of unemployment.
l. Beliefs concerning future price level increases.

BASIC EXERCISE

This exercise is designed to illustrate the nature of the inflation-unemployment trade-off that policymakers must face when planning aggregate demand policy.

1. Figure 16–1 shows an economy with a recessionary gap. Which of the following monetary and fiscal policies could be used to help eliminate this gap?
   - open market (purchase/sale).

   - (increase/decrease) of minimum reserve requirements.

   - (increase/decrease) in taxes.

   - (increase/decrease) in government transfer payments to individuals.

   - (increase/decrease) in government purchases of goods and services.

2. Assume the full-employment level of income is $5000 billion. Draw a new aggregate demand curve, representing one or more of the appropriate policies you identified in Question 1, that will restore full employment for this economy. Following a shift in the aggregate demand curve, prices will rise to _____.

3. Consider the following statement: "The increase in prices that resulted when we restored full employment was a small price to pay for the increased output. Why not try moving even farther along the aggregate supply curve? If we further stimulate the economy to lower unemployment we can increase output to, say, $5200 billion and prices will only rise to 109. We can thus have a permanent increase in output of $200 billion every year in return for a one-time increase in prices of just under 6 percent. That's a pretty favorable trade-off." What is wrong with the reasoning of this argument?

   Is the output-price combination of $5200 billion and 109 a viable long-run equilibrium

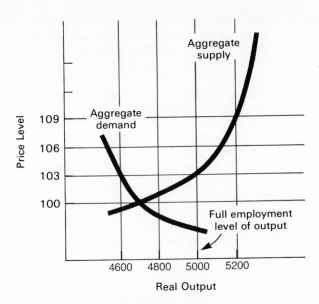

FIGURE 16–1

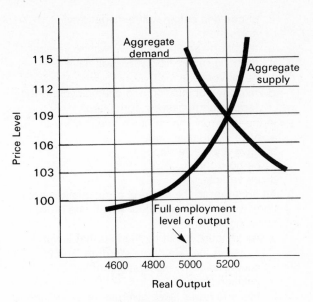

FIGURE 16–2

position? (Figure 16–2 illustrates such a combination. What is apt to happen to the aggregate supply curve? Draw in the new aggregate supply curve that restores full employment.) What would happen if government policymakers tried to keep output at $5200 billion on a permanent basis? (That is, what would happen if every time the aggregate curve shifted, policymakers undertook appropriate expansionary fiscal or monetary policy to shift the aggregate demand curve in an effort to avoid any reduction in output.)

4. Figure 16–3 shows an economy following an adverse shift in the aggregate supply curve. Equilibrium used to be an output of $5000 and a price level of 103.

   a. What is the new equilibrium immediately following the adverse shift in the supply curve?

      Output _____

      Prices _____

   b. If there is to be no decline in employment, the government must undertake (expansionary/restrictive) policies to shift the aggregate demand curve. The government could maintain employment but at the cost of an increase in prices to _____.

   c. Alternatively, the government could avoid any increase in prices. Such a decision would require (expansionary/restrictive) policies and would result in a new equilibrium level of

      output of _____.

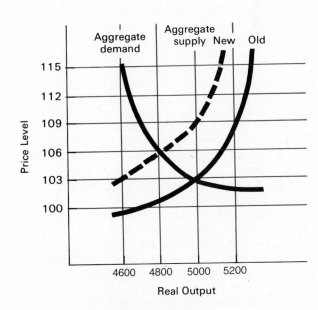

FIGURE 16–3

SELF-TESTS FOR UNDERSTANDING

Test A

Circle the correct answer.

1. If fluctuations in economic activity are caused by shifts in the aggregate demand curve, then

a. prices and output will be negatively correlated.
b. the short-run Phillips curve will be vertical.
c. the long-run Phillips curve will have a negative slope.
d. the rates of inflation and unemployment will tend to be negatively correlated.

2. In the long run, the Phillips curve is likely to
   a. have a negative slope.
   b. have a positive slope.
   c. be horizontal.
   d. be vertical.

3. An adherent to the doctrine of rational expectations would be surprised by which one of the following occurrences?
   a. An announcement by the Fed that it will increase the rate of growth of the money supply leads to expectations of higher inflation.
   b. Plans to lower taxes give rise to expectations of higher prices.
   c. Plans to fight inflation by restrictive policy succeed in reducing the rate of inflation with no increase in unemployment.
   d. An examination of the record shows that people consistently underestimate the rate of inflation during periods when it is increasing.

4. The doctrine of rational expectations implies that increases in output beyond the level of potential output can be produced
   a. by expected increases in prices.
   b. only by unexpected increases in prices.
   c. by any increase in prices whether expected or not.
   d. by preannounced increases in the money supply or reductions in taxes.

5. Using deliberate stabilization policy to cure a recession rather than waiting for the economy's self-correcting mechanism
   a. means that we will end up with the same output and price level, only sooner.
   b. means that we will end up with a permanently higher level of output.
   c. will give us a temporary period of higher employment at the cost of more inflation.
   d. means that the price level will be permanently lower.

6. Which of the following is not a feasible alternative for aggregate demand policy following an adverse shift of the supply curve to the left?
   a. Do nothing and initially experience both higher prices and lower output.
   b. Avoid the reduction in output at the cost of even higher prices.
   c. Avoid the increase in prices at the cost of an even greater decline in output.

d. Avoid both the reduction in output and increase in prices by appropriate policies to shift the aggregate demand curve.

7. Which of the following is not an example of an incomes policy?
   a. Wage–price controls designed to break inflationary expectations.
   b. Open market sales to slow down the increase in the stock of money.
   c. Labor contracts that link wages with profits.
   d. The wage–price guideposts of Presidents Kennedy and Johnson.

8. Wage–price controls
   a. may be effective if they succeed in changing expectations of inflation.
   b. were used with great success by President Nixon.
   c. have little long-run impact on economic efficiency.
   d. can be imposed on some parts of the economy without affecting the rest of the economy.

9. A general policy of indexing
   a. is an attempt to shift the aggregate supply curve downward and to the right.
   b. would help to balance the federal government's budget.
   c. is an attempt to ease the social cost of inflation, not an attempt to improve the terms of the inflation-unemployment trade-off.
   d. runs little risk of accelerating the rate of inflation.

10. Which of the following is an example of indexing?
    a. Tax penalties on firms that grant excessive wage increases.
    b. The adjustment of nominal interest rates in response to expectations of inflation.
    c. The average change in prices on the New York Stock Exchange.
    d. Increases in social security checks computed on the basis of changes in the consumer price index.

Test B

Circle T or F for True or False as appropriate.

1. Inflation occurs only as a result of shifts in the aggregate demand curve.　　T F

2. In contrast to expansionary monetary or fiscal policy, an autonomous increase in private spending will increase output without increasing prices.　　T F

3. If fluctuations in economic activity are predominantly the result of shifts in the aggregate supply curve, the rate of unemployment and the rate of inflation will tend to be positively correlated. **T F**

4. The economy's self-correcting mechanism implies that the only long-run policy choices for the economy lie along a vertical Phillips curve. **T F**

5. The natural rate of unemployment is given by the position of the long-run Phillips curve. **T F**

6. A belief that the economy's self-correcting mechanism works quickly is an argument in favor of activist demand-management policy. **T F**

7. Expectations of inflation that lead to higher wages will be somewhat self-fulfilling as the increase in wages shifts the aggregate supply curve. **T F**

8. One can minimize the inflationary effects of fighting a recession by using fiscal policy rather than monetary policy. **T F**

9. Following an adverse shift in the aggregate supply curve, aggregate demand policies can stop the rise in prices with no increase in unemployment. **T F**

10. The economy's self-correcting mechanism means that, in the face of a recessionary gap, output and prices will eventually be the same with or without expansionary stabilization policy. **T F**

SUPPLEMENTARY EXERCISE

The following statement on wages, prices, and productivity comes from the 1962 *Annual Report of the Council of Economic Advisers*, page 186. If all prices remain stable, all hourly labor costs may increase as fast as economy-wide productivity without, for that reason alone, changing the relative share of labor and non-labor incomes in total output. At the same time, each kind of income increases steadily in absolute amount. If hourly labor costs increase at a slower rate than productivity, the share of non-labor incomes will grow or prices will fall, or both. Conversely, if hourly labor costs increase more rapidly than productivity, the share of labor incomes in total product will increase or prices will rise, or both. It is this relationship among long-run economy-wide productivity, wages, and prices which makes the rate of productivity change an important benchmark for noninflationary wage and price behavior.

This exercise is designed to illustrate some of the ideas associated with the 1962 wage-price guideposts based on increases in labor productivity. In particular, we will see that even if firms do not increase prices there can be *increases in both wages and profits* when wages increase in step with increases in labor productivity.

Column 1 of Table 16–1 illustrates the initial position of the Acme Manufacturing Company, a firm that produces gizmos. In all the remaining columns it is assumed that labor productivity has increased by 10 percent. (In reality, 10 percent would be an unusually large increase; we use it

TABLE 16–1

ACME MANUFACTURING COMPANY

	(1)	(2)	(3)	(4)
1. Employment (people)	100	100	100	100
2. Labor productivity (gizmos per employee)	4,000	4,400	4,400	4,400
3. Total output [(1) × (2)]	400,000	_____	_____	_____
4. Price per gizmo	$ 5.00	$ 5.00	$ 5.00	$ 5.25
5. Total revenue [(4) × (3)]	$2,000,000	_____	_____	_____
6. Hourly wage	$ 8.00	$ 8.80	$ 8.60	$ 9.24*
7. Total wages [(6) × 2000 × (1)]	$1,600,000	$1,760,000	$1,720,000	$1,848,000
8. Profits plus overhead [(5) − (7)]	$ 400,000	_____	_____	_____

*If x is the percentage increase in labor productivity and y is the rate of inflation, the correct adjustment of wages is $(1 + x)(1 + y) - 1 = x + y + xy$. In our case, this formula works out to 15.5 percent, slightly greater than the 15 percent implied by looking just at $x + y$.

here to simplify the calculations. The same principle would apply even if the increase in labor productivity were smaller.)

1. Column 2 assumes that hourly wages increase in step with labor productivity. Fill in the appropriate spaces for total output, total revenue, and profits plus overhead. What is the percentage increase in total wages and in profits plus overhead? Are they equal?

2. Column 3 assumes that hourly wages increase by less than the increase in labor productivity. Fill in the appropriate spaces for total output, total revenue, and profits and overhead. What is the percentage increase in total wages and in profits plus overhead? Are they equal? Are your answers to this and the preceding question consistent with the quotation from the report of the Council of Economic Advisers?

3. Column 4 is meant to illustrate a situation of general inflation. As discussed in Chapter 16 of the textbook, the claim of wage-price guideposts is that wage increases equal to the increase in labor productivity plus the target rate of inflation will, in combination with price increases equal to the target rate, allow equal percentage increases in both wages and profits plus overhead. Prices and wages in column 4 are based on a target rate of inflation of 5 percent. Fill in the appropriate spaces for total output, total revenue, and profits plus overhead to see if the inflation plus productivity standard favors workers or capitalists.

4. If things work so simply, why can't we eliminate inflation overnight by adopting an inflation target of zero?

PART
4

THE
UNITED
STATES
IN THE
WORLD
ECONOMY

17

Productivity and Growth in the Wealth of Nations

LEARNING OBJECTIVES

After completing the material in this chapter you should be able to:

- define, understand, and use correctly the terms and concepts listed below.
- explain why growth in labor productivity is the major determinant of living standards.
- discuss and evaluate arguments about the cause of the slowdown in the growth of labor productivity since the 1960s.
- discuss arguments and evidence about the international convergence of living standards and productivity levels.
- evaluate arguments and evidence about de-industrialization of the American economy.
- evaluate the argument that growth in labor productivity will lead only to increased unemployment.

- explain why productivity growth less than that of other countries need not imply a loss of export competitiveness, but can lower real wages.

IMPORTANT TERMS AND CONCEPTS

Labor productivity
Standard of living
GNP per capita
Gross Domestic Product (GDP)
GDP per labor hour
GDP per capita
Service industry
Deindustrialization

CHAPTER REVIEW

The growth in labor productivity is the major determinant of living standards over long periods of time. Growth in labor productivity explains why, on the average, your parents are wealthier than their parents and their parents' parents. Continued growth in labor productivity will mean that your children and their children will be wealthier than you.

(1) Discussions of productivity usually focus on labor productivity, which is defined as the amount of output per unit of labor input. For a firm producing a single output, measuring labor productivity per hour is a simple matter of dividing output by total labor hours. For the American economy, output is usually measured in terms of real GNP and labor input is preferably measured in terms of total labor hours. An increase in labor productivity means that (more/less) output can be produced with the same number of labor hours. If aggregate output were unchanged, an increase in labor productivity would mean (more/less) unemployment. But remember that total output and the unemployment rate are determined by the intersection of the aggregate _____ and aggregate _____ curves. An increase in productivity means that the production possibilities frontier has shifted (out/in); that is, there has been a(n) (increase/decrease) in potential GNP. It is macroeconomic policy that determines whether we take advantage of new possibilities.

(2) Sustained growth in labor productivity (is/is not) a relatively new phenomenon, tracing back about (2000/200) years. As the following word equation shows, growth in labor productivity is the basic determinant of living standards or output per capita.

$$\left(\frac{\text{Total output}}{\text{Total population}}\right) = \left(\frac{\text{Total output}}{\text{Total hours worked}}\right) \times \left(\frac{\text{Total hours worked}}{\text{Number of workers}}\right) \times \left(\frac{\text{Number of workers}}{\text{Total population}}\right)$$

The expression on the left of the equal sign is output per person or per capita. The first expression on the right side of the equal sign is labor productivity. The second and third expressions measure the number of hours a typical worker works and the proportion of the population that works. (This last term is sometimes referred to as the employment ratio.) Notice that several of the numerators and denominators on the right hand side of the equal sign can be cancelled, establishing the equality of the expression. If the number of hours per worker does not change and the proportion of the population that works is constant—that is if the second and third terms on the right hand side do not change—then the only way that output or GNP per capita can increase is if labor productivity increases. If hours per worker decline, then increases in labor productivity will imply a smaller increase in output per capita. Much of the difference between the growth in labor productivity and the growth in output per capita since 1990 can be accounted for by the decline in the number of hours worked each year by a typical worker.

(3) There is much concern about the growth in labor productivity in different countries. Long-term data for a number of industrial countries shows a (convergence/divergence) in levels of labor productivity. The faster dispersion of new technologies enables all industrial countries to share in the benefits of new innovations. If levels of productivity are converging then it must be true that those countries that start with lower levels of productivity will show a (faster/slower) growth in labor productivity and those countries that start with higher levels of productivity will show a _____ growth in labor productivity. The concept of convergence indicates how difficult it is for any single country to sustain levels of labor productivity far in advance of other countries. It also suggests that a single industrialized country is not doomed to fall further behind the rest of the world. However, there is evidence that many developing countries (are/are not) participating in this process of convergence. See Chapter 38 for more discussion on prospects for these countries.

(4) Popular discussions of changes in the growth of labor productivity and changes in the structure of employment are often based on limited data. When measured just from the end of World War II there has been a dramatic decline in the rate of growth of labor productivity in the United States and other industrialized countries. (Note that a decline in the rate of growth (must/need not) imply a decline in the level of labor productivity.) When viewed over a longer period of time, it is unclear which period is unusual, the 1970s and 1980s when labor productivity growth was 1 to 2 percent per year or the period from 1945 to 1965 when labor productivity grew by over 3 percent per year.

There has been much recent concern about the declining share of manufacturing employment and the increasing share of service employment in the American economy. At least two pieces of evidence are

relevant to a broader consideration of this issue. All major industrialized economies have experienced increases in the size of their service industries. The record of productivity growth for American manufactur-
(5) ing shows (no/a significant) trend toward a declining rate of growth.

While the slowdown in productivity growth has been worldwide, the growth of labor productivity in the United States has been below that of other countries for some time. To the extent that this relative performance reflects the forces of convergence, there is less need for concern. Should this relative performance continue for a prolonged period of time, it would still be possible to sustain high levels of employment with appropriate macroeconomic policy, but there would be serious implications for American competitiveness in international markets. We could continue to export and reap the gains of international specialization described in Chapter 18, but we would do so at the cost of a decline in our standard of living relative to that of the rest of the world. The experience of the British economy comes most immediately to mind.

DEFINITION QUIZ

Choose the letter that is the most appropriate definition for each of the following terms.

1. _____ Labor productivity

2. _____ GNP per capita

3. _____ Gross domestic product

4. _____ Service industry

5. _____ Deindustrialization

a. Total output divided by population.
b. Industry that does not turn out physical goods.
c. GNP minus net exports.
d. Alleged decline in manufacturing due to a country's lagging productivity.
e. Output per unit of labor input.
f. Total output produced within a country's borders.

BASIC EXERCISES

1. Productivity growth compounds like interest on a savings account. Over long periods of time small differences in the growth of productivity compound to quite substantial differences in the level of income. Table 17–1 reports data for GNP per capita for a number of countries. The data is for 1987 and comes from the World Bank. The columns for the year 2087 compound the actual data for 1987 by assumed growth rates of 1 to 2.5 percent per year for 100 years. Note how small differences in the assumed growth rates, even a difference as small as one half of one percent, can compound to significant differences over 100 years.

a. Pick a particular country and calculate how much output per capita increases over 100 years if it grows at 1 percent per year. In 2087 output per capita would be

   _____ as large as it was in 1987. (Try another country to be sure that your answer does not depend upon which country you chose. It shouldn't.)

b. Assume now that output per capita grows at 2 percent per year for 100 years. How does the increase in output per capita compare to the situation where it increased 1 percent per year? Is it twice as large or even larger?

c. If labor productivity in the United States grew at 1 percent per year while it grew at 2 percent per year in the rest of the world, our standard of living would not compare favorably to that of other countries after 100 years. The extrapolation of growth trends is a matter of mathematics, not economics. Economics can offer insights as to whether mechanical trends can be realized. For example, what are the implications of the concept of convergence for the long-term maintenance of a 1 percent differential in the growth of labor productivity?

d. (Optional) Assume that output per capita in the United States grows at 1.5 percent per year while in Japan it grows at 2 percent per year. How many years will it take for output per capita in Japan to catch up with that of the United States?

2. This exercise investigates whether a decline in the growth of labor productivity results in a decline in the level of productivity. Assume that annual labor productivity is originally $11,000 of GNP per worker, and that it grows at an annual rate of 3.9 percent for 20 years, and 1.9 percent for the next 20 years.

a. What is labor productivity at the end of the first 20 years?

   $_____

TABLE 17-1

| | GNP per capita 1987 | GNP per capita in 2087 assuming annual growth rate of | | | |
		1.0%	1.5%	2.0%	2.5%
Poland	$1,930	$5,220	$8,554	$13,982	$22,800
South Korea	$2,690	$7,276	$11,922	$19,488	$31,779
Singapore	$7,940	$21,476	$35,190	$57,522	$93,801
Great Britain	$10,420	$28,184	$46,182	$75,489	$123,099
France	$12,790	$34,595	$56,686	$92,659	$151,097
Germany	$14,400	$38,949	$63,821	$104,323	$170,118
Japan	$15,760	$42,628	$69,849	$114,176	$186,184
United States	$18,530	$50,120	$82,126	$134,243	$218,908

Source: World Bank, World Development Report, 1989, Table 1, p. 165.

Note: All figures expressed in terms of American dollars.

b. What is labor productivity at the end of 40 years?

$_____

c. Does the decline in the rate of growth of productivity lead to a decline in the level of productivity?

SELF-TESTS FOR UNDERSTANDING

Test A

Circle the correct answer.

1. There is some evidence that by the time of the American Civil War, average living standards were
   a. lower than at the time of the American Revolution.
   b. quite similar to living standards today.
   c. starting a decline that lasted to the end of the 19th century.
   d. about equal to those of Ancient Rome.
2. If more output can be produced with the same number of labor hours, we would say that labor productivity
   a. has decreased.
   b. is unchanged.
   c. has increased.
3. Declines in the number of hours worked per year by an average worker will mean that compared to the growth in labor productivity, the growth in GNP per capita will be
   a. smaller.
   b. about the same.
   c. larger.

4. Lagging productivity growth in a single country is likely to lead to
   a. massive unemployment.
   b. greater exports.
   c. lower exports.
   d. a lower standard of living relative to other countries.
5. The share of the employment in service employment in the United States has grown
   a. less rapidly than that of other countries.
   b. about the same as in other countries.
   c. by more than that of other countries.
6. Historical evidence shows that since 1800 productivity in the United States has increased at an average annual rate of
   a. less than 1 percent.
   b. about 1.5 percent.
   c. slightly less than 2 percent.
   d. 3.9 percent.
7. A major factor leading to the convergence of growth rates across countries is probably
   a. the use of the dollar as the international currency of commerce.
   b. the increased levels of GNP devoted to military spending in many countries.
   c. the quick pace by which new technologies are spread among countries.
   d. the emergence of Japan as a major industrial country.
8. The record of productivity growth in the United States
   a. has exceeded that of other countries ever since World War II.
   b. has been slower than that of a number of other countries for many decades.
   c. has been higher in service industries than in manufacturing industries.

d. dooms us to a future of high unemployment and dwindling exports.

9. The convergence of productivity levels reflects the fact that
   a. high-productivity countries have high wages.
   b. low-productivity countries can increase growth rates by borrowing established technologies from high-productivity countries.
   c. the dollar has been the world's leading currency.
   d. macroeconomic policy in all countries has converged to a common set of actions.

10. In the absence of increases in productivity, American goods can be made competitive in international trade if
   a. there is a reduction in the real wages of American workers relative to workers in other countries.
   b. inflation increases.
   c. the United States increases tariffs on foreign goods.
   d. foreign currency becomes less expensive in terms of dollars.

Test B

Circle T or F for True or False as appropriate.

1. Over the long haul it makes little difference whether productivity grows at 1 percent per year or at 3 percent per year.   T F

2. Output per worker has been increasing more or less steadily for the last two millenia.   T F

3. Although productivity growth has slowed in the United States, it still remains higher than in most other industrialized countries.   T F

4. Since 1970 the growth in productivity in the United States has been about three times as high as it was right after World War II.   T F

5. There is clear evidence of a long-term decline in the productivity of American manufacturing workers.   T F

6. The historical record shows a convergence of living standards in the major industrial countries.   T F

7. Most third world developing countries are seeing their living standards converge to living standards in the industrial world.   T F

8. A decline in the rate of growth of American labor productivity means a decline in the productivity of American workers.   T F

9. The experience of Great Britain suggests that growth in labor productivity will only lead to massive unemployment.   T F

10. If productivity growth in the United States is lower than that of our major international competitors, we will lose export markets as foreigners can undersell us in everything. T F

18

International Trade and Comparative Advantage

LEARNING OBJECTIVES

After completing the material in this chapter you should be able to:

- define, understand, and use correctly the terms and concepts listed below.
- list the important factors that lead countries to trade with one another.
- explain how voluntary trade, even if it does not increase total production, can be mutually beneficial to the trading partners.
- explain in what ways international and intranational trade are similar and in what ways they are dissimilar.
- distinguish between absolute and comparative advantage.
- explain how absolute advantage and comparative advantage are related to the location and slope of a country's production possibilities frontier.
- explain how trade means that a country's consumption possibilities can exceed its production possibilities.

- explain how world prices are relevant for determining a country's consumption possibilities.
- explain how specialization, consistent with the law of comparative advantage, can increase total world production.
- explain how world prices are determined by the interaction of demand and supply curves for trading partners.
- use a pair of demand and supply diagrams to illustrate the impact of quotas and tariffs.
- contrast the efficiency and distribution effects of tariffs and quotas.
- analyze the arguments used to advocate trade restrictions.
- explain the role of adjustment assistance in a country favoring free trade.
- explain the fallacy in the ''cheap foreign labor'' argument.

IMPORTANT TERMS AND CONCEPTS

Imports
Exports
Specialization
Mutual gains from trade
Absolute advantage
Comparative advantage

"Cheap Foreign Labor" argument
Tariff
Quota
Export subsidy
Trade adjustment assistance
Infant-industry argument
Strategic trade protection
Dumping

CHAPTER REVIEW

The material in this chapter discusses the basic economic forces that influence the international division of labor in the production of goods and the resulting pattern of international trade. The basic economic principle

(1) underlying an efficient international distribution of production is (absolute/comparative) advantage. It is important to remember that actual production and trade decisions are also affected by important policy interventions such as tariffs, quotas, and export subsidies.

Exchange rates—that is, the number of units of one country's currency that are changeable for another country's currency—are an important determinant of international trade and will be discussed in the next chapter. However, the real terms of trade—that is, how many import goods a country can get indirectly through export production rather than through direct domestic production—are the important measure of the benefits of trade, and they are considered here in some detail.

Individual countries can try to meet the consumption needs of their citizens without trade by producing everything their populations need. Alternatively, they can specialize in the production of fewer commodities and trade for commodities they do not produce. Even if there were no differences between countries, special-

(2) izing and trading would still make sense if there were important economies of _____ in production.

The most important reason for trade is that differences in oil deposits, fertile soil, and other natural resources, as well as differences in labor inputs and productive capital, will affect the efficiency with which

(3) countries can produce different goods. It is the law of (absolute/comparative) advantage that then indicates where countries should concentrate their production to maximize the potential gains from trade.

If country A can produce 2000 bushels of wheat if it produces one less car while country B can produce only 1200 bushels of wheat, then, for the same world production of cars, world production of wheat will

(4) increase if country (A/B) produced 10 fewer cars and country _____ produces

10 more cars. (World wheat production would increase by _____ bushels.) In

this case country A has a comparative advantage in producing _____.

Looking only at its own domestic production opportunities, the opportunity cost of one more car in

(5) country A is _____ bushels of wheat. Country B can produce one more car by

giving up only _____ bushels of wheat. Thus it should not be surprising if

country B concentrates on the production of _____ and trades with country A,

which concentrates on the production of _____.[1]

As countries concentrate production on those goods in which they have a comparative advantage, equilibrium world prices and trade flows—that is, exports and imports—will be determined at the point where

[1]Does the law of comparative advantage imply that all countries should completely specialize in the production of just a few commodities? No, it does not, for several reasons. One important reason is that production possibilities frontiers are likely to be curved rather than straight lines. The implication of the curved frontier is that the opportunity cost of cars in terms of wheat for country B will rise as B produces more cars. Simultaneously, the opportunity cost of cars in terms of wheat for country A will fall as A concentrates on wheat. In equilibrium, the opportunity cost, or slope of the production possibilities frontier, in both countries will be equal. At this point neither country has an incentive for further specialization. Exactly where this point will occur will be determined by world demand and supply for cars and wheat.

(6) world _____ equals world _____. This price is not at the intersection of domestic demand and supply curves; instead, it occurs at a point where the excess supply from (importing/exporting) countries (domestic supply minus domestic demand) equals the excess demand by

_____ countries (domestic demand minus domestic supply).

Just as Chapter 26 discusses the efficiency of competitive markets for self-contained economies, advanced courses in international trade show how prices derived under conditions of free trade will lead profit-maximizing firms to exploit the comparative advantage of individual countries. Most countries do not

(7) have unrestricted free trade. Rather, imports are often restricted by the use of _____

and _____, and exports are often promoted through the use of export _____.

Tariffs reduce the quantity of imports by raising their _____ while quotas raise

the price of imports by restricting _____. Either a tariff or a quota could be used to achieve the same reduction in imports, but the choice between the two has other consequences.

(8)   Tariff revenues accrue directly to the _____ while the benefits of higher prices under a quota are likely to accrue to private producers, both foreign and domestic. (The government might be able to capture some of these profits by auctioning import licenses, but this is not usually done.)

Tariffs still require foreign suppliers to compete among themselves. This competition will favor the

(9) survival of (high/low)-cost foreign suppliers. (What about domestic firms? They (do/do not) have to pay the tariff and so high-cost domestic suppliers (can/can not) continue in business.) Quotas are apt to be distributed on almost any grounds except efficiency, and thus have no automatic mechanism that works in favor of low-cost foreign suppliers.

Why do countries impose tariffs and quotas? Many trade restrictions reflect the successful pleadings of high-cost domestic suppliers. Free trade and the associated reallocation of productive resources in line with the law of comparative advantage would call for the elimination of these firms in their traditional lines of business. It is not surprising that managers and workers resist these changes. If everyone is to benefit from

(10) the increased output opportunites offered by free trade, then a program of trade _____ assistance will be necessary to help those most affected by the realignment of productive activities.

(11)   Other traditional justifications for trade restriction include the national _____

argument and the _____-industries argument. In both cases it is extremely difficult to separate firms with legitimate claims from those that are looking for a public handout. Recently some have argued that the threat of trade restrictions should be used in a strategic manner to convince others not to impose restrictions.

DEFINITION QUIZ

Choose the letter that is the most appropriate definition for each of the following terms.

1. _____ Imports

2. _____ Exports

3. _____ Specialization

4. _____ Absolute advantage

5. _____ Comparative advantage

6. _____ Tariff

7. _____ Quota

8. _____ Trade adjustment assistance

9. _____ Dumping

a. Maximum amount of a good that can be imported per unit of time.
b. Ability of one country to produce a good using fewer resources than another country requires.
c. Selling goods in a foreign market at higher prices than those charged at home.
d. Domestically produced goods sold abroad.
e. Selling goods in a foreign market at lower prices than those charged at home.
f. Tax on imports.
g. Decision by a country to emphasize production of particular commodities.
h. Provision of special aid to those workers and firms harmed by foreign competition.
i. Ability of one country to produce a good less inefficiently (relative to other goods) than another country.
j. Foreign-produced goods purchased domestically.

BASIC EXERCISES

1. This exercise is designed to review the law of comparative advantage.
   a. Assume that the following hours of labor are the only input necessary to produce hand calculators and backpacks in Canada and Japan.

	Calculators	Backpacks
Canada	6	4
Japan	2	3

   Which country has an absolute advantage in the production of hand calculators?

   _____

   Which country has an absolute advantage in the production of backpacks?

   _____

   b. If labor in Canada is reallocated from the production of calculators to the production of backpacks, how many calculators must be given up in order to produce one more

   backpack? _____
   What about Japan? How many calculators must it give up in order to produce one more

   backpack? _____
   Which country has a comparative advantage in the production of backpacks?

   _____

   Which country has a comparative advantage in the production of calculators?

   _____

   According to the law of comparative advantage,

   _____ should concentrate on the production of backpacks

   while _____
   concentrates on the production of calculators.
   c. Assume each country has 12 million hours of labor input that initially is evenly distributed in both countries between the production of backpacks and calculators: 6 million for each. Fill in the following table of outputs.

	Output of Calculators	Output of Backpacks
Canada	_____	_____
Japan	_____	_____
Total	_____	_____

   d. Assume that Canada now reallocates 1.8 million labor hours away from the production of calculators and into the production of backpacks. The change in Canadian calcula-

   tor output is   – _____
   The change in Canadian backpack output is

   + _____
   e. What reallocation of labor in Japan is necessary to be sure that world output of calculators (Japan plus Canada) remains unchanged?

   _____ labor hours. What are the changes in Japanese output from this reallocation?
   The change in Japanese calculator output is

   + _____.
   The change in Japanese backpack output is

   – _____.
   f. By assumption, the world output of calculators has not changed, but the net change in the world output of backpacks is a(n) (increase/

   decrease) of _____
   backpacks.
   g. Questions c through f showed how specialization according to the law of comparative advantage could increase the output of backpacks without decreasing the output of calculators. Adjustments in line with the law of comparative advantage could alternatively increase the output of both goods. Suppose Japan had reallocated 900,000 labor hours to the production of calculators. Fill in the following table, and compare total outputs with your answers to Question c.

   Calculators

	Labor Input (millions of hours)	Output
Canada	4.2	_____
Japan	6.9	_____
Total		_____

   Backpacks

	Labor input (millions of hours)	Output
Canada	7.8	_____
Japan	5.1	_____
Total		_____

h. (Optional) Work through Questions d and e again, but assume this time that the initial reallocation of 1.8 million labor hours in Canada is away from backpacks and to the production of calculators. Calculate the reallocation in Japan necessary to maintain world backpacks output. What happens to the total output of calculators? Why?

i. (Optional) Assume that the production of backpacks in Canada requires 9 hours rather than 4 hours. Work through the original output levels in Question c and the reallocation of labor in Questions d and e to see what now happens to total output of calculators and backpacks. Does your answer to Question f differ from your original answer? Why?

2. This exercise is designed to give you practice in analyzing the impact of quotas and tariffs. To simplify the analysis, the question assumes that the world is composed of only two countries, the United States and India.

a. Figure 18–1 shows the demand and supply for shirts in the United States and India. (Prices in India are expressed in terms of American dollars.) In the absence of international trade, what are the domestic price and quantity of shirts in India and the United States?

	Price	Quantity
India	_____	_____
United States	_____	_____

b. Assume now that India and the United States are free to trade without restrictions. What is the world price? _____.
What happens to the production of shirts in India? _____. What happens to the production of shirts in the United States? _____.
Who exports and who imports how many shirts? _____.

c. Assume now that American producers are able to persuade the government to impose a quota limiting shirt imports to 200 million shirts. Following the imposition of the quota, what are prices and production in India and the United States?

	Price	Quantity
India	_____	_____
United States	_____	_____

Compared to the free trade equilibrium described in b, shirt prices have increased in (India/the United States) and decreased in _____. The production of shirts has increased in _____ and decreased in _____.
For the world as a whole, shirt production has (increased/decreased).

India

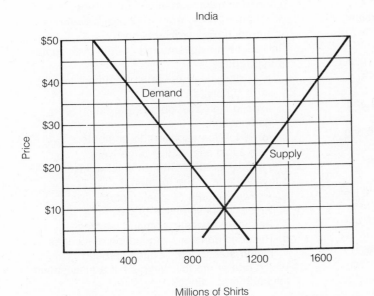

United States

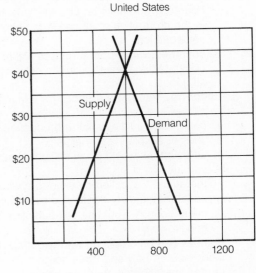

FIGURE 18–1

d. What tariff would have yielded the same results as the quota of 200 million shirts?

_____

e. Discuss the reasons for choosing between a tariff and a quota.

SELF-TESTS FOR UNDERSTANDING

Test A

Circle the correct answer.

1. Which of the following is an example of comparative advantage?
   a. Wages of textile workers are lower in India than in America.
   b. The slope of the production possibilities frontier between tomatoes and airplanes differs for Mexico and the United States.
   c. American workers must work an average of only 800 hours to purchase a car, while Russian workers must work 1600 hours.
   d. In recent years Swedish income per capita has exceeded that of the United States.
2. Economists argue that
   a. efficiency in international trade requires countries to produce those goods in which they have an absolute advantage.
   b. efficiency in international trade requires countries to produce those goods in which they have a comparative advantage.
   c. efficiency in international trade requires countries that have an absolute advantage in the production of all goods to become self-sufficient.
   d. countries with export surpluses will have a comparative advantage in the production of all goods.
3. Under free trade, world prices for exports and imports would be such that
   a. countries would specialize production along lines of absolute advantage.
   b. all countries would show a slight export surplus.
   c. the quantity supplied by exporters would just equal the quantity demanded by importers.
   d. every country would be self-sufficient in all goods.
4. If shoes can be produced with two hours of labor input in Italy and three hours of labor input in the United States, then it is correct to say that

a. Italy has an absolute advantage in the production of shoes.
b. Italy has a comparative advantage in the production of shoes.
c. the United States has an absolute advantage in the production of shoes.
d. the United States has a comparative advantage in the production of shoes.

5. Assuming that shoes are produced as in Question 4 and shirts can be produced with four hours of labor in both countries, then it is correct to say that
   a. the United States has a comparative advantage in the production of shirts.
   b. Italy has a comparative advantage in the production of shirts.
   c. Italy has an absolute advantage in the production of shirts.
   d. the United States has an absolute advantage in the production of shirts.
6. All but which one of the following have been used to restrict trade?
   a. Export subsidies.
   b. Tariffs.
   c. Quotas.
   d. "Voluntary" export agreements.
7. Which of the following is an example of a tariff?
   a. Japanese car manufacturers agree to limit exports to the United States.
   b. U.S. law limits the imports of cotton shirts to 20 million.
   c. Television manufacturers outside of Great Britain must pay a 5 percent duty on each set they ship to Great Britain.
   d. Foreign bicycle manufacturers receive a rebate of taxes from their own government for each bicycle they export.
8. One economic advantage of tariffs over quotas is that tariffs
   a. typically give preferential treatment to long-term suppliers.
   b. expose high-cost domestic producers to competition.
   c. force foreign suppliers to compete.
   d. help avoid destructive price wars.
9. The imposition of a tariff on steel will lead to all but which one of the following?
   a. A lower volume of steel imports.
   b. Higher domestic steel prices.
   c. Reduced domestic demand for steel.
   d. Reduced domestic production of steel as higher steel prices reduce demand.
10. Which one of the following is not a justification for trade restrictions?

a. Some industries would be so vital in times of war that we cannot rely on foreign suppliers.

b. A temporary period of protection is necessary until an industry matures and is able to compete with foreign suppliers.

c. Competition from foreign suppliers will help keep prices to consumers low.

d. The threat of trade restrictions may prevent the adoption of restrictions by others.

Test B

Circle T or F for True or False as appropriate.

1. A country with an absolute advantage in producing all goods is better off being self-sufficient than engaging in trade.　　T F

2. Countries gain from trade only when it allows them to adjust productive resources to take advantage of economies of scale.　　T F

3. A country with an absolute advantage in the production of all goods should only export commodities.　　T F

4. The unequal distribution of natural resources among countries is one important reason why countries trade.　　T F

5. Which of two countries has a comparative advantage in the production of wine rather than cloth can be determined by comparing the slopes of the production possibility frontiers of both countries.　　T F

6. It is possible for all countries to simultaneously expand exports and reduce imports.　　T F

7. A quota on shirts would reduce the volume of imported shirts by specifying the quantity of shirts that can be imported.　　T F

8. The infant-industry argument is used to justify protection for industries that are vital in times of war.　　T F

9. Dumping of goods by the United States on Japanese markets would necessarily harm Japanese consumers.　　T F

10. If foreign labor is paid less, foreign producers will always be able to undersell American producers.　　T F

SUPPLEMENTARY EXERCISES

1. During 1979 and 1980 there was much concern about the exporting of cars from Japan. It was argued that competition from Japanese car manufacturers was unfair and that American car manufacturers needed temporary protection from imports in order to retool. In 1980 William Niskanen, chief economist for Ford Motor Company, was fired for arguing against import restrictions. In the spring of 1981, at about the same time that President Reagan appointed Niskanen to his Council of Economic Advisers, the Reagan administration announced that Japanese manufacturers had agreed to "voluntarily" limit their exports. For more on this interesting series of events, you might enjoy reading the article "Ford Fires an Economist," by Robert L. Simison, in *The Wall Street Journal*, July 30, 1980, p. 18. Experience with the voluntary restraint is reviewed by Robert W. Crandall in "Import Quotas and the Automobile Industry: The Costs of Protection" *The Brookings Review*. Summer 1984, pages 8–16, and in *Has Trade Protection Revitalized Domestic Industries?* Congressional Budget Office, November 1986.

2. Demand and supply for widgets in Baulmovia and Bilandia are as given below.

   Baulmovia
   Demand: $Q = 156 - 7P$
   Supply: $Q = -44 + 18P$

   Bilandia
   Demand: $Q = 320 - 10P$
   Supply: $Q = -20 + 10P$

   a. In the absence of trade, what is the price of widgets in Baulmovia? In Bilandia? What quantity is produced in Baulmovia? In Bilandia?

   b. With free trade what is the one common world price for widgets? Which country exports widgets? Which country imports widgets? What is the volume of exports and imports?

   c. Manufacturers in the importing country have convinced the government to impose a tariff on widget imports of $4.50 a widget. What will happen to trade and the price of widgets in the two countries?

d. What quota would have the same impact on trade?

e. What factors might lead one to prefer a tariff over a quota?

3. Ricardia is a small country that produces wine and cloth. The production possibilities frontier for Ricardia is

$$W = \sqrt{324 - C^2}$$

where W = millions of barrels of wine and C = millions of bolts of cloth.

a. Use a piece of graph paper. Label the vertical axis "wine" and the horizontal axis "cloth." Draw the production possibilities frontier.

b. Since Ricardia is a small country, it can export or import cloth or wine without affecting world prices. World prices are such that Ricardia can export one million barrels of wine for 750,000 bolts of cloth or it can export 750,000 bolts of cloth for one million barrels of wine. The government's chief economist argues that regardless of consumption preferences, Ricardia should produce 14.4 million bolts of cloth and 10.8 million barrels of wine. Do you agree with her? Why? (Hint: Consider what the consumption possibilities look like. For any production combination of wine and cloth, Ricardia's consumption possibilities are given by a negatively sloped straight line through the production point. The slope of the consumption possibilities line reflects world prices. A movement up the straight line to the left of the production point would imply exporting cloth in order to consume more wine. A movement down the straight line to the right would reflect exporting wine in order to consume more cloth. Exactly what Ricardia chooses to consume is a matter of preferences, but its choice is constrained by its consumption possibilities line, which, in turn, is determined by Ricardia's production choice and world prices for cloth and wine. Why does the production point 10.8 million barrels of wine and 14.4 million bolts of cloth offer the greatest consumption possibilities?)

19

The International Monetary System: Order or Disorder?

LEARNING OBJECTIVES

After completing the material in this chapter you should be able to:

- define, understand, and use correctly the terms and concepts listed below.
- identify the factors that help determine a country's exchange rate under a system of floating exchange rates.
- distinguish between long-, medium-, and short-run factors that help determine the demand and supply of currencies.
- use a demand and supply diagram to show how changes in GNP, inflation, or interest rates can lead to an appreciation or depreciation of the dollar under a system of floating exchange rates.
- show, on a supply-demand graph, how fixed exchange rates can lead to a balance of payments deficit or surplus.
- explain why, under the gold standard, countries lost control of their domestic money stock.
- describe the options, other than changing the exchange rate, that were available under the Bret-

ton Woods system to a country wanting to eliminate a balance of payments deficit or surplus.
- explain why, under a system of fixed exchange rates, there was very little risk in speculating against an overvalued currency.
- explain how speculators can reduce the uncertainty exporters and importers face under a system of floating exchange rates.

IMPORTANT TERMS AND CONCEPTS

International monetary system
Exchange rate
Appreciation
Depreciation
Devaluation
Revaluation
Supply of and demand for foreign exchange
Floating exchange rates
Purchasing-power parity theory

Fixed exchange rates
Balance of payments deficit and surplus
Current account
Capital account
Balance of trade
Gold standard

Gold-exchange system (Bretton Woods system)
International Monetary Fund (IMF)
Exchange controls
"Dirty" or "managed" floating
The European Monetary System (EMS)
The LDC debt problem

CHAPTER REVIEW

Meeting: President Richard M. Nixon and H. R. Haldeman, Oval Office, June 23, 1972 (10:04–11:39 A.M.)

Haldeman: Burns is concerned about speculation against the lira.
Nixon: Well, I don't give a (expletive deleted) about the lira . . . There ain't a vote in it.

(Statement of Information: Appendix III, Hearings before the Committee on the Judiciary,
House of Representatives, Ninety-third Congress, Second Session, May–June 1974, page 50)

Soon after 1972 even American presidents paid attention to exchange rates. So should you. Even if you are never President, exchange rates have important impacts on all Americans. Consumers are affected by the price of imports, and jobs for workers can be affected by the price of exports and imports. This chapter discusses exchange rates, that is, the price of one currency in terms of another. The discussion in the text covers the economic factors that determine exchange rates, the implications of attempts by governments to fix exchange rates, and a review of recent history focusing on the evolution of the world's current mixed international monetary system.

Discussions of international monetary arrangements involve a whole new vocabulary of fixed and floating exchange rates, current and capital accounts, appreciating and depreciating currencies and devaluations and revaluations. It may help you to keep the vocabulary straight if you remember that most of the analysis of international monetary arrangements is merely an application of the supply-demand analysis originally introduced in Chapter 4.

Find out how much it would cost, in dollars, to buy one German mark. This figure is the current dollar/

(1) mark _____ rate, expressed in dollars. Many newspapers now publish exchange rates on a daily basis. A student in Germany could do the same thing and get a price for dollars in terms of marks. If you both call on the same day you should both get the same price (ignoring sales commissions.)[1] If the dollar price of one mark increases, so that it takes more dollars to buy one mark, we say that the dollar

has _____ relative to the mark. Alternatively, we could say that the mark has

_____ relative to the dollar.

Under a system of floating exchange rates, exchange rates will be determined by market forces of

(2) _____ and _____. Consider an example using two countries, Germany and the United States. The demand for German marks has three major sources:

(1) the demand by Americans for German exports, such as cars, cameras, and clocks;
(2) the demand by Americans for German financial assets, such as stocks and bonds; and
(3) the demand by Americans for German physical assets, such as factories and machines.

The supply of German marks also has three sources: the demand by Germans for American (exports/imports),

American _____ assets, and American _____

assets. (Note that the demand and supply of marks has an interpretation in terms of the demand and supply

of dollars. The demand for marks by Americans is simultaneously a _____ of

dollars. Understanding this mirror-image aspect of exchange rates may help keep the vocabulary and analysis straight.)

---

[1] In the United States you might get a price like 62.5 cents for one mark. The German student would get a price like 1.6 marks for one dollar. If x is the dollar price of one mark, than $1/x$ is the mark price of one dollar.

Under a system of floating rates, the equilibrium exchange rate will be at a level where demand equals supply. A change in any factor that affects demand or supply will change the exchange rate. For example, a

(3) sudden demand for German wines on the part of Americans would shift the (demand/supply) curve for marks. The dollar price of marks will (increase/decrease), a result economists call a(n) (appreciation/depreciation) of the mark in terms of the dollar. Conversely, a sudden demand for California wines on the part of Germans

would shift the _____ curve of marks and would mean a(n) (appreciation/depreciation) of the mark in terms of the dollar. A simultaneous boom in the United States and recession in Germany are

likely to lead to a(n) _____ of the mark in terms of the dollar.

In the long run, the exchange rate should be dominated by the relative movement of domestic prices

(4) according to the theory of _____ _____ _____. In order that its goods remain competitive on world markets, a country with a very high rate of inflation will see its exchange rate (appreciate/depreciate). In the medium run, a country that experiences an economic boom will

find its imports rising and its exchange rate _____. In the short run, exchange rates will be affected by the movement of large pools of investment funds that are sensitive to differences in interest rates. Restrictive monetary policy that increases interest rates will attract funds, (appreciating/depreciating) the exchange rate.

Governments may try to peg the exchange rate. In fact from the end of World War II until 1973, the world

(5) operated on a system of fixed exchange rates, established at the _____ Woods conference. At the time, it was thought that fixed exchange rates were necessary to stimulate the growth of international trade, so countries could reap the benefits of specialization according to the law of comparative advantage. Pegging an exchange rate is very similar to any other sort of price control and is subject to similar problems.

If, say, the Japanese government pegs the exchange rate at too high a level, the supply of Japanese yen

(6) will exceed the demand for yen, and Japan will experience a balance of payments (deficit/surplus). If the

government pegs the rate too low, then (demand/supply) will exceed _____ and

the result will be a balance of payments _____.

A government pegging its exchange rate and faced with a deficit will need to use its holdings of inter-

(7) national reserves, that is, gold or foreign currencies, in order to (buy/sell) its own currency. A country faced with a surplus will need to supply its own currency. As a result it will find its international reserves (increasing/decreasing).

Under fixed exchange rates, most of the pressure for adjustment is placed on countries experiencing a

(8) balance of payments (deficit/surplus). If nothing else, such a country will eventually run out of international reserves. If a country does not want to change its exchange rate, other adjustment options include monetary and fiscal policies that (increase/decrease) interest rates, (increase/decrease) the rate of inflation, or induce a general (contraction/expansion) in the level of economic activity. Many of these adjustments occurred automatically under the gold standard as a balance of payments deficit led to an outflow of gold and a(n) (increase/reduction) in the stock of money.

A major weakness of the Bretton Woods system of fixed exchange rates was that deficit countries

(9) (liked/disliked) adjusting their domestic economies for balance of payments reasons rather than for domestic political and economic reasons. Another weakness was the special role accorded the U.S. dollar.

In recent years the world's major industrialized countries have operated under a mixed system of floating rates. Exchange rates are allowed to change on a daily basis in response to market forces. At the same time, many governments intervene by buying or selling currencies, hoping to influence the exchange rate to their advantage. Some have worried that floating exchange rates would be so volatile as to destroy world trade. However, market-determined prices need not be volatile, and importers and exporters can often

(10) relieve the business risk of changes in exchange rate by dealing with _____.

DEFINITION QUIZ

Choose the letter that is the most appropriate definition for each of the following terms.

1. _____ International monetary system
2. _____ Exchange rate
3. _____ Appreciation
4. _____ Depreciation
5. _____ Devaluation
6. _____ Revaluation
7. _____ Floating exchange rates
8. _____ Purchasing-power parity theory
9. _____ Fixed exchange rates
10. _____ Balance of payments deficit
11. _____ Balance of payments surplus
12. _____ Current account
13. _____ Capital account
14. _____ Balance of trade
15. _____ Gold standard
16. _____ Gold-exchange system
17. _____ International Monetary Fund
18. _____ Exchange controls
19. _____ Dirty float

a. Value of currencies linked to dollars whose value was linked to gold.
b. Price of one currency in terms of another.
c. Exchange rates determined in free market via supply and demand.
d. Difference between merchandise exports and imports.
e. Set of institutions that facilitate international movements of currencies.
f. System where exchange rates change in response to market forces but with intervention by central banks.
g. International agency that extends loans for infrastructure to developing countries.
h. Amount by which quantity supplied of a country's currency exceeds quantity demanded in a given year.
i. Balance of trade involving purchases and sales of assets.
j. International agency that monitors exchange rate policies of member countries.
k. Reduction in official value of a currency.
l. Balance of trade in goods and services plus unilateral transfers.
m. System where exchange rates are set in terms of gold.
n. Increase in the amount of foreign currency a unit of a given currency can buy.
o. Exchange rates set by the government.
p. Laws restricting exchange of one nation's currency for that of another.
q. Amount by which quantity demanded of a country's currency exceeds quantity supplied.
r. Idea that exchange rates adjust to reflect price level differences.
s. Drop in the amount of foreign currency a unit of a given currency can buy.
t. Increase in official value of a currency.

BASIC EXERCISES

1. This exercise is designed to contrast the impact of similar events under systems of fixed and floating exchange rates.

   Assume that the world is divided into two countries, the United States and France. Table 19–1 lists a number of events. Fill in the missing blank spaces in the table to analyze the impact of these events on (1) the dollar-franc exchange rate under a system of floating rates, and (2) the French balance of payments under a system of fixed exchange rates. Assume that each event takes place from an initial equilibrium that under fixed exchange rates entails neither a deficit nor a surplus. Figure 19–1 illustrates such an equilibrium, with an initial exchange rate of 16 cents per franc.

2. This exercise is designed to illustrate the theory of purchasing power parity.

   Assume that the United States and France are the only suppliers of wine on the world market. Consumers of wine are indifferent between French and California wines and buy whichever is cheaper. Initially, the dollar-franc exchange rate is assumed to be 16 cents to the franc and California wine sells for $4.80 a bottle.

 Ignoring transportation costs, the initial dollar price of French wines must be $4.80. Accordingly, we know that the initial franc price of French wine is _____ francs.

 Assume now that inflation in the United States has raised the price of California wine to $7.20 a bottle, while inflation in France has raised the price of French wine to 40 francs. Based on this data, answer each of the following:

a. If the exchange rate is fixed at 16 cents to the franc, what is the new dollar price of French wine? $_____ What would happen to the sales of French and California wines? What happens to the American balance of payments?

b. If the dollar–franc exchange rate is free to adjust, what is the new exchange rate; that is, what dollar price of a franc is necessary to equalize the dollar (or franc) price of both wines? _____
This change in the dollar price of a franc is an (appreciation/depreciation) of the franc and a _____ of the dollar.

TABLE 19-1

Event	Shift in Demand Curve for Francs (left, right, no shift)	Shift in Supply Curve for Francs (left, right, no shift)	Floating Rates — Appreciation or Depreciation of Franc	Fixed Rates — Change in French Balance Payment*
a. Federal reserve policy raises interest rates in the United States.				
b. A change in tastes increases American demand for haute couture fashions from Paris.				
c. The U.S. economy enters a recession.				
d. Major labor strikes in France have resulted in a sudden increase in the (franc) price of French goods.				

*Appropriate answers would be deficit, surplus, or no change.

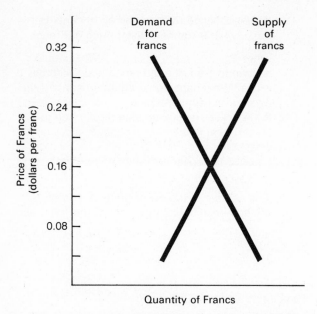

FIGURE 19-1

c. Assuming that the change in the price of wine is typical of the change in other prices, which country had the higher rate of inflation?

_____

d. From Questions a and c, it is seen that the purchasing-power parity theory implies that under fixed exchange rates, a country with more inflation will experience a balance of payments (deficit/surplus).

e. From Questions b and c, it is seen that the purchasing-power parity theory implies that under floating exchange rates a country with more inflation will have a(n) (appreciating/ depreciating) currency.

SELF-TESTS FOR UNDERSTANDING

Test A

Circle the correct answer.

1. If under a system of floating exchange rates the Mexican peso used to cost 2 cents and now costs less than a penny, one would say that
   a. the peso has appreciated relative to the dollar.
   b. the peso has depreciated relative to the dollar.
   c. there has been a devaluation of the peso relative to the dollar.

d. there has been a revaluation of the peso relative to the dollar.

2. If the German mark appreciates relative to the British pound, then a mark will buy
   a. fewer pounds than before.
   b. more pounds than before.
   c. the same number of pounds as before.

3. Under a system of floating exchange rates, which one of the following conditions will tend to depreciate the French franc relative to the German mark?
   a. An economic boom in Germany.
   b. A higher level of inflation in France than in Germany.
   c. An increase in interest rates in France.
   d. A sudden increase in German demand for imports from France.

4. Consider a country that is attempting to peg its currency at an unrealistically high exchange rate under a system of fixed exchange rates. Which one of the following is *not* true?
   a. The exchange rate will be said to be overvalued.
   b. The supply of its own currency will exceed demand.
   c. The country will have a balance of payments surplus.
   d. The country will be forced to use foreign exchange reserves—gold and holdings of other currencies—in order to buy its own currency.

5. Which one of the following policies would *not* help to eliminate a deficit under a system of fixed exchange rates?
   a. Monetary and fiscal policies to raise the level of unemployment.
   b. A devaluation of the exchange rate.
   c. Monetary and fiscal policies to increase the rate of inflation.
   d. A change in monetary policy that increases interest rates.

6. Purchasing-power parity theory says that
   a. only the volume of exports and imports determines exchange rates; interest rates have nothing to do with exchange rates.
   b. all countries are better off with a system of fixed exchange rates.
   c. adjustment of fixed exchange rates should be symmetrical as between deficit and surplus countries.
   d. in the long run, exchange rates adjust to reflect differences in price levels between countries.

7. If inflation in Germany is at an annual rate of 2 percent and inflation in the United States is at 8 percent, then the purchasing-power parity

theory suggests that in the long run the dollar price of one mark will

a. increase at an annual rate of 8 percent.
b. decrease at an annual rate of 6 percent.
c. increase at an annual rate of 6 percent.
d. increase at an annual rate of 2 percent.

8. In Question 7 above, one would say that the higher rate of inflation in the United States results in a(n)

a. depreciation of the mark relative to the dollar.
b. appreciation of the mark relative to the dollar.
c. appreciation of the dollar relative to the mark.
d. cross subsidy of the mark by the dollar.

9. Assume that the mark–dollar exchange rate is fixed, that Germany and the United States are the only two countries in the world, and that inflation rates differ as described in Question 7. Which country will have a balance of payments surplus?

a. The United States.
b. Germany.

10. If it takes 16 cents to buy one Swedish krona and 48 cents to buy one Dutch guilder, then how many kronor should it take to buy one guilder?

a. $(16 \div 48) = .33$.
b. $(48 \div 16) = 3$.
c. $(1.0 \div 16) = 6.25$.
d. $(1.0 \div .48) = 2.08$.

Test B

Circle T or F for True or False as appropriate.

1. If one mark used to cost 60 cents and now costs 40 cents, the dollar has appreciated relative to the mark.   T F

2. A pure system of floating exchange rates requires government intervention—purchases and sales of its own currency—in order to work properly.   T F

3. Under a system of floating exchange rates a sudden increase in the demand for U.S. exports will lead to appreciation of the dollar relative to other currencies.   T F

4. Under a system of fixed exchange rates a sudden increase in American imports would increase the American balance of payments deficit (or reduce the size of the surplus).   T F

5. Purchasing-power parity is a theory of the short-run determination of exchange rates.   T F

6. Under a system of fixed exchange rates, a country that attempts to peg its exchange rate at an artificially low level will end up with a balance of payments surplus.   T F

7. Today, world international monetary relations are based on the gold standard.   T F

8. A major advantage of the gold standard was that countries could control their own domestic money stock.   T F

9. The Bretton Woods gold-exchange system established a system of fixed exchange rates based on the convertibility of dollars into gold.   T F

10. Under the Bretton Woods system of fixed exchange rates, both surplus and deficit countries felt the same pressure to correct any imbalance in their balance of payments.   T F

SUPPLEMENTARY EXERCISES

1. **The Risks of Speculation Against Fixed Exchange Rates**

Assume that in the mid-1960s you are treasurer for a large multinational corporation with 10 million British pounds to invest. The fixed official exchange rate vis-a-vis the U.S. dollar has been $2.80. At this exchange rate Britain has been experiencing large and growing deficits in its balance of payments and has been financing this deficit by buying pounds with foreign currencies. Britain's holdings of foreign currencies are running low, and there is a general feeling that Britain will have to devalue the pound. Exactly how large the devaluation will be and exactly when it will occur are uncertain, but given the history of chronic deficits, there is absolutely no chance that the pound will be revalued.

Fill in Table 19–2 to measure the risks of speculating against the pound. (Changing from pounds to dollars and back again will involve transactions costs. Table 19–2 abstracts from these costs, which are apt to be small.)

What is the worst outcome?

As the talk of devaluation heats up, what are you apt to do? How will your actions affect the British deficit and the pressures for devaluation?

TABLE 19-2

	(1)	(2)	(3)
Initial holdings of pounds	10,000,000	10,000,000	10,000,000
Current exchange rate	$2.80	$2.80	$2.80
Number of dollars if you sell pounds for dollars	_____	_____	_____
Possible new exchange rate	$2.80*	$2.60	$2.40
Number of pounds following reconversion to pounds after devaluation	_____	_____	_____

*This exchange rate assumes Britain takes other steps and does not devalue the pound.

2. World Trade Under Fixed and Flexible Exchange Rates

Some observers worried that the introduction of a system of floating exchange rates would have adverse effects on the volume of world trade, as exporters and importers would have trouble coping with short-run fluctuations in exchange rates. Go to the library and look up data on the volume of international trade. (You might try data from one of a variety of international organizations, including the United Nations, the International Monetary Fund, or the World Bank.) What is the percentage change in the annual physical volume of trade since the establishment of the current mixed system of floating exchange rates in 1973? How does the growth in trade compare with the growth in world output, that is, the sum of all countries' GNP?

20

Macroeconomics in a World Economy

LEARNING OBJECTIVES

After completing the material in this chapter you should be able to:

- define, understand, and use correctly the terms and concepts listed below.
- explain how an appreciation or depreciation in the exchange rate affects net exports, the aggregate demand curve and the aggregate supply curve.
- explain why the reaction of international capital flows to changes in interest rates works to offset the impact of changes in fiscal policy.
- explain why the reaction of international capital flows to changes in interest rates works to enhance the impact of changes in monetary policy.
- explain the J curve and its relevance to an understanding of the impact of a change in exchange rates.
- explain in what way government deficits and trade deficits are linked.
- explain how a change in the mix of fiscal and monetary policy affects macroeconomic variables such as GNP, real interest rates, prices, the trade deficit, and the exchange rate.

- evaluate the likely impact of proposals to reduce the U.S. trade deficit.

IMPORTANT TERMS AND CONCEPTS

Exports
Imports
Net exports
Closed economy
Open economy
Exchange rate
Appreciation
Depreciation
Trade deficit
J curve
International capital flows
Budget deficits and trade deficits
$G - T = (S - I) - (X - IM)$

CHAPTER REVIEW

This chapter integrates the discussion of international trade and exchange rates of the last two chapters with the earlier discussions of income determination and fiscal and monetary policy. An economy that did

(1) not trade with any other economy would be called a _____ economy. Today all industrial economies and most developing economies have extensive links with other economies through

trade in goods and services and financial assets. Such economies are called _____ economies. These international linkages can affect important macroeconomic outcomes such as GNP and prices. A complete and rigorous examination of these linkages is the stuff of more advanced courses in economics, but with a few minor modifications we can use the model of income determination that we developed in earlier chapters to shed light on a number of important issues.

We start with a review of factors affecting the demand for exports and imports. As we saw in Chapter 8, the demand for exports and imports is influenced by income and prices. An increase in foreign income will

(2) (decrease/increase) the demand for American exports and is an important reason why economic fluctuations abroad (are/are not) felt in the United States. Exports and imports are also influenced by changes in the exchange rate as these changes alter the relative price of foreign and domestic goods. An appreciation of the dollar makes foreign goods (less/more) expensive. The result is likely to be a(n) (decrease/increase) in

American imports and a(n) _____ in American exports. Putting these two effects together shows that an appreciation of the exchange rate will lead to a(n) (decrease/increase) in net exports, ($X - IM$). Similar reasoning shows that a depreciation of the dollar will lead to a(n)

_____ in exports, a(n) _____ in imports and a(n)

_____ in net exports.

A change in net exports that comes from a change in exchange rates is analogous to any other autonomous change in spending. It shifts the expenditure schedule and leads to a (movement along/shift in)

(3) the aggregate demand curve. More precisely, following an appreciation of the dollar net exports (decline/increase), the expenditure schedule shifts (down/up), and the aggregate demand curve shifts to the (left/right). Exactly opposite results follow from a depreciation of the dollar.

A change in exchange rates can also lead to a shift in the aggregate supply curve through its impact

(4) on the price of imported intermediate goods. An appreciation of the dollar makes imported inputs (less/more) expensive. This result can be modeled as a(n) (downward/upward) shift in the aggregate supply curve. A

depreciation of the dollar makes imported inputs _____ expensive and leads to

a(n) _____ shift in the aggregate supply curve.

Once we understand the impact of a change in interest rates on international capital flows and on the exchange rate, we will have all the pieces necessary to examine the impact of changes in fiscal and

(5) monetary policy. We saw in Chapter 19 that an increase in interest rates is apt to (decrease/increase) the demand by foreigners for American financial assets. This change in the demand for dollars should lead to a(n) (appreciation/depreciation) of the dollar. Tracing through the impact of this capital flow induced change in the exchange rate is the key to understanding how fiscal and monetary policy work in an open economy.

(6) To review, consider a change in fiscal policy. A move to expansionary fiscal policy, say a(n) (decrease/increase) in taxes, would shift the expenditure schedule (up/down) and shift the aggregate demand curve to the (right/left). With no changes in monetary policy (that is, no shift in the supply of money schedule), there will be a(n) (decrease/no change/increase) in interest rates. The impact of this change in interest rates on international capital flows will lead to a(n) (appreciation/depreciation) in the exchange rate. This change in the exchange rate will shift the aggregate demand curve to the (left/right) and shift the aggregate supply curve (down/up). The shift in the aggregate demand curve, induced by the change in the exchange rate, works to (enhance/offset) the original expansionary change in fiscal policy. The shift in the aggregate supply curve works to (lower/raise) prices and to (increase/decrease) output. If the shift in the aggregate supply curve induced by the change in exchange rates were large enough it could offset the impact on output from the exchange-rate-induced shift in the aggregate demand curve. Evidence suggests that the shift in the aggregate supply curve is small and that, on net, the shifts in the two curves work to (enhance/offset) the impact of expansionary fiscal policy on output.

(7)   A move to restrictive monetary policy can be analyzed in the same way. The initial impacts will include an increase in interest rates that leads to a(n) <u>(appreciation/depreciation)</u> of the exchange rate. The impact of the change in the exchange rate will <u>(enhance/offset)</u> the original restrictive change in monetary policy.

     Our equilibrium condition that $Y = \overline{C + I + G + (X - IM)}$ can be manipulated to illustrate the important link between government budget deficits and trade deficits. Remembering that GNP equals disposable income plus taxes and that disposable income equals consumption spending plus savings enables us to rewrite this equilibrium condition[1] as

$$G - T = (S - I) - (X - IM).$$

If the government runs a deficit—that is, if the government wants more output than it can command through taxes—then either private savings must exceed private investment, $(S - I)$, or additional output must be forthcoming from foreigners—that is, imports must exceed exports. It is changes in income, interest rates, exchange rates, and prices that enforce equilibrium and the link between budget deficits and trade deficits.

     The impact of a change in exchange rates on imports and exports usually takes some time. Economists refer to the lag in the adjustment of the balance of trade following a change in exchange rates as the

(8)   _____ curve. Is the Ameridan trade deficit a problem? One's answer to this question depends upon whether one views capital inflows over the 1980s as a market response to extravagant spending requiring high interest rates in the United States to attract foreign capital or as the result of an autonomous increase in foreign demand for investment in the United States. Many feel that evidence on interest rates and consumption spending is more consistent with the first rather than the second view.

     A number of suggestions have been made to reduce the trade deficit. Many argue that the United

(9)   States should alter the mix of fiscal and monetary policy. According to this view <u>(contractionary/expansionary)</u>

fiscal policy and _____ monetary policy were responsible for the increase in

the trade deficit during the 1980s. Reversing these actions, that is, a move to _____

fiscal policy and _____ monetary policy, could work in reverse and lower the trade deficit. Rapid economic growth abroad would increase American <u>(exports/imports)</u>. Protectionism could lower imports, but retaliation by foreign governments would <u>(lower/raise)</u> American exports with little change in net exports. One also needs to consider the impact of protectionism on exchange rates. For any of these measures to work, the equilibrium condition described above, $G - T = (S - I) - (X - IM)$, shows us that a reduction in the trade deficit must be accompanied by a combination of lower budget deficits, higher savings, or lower investment.

DEFINITION QUIZ

Choose the letter that is the most appropriate definition for each of the following terms.

1. _____ Exports

2. _____ Imports

3. _____ Net imports

4. _____ Closed economy

5. _____ Open economy

6. _____ Trade deficit

7. _____ J curve

a. Domestically produced goods sold abroad.

b. Graph depicting response of inflation to changes in the value of currency.

c. Economy that trades with other economies.

d. Graph depicting response of net exports to changes in the exchange rate.

e. Foreign-produced goods purchased domestically.

f. Economy that does not trade with other economies.

g. Amount by which imports exceed exports.

h. Domestic goods sold abroad minus foreign goods bought domestically.

[1]This condition can also be written as $G + I + X = S + T + IM$. In terms of the circular flow diagram of Figure 7–1 in the text, this formulation says that injections must equal leakages.

BASIC EXERCISE

This exercise is designed to review how the operation of fiscal and monetary policy is affected by interest-sensitive capital flows in an open as compared to a closed economy.

Table 20–1 reviews the impact of an appreciation and depreciation in the exchange rate on various macroeconomic variables. Note that the shift in the aggregate supply curve could offset the impact on GNP of the shift in the aggregate demand curve. As in the text, we will assume that the shift in the aggregate supply curve following a change in the exchange rate is small relative to the shift in the aggregate demand curve.

1. Table 20–2 shows the impact on GNP and prices of various changes in fiscal and monetary policy. The completed upper portion of the table ignores any impact on exchange rates. Remembering that changes in interest rates are likely to influence the international investment of funds and hence the demand for dollars, complete Table 20–2 to determine whether capital flows offset or enhance these changes in monetary and fiscal policy. You should specify the change in interest rates, determine how the exchange rate is affected, consider the impact of the change in the exchange rate on GNP and prices, and finally combine your results from the change in policy

TABLE 20-1

Macroeconomic Variable	Exchange Rate Appreciation	Exchange Rate Depreciation
Exports	Decrease	Increase
Imports	Increase	Decrease
Net Exports	Decrease	Increase
Aggregate Demand Curve	Shifts to the left	Shifts to the right
Aggregate Supply Curve	Shifts down	Shifts up
Real GNP	Down	Up
Price Level	Down	Up

and the change in exchange rates to determine the overall impact. Figure 20–1 may be helpful when completing Table 20–2.

2. What general conclusion can you draw about the effectiveness of monetary and fiscal policy in a world of interest-sensitive capital flows and flexible exchange rates?

TABLE 20-2

	Increase in G	Decrease in G	Open Market Sale	Open Market Purchase
Aggregate Demand Curve	Right	Left	Left	Right
Real GNP	Up	Down	Down	Up
Price Level	Up	Down	Down	Up
Interest Rate	_____	_____	_____	_____
Exchange Rate	_____	_____	_____	_____
Real GNP	_____	_____	_____	_____
Price Level	_____	_____	_____	_____
Overall Impact				
Real GNP	_____	_____	_____	_____
Price Level	_____	_____	_____	_____

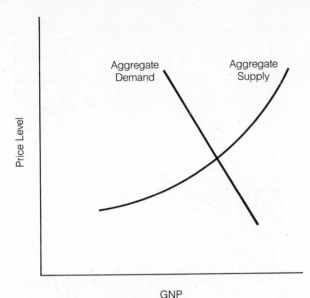

FIGURE 20-1

SELF-TESTS FOR UNDERSTANDING

Test A

Circle the correct answer.

1. In an open economy, $C + I + G$
   a. is always less than Y.
   b. must always equal Y.
   c. is always greater than Y.
   d. none of the above.
2. An increase in foreign GNP is likely to lead to
   a. a decrease in our exports.
   b. little if any change in our exports.
   c. an increase in our exports.
3. An increase in foreign GNP is likely to lead to
   a. a decrease in our net exports.
   b. little if any change in our net exports.
   c. an increase in our net exports.
4. An increase in domestic interest rates should lead to which one of the following?
   a. Capital outflow.
   b. Appreciation of the dollar.
   c. Increase in exports.
   d. Upward shift in the expenditure schedule.
5. An appreciation in the dollar vis-a-vis other currencies should lead to all but which one of the following?
   a. A decrease in exports.
   b. An increase in imports.
   c. A shift of the aggregate demand curve to the right.
   d. A downward shift of the aggregate supply curve.
6. A move to expansionary fiscal policy will lead to all but which one of the following?
   a. An increase in interest rates.
   b. An appreciation of the dollar.
   c. An increase in American exports.
   d. An increase in the American trade deficit.
7. A move to expansionary monetary policy will lead to all but which one of the following?
   a. A decrease in interest rates.
   b. An appreciation of the dollar.
   c. An upward shift in the expenditure schedule.
   d. An increase in inflationary pressures.
8. The J curve refers to
   a. What Julius Erving does with his body when he drives for the bucket.
   b. the delayed impact of higher rates of inflation on interest rates.
   c. the delayed impact of a change in the exchange rate on a country's trade deficit.
   d. the pitch that won the 1983 World Series.
9. In an open economy equilibrium requires that
   a. $G - T = I + S + X - IM$.
   b. $G - T = S - I - X + IM$.
   c. $G - T = I + X - S - IM$.
   d. $G - T = S - X - (I + IM)$.
10. If there is no change in the balance of domestic savings and investment, then any increase in the government deficit must be matched by
    a. an increase in the trade deficit.
    b. a reduction in the equilibrium level of output.
    c. a capital outflow.

Test B

Circle T or F for True or False as appropriate.

1. International trade means that an economic boom in the United States is likely to lead to recession in the rest of the world.　　　T F
2. A change in exports has no multiplier impacts.　　　T F
3. A shift in the expenditure schedule coming from an autonomous change in domestic investment spending would be expected to have no impact on a country's trade deficit.　　　T F
4. A depreciation in the exchange rate is inflationary.　　　T F
5. A depreciation in the exchange rate should help to reduce a country's trade deficit.　　　T F

6. Under floating exchange rates, a country with a trade surplus will also experience a capital outflow.   T F

7. International capital flows make monetary policy less effective.   T F

8. International capital flows are unaffected by changes in fiscal policy.   T F

9. Increased protectionism may only lead to an appreciation of the dollar.   T F

10. The only way to reduce the trade deficit is by reducing the government's budget deficit.   T F

Appendix

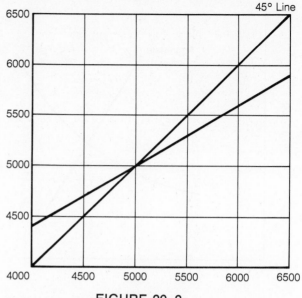

FIGURE 20-2

BASIC EXERCISES

This problem is designed to illustrate the major lesson from the appendix: When imports increase with income, the expenditure schedule is flatter and the multiplier is smaller than before.

Figure 20-2 shows the expenditure schedule consistent with Table 11-1 where imports, and hence net exports, do not vary with income. Table 20-3 repeats Table 11-1 except that imports are assumed to increase with income and thus net exports decline as income increases.

1. Calculate total expenditures, $C + I + G + (X - IM)$ for Table 20-3 and enter this data in the second column of Table 20-4. Plot the expenditure data you just calculated in Figure 20-2 to compare this expenditure schedule with the one

based on data from Table 11-1 which assumes that net exports do not vary with income. Which expenditure schedule is flatter? Explain why.

2. What happens to the multiplier when net exports vary with income? Use column (3) of Table 20-4 to record total expenditures on the assumption that government purchases are $1,450 billion rather than $1,200 billion. What is the new equilibrium level of GNP? What is the value of the multiplier? What explains the difference in this multiplier and the multiplier of 2.5 for the model in Chapter 11?

3. (Optional) Use the data in Table 20-3 to calculate the marginal tax rate, the marginal propensity to consume, and the marginal propensity to import. Use these parameters and the formula described in footnote 10 on page 438 of the text to calculate the multiplier. How does this calculation compare with your answer to question 2?

TABLE 20-3

($ billions)

National Income	Income Taxes	Disposable Income	Consumption Spending	Investment Spending	Government Purchases	Net Exports
4000	1000	3000	2500	800	1200	0
4500	1125	3375	2800	800	1200	− 50
5000	1250	3750	3100	800	1200	− 100
5500	1375	4125	3400	800	1200	− 150
6000	1500	4500	3700	800	1200	− 200

TABLE 20-4

National Income	(1) Total Expenditures (Table 11–1)	(2) Total Expenditures (Table 20–3 $G = \$1200$)	(3) Total Expenditures (Table 20–3 $G = \$1450$)
$4000	$4400	_____	_____
4500	4700	_____	_____
5000	5000	_____	_____
5500	5300	_____	_____
6000	5600	_____	_____

PART

5

ESSENTIALS OF MICRO- ECONOMICS: CONSUMERS AND FIRMS

21

Consumer Choice and the Individual's Demand Curve

LEARNING OBJECTIVES

After completing the material in this chapter you should be able to:

- define, understand, and use correctly the terms and concepts listed below.
- distinguish between total and marginal utility.
- explain the role of marginal utility as a guide to the maximization of total utility.
- explain how the law of diminishing marginal utility can be used to derive an optimal purchase rule.
- explain how the optimal purchase rule can be used to derive a demand curve.
- explain what economists mean by inferior goods and why inferior goods may have demand curves that slope upward.

- distinguish between the income and substitution effects of a price change.

IMPORTANT TERMS AND CONCEPTS

Diamond–water paradox
Marginal analysis
Total utility
Marginal utility
The "law" of diminishing marginal utility
Optimal purchase rule ($P = MU$)
Scarcity and marginal utility
Consumer's surplus
Inferior goods
Income effect
Substitution effect

CHAPTER REVIEW

This chapter discusses economic models of consumer choice. These models are what lie behind negatively sloped demand curves. The appendix to the chapter discusses indifference curve analysis, which is a more sophisticated treatment of the same material.

Economists derive implications for individual demand curves by starting with some assumptions about individual behavior. One relatively innocent assumption should be sufficient. This assumption concerns consumer preferences and is called the ''law'' of diminishing marginal utility. Perhaps we should first start with utility.

Economists use the term *utility* to refer to the benefits people derive from consuming goods and services. The actual utility, or benefits, that individuals derive from consuming commodities is unique to each one of us and thus incapable of being measured. To get around the measurement problems associated with personal satisfaction, we will use the term *total utility* to refer to the maximum amount of money that a consumer will pay for a given quantity of the commodity. (It should be obvious that this amount of money will be influenced by a person's income and preferences.) Rather than focusing on total utility, however, economists have found it useful to pay attention to the additional amount of money that a consumer would

(1) pay for one more unit of the commodity, or _____ utility, measured in money terms. (Marginal utility (will/will not) also be influenced by a person's income and preferences.) The law of diminishing marginal utility is a hypothesis about consumer preferences. It says that normally additional units of any commodity provide less and less satisfaction. As a result, the additional amount a consumer will pay for an additional unit of some commodity will (increase/decrease) the more units he or she is already consuming.

The law of diminishing marginal utility can be used as a guide to optimal commodity purchases. Optimal purchases are ones that maximize the difference between total utility and total expenditures on a commodity.

This difference is called _____ surplus. That is, optimal purchases yield

(2) maximum total utility for a given level of income and maximum _____

_____. Our optimal purchase rule says that an individual consumer should buy additional units of a commodity as long as the marginal utility of the additional units exceeds the

_____ of the commodity. If marginal utility exceeds price, the addition to total utility from consuming one more unit will be (greater/less) than the addition to total spending, and the difference between total utility and expenditures will (increase/decrease).

Now, with our optimal purchase rule it is easy to derive an individual *demand curve*. A demand curve shows the quantity demanded at different possible prices, holding all other things constant. (Look back at Chapter 4 if necessary.) To derive an individual demand curve we simply confront our consumer with different prices and see how the quantity demanded changes. Our optimal purchase rule tells us that she will

(3) purchase more units as long as the marginal utility of the unit being considered is (greater/less) than the price of the unit. She will stop when the two are equal. If we now lower the price, we know that she will

again try to equate price and _____ utility, which she does by considering buying (more/less). Thus, as price goes down the quantity demanded goes (down/up), and this individual demand curve has a (positive/negative) slope.

Price is not the only variable that affects an individual's demand for various commodities. Income is also

(4) an important variable. We saw in Chapter 4 that a change in income will mean a (shift in/movement along) the demand curve. In terms of the concepts of this chapter, a change in income will influence how much a person would be willing to spend to buy various commodities; that is, a change in income will influence

total and marginal _____. Following a change in income we could again conduct our demand curve experiment of the last paragraph, and it would not be surprising if the resulting demand curve had shifted. An increase in income will typically mean an increase in the demand for most commodities, but occasionally one will find that the demand for some commodity decreases following an increase in income. Commodities whose consumption increases as a consumer's income increases are called

_____ goods and commodities whose consumption decreases are called

_____ goods.

We can now use the possibility of inferior goods to see why the quantity demanded might decrease following a reduction in price. We start by noting that the impact of a price change can be divided into an *income effect* and a *substitution effect*. Consider a price reduction on some good, say potatoes. The fact that potatoes are now cheaper relative to other goods implies an increase in demand for potatoes. This relative

(5) price effect is also called the _____ effect. But that is not the whole story.

Following the price decline a consumer could buy exactly the same amount of all commodities, including potatoes, as she did before and still have money left over. This leftover money comes from the decline in the price of potatoes, and it is similar to an increase in income, which will, as noted above, affect her demand for

all goods. This leftover money effect is also called the _____ effect of a price change. If potatoes were an inferior good, then increased income would lead our consumer to demand (fewer/more) potatoes. The final change in demand for potatoes, or any other commodity following a

price change will be determined by the net effect of the _____ and

_____ effects of a price change. Demand curves for normal goods will always have a (positive/negative) slope as the substitution and income effects of a price change work in the same direction. Demand curves for inferior goods will also have a negative slope as long as the

_____ effect is stronger than the _____ effect.

DEFINITION QUIZ

Choose the letter that is the most appropriate definition for each of the following terms.

1. _____ Marginal analysis
2. _____ Total utility
3. _____ Marginal utility
4. _____ "Law" of diminishing marginal utility
5. _____ Consumer's surplus
6. _____ Inferior good
7. _____ Income effect
8. _____ Substitution effect

a. Impact on demand from change in purchasing power when the price of a good changes.
b. Difference between total utility and total expenditures for given quantity of some commodity.
c. Change in quantity demanded of a good resulting from change in its relative price holding real income constant.
d. Evaluation of the effects of small changes.
e. Maximum amount of money a consumer will pay for an additional unit of some commodity.
f. Quantity demanded increases when consumer real income rises.
g. Quantity demanded falls when consumer real income rises.
h. Maximum amount of money a consumer will give in exchange for a fixed quantity of some commodity.
i. Observation that additional units of a given commodity generally have decreasing value for a consumer.

BASIC EXERCISE

This exercise reviews how one can use the law of diminishing marginal utility to derive a negatively sloped demand curve. Table 21–1 presents data on Dolores's evaluation of different quantities of dresses.
1. Use these data to compute the marginal utility of each dress.
2. The optimal purchase rule says to buy more dresses as long as the marginal utility of the next dress exceeds the price of the dress. According to this rule, how many dresses should Dolores buy if they cost

$90 each? _____ ;
$60 each? _____ ;
$40 each? _____ ?

3. Now, fill in columns 3, 5, and 7 of Table 21–2 to compute the difference between total utility and total expenditures for each different price. What quantity maximizes the difference between total utility and total expenditures when price equals

$90 _____ ;
$60 _____ ;
$40 _____ ?

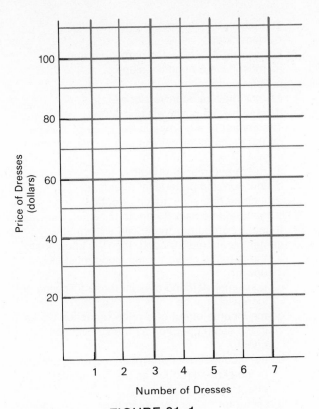

Price of Dresses (dollars)

Number of Dresses

FIGURE 21-1

difference between what she would be willing to pay and what she has to pay is called

_____ surplus. How do the quantities determined using the optimal purchase rule in question 2 compare with those determined by maximizing consumer surplus in question 3?

5. Use the information in Table 21–1 to plot Dolores's demand curve for dresses in Figure 21–1. Is your demand curve consistent with your answers to Questions 2 and 3? (It should be.)

4. The text defines total utility as the maximum amount of money that Delores would be willing to pay for various quantities of dresses. The

TABLE 21-1

Dresses	Total Utility (measured in dollars)	Marginal Utility (measured in dollars)
1	110	_____
2	210	_____
3	290	_____
4	360	_____
5	410	_____
6	440	_____
7	460	_____

TABLE 21-2

	Price = $90		Price = $60		Price = $40	
Dresses	Total Expenditure	Difference*	Total Expenditure	Difference*	Total Expenditure	Difference*
1	$ 90	_____	$ 60	_____	$ 40	_____
2	180	_____	120	_____	80	_____
3	270	_____	180	_____	120	_____
4	360	_____	240	_____	160	_____
5	450	_____	300	_____	200	_____
6	540	_____	360	_____	240	_____
7	630	_____	420	_____	280	_____

*Differences between total utility and total expenditures.

SELF-TESTS FOR UNDERSTANDING

Test A

Circle the correct answer.

1. The total utility of any commodity bundle
   a. should be the same for all individuals.
   b. is defined as the maximum amount of money that a consumer will spend for the bundle.
   c. will be equal to expenditures on the commodity in question.
   d. is not likely to change even if a consumer's income changes.

2. Rick is willing to spend up to $200 for one ski trip this winter and up to $250, in total, for two trips. The marginal utility of the second trip to Rick is
   a. $50.   b. $200.   c. $250.   d. $450.

3. The law of diminishing marginal utility
   a. implies that total utility declines as a consumer buys more of any good.
   b. is an important psychological premise that helps to explain why all demand curves have a negative slope.
   c. must hold for every commodity and every individual.
   d. says that increments to total utility will decrease as an individual consumes more of the commodity in question.

4. The optimal purchase rule says that to maximize the difference between total utility, measured in money terms, and total expenditures, a consumer should purchase additional units
   a. as long as total utility is increasing.
   b. until marginal utility equals zero.
   c. as long as marginal utility exceeds price.
   d. until marginal utility equals total utility.

5. The diamond–water paradox indicates that
   a. contrary to economists' assumptions, consumers are really irrational.
   b. price is more closely related to marginal utility than to total utility.
   c. water is an inferior good.
   d. the demand for diamonds is very elastic.

6. When economists say that some commodity is an inferior or a normal good, they are referring to the impact of
   a. a change in price on the quantity demanded.
   b. an increase in the quantity consumed on total utility.
   c. an increase in the quantity consumed on marginal utility.
   d. a change in income on the quantity demanded.

7. For an inferior good, the demand curve
   a. must have a negative slope.
   b. is likely to be horizontal.
   c. must have a positive slope.
   d. may have a positive slope.

8. The impact of a change in the price of cheese on the demand for cheese can be decomposed into
   a. micro and macro effects.
   b. inflation and price-level effects.
   c. income and substitution effects.
   d. general and partial effects.

9. If cheap hamburger meat with a high fat content is an inferior good, then we know that
   a. the demand curve for this good must slope upward.
   b. consumer demand may increase following an increase in price.
   c. the income effect of a price reduction works in the same direction as the substitution effect.
   d. the income effect of a price increase works in the same direction as the substitution effect.

10. If restaurant meals are not inferior goods, then the income effect of a price change
    a. will work in the same direction as the substitution effect.
    b. will work in the opposite direction from the substitution effect.
    c. implies, on balance, that people will demand fewer restaurant meals following a price reduction.
    d. means that at higher prices people may demand more not fewer, restaurant meals.

Test B

Circle T or F for True or False as appropriate.

1. The diamond–water paradox can be resolved by realizing that scarcity reduces total utility and simultaneously increases marginal utility.   T F

2. The term *marginal utility* refers to the total amount of dollars that consumers would pay for a particular commodity bundle.   T F

3. The term *inferior good* refers to those commodities that economists do not like.   T F

4. If the law of diminishing marginal utility holds for pizza, and if pizzas are not an inferior good, then the demand curve for pizza will have a negative slope.   T F

5. If, following a reduction in price, the quantity of potatoes demanded declines, we can conclude that potatoes are an inferior good.　**T F**

6. If a consumer is interested in maximizing the difference between total utility and expenditures, it is optimal to consume more of a commodity as long as the marginal utility of additional units exceeds the market price.　**T F**

7. The income and substitution effects of a change in price always work in the same direction, implying that a reduction in price must increase the quantity demanded.　**T F**

8. Part of the impact of an increase in the price of any good can be analyzed as a reduction in income.　**T F**

9. If a consumer is rational he will never buy an inferior good.　**T F**

10. Consumer's surplus is defined as the difference between price and marginal utility.　**T F**

Appendix: Indifference Curve Analysis

LEARNING OBJECTIVES

After completing the material in this appendix you should be able to:

- define, understand, and use correctly the terms and concepts listed below.
- draw a budget line, given data on prices and money income.
- explain why economists usually assume that indifference curves (1) never intersect, (2) have a negative slope, and (3) are bowed in toward the origin.
- determine optimal commodity bundle(s) for a consumer, given a budget line and a set of indifference curves.
- explain why, if indifference curves are smooth and bowed in to the origin, the optimal commodity bundle is the one for which the marginal rate of substitution equals the ratio of commodity prices.
- use indifference curve analysis to derive a demand curve, that is, show the change in the quantity demanded of a good as its price changes.
- use indifference curve analysis to analyze the impact on commodity demands of a change in income.

IMPORTANT TERMS AND CONCEPTS

Budget line
Indifference curves
Marginal rate of substitution
Slope of an indifference curve
Slope of a budget line

APPENDIX REVIEW

Indifference curve analysis is a more rigorous treatment of the material covered in Chapter 21. As the appendix shows, we can study consumer choices by confronting a consumer's desires or preferences, indicated by indifference curves, with a consumer's opportunities, indicated by a budget line. This approach clearly shows how total purchases are constrained by income.

(1) The *budget line* represents all possible combinations of commodities that a consumer can buy, given her money income. The arithmetic of a budget line for two commodities shows that it is a (straight/curved) line with a (positive/negative) slope. An increase in money income will produce a change in the (intercept/slope)

of the budget line. A change in the price of either commodity will mean a change in the _____ of the budget line. The slope of the budget line is equal to the ratio of the prices of the two commodities. (The price of the commodity measured along the horizontal axis goes on top.)

The budget line indicates only all the different ways a consumer could spend her money income. In order to figure out what consumption bundle is best for her, we must examine her own personal preferences.

(2) Economists use the concept of _____ curves to summarize an individual's

161

preferences. These curves are derived from a person's ranking of alternative commodity bundles. For two commodities, a single indifference curve is a line connecting all possible combinations (bundles) of the two

commodities between which our consumer is _____. From the assumption that more is better, we can deduce (1) that higher indifference curves (are/are not) preferred to lower indifference curves, (2) that indifference curves (never/often) intersect, and (3) that indifference curves will have a (positive/negative) slope.

(3)   Indifference curves are usually assumed to be curved lines that are bowed (in/out). The slope of an indifference curve indicates the terms of trade between commodities that our consumer is indifferent about. For a given reduction in one commodity the slope tells us how much (more/less) of the other commodity is necessary to keep our consumer as well off as before. The slope of the indifference curve is also known as

the marginal rate of _____. If indifference curves are bowed in, or convex to the origin, it means that the marginal rate of substitution (increases/decreases) as we move from left to right along a given indifference curve. This change in the marginal rate of substitution is a psychological premise that is similar to our earlier assumption about declining marginal utility, and it is what makes the indifference curves convex to the origin.

      We are now in a position to determine optimal consumer choices. The optimal choice is the commodity bundle that makes our consumer as well off as possible, given her opportunities. In this case opportunities

(4)   are represented by the _____ line and the evaluation of alternative commodity

bundles is given by the _____ curves. The best choice is a commodity bundle that puts our consumer on her (highest/lowest) possible indifference curve. This consumption bundle is

indicated by the indifference curve that is just tangent to the _____.
      From the definition of the slope of a curved line (review the material in Chapter 2 if necessary) we know that at the point of tangency the slope of the associated indifference curve will just equal the slope of the budget line. Since the slope of the budget line is given by the ratio of the prices of the two goods, we know that at the optimal decision the slope of the indifference curve, or the marginal rate of substitution, will just equal the ratio of prices.

      The marginal rate of substitution tells how our consumer is willing to trade goods and the price ratio tells us how she can trade goods in the market by buying more of one good and less of the other. If these two trading ratios are different, our consumer can make herself better off by changing her purchases. It is only when the two trading ratios are equal that her opportunities for gain have been eliminated.

      Once you master the logic and mechanics of indifference curve analysis you can use it to investigate the impact on demand of changes in price or incomes. A change in either income or prices will shift the

(5)   _____ _____. It is the resulting change in the optimal commodity bundle that helps trace out a movement along the demand curve in the case of a change in prices, and the shift in the demand curve, in the case of a change in income. (It is possible to show the income and substitution effects on the indifference curve diagram. If interested, ask your instructor.)

DEFINITION QUIZ

Choose the letter that is the most appropriate definition for each of the following terms.

1. _____ Budget line

2. _____ Indifference curves

3. _____ Marginal rate of substitution

4. _____ Slope of budget line

a. Maximum amount of one commodity a consumer will forego for an extra unit of another commodity.
b. Lines connecting all combinations of commodities on a consumer's utility function.
c. Graph of all possible combinations of two commodities a consumer can purchase given prices and the consumer's income.
d. Lines connecting all combinations of commodities that a consumer finds equally desirable.
e. Ratio of commodity prices.

BASIC EXERCISES

These problems are designed to review the logic of the rule for optimal consumer choice using indifference curve analysis, which says that a consumer should choose the commodity bundle associated with the point of tangency between the budget line and the highest indifference curve.

1. Figure 21–2 shows a set of indifference curves for Gloria between books and hamburgers.

    a. Gloria has an income of $80 that she will spend on books and hamburgers. Hamburgers cost $2 each and paperback books cost $4 each. Draw the budget line in Figure 21–2 that constrains Gloria's choices. (You might first compute the maximum number of hamburgers Gloria can buy; then determine the maximum number of books; and then connect these two points with a straight line.)

    b. How many hamburgers will Gloria buy?

    _____ How many books will she buy? _____ In Figure 21–2, label this combination B for best choice. (If you drew the budget line correctly this point should lie on indifference curve I_3.)

    c. The combination of 30 hamburgers and 5 books, point Z, is obviously not a better choice as it lies on a lower indifference curve. Assume for the moment that Gloria tentatively chooses point Z and is considering whether this choice is best. If you put a ruler along indifference curve I_2 and look very carefully you should be able to verify that at point Z the marginal rate of substitution of hamburgers for books is 3. This means that Gloria would be willing to give up _____ hamburgers in order to be able to buy one more book. (You can check this by noting that the combination of 27 hamburgers and 6 books is on the same indifference curve.[1] However, since books cost only $4 while hamburgers cost $2 Gloria has only to give up _____ hamburgers in order to buy 1 book. This is clearly a good deal for Gloria, and she will reduce her consumption of hamburgers in order to buy more books; that is, she will move down the budget line away from point Z.

    d. Consider point W, on indifference curve I_1. Tell a similar story that convinces both your-self and someone to whom you explain this analysis, that Gloria will be better off moving to the left along the budget line away from point W.

    e. Arguments similar to those in c and d above indicate that for smooth indifference curves as in Figure 21–2, the optimal consumer choice cannot involve a commodity bundle for which the marginal rate of substitution differs from the ratio of market prices. The conclusion is that the optimal decision must be the commodity bundle for which the marginal rate of substitution _____

    _____ .

2. Use Figure 21–3 to answer the following questions. Figure 21–3 assumes that Sharon spends all of her income on pizza and baseball tickets. The budget line P_1B_1 reflects Sharon's initial income and market prices for pizza and baseball tickets. Sharon's preferences are shown by the curved indifference curves. Initially Sharon chooses to consume at point X.

    a. Change in income. Where will Sharon consume following a change in income that shifts the budget line to P_2B_2? _____

    b. Change in price. Where will Sharon consume following a reduction in the price of pizzas that shifts the budget line to P_3B_1?

    _____

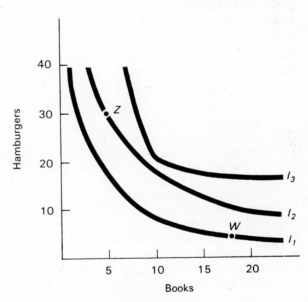

FIGURE 21–2

GLORIA'S INDIFFERENCE CURVES

[1]Most indifference curves that economists draw do not have straight-line segments. The straight-line segment is used for convenience, the general argument is still correct.

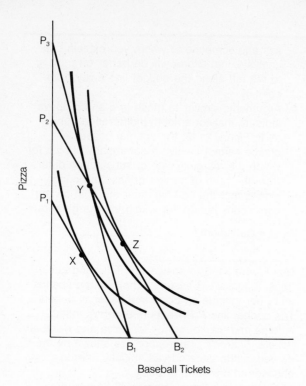

FIGURE 21-3

b. used by economists to represent a person's preferences among different commodity bundles.
c. the same for everyone.

4. The slope of an indifference curve.
   a. is constant if the indifference curve is convex to the origin.
   b. is always equal to the slope of the budget line.
   c. indicates what commodity trades an individual would be indifferent about.

5. Indifference curve analysis of the choice between two commodities shows that an increase in the price of one commodity will
   a. change the slope of the budget line.
   b. lead a consumer to choose a new commodity bundle, but one that is on the same indifference curve.
   c. shift consumer preferences.
   d. necessarily lead to a reduction in the demand for both commodities.

6. The assumption that more is preferred to less is sufficient to prove all but which one of the following?
   a. Indifference curves never intersect.
   b. Indifference curves bow in toward origin.
   c. Higher indifference curves are preferred to lower ones.
   d. Indifference curves have a negative slope.

SELF-TESTS FOR UNDERSTANDING

Test A

Circle the correct answer.

1. The budget line
   a. determines an individual's optimal consumption bundle.
   b. will not shift at all if prices of both commodities increase and money income is unchanged.
   c. determines an individual's possible consumption bundles.
   d. is a straight line whose slope is given by the rate of inflation.

2. Following an increase in income
   a. a consumer's indifference curves will shift.
   b. the slope of the budget line will increase.
   c. individual commodity demand curves will not shift.
   d. the budget line will shift in a parallel fashion.

3. A set of indifference curves is
   a. usually assumed to have a positive slope.

Test B

Circle T or F for True or False as appropriate.

1. The budget line is a curved line, convex to the origin.   T F

2. A change in the price of one commodity will change the slope of the budget line.   T F

3. The assumption that consumers prefer more to less is sufficient to establish that indifference curves will be convex to the origin.   T F

4. The slope of indifference curves at any point is given by the ratio of prices.   T F

5. The slope of an indifference curve is also called the marginal rate of substitution.   T F

6. Optimal decision making implies that a consumer should never choose a commodity bundle for which the marginal rate of substitution equals the ratio of market prices.   T F

7. Indifference curve analysis shows us that the demand for all goods is interrelated in the sense that changes in the price of one good can affect the demand for other goods.   T F

8. Indifference curve analysis suggests that a doubling of all prices and of money income will not change optimal consumption bundles.

T F

SUPPLEMENTARY EXERCISE

Consider a consumer whose total utility can be represented as

$$U = (F + 12)(C + 20)$$

where F = quantity of food, C = quantity of clothing, and U = the arbitrary level of utility associated with a particular indifference curve. (A different value for U will imply a different indifference curve.)

1. On a piece of graph paper draw a typical indifference curve. (Try $U = 7840$.)

2. Can you derive an expression for the demand for food? For clothing? (Can you use the equation for the indifference curves and what you know about optimal consumer choice to derive an equation that expresses F or C as a function of prices and income? The particular form of these demand curves comes from the mathematical specification of the indifference curves. A different specification of the indifference curves would lead to a different demand function.)

3. If the price of food is $1.50, the price of clothing is $3, and total money income is $300, what combination of food and clothing will maximize utility?

4. Assume the price of food rises to $2. Now what combination of food and clothing maximizes utility?

5. Assume income increases to $330 while prices are as given in Question 3. What happens to the demand for food and clothing? Is either good an inferior good?

22

Market Demand and Elasticity

LEARNING OBJECTIVES

After completing the material in this chapter you should be able to:

- define, understand, and use correctly the terms and concepts listed below.
- explain how to derive a market demand curve from individual demand curves.
- define the "law" of demand and discuss why there may be exceptions to it.
- compute the elasticity of demand, given appropriate data from a specific demand curve.
- describe how the elasticity of demand is affected by various factors.
- explain how the impact of a change in any excise tax will be affected by the price elasticity of demand.
- explain how the impact of a change in price on consumer expenditures depends on the price elasticity of demand.
- explain how the concept of cross elasticity of demand relates to the concepts of substitutes and complements.
- explain how factors other than price can affect the quantity demanded.
- distinguish between changes in the quantity demanded that come from a shift in the demand curve from those that come from a movement along the demand curve.

IMPORTANT TERMS AND CONCEPTS

Market demand curve
Excise tax
"Law" of demand
(Price) elasticity of demand
Elastic, inelastic, and unit-elastic demand curves
Complements
Substitutes
Cross elasticity of demand
Shift in a demand curve

CHAPTER REVIEW

The material in this chapter offers a more intensive look at demand curves. In effect, it is an extension of the material presented in Chapters 4 and 21. Demand curves provide important information for analyzing business decisions, market structures, and public policies.

In Chapter 21 we saw how the logic of consumer choice leads to individual demand curves. Business firms are usually less interested in individual demand curves than they are in market demand curves. It is the market demand curve that tells a firm how much of its product it can sell, in total, at different prices. Given individual demand curves, and assuming that the one person's demand does not depend upon the actions of

(1) another, we can derive the market demand curve by (horizontal/vertical) summation of all individual demand curves.

In Chapter 21 we saw that individual demand curves will usually have a (positive/negative) slope. If all individual demand curves have a negative slope, the market demand curve will necessarily have a

(2) _____ slope. Even if some or many individual demand curves are vertical—that is, if they show no change in the quantity demanded to a change in price—the market demand curve can still have a negative slope if a reduction in prices induces new customers to enter the market. The result that

market demand curves usually have a negative slope is called the "_____" of demand and is an important reason why demand is not a fixed amount, but rather should be thought of as a schedule that depends upon many factors, including price. It may be easy to think of exceptions to the "law"; snob appeal and a tendency to judge quality by price are two examples. However, there is overwhelming evidence that the "law" of demand is valid for most goods and services.

The price of a commodity is not the only variable influencing demand for it. Changes in other factors,

(3) say, consumers' income, tastes, or the price of a close substitute, will mean a (shift in/movement along) a demand curve drawn against price. Finally, remember that a demand curve refers to a particular period of time.

An important property of demand curves is the responsiveness of demand to a change in price. If a firm raises its price, how big a drop in sales is likely to occur? Or if a firm lowers its price, how large an increase in sales will there be?

To avoid problems with changing units, economists have found it useful to measure these changes as percentages. If, for a given change in price, one divides the percentage change in the quantity demanded by the percentage change in the price producing the change in quantity and ignores the negative sign, one has

(4) just computed the price _____ of _____. Remember, this calculation ignores minus signs and uses the average price and quantity to compute percentage changes.

It is useful to know the elasticity properties of certain, special types of demand curves. If the demand curve is truly a vertical line, then there is no change in the quantity demanded following any change in price,

(5) and the elasticity of demand is _____. (No demand curve is likely to be vertical for all prices, but it may be for some.) The other extreme is a perfectly horizontal demand curve where a small change in price produces a very large change in the quantity demanded. Such a demand curve implies that if price declines, even just a little, the quantity demanded will be infinite while if the price rises, even a little, the quantity demanded will fall to zero. In this case a very small percentage change in price produces a very large percentage change in the quantity demanded, and the price elasticity of demand is, in the limit,

_____. The price elasticity of demand along a negatively sloped straight-line demand curve (is constant/changes). One of the basic exercises illustrates just this point.

(6) A demand curve with a price elasticity of demand greater than 1.0 is commonly called _____

while demand curves with a price elasticity of demand less than 1.0 are called _____.

If the price elasticity of demand is exactly 1.0 the demand curve is said to be a _____

_____ demand curve.

Some simple arithmetic, not economics, can show that there is a connection between the price elasticity of demand and the change in total consumer expenditure (or, equivalently, the change in sales revenue) following a change in price. We know that total expenditures or revenues are simply price times quantity, or

$$\begin{array}{ccc} \text{Total} & & \text{Total} \\ \text{expenditures} & = & \text{revenues} \end{array} = p \times q.$$

A decrease in price will increase quantity as we move along a given demand curve. Whether total revenue increases clearly depends on whether the increase in quantity is big enough to outweigh the decline in price. (Remember the old saying: "We lose a little on each sale but make it up on volume.")

Again, it is mathematics, not economics, that tells us that the percentage change in total expenditures or revenue is equal to the *sum* of the percentage change in price and the percentage change in quantity.[1] Remember that as we move along a given demand curve, a positive change in price will lead to a negative change in quantity, and vice versa.

If the absolute value of the percentage change in quantity is equal to the absolute value of the per-
(7) centage change in price, then total revenue (will/will not) change following a change in price. In this case, the

price elasticity of demand is equal to _____.

If the price elasticity of demand is greater than 1.0, and if we ignore any negative signs, a given per-
(8) centage change in price will result in a (greater/smaller) percentage change in quantity demanded. From the equation above we can also see that if the price elasticity of demand is greater than 1.0, a reduction in price

will (increase/decrease) total revenue and an increase in price will _____ total revenue. Exactly opposite conclusions apply when the price elasticity of demand is less than 1.0.

The price elasticity of demand refers to the impact on the quantity demanded of a change in a commodity's price. There is a related elasticity concept that compares the change in the quantity demanded

(9) of one good with a change in the price of another good. This quotient is called the _____ elasticity of demand. In this case we must keep track of any negative signs.

Some goods, such as tables and chairs, hot dogs and buns, are usually demanded together. Such pairs

(10) are called _____ and are likely to have a (positive/negative) cross elasticity of

demand. Other goods, such as different brands of toothpaste, are probably close _____

and are likely to have a _____ cross elasticity of demand. (What is the likely impact on the demand for Colgate toothpaste of a change in the price of Crest?)

DEFINITION QUIZ

Choose the letter that is the most appropriate definition for each of the following terms.

1. _____ Market demand curve

2. _____ Excise tax

3. _____ "Law" of demand

4. _____ Price elasticity of demand

5. _____ Elastic demand curve

6. _____ Inelastic demand curve

7. _____ Unit-elastic demand curve

8. _____ Complements

9. _____ Substitutes

10. _____ Cross elasticity of demand

a. Ratio of percent change in quantity demanded of one product to the percent change in the price of another.
b. A change in price leads to a less than proportionate change in quantity demanded.
c. Graph depicting how total quantity demanded changes as price changes, holding other things constant.
d. Good for which an increase in price leads to higher demand.
e. Goods for which an increase in price of one decreases the demand for the other.
f. A change in price leads to a more than proportionate change in quantity demanded.
g. Ratio of percent change in quantity demanded to percent change in price.
h. Notion that demand tends to be higher at lower prices.
i. A change in price accompanied by an exactly proportionate change in quantity demanded.
j. Tax levied as a fixed amount of money per unit sold or fixed percentage of price.
k. Goods for which an increase in the price of one increases the demand for the other.

[1]This result is strictly true only for very small changes in *p* and *q*. Total revenue always equals $p \times q$, but this simple way of calculating the percentage change in total revenue is only true for small changes.

BASIC EXERCISES

These exercises are designed to give you some practice in the calculation and interpretation of price elasticities of demand.

1. The Price Elasticity of Demand

a. Table 22–1 has some data on possible prices and the associated demand for both schmoos and gizmos. Use these data to plot the demand curves in Figures 22–1 and 22–2. Looking at these demand curves, which curve looks more elastic? More inelastic?

b. Now use the data in Table 22–1 to calculate the elasticity of demand for schmoos for a

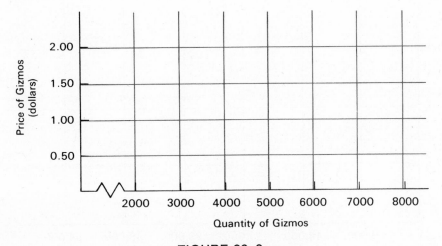

FIGURE 22-1

THE DEMAND FOR SCHMOOS

TABLE 22–1

The Demand for Schmoos		The Demand for Gizmos	
Price (dollars)	Quantity	Price (dollars)	Quantity
60	200	2.00	2000
50	240	1.25	3200
48	250	1.00	4000
40	300	0.50	8000

FIGURE 22-2

THE DEMAND FOR GIZMOS

change in price from $60 to $50.[2] It is

_____.

c. Use the same data to calculate the elasticity of demand for gizmos for a change in price from $1 to 50 cents. It is

_____.

d. For these changes, which demand curve is more elastic? In fact, if you look more closely at the underlying data for both curves—for example, by computing the total revenue— you will see that for both curves the elasticity of demand is _____.

2. Table 22–2 contains data on possible prices and

the associated quantity of demand for jeans in Collegetown. Plot this demand curve in

Figure 22–3. It is a _____ line.

a. Using the data in Table 22–2, compute the elasticity of demand for each change in price.[3] What general conclusion can you draw about the elasticity of demand along a straight-line demand curve? The elasticity of demand (increases/decreases) as one moves down and to the right along a straight-line demand curve.

b. Use the same data to compute total revenue for each price-quantity pair in Table 22–2. Compare the change in total revenue to the elasticity of demand. What conclusion can you draw about this relationship?

[2]When computing the elasticity of demand, remember to use the average of the two prices or quantities when computing each percentage change. For example, compute the elasticity of demand when the price changes from $60 to $50 as

$$\left[\frac{40}{220}\right] \div \left[\frac{10}{55}\right]$$

[3]Again, remember to use the average of the two prices and quantities. For a change in price from $18 to $15 compute the elasticity of demand as

$$\frac{9000}{31,500} \div \frac{3}{16.50}$$

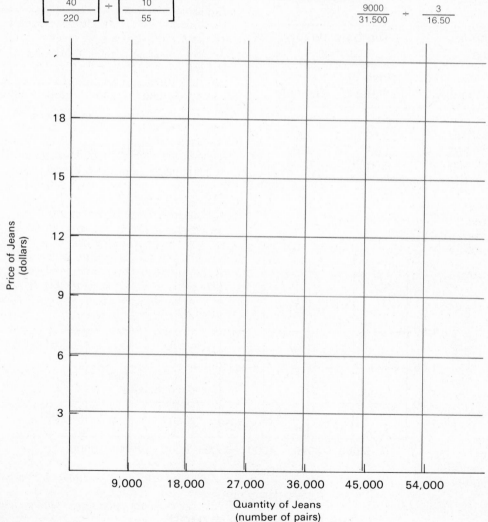

FIGURE 22–3

TABLE 22-2

THE DEMAND FOR JEANS

Price (dollars)	Quantity	Elasticity of Demand	Total Revenue
18	27,000		_____
		_____	
15	36,000		_____
		_____	
12	45,000		_____
		_____	
9	54,000		_____

SELF-TESTS FOR UNDERSTANDING

Test A

Circle the correct answer.

1. Which of the following would be an exception to the "law" of demand?
   a. Increased advertising expenditures for Fords result in increased sales.
   b. An increase in the price of a particular 35 mm camera, with no change in the camera itself, results in increased sales.
   c. Sales of Sears refrigerators decline when Wards reduces the price on its refrigerators.
   d. Total sales receipts increase when price increases.
2. Which of the following will *not* lead to a shift in the demand curve for Chevrolets?
   a. A limit on the number of Japanese cars that can be imported into the United States.
   b. A reduction in the price of Fords.
   c. An increase in the price of Chevrolets.
   d. A dramatic decline in the price of gasoline.
3. Which of the following will lead to a movement along the demand curve for Fords?
   a. A limit on the number of Japanese cars that can be imported into the United States.
   b. A reduction in the price of Fords.
   c. An increase in the price of Chevrolets.
   d. A dramatic decline in the price of gasoline.
4. If a 20 percent decrease in the price of long distance phone calls lead to a 35 percent increase in the quantity of calls demanded, we can conclude that the demand for phone calls is
   a. elastic.
   b. inelastic.
   c. unit elastic.

5. From the data given above what would happen to total revenue following a 20 percent decrease in the price of long distance phone calls? It would
   a. increase.
   b. decrease.
   c. remain the same.
6. If a 10 percent increase in price leads to a 12 percent decline in the quantity demanded, the price elasticity of demand is
   a. $(10 \div 12) = .83$.
   b. $(12 \div 10) = 1.2$.
   c. $(12 - 10) = 2$.
   d. $(12 + 10) = 22$.
7. Which one of the following pairs is *not* a likely example of substitutes?
   a. A flight from New York to Chicago on United and the same trip on American.
   b. Stereo tuner-amplifiers and pairs of speakers.
   c. Calculators made by Texas Instruments and calculators made by Hewlett-Packard.
   d. Gasoline from the Texaco station and gasoline from the Mobil station across the street.
8. If the cross elasticity of demand between two goods is positive, we would conclude that the two goods are
   a. substitutes.
   b. complements.
   c. necessities.
   d. both likely to have inelastic demand curves.
9. If following an increase in the price of schmoos, the quantity demanded of gizmos declined, we would conclude that
   a. the demand for gizmos is inelastic.
   b. gizmos and schmoos are substitutes.
   c. gizmos and schmoos are complements.
   d. schmoos are likely to be a luxury good.
10. If skis and boots are complements, then which one of the following statements is false?
    a. A reduction in the price of skis is likely to increase the sales of boots.
    b. Sales revenue of ski manufacturers will increase following a reduction in the price of ski boots.
    c. An increase in the price of boots is likely to reduce the sales of skis.
    d. The cross elasticity of demand between skis and boots is likely to be positive.

Test B

Circle T or F for True or False as appropriate.

1. The "law" of demand states that for most commodities people will buy more at a lower price.   T F

2. If each individual's demand for a particular commodity is independent of the actions of others, then an aggregate demand curve for all individuals can be derived by horizontal summation of individual demand curves.   T F

3. The price elasticity of demand is defined as the change in quantity divided by the change in price.   T F

4. The elasticity of demand will be the same at all points along a straight-line demand curve.   T F

5. A vertical demand curve would have a price elasticity of zero.   T F

6. A demand curve is elastic if, following a decrease in price, the quantity demanded increases.   T F

7. If the demand for airplane travel is elastic, then a reduction in the price of airline tickets will increase total expenditures on airplane trips.   T F

8. If two goods are substitutes, then an increase in the price of one good is likely to reduce the demand for the other good.   T F

9. The cross elasticity of demand between complements is normally negative.   T F

10. If sales of Whoppers at Burger King increase following an increase in the price of Big Macs at McDonald's, we can conclude that Whoppers and Big Macs are complements.   T F

Appendix:

BASIC EXERCISES

Completing these exercises should help underscore the necessity and difficulty of distinguishing between a demand curve and observations on price and quantity that are determined by the intersection of demand and supply curves.

1. Consider the data on cheese consumption and prices for the period 1970 to 1980 in Table 22–3. Use a piece of graph paper to plot these data. What does this tell you about the demand for cheese? Why?

TABLE 22–3

Year	Quantity (millions of pounds)	Price (dollars per pound)
1970	2356	0.65
1971	2490	0.67
1972	2757	0.71
1973	2891	0.84
1974	3077	0.97
1975	3017	1.04
1976	3423	1.16
1977	3577	1.19
1978	3794	1.30
1979	3888	1.41
1980	4149	1.56

Source: Computed from *Survey of Current Business*, various issues.

2. Assume that the demand for tomatoes depends upon consumer income and price as follows:

$$Q^D = -1600 + 3Y - 50P$$

where Q^D = quantity demanded (millions of pounds), Y = consumer income (billions of 1982 dollars), and P = price (cents per pound, 1982 prices).

Supply is assumed to be determined as follows:

$$Q^S = 2400 + 10P$$

where Q^S = quantity supplied (millions of pounds).

a. Compute the equilibrium price and quantity for 1984, 1985, and 1986 given that consumer income was as follows:

Year	Consumer Income
1988	$2,370.6
1989	2,528.0
1990	2,603.7

Plot these price–quantity pairs for each year on a two variable diagram. Are these points a good estimate of the demand curve? Why? Why not?

b. Assume now that the supply curve for tomatoes shifts each year in response to yield-enhancing technical advances. To capture these technical advances, we need a new supply curve for each year as follows:

1988	$Q^S = 2400 + 10P$
1989	$Q^S = 2800 + 10P$
1990	$Q^S = 3200 + 10P$

Compute and plot equilibrium price and quantity for each year. (Remember to include the change in consumer income in the demand curve.) Are these points a good estimate of the demand curve? Why? Why not?

SUPPLEMENTARY EXERCISE

Completing this exercise will give you practice in computing elasticities of individual and market demand curves.

Angela's annual demand for apples is given by

$$Q = 300 - 10P$$

where Q = quantity of apples, and P = price of apples (20 cents = 20). Dan's demand curve is also given by

$$Q = 300 - 10P$$

1. Write down an expression for the market demand curve on the assumption that Angela and Dan constitute the total market.
2. How does the slope of the market demand curve compare with the slope of the individual demand curves? Is it flatter, steeper, or the same?
3. Calculate the price elasticity of demand for the individual and the market demand curves when the price of apples changes from 20 to 25 cents. How does the price elasticity of demand of the market demand curve compare with the price elasticity of the individual demand curves? Is it larger, smaller, or equal?
4. Let Dan's demand be given by:
   $Q = 300 - 8P$. Reanswer a, b, and c.

23

Input Decisions and Production Costs

IMPORTANT TERMS AND CONCEPTS

Total physical product
Average physical product (APP)
Marginal physical product (MPP)
Marginal revenue product (MRP)
"Law" of diminishing marginal returns
Total cost curve
Average cost curve
Marginal cost curve
Fixed cost
Variable cost

Increasing (decreasing) average cost
Sunk cost
Short and long runs
Substitutability of inputs
Cost minimization
Rule for optimal input use
Production function
Economies of scale
 (increasing returns to scale)
Constant returns to scale
Decreasing returns to scale
Historical versus analytical cost relationships

CHAPTER REVIEW

In this chapter we will again make extensive use of the concept of *marginal analysis* as a guide to optimal decision making. In Chapter 21 we saw that the optimal purchase rule for a consumer implied that he or she should purchase additional units of a commodity until marginal utility equals the price of the commodity. In this chapter we will see how marginal analysis can help a firm make optimal decisions about the use of production inputs and how these decisions in turn can be used to derive cost curves.

This chapter introduces a potentially bewildering array of curves and concepts, for example, marginal physical product, marginal revenue product, fixed costs, variable costs, long run, and short run. All these curves and concepts relate to each other and underlie optimal firm decisions. Spending time now to get these relationships clear will save you time in later chapters and the night before the exam.

(1) In deciding whether to use an additional unit of some input, say, hiring more workers, a firm should look at the contribution of the additional workers to both total revenue and total cost. If the increase in revenue is greater than the increase in cost, then profits will (increase/decrease). The increase in revenue comes from producing and selling additional units of output. Economists call the amount of additional output from the use of one more unit of input the marginal (physical/revenue) product of the input. For a firm selling its output at a constant price, the increase in revenue comes from multiplying the additional output by the price at which it

can be sold. Economists call this the marginal _____ product.

(2) Common sense tells us that a profit-maximizing firm should use additional units of any input if the addition to total revenue exceeds the addition to total cost. Another way of saying the same thing is that the firm should consider using more of an input as long as the marginal (physical/revenue) product exceeds the

_____ of the input. One has clearly gone too far if additions to revenue are less than additions to cost. Thus a profit-maximizing firm should expand the use of any factor until the marginal revenue product equals the price of the input. (This condition is completely analogous to the marginal rule given in Chapter 21.)

If the price of an input is constant, firms will use more and more units of this input until the marginal revenue product falls to a point where it is equal to the input price. As a result, firms will usually expand the use of any input past any region of increasing marginal returns and into the region of decreasing returns to the one input.

We have talked about the optimal use of one input. Our rule still holds true for more than one input. The idea is to adjust the combination of inputs until the ratio of input prices equals the ratio of marginal physical products. In symbols, assuming the two inputs are A and B, we have

$$\frac{P_A}{P_B} = \frac{MPP_A}{MPP_B}$$

as the condition for an optimal input combination. This expression can be rewritten by multiplying both sides of the equation by P_B and dividing both sides by MPP_A.

$$\frac{P_A}{MPP_A} = \frac{P_B}{MPP_B}$$

These new ratios can be interpreted as the price of changes in output from the changes in the use of inputs A and B. For example, an increase in the use of input A by one unit will cost P_A and will increase output by MPP_A. Thus the ratio P_A/MPP_A is the cost of changing output by changing the use of input A.

If P_A/P_B exceeds MPP_A/MPP_B, then P_A/MPP_A exceeds P_B/MPP_B. In this case, reducing the use of input A and increasing the use of input B saves more, P_A/MPP_A, than it costs P_B/MPP_A. It makes obvious sense to adjust the use of inputs in this way, and we can conclude that the original combination was not optimal. Making this adjustment will tend to increase MPP_A and reduce MPP_B, driving both ratios toward equality, our condition for optimal input combination and the point at which further adjustments are not profitable. (The appendix to this chapter uses geometry to illustrate this case.)

What about our original result that one should adjust the use of a single input until marginal revenue product equals the price of the input? Is it still valid when there is more than one input? Yes. Remember that for input A, $MRP_A = MPP_A \cdot P_{OUTPUT}$. Following our earlier rule we would adjust the use of input A until $P_A = MRP_A$ or until $P_A = MPP_A \cdot P_{OUTPUT}$. The use of input B should be adjusted until $P_B = MPP_B \cdot P_{OUTPUT}$. Dividing these last two expressions gives us the result discussed above and on page 497 of the text.

If the price of an input changes, it is natural to expect the firm's optimal input combination to change.

(3) Specifically, it is natural to expect that a profit-maximizing firm will (reduce/increase) the use of any factor whose price has risen. Changing the quantity of one input will typically affect the marginal physical product of other inputs. As a result, a firm will want to rethink its use of all inputs following a change in price of any one input. It is quite likely that following an increase in the price of one input, a profit-maximizing firm will decide

to use relatively (less/more) of the more expensive input and relatively _____ of the inputs with unchanged prices.

The relationship between inputs and outputs has been formalized by economists into something that measures the maximum amount of output that can be produced from any specified combination of inputs

(4) given current technology, or, for short, the _____ function. Information about the marginal physical product for a single factor comes from the production function. (The appendix to this chapter discusses one geometrical representation of such a function through the use of a contour-line diagram.) The concept of a production function is also useful in separating what happens if one increases the use of all factors or of just one factor. If all inputs are increased by the same percentage amount, then the percentage increase in output is used to indicate the degree of *economies of scale*. If output increases by more than the common percentage increase in all inputs, the production function exhibits

_____ returns to scale. If output increases by less, there are

_____ returns to scale, and if output increases by the same percentage,

we would say that returns to scale are _____.

Information from the production function can be used to construct *cost curves* for a firm. When talking about costs economists find it important to make a distinction between various periods of time. Over a very short time horizon, previous commitments may limit a firm's ability to adjust all inputs. These commitments often imply that at least one input is predetermined and cannot be adjusted immediately. Imagine a farmer with a five-year lease on a particular parcel of land and unable to rent additional land. The interval of

(5) time over which none of a firm's fixed commitments can be adjusted is called the (long/short) run.

The total cost of producing any given level of output in the short run can be computed with the help of the production function, input prices and any relevant opportunity costs. We will be interested only in minimum total costs for any level of output. We can use what we know about optimal factor use to help figure out minimum total cost. As an example, assume that production requires two inputs, one of which is fixed in the short run. To compute total cost, the firm must first use the production function to see what amount of the variable input is necessary to produce different levels of output. Then it can compute total cost for each level of output by multiplying the quantity of the fixed input and the optimal quantity of the variable input by their prices remembering relevant opportunity costs, and adding the results. After computing total cost the

(6) firm can compute average cost by dividing total cost by the associated level of _____.
The firm can also compute marginal cost by examining the way (average/total) cost changes when output changes. We will make extensive use of the marginal cost curve in Chapter 24 when we examine supply curves.

(7)   The period of time over which a firm can adjust all its fixed commitments is called the _____

_____. Long-run cost curves can be derived by either of two equivalent methods. One procedure would first derive short-run cost curves for each possible amount of the fixed input. One would then deter-

mine the long-run cost curve by joining the _____ segments of the short-run cost curves. An alternative and equivalent method would treat both factors as variable. One would first use the production function and input prices to determine the optimal level of both inputs to produce any given level of output. Total cost for each level of output is computed from input prices and from optimal input levels by multiplication and addition. Average and marginal cost are then easily computed.

     Since in the long run all factors can be changed, the shape of the long-run average cost curve is related to economies of scale. Constant returns to scale imply that a doubling of output requires twice as much of all

(8)   inputs. In this case, total costs also double and average cost (falls/is unchanged/rises). Increasing returns to scale mean that twice the output can be produced with (more/less) than twice the inputs and average cost

will (fall/rise). With decreasing returns to scale, twice the output requires _____

than twice the inputs and average cost _____.

     We've covered a lot of ground and a lot of curves. You may want to take a deep breath before a quick review. The production function contains the basic technical information about inputs and output. From this information one can derive total physical product and marginal physical product for a single input. Knowing the price of output will let us compute marginal revenue product. Comparing marginal revenue product with input prices will determine the optimal input quantities. Optimal input quantitites, in turn, determine (minimum) total cost for alternative levels of output. Once we know total cost, we can easily compute average and marginal cost. In the short run there may be fixed costs. In the long run all inputs, and hence all costs, are variable. In either run the same optimizing principles apply.

DEFINITION QUIZ

Choose the letter that is the most appropriate definition for each of the following terms.

1. _____ Total physical product

2. _____ Average physical product

3. _____ Marginal physical product

4. _____ "Law" of diminishing marginal returns

5. _____ Total cost curve

6. _____ Average cost curve

7. _____ Marginal cost curve

8. _____ Fixed costs

9. _____ Variable costs

10. _____ Sunk cost

11. _____ Short run

12. _____ Long run

13. _____ Production function

14. _____ Economies of scale

15. _____ Returns to scale

16. _____ Marginal revenue product

a. Graph depicting cost per unit, at each level of output.
b. Observation that marginal physical product eventually declines.
c. Cost of indivisible inputs necessary for any production.
d. Savings acquired through increases in quantities produced.
e. Period of time long enough for all of a firm's commitments to end.
f. Dollar value of output produced by an extra unit of input.
g. Graph of output generated by various quantities of one input, holding all inputs factors fixed.
h. Total output divided by total quantity of input.
i. Cost to which a firm is precommitted.
j. Maximum amount of product obtainable from any specified combination of inputs, given the current state of knowledge.
k. Increase in output that results from an extra unit increase in a given input, holding other inputs constant.
l. Graph depicting the amount a firm must spend, including opportunity costs, to produce each possible quantity of output.
m. Graph depicting increase in firm's total cost from producing an additional unit of output.
n. Period of time during which some, but not all, of a firm's commitments will have ended.
o. Costs that change as the level of production changes.
p. Relation of percentage change in output to proportionate change in all inputs.
q. Change in profits resulting from a change in price.

BASIC EXERCISE

These questions review the concept of a production function and optimal input decisions.

Megan and Jamie have invested in Greenacre Farms to grow cornbeans. Since they both work in the city, they will need to hire workers for the farm. Table 23–1 has data on various input combinations and the resulting output of cornbeans.

1. Use the data in Table 23–1 to draw, on Figure 23–1, the relationship between total output and labor input for 100 acres of land. What is the region of increasing marginal returns?

   _____

   What is the region of decreasing marginal returns?

   _____

   What is the region of negative marginal returns?

   _____

2. Use Figure 23–1 to draw the relationship between total output and labor input, assuming the use of 200 acres of land. Identify the regions of increasing, decreasing, and negative returns.

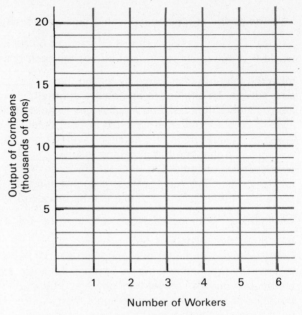

FIGURE 23–1

TOTAL OUTPUT OF CORNBEANS

TABLE 23–1

TOTAL OUTPUT OF CORNBEANS
(thousands of tons)

Number of Workers

		1	2	3	4	5	6
Acres	100	1	4	6	7	6	4
of	200	2	6	9.5	12	13	12
Land	300	3	7.5	11	14	16	17

Marginal Physical Product of Labor

		1	2	3	4	5	6
Acres	100	—	—	—	—	—	—
of	200	—	—	—	—	—	—
Land	300	—	—	—	—	—	—

Marginal Revenue Product of Labor

		1	2	3	4	5	6
Acres							
of							
Land	200	—	—	—	—	—	—

Do the same assuming the use of 300 acres of land. How does the output–labor curve shift when more land is used?

3. Fill in the middle part of Table 23–1 by computing the marginal physical product of each worker. Check to see that the regions of increasing, diminishing, and negative returns that you identified above correspond to information about the marginal physical product of labor. (You might also check to see that your entries in the middle of Table 23–1 equal the slopes of the total product curves you drew in Figure 23–1.)

4. Your answers to Questions 1, 2, and 3 should confirm that the production function for cornbeans eventually shows decreasing returns to labor for all three potential farm sizes. (What about returns to the increased use of land for a fixed amount of labor?)

5. Now consider the following pairs of inputs (acres, workers) and indicate for each whether economies of scale are increasing, decreasing, or constant.

   　　　　　　　　　　　　　ECONOMIES OF SCALE

   (100, 1) to (200, 2)　　_____

   (100, 2) to (200, 4)　　_____

   (100, 3) to (200, 6)　　_____

   (200, 2) to (300, 3)　　_____

   (200, 4) to (300, 6)　　_____

6. Assume that cornbeans can be sold for $5 a ton. Greenacre Farms has 200 acres of land. Calculate the marginal revenue product of labor for 200 acres of land in the bottom part of Table 23–1. Plot the marginal revenue product in Figure 23–2. Hired help costs $8000. Draw a horizontal line in Figure 23–2 at $8000 to indicate the price of labor. How many workers should

Megan and Jamie hire? _____.
At the level of labor input you just determined, what is the difference between the proceeds from selling cornbeans (output) and labor costs?

_____. (Check to see that your labor input choice maximizes this difference by considering the use of one more or one less worker.)

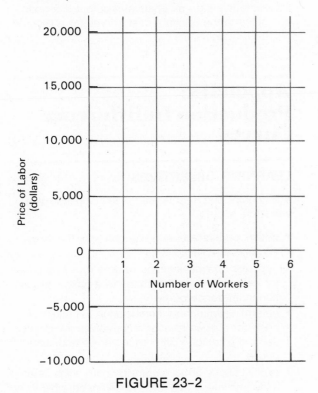

FIGURE 23–2

MARGINAL REVENUE PRODUCT

SELF-TESTS FOR UNDERSTANDING

Test A

Circle the correct answer.

1. The "law" of diminishing marginal returns
   a. says that eventually the marginal physical product of any input must become negative.
   b. applies to only a simultaneous increase in all inputs.
   c. can only be true for a production function with decreasing returns to scale.
   d. refers to what happens to output as only one factor is increased, all other inputs being held constant.

2. Consider the following data on workers and output.

Workers	1	2	3	4	5
Output	10	25	35	42	40

Where do diminishing marginal returns to workers begin to set in?
   a. After the first worker.
   b. After the second worker.
   c. After the third worker.
   d. After the fourth worker.

3. For a firm that sells output at a fixed price, the marginal revenue product of additional units of some input is found by
   a. dividing the marginal physical product by the input price.
   b. multiplying the marginal physical product by the sales price of the output.
   c. multiplying the marginal physical product by the input price.
   d. dividing the price of the output by the price of the input.

4. The rule for optimal input use implies that a firm should use additional units of an input until
   a. average cost equals the price of the input.
   b. marginal physical product is maximized.
   c. marginal revenue product equals the price of the input.
   d. increasing returns to scale are exhausted.

5. The term *economies of scale*
   a. refers to the change over time in average cost as firms grow larger.
   b. is measured by dividing the percentage change in the marginal revenue product by the percentage change of the associated input.
   c. refers to the increase in output when only one input is increased.
   d. refers to what happens to total output following a simultaneous and equal percentage increase in all inputs.

6. If all inputs are doubled and output more than doubles, one would say that the production relationship
   a. shows decreasing returns to scale.
   b. shows constant returns to scale.
   c. shows increasing returns to scale.
   d. violates the "law" of diminishing returns.

7. Assume that on a small farm with 10 workers, the hiring of an 11th worker actually lowers total output. Which of the following statements is not necessarily true?
    a. The marginal physical product of the last worker is negative.
    b. The marginal revenue product of the last worker is negative.
    c. A profit-maximizing firm would never hire the 11th worker.
    d. The production function shows decreasing returns to scale.

8. The optimal choice of input combinations
    a. is a purely technological decision, unaffected by input prices, and better left to engineers than economists.
    b. can be determined by looking at information on the marginal revenue product and the prices of various inputs.
    c. will always be the same in both the short and long run.
    d. is likely to include more of an input if its price rises and if other input prices are unchanged.

9. A change in which of the following will *not* shift the short-run average cost curve?
    a. The price of output.
    b. The price of inputs.
    c. The quantity of fixed factors.
    d. The marginal physical product of variable inputs.

10. In the long run,
    a. inputs are likely to be less substitutable than in the short run.
    b. all production functions will exhibit constant returns to scale.
    c. a firm is assumed to be able to make adjustments in all its fixed commitments.
    d. average cost must decline.

Test B

Circle T or F for True or False as appropriate.

1. The "law" of diminishing returns says that economies of scale can never be increasing.   T F

2. The marginal physical product of an input refers to the increase in output associated with an additional unit of that input when all other inputs are held constant.   T F

3. The marginal revenue product measures the total revenue that a firm will have at different use levels of a particular input.   T F

4. If a production function shows increasing returns to scale from the additional use of all

inputs, it violates the "law" of diminishing returns.   T F

5. If a production function shows decreasing returns to scale, it is likely that long-run average costs will be increasing.   T F

6. The short run is defined as any time less than six months.   T F

7. The curve of average fixed cost is usually U-shaped.   T F

8. Long-run cost curves will always lie above short-run cost curves.   T F

9. Inputs are likely to be more substitutable in the long run than in the short run.   T F

10. Historical data on costs and output is a good guide to the relevant cost curves for a firm's current decisions.   T F

Appendix: Production Indifference Curves

LEARNING OBJECTIVES

After completing the material in this appendix you should be able to:

• define, understand, and use correctly the terms and concepts listed below.
• describe how diminishing returns to a single factor help determine the shape of a typical production indifference curve.
• determine what input combination will minimize costs for a given level of output given information about production indifference curves and input prices.
• explain how a firm's expansion path helps determine (minimum) total cost for every possible level of output.
• use a production indifference curve to explain how a change in the price of one productive factor can affect the least cost combination of inputs.

IMPORTANT TERMS AND CONCEPTS

Production indifference curve
Budget line
Expansion path
Point of tangency between the budget line and the corresponding production indifference curve

APPENDIX REVIEW

A set of *production indifference curves*, or isoquants, is a geometrical device that can be used to represent a production function involving two inputs and one output. The horizontal and vertical axes are used to measure quantities of each input. A line connecting all input combinations capable of producing the same

(1) amount of output is called the _____ _____ curve. Each separate curve represents a particular level of output. Higher curves will mean (more/less) output.

(2) Production indifference curves will usually have a (negative/positive) slope and (will/will not) bow in

towards the origin. This last property follows from the "law" of _____ _____ returns. Like indifference curves for utility functions, production indifference curves do not cross.

Production indifference curves will tell a firm what alternative combinations of inputs can be used to produce the same amount of output. However, an optimizing firm should not be indifferent between these alternatives. In order to make an optimal decision, the firm will need to know the price of each input. From this information the firm can construct a budget line showing various combinations of inputs that can be purchased for the same total cost. (This budget line is analogous to the consumer's budget line of Chapter

(3) 21.) The budget line is a (curved/straight) line. The slope of the budget line is given by the ratio of factor prices. The price of the factor measured on the (horizontal/vertical) axis goes on the top of the ratio. The intercept on each axis comes from dividing the total budget by the price of factor measured on that axis.

To minimize cost for a given level of output, the firm chooses that combination of inputs lying on the

(4) (highest/lowest) budget line consistent with the given level of output. For smooth and convex production indifference curves, one chooses an input combination such that a budget line is just tangent to the relevant production indifference curve. A change in the price of either input will shift the budget line and result in a new optimal input combination.

The procedure we have just described will determine the optimal input combination to minimize cost for a given output target. Using the same procedure to find the lowest cost input combination for different levels

(5) of output defines the firm's _____ path. It also allows us to compute total cost for any level of output. At this point, division and subtraction will allow us to compute average and marginal cost. Which level of output maximizes profits is another question, one that will be addressed in Chapter 24.

Is the solution to the question of optimal input in this appendix consistent with the discussion on page 497 of the text about the ratio of input prices and marginal physical products? Yes. Although it may not be immediately obvious, the slope of the production indifference curve is equal to the ratio of marginal physical products. If we choose an input combination such that the slope of the production indifference curve equals the slope of the budget line, we will set the ratio of marginal products equal to the ratio of input prices. As described in the Chapter Review, this result also insures that MRP = P for each input.

DEFINITION QUIZ

Choose the letter that is the most appropriate definition for each of the following terms.

1. _____ Production indifference curve

2. _____ Budget line

3. _____ Expansion path

a. Locus of firm's cost-minimizing input levels for different output levels.
b. Graph depicting all combinations of output quantities which produce a given level of utility.
c. Graph depicting all combinations of input quantities that yield a given level of output.
d. Representation of equally costly input combinations.

BASIC EXERCISE

Figure 23–3 shows a production indifference curve for producing 6000 tons of cornbeans. This curve is derived from data given in Table 23–1.

1. (Read all of this question before answering.) If land can be rented at $65 an acre a year and if labor costs work out to $8000 a worker, what is the least cost combination for producing 6000 tons of cornbeans? Restrict your answer to the

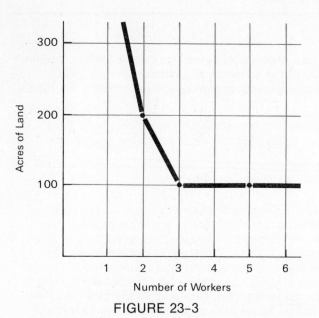

FIGURE 23-3

PRODUCTION INDIFFERENCE CURVE

dots in Figure 23–3 that correspond to data from

Table 23–1. _____ acres and

_____ workers.

If land rents for $125 a year and labor costs $8000 a worker, what is the least cost input combination for producing 6000 tons of

cornbeans? _____ acres and

_____ workers.

Remember that the ratio of input prices determines the slope of the budget line. For a given set of input prices draw the budget lines that pass through each of the three input combinations. Remember that these lines should be parallel. For a given set of input prices, the least cost combination is given by the lowest budget line. Can you explain why?

2. From your answer to the previous question you know that if the cost of using land is relatively low, the least cost input combination will use more land with a smaller number of workers. You also know that if the cost of using land rises enough, an optimizing farmer would be induced to use less land and more workers. What is the rental price of land that just tips the balance away from the input combination of 200 acres and 2 workers to the combination of 100 acres

and 3 workers? $_____.

You should be able to answer this question by "rotating" a budget line around the outside of

the production indifference curve. For given input prices, find the one budget line that just touches, or is tangent to, the production indifference curve. This point will show the lowest cost-input combination. As one input price changes, the slope of the budget line will change and the tangency point will move as the lowest cost-budget line rotates around the outside of the production indifference curve. If the price of land is low, the input combination of 200 acres and 2 workers will be on the lowest budget line. As the price of land rises, the slope of the budget line becomes flatter, and there will come a point where suddenly the input combination of 100 acres and 3 workers is on the lowest budget line.

SELF-TESTS FOR UNDERSTANDING

Test A

Circle the correct answer.

1. Which of the following properties is *not* true of production indifference curves?
   a. They have a negative slope.
   b. Their slope is always equal to the ratio of input prices.
   c. They bow in towards the origin because of the "law" of diminishing returns.
   d. Each curve shows different input levels consistent with the same output.
2. The budget line relevant for choosing the optimal amount of two inputs
   a. has a positive slope, unlike the budget line for the problem of consumer choice.
   b. will shift in a parallel fashion in response to an increase in the price of one input.
   c. is a straight line with a negative slope reflecting relative input prices.
   d. will have a different slope following an equal percentage change in the price of all inputs.
3. Which one of the following will not occur after a reduction in the price of one input?
   a. The budget line will shift in such a way that a fixed production budget can now buy more of the cheaper input.
   b. The optimal input combination for a given level of output is likely to involve the use of more of the cheaper input.
   c. The minimum total cost for producing a given level of output will fall.
   d. Each production indifference curve will show a parallel shift.

Test B

Circle T or F for True or False as appropriate.

1. Production indifference curves have a positive slope because higher output usually requires more of both inputs. **T F**

2. Typically a production indifference curve will bow in at the middle because of the "law" of diminishing returns. **T F**

3. A firm minimizes cost for any level of output by choosing the input combination given by the tangency of the budget line to the production indifference curve. **T F**

4. An increase in the price of either input will make the budget line steeper. **T F**

5. If production requires the use of two inputs, x_1 and x_2 a change in the price of input x_1 will never affect the optimal use of input x_2. **T F**

6. A change in the price of output will change the cost-minimizing input combination for a given level of output. **T F**

7. For given input prices, the tangencies of production indifference curves with alternative budget lines trace out a firm's expansion path. **T F**

SUPPLEMENTARY EXERCISE

Assume that the production of widgets (W) requires labor (L) and machines (M) and can be represented by the production function*

$$W = L^{\frac{1}{2}} M^{\frac{1}{2}}$$

*This particular mathematical representation of a production function is called the Cobb-Douglas production function. Cobb was a mathematician. Douglas was President of the American Economic Association and United States Senator from Illinois from 1948 to 1966. You might enjoy reading the comments by Albert Rees and Paul Samuelson about Douglas and his work in the *Journal of Political Economy*, October 1979, Part 1.

1. Draw a production indifference curve for the production of 500,000 widgets.

2. L measures labor hours and M measures machine hours. In the long run, both machines and labor hours are variable. If machine hours cost $48 and labor hours cost $12, what is the cost-minimizing number of labor and machine hours to produce 500,000 widgets? (Whether it is profitable to produce 500,000 widgets depends upon the price of widgets.)

3. Assume now that the firm has 125 machines capable of supplying 250,000 machine hours.
   a. Draw a picture of total output as a function of the number of labor hours.
   b. Use the production function to derive an expression for the marginal physical product of labor conditional on the 250,000 machine hours. Draw a picture of this function. What, if any, is the connection between your picture of total output and the marginal physical product?
   c. Divide your picture of the marginal physical product into regions of increasing, decreasing, and negative marginal returns to labor. (Note: Not all areas need exist.)
   d. If the price of widgets is $50 and the price of labor is $12 per hour, what is the optimal number of labor hours that the firm should use? How many widgets will the firm produce?

4. Graph the expansion path for this production function on the assumption that labor hours cost $12 and machine hours cost $48.

5. Are returns to scale in the production of widgets constant, increasing, or decreasing?

24

Output–Price Decisions: The Importance of Marginal Analysis

LEARNING OBJECTIVES

After completing the material in this chapter you should be able to:

- define, understand, and use correctly the terms and concepts listed below.
- explain why a firm can make a decision on output *or* price, but not usually on both.
- calculate average and marginal cost from data on total cost.
- explain why the demand curve is the curve of average revenue.
- calculate total and marginal revenue from data on the demand curve.
- use data on costs and revenues to compute the level of output that maximizes profits.
- explain why the point of maximum profit cannot be associated with a positive or negative marginal profit.
- explain why comparing marginal revenue and marginal cost is equivalent to looking at marginal profit.

- explain how and why an economist's definition of profit differs from that of an accountant.
- explain why a change in fixed costs will not affect marginal cost.
- explain how selling at a price above marginal cost can increase profits even if the price is below average cost.

IMPORTANT TERMS AND CONCEPTS

Profit maximization
Satisficing
Total profit
Economic profit
Total revenue and cost
Average revenue and cost
Marginal revenue and cost
Fixed cost
Marginal analysis
Marginal profit

CHAPTER REVIEW

This is the second consecutive chapter to make extensive use of *marginal analysis*, one of the most important tools an economist has. You have already used marginal analysis in deriving a consumer's optimal purchase rule and a firm's optimal use of inputs. In this chapter the concept is used to help decide how much output a firm should produce in order to maximize its profits.

While marginal analysis is a powerful tool for business decision making, it is applicable in many nonbusiness situations as well. For example, how much should the government spend to clean up the environment? Or a related question: To clean up our lakes and rivers, should the government require all industries and towns to reduce their discharges by an equal percentage or is there a more efficient alternative? As discussed in Chapter 34 marginal analysis can help answer these and similar questions.

You may already have had more experience with the concept of marginal analysis than you realize. Have you ever had to pay federal income taxes? If so, you might dig out your records and make two calcula-

(1) tions. Your total taxes divided by your total income would be your (average/marginal) tax rate. Now assume that you had $100 more income. Figure out how much more taxes you would have owed. This increase in taxes divided by the $100 additional income would be your (average/marginal) tax rate.

Your grade point average is another example of the distinction between marginal and average. If you want to raise your overall GPA, what sorts of grades do you need this semester (or quarter)? The grades you earn this semester are the marginal contribution to your overall grade average. Similarly, a baseball player's daily batting record is a marginal measure when compared with his season's batting average.

In whatever context, marginal analysis focuses attention on the effect of changes. For business output decisions, marginal analysis looks at the effect on costs, revenues, and profits as output changes. The

(2) change in total cost from changing output by one unit is called _____ cost. The

change in total revenue from producing and selling one more unit is _____

revenue. Marginal profit is the change in total _____ as output expands by one

unit. Because profits equal revenue minus costs, marginal profit equals marginal _____

minus marginal _____.

(3) Economists usually assume that business firms are interested in maximizing (average/marginal/total) profit. This assumption need not be true for all firms, but economists have found that models based on this assumption provide useful insights into actual events. (You might want to refer back to the discussion in Chapter 1 about the role of abstraction in theory.) Economists are interested in marginal profit not as an end in itself, but because marginal profit is an extremely useful guide to the maximizing of total profit.

It should be common sense that any firm that is interested in maximizing profit will want to expand output as long as the increase in total revenue is greater than the increase in total costs. Rather than looking at total revenue and total cost, one could just as easily look at the changes in revenue and cost as output changes. An increase in output will add to profits if the change in revenue is greater than the change in costs. An economist might make the same point by saying that an increase in output will add to total profits if

(4) (marginal/average) revenue exceeds (marginal/average) cost. We could also say that an increase in output will add to total profits as long as marginal profits are (positive/zero/negative). Total profits will stop rising

when marginal profits fail to _____, that is, when marginal revenue _____ marginal costs.

As discussed in Chapter 23, it is often convenient to divide a firm's costs into two categories: *fixed* and

(5) *variable* costs. Even if output is zero a firm may have to meet certain costs. These are _____ costs. Other costs will vary directly with the level of output, usually rising as output increases. These are

_____ costs. Total cost is the sum of fixed and variable costs. Average cost reflects both fixed and variable costs because it is the average of total costs. Marginal cost measures the

change in total costs and thus reflects only _____ costs. If fixed costs increase and variable costs are unchanged, then total and average costs for each level of output will increase and marginal cost (will/will not) change. Total profits are maximized at the level of output where marginal revenue equals marginal cost. An increase in fixed costs does not change marginal revenue or, as we have just seen, marginal cost. Thus the profit maximizing level of output (will/will not) change following an increase in fixed costs.

DEFINITION QUIZ

Choose the letter that is the most appropriate definition for each of the following terms.

1. _____ Satisficing

2. _____ Total profit

3. _____ Economic profit

4. _____ Total revenue

5. _____ Total cost

6. _____ Average revenue

7. _____ Average cost

8. _____ Marginal revenue

9. _____ Marginal cost

10. _____ Marginal profit

11. _____ Profit maximization

a. Net earnings minus firm's opportunity cost of capital.
b. Total revenue divided by quantity of output.
c. Addition to total profit when producing one more unit of output.
d. Amount firm must spend to produce a given quantity of output.
e. Difference between total revenue and total costs.
f. Addition to total cost when producing one more unit of output.
g. Decision-making rule that seeks no more than satisfactory solutions.
h. Total variable cost divided by total output.
i. Level of output where revenue minus cost is greatest.
j. Total cost divided by quantity of output.
k. Price of output times quantity sold.
l. Addition to total revenue when producing one more unit of output.

BASIC EXERCISES

1. This exercise is designed to review the use of marginal revenue and marginal cost as a guide to the maximization of profits.
   a. Table 24–1 below has data on demand for widgets from Wanda's Widget Company as well as data on the costs of production. Use these data to compute marginal cost and marginal revenue. Ignore the columns on total profits and average cost for now.
   b. From the data on marginal cost and revenue that you just calculated, marginal revenue exceeds marginal cost up to what level of output? _____
   c. Restricting yourself to levels of output listed in Table 24–1, what is the profit maximizing level of output? _____ Why?
   d. At the level of output determined in Question c, total profits are _____ (Check to be sure you have maximized total profits by computing total profits at different output levels.)
   e. Use the data from the third and fourth columns of Table 24–1 to plot the demand curve for widgets in Figure 24–1. Now compute average cost from the data in Table 24–1 and plot that in Figure 24–1.

   Still using Figure 24–1, plot the data on marginal revenue and marginal cost from Table 24–1. Where do these two curves intersect? It should be just beyond, but less than 1 unit beyond, the profit-maximizing output level previously identified.
   f. Identify the profit-maximizing level of output on your graph. Draw the rectangle for total revenue and shade it lightly with positively sloped lines. Draw the rectangle for total cost and shade it lightly with negatively sloped lines. This rectangle should overlap part of the rectangle of total revenue. The nonoverlapped portion of the total revenue rectangle is a picture of total _____.
   Maximizing total profit maximizes this total profit rectangle. It (does/does not) maximize the difference between average revenue and average cost. It (does/does not) imply increases in output whenever price (average revenue) exceeds average cost.
   g. Assume now that the fixed costs Wanda must pay have increased by $1,000, that is, every entry for total cost in Table 24–1 is $1,000 higher. Compute marginal cost, now that fixed costs have increased. How does your answer compare with your entries for marginal cost in Table 24–1? (What about average cost?) What is the new profit maximizing level of output? What are total profits?

TABLE 24-1

WANDA'S WIDGET COMPANY

Marginal Revenue	Total Revenue	Demand Price (dollars)	Output	Total Cost (dollars)	Marginal Cost	Average Cost	Total Profits
	_____	3,500	1	2,000		_____	_____
_____	_____	3,400	2	3,900	_____	_____	_____
_____	_____	3,300	3	5,700	_____	_____	_____
_____	_____	3,200	4	7,400	_____	_____	_____
_____	_____	3,100	5	9,000	_____	_____	_____
_____	_____	3,000	6	10,650	_____	_____	_____
_____	_____	2,900	7	12,600	_____	_____	_____
_____	_____	2,800	8	15,200	_____	_____	_____
_____	_____	2,700	9	18,000	_____	_____	_____
_____	_____	2,600	10	21,000		_____	_____

2. The geometry of marginal revenue
   a. Figure 24-2 shows the demand curve for Medalist bicycles. Draw a rectangle for total revenue on the assumption that 100,000 bicycles are sold. Lightly shade this rectangle with horizontal lines.
   b. Assume now that 120,000 bicycles are sold rather than 100,000. Draw a rectangle for total revenue at this higher level of sales. Lightly shade this rectangle with vertical lines. If you have drawn and shaded the rectangles correctly you should have a large cross-hatched rectangle and two smaller rectangles; one long, horizontal rectangle on the top of the cross-hatched rectangle and one thin, vertical rectangle. The thin vertical rectangle represents revenue from additional sales at the new lower price. This rectangle (is/is not) a complete measure of marginal revenue. It measures the receipts of additional sales but neglects the drop in revenue from the reduction in price that is necessary to expand sales in the first place. This reduction in revenue on previous units is

   represented by the _____

rectangle. The geometric representation of marginal revenue is the (vertical/horizontal)

rectangle minus the _____ rectangle.

SELF-TESTS FOR UNDERSTANDING

Test A

Circle the correct answer.

1. Marginal cost equals
   a. total cost divided by total output.
   b. the change in total cost associated with an additional unit of output.
   c. the change in average cost.
   d. the slope of the average cost curve.
2. The demand curve is the curve of
   a. total revenue.
   b. average revenue.
   c. marginal revenue.
   d. variable revenue.

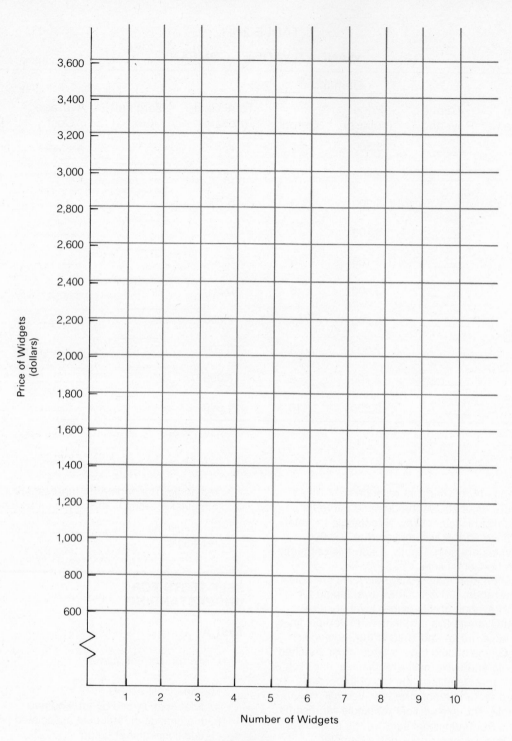

FIGURE 24-1

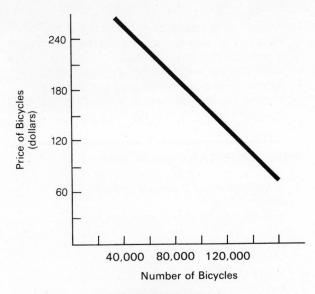

FIGURE 24-2

THE DEMAND FOR MEDALIST BICYCLES

3. Marginal revenue to a firm is
   a. the same as the demand curve for the firm's output.
   b. found by dividing price by output.
   c. found by dividing output by price.
   d. the change in revenue associated with an additional unit of output.

4. When output increases by one unit, marginal revenue will typically be
   a. less than the new lower price.
   b. equal to the new lower price.
   c. greater than the new lower price.

5. Marginal profit equals the difference between
   a. total revenue and total cost.
   b. average revenue and average cost.
   c. marginal revenue and marginal cost.
   d. the demand curve and the marginal cost curve.

6. If a firm has chosen a level of output that maximizes profits, then at the chosen level of output
   a. marginal profits are also maximized.
   b. average cost is minimized.
   c. further increases in output will involve negative marginal profits.
   d. the difference between average revenue and average cost is maximized.

7. Which of the following is consistent with profit maximization?
   a. Produce where marginal cost is minimized.
   b. Produce where average cost is minimized.
   c. Produce where marginal revenue equals marginal cost.
   d. Produce where marginal revenue is maximized.

8. An economist's definition of profit differs from that of an accountant because
   a. the economist is only interested in marginal cost and marginal revenue.
   b. the economist includes the opportunity cost of owner-supplied inputs in total cost.
   c. accountants cannot maximize.
   d. economists cannot add or subtract correctly.

9. An increase in fixed costs will affect which one of the following?
   a. Marginal cost.
   b. Average variable cost.
   c. Average total cost.
   d. Marginal revenue.

10. A decrease in fixed cost will affect which one of the following?
    a. Total profits.
    b. Marginal profits.
    c. The profit-maximizing level of output.
    d. Total revenue at the profit-maximizing level of output.

Test B

Circle T or F for True or False as appropriate.

1. Business firms can decide both the price and quantity of their output. **T F**

2. Firms always make optimal decisions. **T F**

3. The demand curve for a firm's product is also the firm's marginal revenue curve. **T F**

4. Marginal cost is computed by dividing total cost by the quantity of output. **T F**

5. Marginal revenue is simply the price of the last unit sold. **T F**

6. An output decision will generally not be optimal unless it corresponds to a zero marginal profit. **T F**

7. Marginal profit will be zero when marginal revenue equals marginal cost. **T F**

8. Marginal cost should decline continuously as output increases because fixed costs are being spread over a larger number of units. **T F**

9. As long as average revenue exceeds average cost, a firm is making profits and should increase output. **T F**

10. It never pays to sell below average cost. **T F**

Appendix: The Relationships Among Total, Average, and Marginal Data

BASIC EXERCISES

These questions are designed to help you review the relationships between total, average, and marginal measures described in the appendix to Chapter 24.

1. Explain what is wrong with both of the illustrations below.
2. For part (a) of Figure 24–3, assume that the total profit curve is correct and draw an appropriate marginal profit curve.

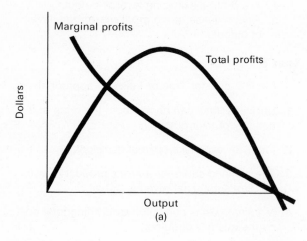

Output
(a)

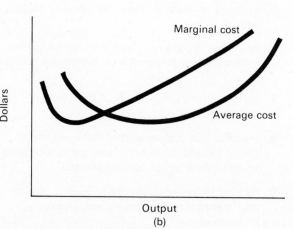

Output
(b)

FIGURE 24–3

3. For part (b) of Figure 24–3, assume that the average cost curve is correct and draw an appropriate marginal cost curve.
4. Verify that the marginal and average cost curves, as well as the marginal and average revenue curves, you drew in Figure 24–1 are consistent with Rule 4 in the Appendix.

SUPPLEMENTARY EXERCISES

1. **A Mathematical Example of Profit Maximization**
   The demand for Acme stereos is

   $$Q = 1200 - 4P,$$

   where Q represents output measured in thousands of sets and P represents price. The total cost of producing stereos is given by

   $$TC = 16,000 + 120Q - .4Q^2 + .002Q^3.$$

   a. What are Acme's fixed costs?
   b. What mathematical expression describes average costs? Marginal costs?
   c. On a piece of graph paper plot average cost and marginal cost. Does your marginal cost curve go through the minimum point of your average cost curve?
   d. Use the information from the demand curve to derive a mathematical expression for marginal revenue.
   e. On the same graph as in c draw the demand curve (the average revenue curve) and the marginal revenue curve.
   f. What does your graph suggest about the profit-maximizing level of output?
   g. Does your answer in f coincide with a direct mathematical solution for Q, where $MR = MC$? It should. (To answer this question you will need to use the expressions you derived for marginal revenue and marginal cost.)
   h. What is Acme's maximum profit?
   i. Shade in the portion of your graph that represents maximum profit.
   j. What if fixed cost were $20,000? How, if at all, do your answers to b, c, d, g, and h change?

2. **Profit Maximization and the Elasticity of Demand**
   A profit-maximizing firm will not try to produce so much output that it is operating in the inelastic portion of its demand curve. Why not? In Chapter 22 we saw that if demand is inelastic, total revenue will

increase following a reduction in output. (The higher price more than compensates for the reduction in output.) Total costs will decline if output is reduced. Thus, profits—revenue minus costs—must increase following a decline in output if a firm is originally operating in the inelastic portion of its demand curve. What are the elastic and inelastic portions of the demand for Acme stereos? (Check to be sure that the profit-maximizing output you determined in Question 1 is not in the inelastic region.)

3. **Profit Maximization and the Production of Widgets**

   Use the production function for widgets from Chapter 23. Assume that the demand for widgets is given by

$$W = 2,500,000 - 25,000P_W$$

where W = widgets and P_W = price of widgets.

a. If labor costs $12 per hour and the machines cost $48 per hour, what is the marginal cost? What is the profit maximizing level of output? What is the market price of widgets?

b. Assume now that the firm owns 100 machines that supply 200,000 machine hours and that the firm can purchase labor at a cost of $12 per hour. Derive an expression for marginal cost and determine the profit maximizing level of output. What is the market price of widgets?

PART
6

THE MARKET SYSTEM: VIRTUES AND VICES

25

The Firm and the Industry Under Perfect Competition

LEARNING OBJECTIVES

After completing the material in this chapter you should be able to:

- define, understand, and use correctly the terms and concepts listed below.
- describe the conditions that distinguish perfect competition from other market structures.
- explain why the study of perfect competition can be profitable even if few industries satisfy the conditions of perfect competition exactly.
- explain why under perfect competition the firm faces a horizontal demand curve while the industry faces a downward-sloping demand curve.
- explain the relation of price, average revenue and marginal revenue as seen by individual firms under perfect competition.
- find the profit-maximizing level of output for a perfectly competitive firm given information on the firm's marginal cost curve and the market price for its output.

- explain why a perfectly competitive firm's short-run supply curve is the portion of its marginal cost curve that is above average variable costs.
- derive an industry's short-run supply curve given information on the supply curves for individual firms.
- use the concept of opportunity cost to reconcile economic and accounting profits.
- explain how freedom of entry and exit imply that in the long run firms operating under perfect competition will earn zero economic profit.
- explain how freedom of entry and exit imply that in the long run firms operating under perfect competition will earn zero economic profit.
- explain why the long-run supply curve for a competitive industry is given by the industry's long-run average cost curve.
- explain how perfect competition implies the efficient production of goods and services.

IMPORTANT TERMS AND CONCEPTS

Market
Perfect competition
Pure monopoly
Monopolistic competition
Oligopoly
Price taker
Horizontal demand curve

Short-run equilibrium
Sunk cost
Variable cost
Supply curve of the firm
Supply curve of the industry
Long-run equilibrium
Opportunity cost
Economic profit

CHAPTER REVIEW

This chapter uses the concepts developed in earlier chapters to study in more detail the supply decisions of firms. While this discussion makes use of these concepts it also adds important material about *market structures*. The decisions of individual firms depend not only upon their production functions and cost curves, but also upon the type of market structure the firm faces. Among other things, different market structures have important implications for demand conditions that firms face. This chapter focuses on the abstraction of the market structure of perfect competition. Later chapters will investigate other market structures — monopolistic competition, oligopoly, and pure monopoly.

Perfect competition is distinguished from other market structures by four conditions

(1) 1. (Few/Many) buyers and sellers.
2. (Differentiated/Identical) product.
3. (Easy/Difficult) entry and exit.
4. (Perfect/Imperfect) information.

Conditions 1, 2, and 4 imply that the actions of individual buyers and sellers (do/do not) affect the market price for the one identical product. Condition 3 implies that the number of firms can easily expand or contract and leads to the condition that long-run equilibrium will be characterized by (positive/zero/negative) economic profits.

(2) An important first step to analyzing the firm's decisions in a particular market structure is to be careful about what the market structure implies for the firm's demand curve and its marginal revenue. Let us first consider the short-run supply decision of an individual firm under perfect competition. Since the actions of this firm will not affect the market price, the firm can sell as much or as little as it wants at the prevailing market price. Alternatively, we may say that the firm faces a (horizontal/vertical) demand curve. In Chapter 24 we saw that the demand curve is also the curve of average revenue. If the demand curve is horizontal,

then besides being the curve of average revenue it is also the curve of _____ revenue. (Remember the picture of marginal revenue in the Basic Exercise to Chapter 24 of this study guide. If the demand curve is horizontal, there is no horizontal rectangle to subtract.) As we saw in the last chapter, the firm maximizes profits by producing where MC = MR. Under perfect competition, MR = P, thus under perfect competition the firm should produce where MC = MR = P.

We can now derive the short-run supply curve for the firm by imagining that the firm faces a variety of possible prices and considering what output the firm would supply at each price. These price-output pairs will define the firm's short-run supply curve. For many possible prices short-run supply will be given by the

(3) intersection of price and the (average/marginal) cost curve. If price drops below the minimum of the average total cost curve, the MC = P rule maximizes profits by minimizing _____. Even if price is less than average total cost, the firm should continue to produce as long as price is above average

_____ cost. If the firm decides to produce nothing it still must cover its (variable/sunk) costs. As long as price exceeds average variable cost, there will be something left over to help cover sunk costs. Putting all of this together, we can conclude that under perfect competition a firm's

short-run supply curve is given by the portion of the _____ _____

curve above average _____ cost.

(4)   The industry short-run supply curve is given by the (horizontal/vertical) summation of individual firms' supply curves. Market price, the variable so crucial to individual firms' decisions, will be given by the intersection of the market _____ and _____ curves. In the short run, the number of firms in the industry is fixed; and the short-run industry supply curve will come from the supply decisions of existing firms.

     In the long run, there will be more (fewer) firms if the short-run equilibrium involves economic profits (losses). For example, if general market returns are around 12 percent and investments in the firm show a

(5) return of 10 percent, an economist would conclude that the firm has an economic (loss/profit) of

_____ percent. In this case, by investing elsewhere and earning 12 percent, the firm's owners would be (better/worse) off. The 12 percent is the _____ cost of capital to the firm and it is an important part of costs as counted by the economist. Thus, economists focus on economic profits as the indicator of entry or exit rather than on accounting profits. The condition

of long-run equilibrium that (accounting/economic) profits be zero is consistent with _____ profits equal to general market rates of return.

     As firms enter or leave, the industry short-run supply curve will shift appropriately, price will adjust as we move along the industry demand curve, and industry long-run equilibrium will be achieved when there are no further incentives for entry or exit. Figure 25–1(a) illustrates a firm in a perfectly competitive industry. Figure 25–1(b) shows the industry demand and supply. The illustrated firm will be making economic

(6) (profits/losses). Shade in the appropriate rectangle showing economic profits or losses. There will be an incentive for some firms to (enter/leave) the industry. As the number of firms in the industry changes, the supply curve in Figure 25–1(b) will shift to the (right/left) and price will (rise/fall). If the cost curves in Figure 25–1(a) are representative of long-run costs for all current and potential firms in the industry, long-run equilibrium will involve a price of $_____. Note that at all times our representative firm is producing where MC = P. But in the long-run equilibrium, MC = P = minimum

_____ _____ _____ cost. It is this last condition that explains the efficiency of perfectly competitive markets.

DEFINITION QUIZ

Choose the letter that is the most appropriate definition for each of the following terms.

1. _____ Market
2. _____ Perfect competition
3. _____ Pure monopoly
4. _____ Monopolistic competition
5. _____ Oligopoly
6. _____ Price taker
7. _____ Supply curve of the industry

a. Industry composed of a few large rival firms.
b. Industry with only one supplier.
c. Single buyer in a market.
d. Set of all sale and purchase transactions affecting the price of some commodity.
e. Sum of quantities supplied by each of the firms in an industry, at each possible price.
f. Agent too small to affect the market price for a given commodity.
g. Many small firms selling an identical product.
h. Many small firms selling slightly differentiated products.

BASIC EXERCISE

This exercise is designed to explore the short-run supply curve for a firm under perfect competition.

Assume that widgets are produced by perfectly competitive firms. The data in Table 25–1 are consistent with Figure 25–1 and are for a representative widget firm. Although not listed separately in Table 25–1, the production of widgets involves fixed costs of $10,140.

1. If the price of widgets is $19.10, what is the profit-maximizing level of output?

_____.

What are economic profits at this level of output?

$_____. Check to be sure that this level of output maximizes profits by calculating profits for output levels 100 units higher and lower.

Economic profits at higher output = $_____

Economic profits at lower output = $_____

2. What is the profit-maximizing level of output if the price of widgets falls to $11.50, below all values for average cost?

_____.

What are economic profits at this level of output?

$_____. Check to be sure that this level of output maximizes profits or minimizes losses by considering output levels 100 units higher, 100 units lower, and no production.

Economic losses at higher output = $_____

Economic losses at lower output = $_____

Economic losses at zero output = $_____

3. If the price of widgets is $6.00, what is the profit-maximizing level of output?

_____.

4. What general conclusion can you draw about the short-run supply curve for a firm operating under conditions of perfect competition?

_____

_____

_____

TABLE 25-1

COSTS OF PRODUCING WIDGETS

Quantity	Average Cost (dollars)	Average Variable Cost (dollars)	Marginal Cost (dollars)
900	17.67	6.40	4.60
1000	16.44	6.30	6.30
1100	15.62	6.40	8.60
1200	15.15	6.70	11.50
1300	15.00	7.20	15.00
1400	15.14	7.90	19.10
1500	15.56	8.80	23.80

5. Note that in question 1, when the market price was assumed to be $19.10, the profit-maximizing level of output was at a point where price exceeded both average cost and average variable cost. Remembering that under perfect competition a firm can sell as much output as it wants to at the given market price, why isn't it profitable for the firm to expand output as long as price is greater than average costs?

_____

_____

6. If many firms can produce with the same cost functions, what is the long-run equilibrium price of widgets? $_____. What is the associated level of production for the representative firm? _____.

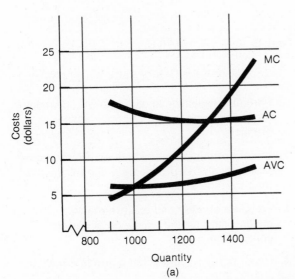

(a)

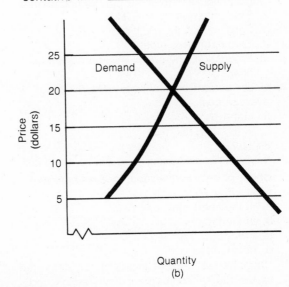

(b)

FIGURE 25-1

SELF-TESTS FOR UNDERSTANDING

Test A

Circle the correct answer.

1. Which of the following is not a condition for perfect competition?
   a. Perfect information about products.
   b. One firm producing many products.
   c. Freedom of entry.
   d. Freedom of exit.

2. If production is limited to a few large firms, the resulting market structure is called
   a. perfect competition.
   b. monopolistic competition.
   c. oligopoly.
   d. pure monopoly.

3. Which one of the following is not true under perfect competition?
   a. The firm's demand curve is horizontal.
   b. The firm's demand curve is also the curve of average revenue.
   c. The firm's demand curve is also the curve of marginal revenue.
   d. The firm's demand curve is inelastic.

4. The short-run supply curve for a firm under perfect competition is the portion of the firm's marginal cost curve that is above the
   a. average total cost curve.
   b. average fixed cost curve.
   c. average variable cost curve.
   d. minimum of the marginal cost curve.

5. Which of the following is not a characteristic of long-run equilibrium under perfect competition?
   a. Production where $P = MC$.
   b. Zero accounting profits.
   c. Zero economic profits.
   d. Production where P = minimum average cost.

6. Under perfect competition, price will equal average cost
   a. in the short run.
   b. in the long run.
   c. always.
   d. never.

7. Under perfect competition, firms will produce where $P = MC$
   a. in the short run.
   b. in the long run.
   c. always.
   d. never.

8. Under perfect competition, price is determined by the intersection of the industry supply and demand curves

   a. in the short run.
   b. in the long run.
   c. always.
   d. never.

9. Imagine that pencils are produced by firms with U-shaped average costs under conditions of perfect competition. A large expansion of federal government aid to education has disturbed the original long-run equilibrium by shifting the demand curve for pencils to the right. Which one of the following is not a likely response?
   a. Pencil prices rise initially in response to the increase in demand.
   b. Existing firms are likely to earn positive economic profits in the short run.
   c. Existing firms in the industry initially expand output to the point where average cost equals the new, higher price.
   d. New firms are likely to enter the industry in response to earnings above the opportunity cost of capital.

10. Widgets are produced by perfectly competitive firms. The demand curve for widgets has a negative slope. A technological innovation dramatically reduces average and marginal costs for current and potential widget manufacturers. All but which one of the following will occur?
    a. The quantity supplied increases in the short run.
    b. The price of widgets declines in the short run.
    c. Economic profits increase in the short run.
    d. Economic profits will be positive in the long run.

Test B

Circle T or F for True or False as appropriate.

1. Perfect competition is characterized by many firms producing similar but not identical products.   T F

2. Under perfect competition firms will maximize profits by always producing at the minimum of their average cost.   T F

3. Freedom of entry and exit are really unnecessary for the existence of perfect competition.   T F

4. Under perfect competition a firm is always guaranteed to earn positive economic profits if it produces where $MC = P$.   T F

5. Under perfect competition the demand curve facing the industry is horizontal. **T F**

6. A competitive firm should always expand output as long as price exceeds average cost. **T F**

7. The firm's short-run supply curve is given by the portion of its marginal cost curve with a positive slope. **T F**

8. In long-run equilibrium, perfectly competitive firms will show positive accounting profits but zero economic profits. **T F**

9. If price is less than average total cost, a firm is always better off shutting down. **T F**

10. Perfect competition is studied because a very large proportion of markets satisfy the conditions for perfect competition. **T F**

SUPPLEMENTARY EXERCISE

Consider a firm with the following total cost curve:

$$TC = 10{,}140 + .00001\,Q^3 - .02\,Q^2 + 16.3\,Q.$$

where Q is output. (This cost curve is consistent with the Basic Exercise.)

1. Derive equations for the firm's
   a. average cost.
   b. average variable cost.
   c. marginal cost.
2. Draw a picture showing these various measures of cost as a function of output.
3. Verify that the marginal cost curve goes through the bottom of the average cost curve and the average variable cost curve.
4. Assume this firm operates in a perfectly competitive market. Derive a mathematical expression for the firm's supply curve.

26

The Price System and the Case for Laissez Faire

LEARNING OBJECTIVES

After completing the material in this chapter you should be able to:

- define, understand, and use correctly the terms and concepts listed below.
- list three coordination tasks that must be solved by any system of resource allocation.
- explain the difference between an efficient and inefficient allocation of resources.
- explain how competitive markets, in which all producers and consumers respond to common market prices, can achieve an efficient allocation of resources.
- describe situations in which price increases may be in society's best interest.

- describe the conditions under which an inefficient allocation of resources might be preferred to an efficient allocation.

IMPORTANT TERMS AND CONCEPTS

Efficient allocation of resources
Coordination tasks: output selection, production planning, distribution of goods
Laissez faire
Input–output analysis
MC = P requirement of perfect competition
MC = MU efficiency requirement

CHAPTER REVIEW

This chapter discusses the role of prices in the economy; specifically, how prices work to allocate resources and how they affect the efficiency of the economy. In particular, it is shown that in a competitive economy, the self-serving actions of utility-maximizing individuals and profit-maximizing firms can lead to an efficient allocation of the economy's resources. The complete, rigorous proof of this proposition is usually discussed only in graduate courses in economic theory and involves the use of some fairly advanced mathematics. The discussion in this chapter is a simpler introduction to this material.

The efficiency implications of a laissez-faire, competitive economy are important reasons why economists have a great deal of respect for the workings of the price system. But the proof of this abstract proposition is not a proof that we should dismantle the federal government and that all markets should be unregulated. The proposition refers to the efficiency of a perfectly competitive economy. There are many

(1) aspects of the American economy that (are/are not) consistent with the requirements for a competitive economy. The implications of these real-world imperfections are the subject of Chapters 27–34. Also, efficiency is not the only way to judge the workings of an economy. Notions of fairness, or equity, are also important and may at times lead one to prefer less efficient, but fairer, nonmarket procedures.

All economies must somehow answer three questions. First there is the question of output

(2) _____: How much of each type of good and service should be produced in the aggregate? Next, there is the question of production _____: How should various productive inputs be allocated among the millions of firms and plants in order to meet the original output decisions? Finally, there is the question of the _____ of products: How are the available goods and services to be divided among consumers? How does one evaluate the job that an economy does in answering these questions? Economists typically use two yardsticks: efficiency and equity. The discussion in this chapter concentrates on efficiency.

Economic efficiency is a very important but relatively abstract concept. If by redistributing the commodities that are produced we can make everyone better off in his or her own estimation, we would say that the

(3) initial allocation of commodities (was/was not) efficient. It is only when there are no more opportunities to make some individuals better off while not worsening the situation of others that economists would character-

ize the operation of the economy as _____.

You should realize that for any economy there are many possible efficient allocations of resources. Each

(4) point on an economy's production possibilities frontier is (efficient/inefficient) in terms of the production of output. If an economy is operating on this frontier, it is impossible to increase the output of one good without

_____ the output of one or more other goods. Whether the economy is efficient or fair in terms of distributing this output is another question.

Let us consider in more detail how a competitive economy achieves efficiency in the selection of output. (The appendix to this chapter discusses efficiency in production planning and output distribution.) Efficiency in

(5) the selection of output requires that, for the quantity produced, the marginal _____

of the last unit to consumers must equal the marginal _____ of producers.

Why is this condition necessary for an efficient output selection? Remember that the definition of efficiency refers to consumers' evaluations of their own well-being, an evaluation that economists assume consumers are making when they maximize the difference between total utility and spending. If the marginal utility of some good exceeds the marginal cost of producing more units, then the production of at least one

(6) more unit of output will result in a net (increase/decrease) in consumer well-being. Consumers benefit by the increase in their utility while the cost to society of additional production is given by the marginal

_____. If marginal utility exceeds marginal cost the benefit to consumers from increased production will be (greater/less) than the cost to society and the initial output selection (is/is not) efficient. It is only when marginal utility (exceeds/equals/is less than) marginal cost that there are no more opportunities for net gains.

It is one of the beauties of a competitive economy that utility-maximizing individuals and profit-maximizing firms will, while pursuing their own self-interests, make decisions that result in marginal utility being equal to marginal cost. Our optimal purchase rule of Chapter 21 showed that utility-maximizing consumers will purchase additional units until the marginal utility of the last unit consumed equals the

(7) _____ of the commodity. The discussion in Chapter 24 showed that profit-

maximizing firms will equate marginal revenue and _____ _____. The discussion in Chapter 25 showed that for a firm under perfect competition, marginal revenue is equal to

_____. Thus a profit-maximizing firm under perfect competition, producing where marginal cost equals marginal revenue, will be producing where the marginal cost of the last unit

produced equals the _____ of the commodity.

(8)   To summarize, utility-maximizing consumers set marginal _____ equal to

price and profit-maximizing competitive firms set marginal _____ equal to price.
The result is that marginal utility (exceeds/equals/is less than) marginal cost, our condition for efficiency in
the selection of output.

A centrally planned economy attempts to answer the three basic questions of output selection, production planning, and product distribution by direct decree, without the use of prices. Often in these economies decisions about output selection are made with little attention to individual consumer preferences. More weight is given to the planners' preferences for such things as increased production of steel and electricity, although periodic newspaper accounts of a readjustment of production goals in response to consumer unrest indicate that even planners cannot forget entirely about consumers.

Once decisions about output levels have been made, a central planner must be sure that productive inputs are allocated to ensure that the production goals can in fact be achieved. One type of analysis that takes account of the interindustry flows of inputs necessary for the production of goods for final use is

(9)   _____ — _____ analysis. A major limitation of this analysis is the
enormity and complexity of the sets of equations. It is a major conceptual advantage that the price system in
a competitive economy does not require that this information be centralized.

DEFINITION QUIZ

Choose the letter that is the most appropriate definition for each of the following terms.

1. _____ Efficient allocation of resources

2. _____ Output selection

3. _____ Production planning

4. _____ Distribution of output

5. _____ Laissez faire

6. _____ Input-output analysis

a. Decisions on what quantities of each input to use to produce each good.
b. Technique of simultaneously solving equations that link necessary inputs to output for all industries.
c. Situation that takes advantage of every opportunity to make some individuals feel better off without harming anyone else.
d. Situation in which an agent's welfare can be improved without injury to anyone else.
e. Decisions on the division of output among consumers.
f. Decisions on how much of each commodity to produce.
g. Program of minimal interference with the workings of the free market.

BASIC EXERCISE

This problem is designed to illustrate the logic of the rule for efficiency in output selection. The discussion in the chapter indicated that efficiency in the selection of output requires that marginal utility equals marginal cost for all commodities. If not, it is possible, by changing the selection of output, to improve consumers' well-being.

Consider an economy that produces records, among other things. At the current level of record output, the marginal utility of records is $7 and the marginal cost is only $5.

1. The production of one more record will increase total utility by $_____. The production of one more record will cost society $_____.

2. In Chapter 21 we saw that utility-maximizing consumers will maximize the difference between total utility and total spending. It is this difference that is the money value of their well-being. For the economy as a whole, the relevant measure of consumer well-being is the difference between total utility and total social costs. Looking at the

change in both utility and cost, we can see that the production of one more record will increase

consumer well-being by $_____.
Efficiency in the production of records requires (more/less) records.

3. What if the marginal utility of an additional record was $3 and the marginal cost was $5? Then the production of an additional record will (increase/

decrease) consumer well-being by $_____.
and efficiency in the production of records will call for (more/fewer) records.

4. If the marginal cost of additional records is constant at $5, then in order that there be no opportunity for a change in the production of records to increase consumer well-being, enough records should be produced so that the marginal

utility of an additional record is $_____.

SELF-TESTS FOR UNDERSTANDING

Test A

Circle the correct answer.

1. For any economy that uses the price system which of the following is not necessarily true?
   a. Prices play an important role in shaping the allocation of resources.
   b. Prices play an important role in shaping the distribution of income and wealth.
   c. Prices will reflect the preference and incomes of consumers.
   d. Prices of necessities will be low and prices of luxuries will be high.
2. The price system distributes goods and services on the basis of income and
   a. scarcity.
   b. consumer preferences.
   c. education.
   d. planner preferences.
3. The condition for optimal output selection is
   a. MC = P.
   b. MC = MU.
   c. MRP = P.
   d. MU = P.
4. If the marginal utility of color television sets is $400 and the marginal cost is $300, then efficiency in output selection requires that the production of color television sets

a. be increased.
b. be decreased.
c. should be neither increased nor decreased.
5. The change in the production of color television sets from question 4 will likely
   a. increase marginal cost and marginal utility.
   b. increase marginal cost and decrease marginal utility.
   c. decrease marginal cost and marginal utility.
   d. decrease marginal cost and increase marginal utility.
6. An efficient allocation of resources
   a. will always be fair.
   b. is the best allocation possible.
   c. would mean the economy is operating somewhere on its production opportunity frontier.
   d. is always better than an inefficient allocation.
7. Leon does not now own a motorcycle. He would be willing to pay up to $800 for one. Motorcycles produced by competitive firms in long-run equilibrium, earning zero economic profit, cost $2,000 to produce. Which of the following is false?
   a. Leon is not likely to buy a motorcycle.
   b. Since Leon's marginal utility is less than the marginal cost of production, there would be a social gain if direct government controls reduced the production of motorcycles.
   c. The marginal utility of a motorcycle to someone must be at least $2,000.
8. If resources have been allocated in a way that meets the requirements of economic efficiency, then we know that
   a. output is being produced in accordance with the preferences of the Council of Economic Advisers.
   b. production occurs at a point inside the economy's production possibilities frontier.
   c. there is no reallocation of resources that can make some individuals better off without making others worse off.
   d. the marginal cost of producing every commodity has been minimized.
9. Efficiency in the distribution of output among consumers requires that
   a. all consumers must face the same price for any single commodity.
   b. the price of all goods must be the same.
   c. marginal cost equal marginal revenue.
   d. income be equally distributed among all consumers.
10. Efficiency in the distribution of output requires that
    a. the price of all goods be the same.
    b. all firms are able to sell a given product at the same price.

c. firms set marginal utility equal to marginal revenue product.

d. marginal cost be minimized.

Test B

Circle T or F for True or False as appropriate.

1. The term *laissez faire* refers to an economy with minimal economic regulation by government. **T F**

2. If resources are being allocated efficiently, we know that there is no better allocation possible. **T F**

3. Efficient resource allocation always requires the intervention of a central planner to set prices correctly. **T F**

4. Efficiency in the selection of output requires that the marginal utility of every commodity be equal to its marginal cost. **T F**

5. An unregulated competitive economy is simply incapable of seeing that appropriate efficiency conditions are achieved for all commodities. **T F**

6. Input–output analysis is a mathematical tool to aid in the distribution of output among consumers without using the price system. **T F**

7. Charging higher prices on public transportation during rush hours is an example of using the price system to increase efficiency. **T F**

8. Considerations of fairness may sometimes lead a society to prefer an inefficient allocation to an efficient one. **T F**

9. Efficiency in the distribution of goods implies that everyone will get an equal share of all goods. **T F**

10. Competitive markets promote efficiency in output selection because both firms and consumers respond to the same price. **T F**

Appendix: The Invisible Hand in the Distribution of Goods and in Production Planning

BASIC EXERCISES

These exercises are designed to illustrate and help you review the implications of the rules for efficiency in the allocation of productive inputs and in the allocation of output between consumers, as discussed in the Appendix to Chapter 26.

1. **Efficiency in the Distribution of Output Among Consumers**

The rule for efficiency in the distribution of output among consumers is that _____

_____

_____

_____

Imagine that Todd and Nicole both consume steaks and pizzas. The initial allocation of steak and pizza has resulted in the following marginal utilities:

MARGINAL UTILITY

	Todd	Nicole
Steaks	$9.00	$6.00
Pizzas	4.00	4.00

a. Is the condition for efficiency in the distribution of output satisfied? _____. If not there should be some, possibly many, reallocations of output that will increase either Todd's or Nicole's total utility (or both) without reducing total utility for the other.

b. Imagine that Nicole gives Todd one steak in exchange for two pizzas. On net, considering the full effects of the trade, what is the change in Todd's utility? (increase/decrease) $_____

Nicole's utility? (increase/decrease) $_____
An implication of the utility changes of the reallocation is that the initial allocation was (efficient/inefficient).

c. How do competitive markets work to ensure that uncoordinated individual demands will satisfy the condition for efficiency in the distribution of output among consumers?

2. **Efficiency in the Allocation of Productive Inputs**

Our rule for efficiency says that if two inputs, labor and land, are both used to produce corn and tomatoes, then inputs should be assigned to

each output until the _____

_____

_____

_____

_____

a. We know from Chapter 23 that this condition will be automatically satisfied under perfect competition for profit-maximizing firms that can buy inputs at given prices. What is perhaps less clear is that if this condition is not satisfied, then it would be possible to reallocate inputs among firms and produce more total output—with the same amount of inputs. Consider the following table showing the initial marginal physical products of land and labor in the production of corn and tomatoes.

MARGINAL PHYSICAL PRODUCT OF LABOR AND LAND IN THE PRODUCTION OF CORN AND TOMATOES

	Corn (bushels)	Tomatoes (pounds)
Labor (person)	120	1200
Land (acre)	40	200

Consider the reallocation of one worker from corn production to tomato production. As a result of this reallocation of labor, the production of corn will fall by _____ bushels and the production of tomatoes will rise by _____ pounds. Now consider moving 4 acres of land from tomato production to corn production. As a result of the reallocation of land, the production of corn will rise by _____ bushels and the production of tomatoes will fall by _____ pounds. In total, counting the reallocation of both land and labor, the production of corn changes by

_____ bushels and the production of tomatoes changes by

_____ pounds.

b. Efficiency in the selection of inputs helps to achieve efficiency in the choice of outputs. We have seen that efficiency in the selection of outputs requires that MU = MC. In competitive markets, MU = MC because utility-maximizing individuals see to it that MU = P. Efficiency in the selection of input sets MC = P.

We saw in Chapter 23 that our rule for optimal use of inputs could also be expressed in terms of marginal revenue product. Using symbols, our optimal input rule says

$$P_Q \, MPP_X = P_X,$$

where P_Q is the product price, P_X is the input price, and MPP_X is the marginal physical product of input X in the production of Q. If we divide both sides of the equation by MPP_X we get

$$P_Q = \frac{P_X}{MPP_X}$$

As the discussion in the Chapter Review for Chapter 23 showed, P_X/MPP_X is the marginal cost of producing more output by using more of input X. Note that a profit-maximizing firm will use the optimal input rule for all its inputs. Thus, the marginal cost of an output expansion by the use of any single input, of the many that a firm may use, will be equal to the marginal cost from the additional use of any other input.

c. How do competitive markets work to insure that the uncoordinated decisions of firms satisfy the condition for efficiency in the allocation of productive inputs?

SUPPLEMENTARY EXERCISE

Go to the library and look up information about the most recent input–output table for the U.S. economy. (Information about input–output tables can be found about once a year in the *Survey of Current Business*, a monthly publication of the U.S. Commerce Department.)

There are several input–output tables. One table indicates which industries use which commodities. Another table indicates which industries produce which commodities. The table of direct requirements shows what direct inputs are necessary per unit of output of each industry. The table of direct and indirect requirements solves all the input–output relationships and shows how the output of every industry must adjust in order to increase the output of any one industry. It is this table that takes account of such indirect requirements as increased electricity to make more steel in order to increase the output of cars.

1. How many separate pieces of information do these input–output tables contain? How long do you think it would take to construct such a table? (The table described in the February 1989 *Survey of Current Business* is for 1983. Why did it take six years to publish this table?) How long do you think it would take you to solve all the interrelationships and produce a table of direct and indirect requirements?

2. Which industries produce mainly for final uses and which produce mainly intermediate outputs, that is, inputs for other industries?

3. The November 1969 *Survey of Current Business* contains data for the 1963 input–output table. Compare these data to the most recent table you can find. Pick one or two favorite industries and see how total and direct requirements have changed over time. If you were a planner concerned with the year 2000 how should you determine what input–output requirements are relevant?

27

Monopoly

LEARNING OBJECTIVES

After completing the material in this chapter you should be able to:

- define, understand, and use correctly the terms and concepts listed below.
- calculate a monopolist's profit-maximizing price and output, given information on costs and the demand for output.
- explain why for a monopolist marginal revenue is less than price.
- describe what factors allow a particular monopoly to persist.
- explain why, unlike the case of a competitive firm, there is no supply curve for a monopolist.
- explain why a monopolist will receive positive economic profits in both the short and long runs.
- describe why a monopolist's demand and cost

curves may differ from those of a comparable competitive industry.
- explain how a monopoly can give rise to an inefficient allocation of resources.
- explain why a monopolist cannot pass on all of any pollution charge or other increase in cost.

IMPORTANT TERMS AND CONCEPTS

Pure monopoly
Barriers to entry
Patents
Natural monopoly
Monopoly profits
Inefficiency of monopoly
Shifting of pollution charges

CHAPTER REVIEW

In Chapter 25 we studied the decisions of firms operating in markets characterized as perfect competition; that is, markets with lots of firms competing to produce and sell one good. Chapter 23 considered optimal firm

(1) decisions and Chapter 26 considered the implications of these decisions for the efficiency of resource allocation. In this chapter we will consider a *pure monopoly*, a market with (one/many) firm(s) producing a single good with (no/lots of) close substitutes. The essence of a pure monopoly is one producer without effective competition.

A pure monopoly could arise for one of two reasons. If the technology of large-scale production implies that one firm can produce enough to satisfy the whole market at lower average costs than a number of

(2) smaller firms, we say that the result is a _____ monopoly. Legal restrictions such as exclusive licensing or patents, or advantages that the monopolist acquires for himself, such as control of a vital input or technical superiority, could also create a pure monopoly. All of these factors would deter poten-

tial competitors and are called _____ to _____.

The study of pure monopoly often starts by assuming that some enterprising entrepreneur is able to monopolize a previously competitive industry. It is also traditional to assume that the monopolist initially faces the previous industry demand curve and operates with the same cost curves.

Under pure competition, individual firms face demand curves that are horizontal; that is, the firm can sell as much as it wants to at the market price. A monopolist will face the industry demand curve with a

(3) (positive/negative/zero) slope. If the monopolist wants to sell more she must (raise/lower) her price.

The monopolist maximizes profit just like any other profit-maximizing firm; that is, the monopolist

(4) chooses the level of output at which (marginal/average) cost equals (marginal/average) _____.
Now the only trick is to figure out what the relevant cost and revenue curves look like. Marginal cost comes from the monopolist's total costs in exactly the same way that it does for anyone else. The tricky part is marginal revenue. Marginal revenue is the addition to total revenue from producing and selling one more unit of output. Under pure competition, the actions of an individual firm have no effect on the market price and

marginal revenue equals _____. But in the case of a monopolist, quantity decisions do affect price and marginal revenue (is/is not) equal to price.

(5)   Remember from Chapter 24 that the demand curve is the curve of (average/total) revenue. From Rule 4 in the Appendix to Chapter 24, we know that when average revenue is declining, marginal revenue will be (less/more) than average revenue. In other words, for the monopolist with a downward-sloping demand curve, the curve of marginal revenue will lie (above/below) the curve of average revenue. (Remember the geometry of marginal revenue in the exercise to Chapter 24 in the Study Guide or in Figure 27–3 in the text.) (A similar

use of Rule 4 indicates that when average cost is rising, the marginal cost curve will lie _____ the average cost curve.)

Once we have used the marginal cost and marginal revenue curves to compute the monopolist's profit-
(6) maximizing level of output we can use the (demand/supply) curve to figure out what price she should charge. We know that since the curve of marginal revenue lies below the demand curve the monopolist's market price will be (greater/less) than both marginal revenue and marginal cost. We also know that if average cost is rising, average cost will be (greater/less) than marginal cost and hence also (greater/less) than the market price given by the demand curve. Thus, for a profit-maximizing monopolist, operating at a level where average cost is rising, price will be greater than average cost and the monopolist will receive positive economic profits. Since, by definition, the monopolist is the only supplier, there (will/will not) be entry of new firms to compete away these profits. Compared with results under pure competition, the monopolist's profit-maximizing behavior will result in a (higher/lower) price and a (higher/lower) level of output in both the short and long run. (If average costs are not rising, the long-run viability of the monopolist requires that price exceed average cost.)

In Chapter 26 we saw that pure competition leads to an efficient allocation of resources. Efficient resource allocation requires that the marginal utility (MU) of each commodity be equal to its marginal cost

(7) (MC). Optimal consumer decisions lead to the result that MU equals _____.

Under perfect competition, optimal firm decisions imply that MC equals _____. The upshot is clearly that under pure competition MU equals MC. With a pure monopoly, as outlined above—that is, with the same demand and cost curves—we know that while consumers will continue to equate MU and

P, the monopolist will equate MC to _____ _____, which is (greater/less) than P. The result is that with a pure monopoly, MU is (greater/less) than MC. Increased quantity of the monopolized commodity would yield marginal benefits, measured by MU, that are (greater/less) than marginal costs. In this sense the monopoly leads to an inefficient allocation of resources.

An important part of the comparison above is that the monopolist faces demand and cost curves that are the same as those of the previously competitive industry. There are, however, several factors that could shift these curves following a change in market structure. Advertising might shift demand and cost curves.

(8) Savings from centralizing various operations and avoiding duplication might shift the cost curves (up/down). Greater inefficiencies from greater size would have the opposite effect. Particular results will depend upon particular circumstances.

Why do we say there is no supply curve for a monopolist? Remember that the supply curve shows the relationship between each possible market price and the quantity supplied. Under pure competition a firm takes price as given and then decides how much to produce, knowing that its individual quantity decision

(9) (will/will not) affect the market price. The firm's supply curve comes from considering its reaction to different possible prices. But the monopolist (does/does not) take price as given. The monopolist is interested in trading off the revenue implications of different price-quantity combinations, as given by the demand curve, against the cost implications of producing those different amounts. The monopolist chooses the *one* quantity that maximizes profits and receives the price given by the point on the demand curve consistent with the quantity. The monopolist is a price (maker/taker).

DEFINITION QUIZ

Choose the letter that is the most appropriate definition for each of the following terms.

1. _____ Pure monopoly

2. _____ Barriers to entry

3. _____ Patents

4. _____ Natural monopoly

a. Impediments preventing potential rivals from entering industry.
b. Industry in which advantages of large-scale production enable a single firm to supply the market demand at a lower average cost than a number of smaller firms could.
c. Industry with a single buyer for the entire market.
d. Temporary government grants of exclusive production rights to products' inventors.
e. Industry with single supplier of a product for which there are no close substitutes.

BASIC EXERCISE

This exercise is designed to give you practice computing the profit-maximizing quantity and price for a monopolist. Mario has a monopoly in the production of widgets.

1. Table 27–1 contains relevant data on the demand for widgets and the cost of producing widgets. Use this data to compute Mario's profit-maximizing quantity and the associated price. There are essentially two ways to do this.
   a. One way is to fill in columns 2 and 5 of Table 27–3 by computing total revenue and total cost. Next, choose the level of output that maximizes the difference. That level of output is _____ widgets.
   b. The second way is to fill in columns 3 and 4 of Table 27–3 by computing marginal revenue

and marginal cost. Mario could maximize profits by increasing production as long as

marginal _____ exceeds

marginal _____. In this case, Mario maximizes profits by producing

_____ widgets.
   c. To maximize profits Mario should charge a

price of $_____.

   d. His profits are $_____.

2. Unfortunately, the production of widgets involves significant pollution, and the government has decided to fight pollution by imposing pollution charges. In Mario's case, this means a pollution charge of $1,000 a widget. Table 27–2 contains the original data on demand along with the new average cost data that reflect the $1,000 a widget pollution charge.

TABLE 27-1

Quantity	Average Revenue (Price)	Average Cost
12	9,500	$7,068.00
13	9,300	6,957.00
14	9,100	6,894.00
15	8,900	6,869.40
16	8,700	6,876.00

TABLE 27-2

Quantity	Average Revenue (Price)	Average Cost
12	$9,500	$8,068.00
13	9,300	7,957.00
14	9,100	7,894.00
15	8,900	7,869.40
16	8,700	7,876.00

TABLE 27-3

(1) Quantity	(2) Total Revenue	(3) Marginal Revenue	(4) Marginal Cost	(5) Total Cost
12				
13				
14				
15				
16				

a. Use Table 27–4 to compute the new profit-maximizing level of output. Mario's new profit-maximizing level of output is _____

and the associated price is $_____.
How much pollution tax in total does Mario

pay? $_____. Note that while the pollution charge is $1,000 a widget, Mario's profit-maximizing price increases by only

$_____. Why doesn't Mario simply raise his price by the full $1,000?
b. What is the new level of profits?

$_____

3. (Optional) Your answer to Question 2 should indicate that the pollution tax has reduced both the output of widgets and the associated volume of pollution. What would have happened if, instead of a per-unit tax, the government had simply fined Mario $13,000 for polluting and imposed no further charges? Compared with the initial situation in Question 1, what happens to Mario's profit-maximizing level of output, the associated level of pollution output, and actual profits with this lump-sum pollution charge? (When answering this question be sure you are working with the correct

cost curves. Adjust Table 27–3 remembering that at each level of output, total costs will now be $13,000 higher than the entries in column 5.)

SELF-TESTS FOR UNDERSTANDING

Test A

Circle the correct answer.

1. Pure monopoly is characterized by
   a. many firms producing slightly different products.
   b. many firms producing slightly different products that are close substitutes.
   c. such a small number of firms that each must figure out how the others will respond to its own actions.
   d. one firm, with no competitors, producing a product with no close substitutes.
2. Which one of the following is *not* likely to lead to a monopoly?
   a. Patents.
   b. Control of the sole source of an important commodity.

TABLE 27-4

(1) Quantity	(2) Total Revenue	(3) Marginal Revenue	(4) Marginal Cost	(5) Total Cost
12				
13				
14				
15				
16				

c. A commodity with many close substitutes.

d. Significant increasing returns to scale.

3. A natural monopoly arises when

   a. natural resources are an important input.

   b. there are significant cost advantages to large-scale production.

   c. the government prohibits entry.

   d. patents protect a firm's technology.

4. If in order to sell more, a firm must reduce the price on all units sold, we can conclude that marginal revenue will

   a. exceed average revenue.

   b. equal average revenue.

   c. be less than average revenue.

5. A monopolist maximizes profit by producing where

   a. marginal cost equals marginal revenue.

   b. marginal cost equals marginal utility.

   c. average cost equals average revenue.

   d. the difference between average cost and average revenue is greatest.

6. A monopolist's economic profits will

   a. be competed away in the long run.

   b. be driven to the opportunity cost of capital.

   c. persist in the long run.

   d. be limited by usury laws.

7. An entrepreneur who monopolizes a previously competitive industry and now faces the same demand curve and produces with the same cost function will typically maximize profits by

   a. forcing consumers to buy more at a higher price.

   b. producing less but charging a higher price.

   c. increasing volume.

   d. lowering both output and price.

8. An increase in a monopolist's average cost will lead to a(n)

   a. increase in price by the same amount, as the monopolist simply passes on the price increase.

   b. increase in price only if marginal cost also increases.

   c. decrease in price as the monopolist needs to sell more in order to cover increased costs.

   d. increase in price only if the elasticity of demand is less than 1.0.

9. An increase in a monopolist's fixed cost will

   a. reduce the profit-maximizing level of output.

   b. not affect the profit-maximizing level of output.

   c. increase the profit-maximizing level of output as the monopolist needs to sell more to cover costs.

10. If marginal cost is greater than zero, we know that a monopolist will produce where the elasticity of demand is

   a. greater than unity.

   b. equal to unity.

   c. less than unity.

Test B

Circle T or F for True or False as appropriate.

1. A pure monopoly results when there are only a few firms supplying a particular commodity for which there are no close substitutes.   T F

2. Significant increasing returns to scale, which reduce average costs as output expands, may result in a natural monopoly.   T F

3. A pure monopolist can earn positive economic profits only in the long run.   T F

4. An entrepreneur who successfully monopolizes a competitive industry will face a horizontal demand curve just like each of the previous competitive firms. T F

5. A monopolist maximizes profits by producing at the point at which marginal cost equals marginal revenue. T F

6. If in a monopolistic industry, demand and cost curves are identical to a comparable competitive industry, and the demand curve slopes downward while the average cost curve slopes upward, then the monopolist's price will always exceed the competitive industry's price but the monopolist's output will be larger. T F

7. A monopolist has a greater incentive to advertise than does an individual firm under pure competition. T F

8. If market price is greater than average cost, a monopolist can always increase profits by producing more. T F

9. A monopolist will be able to increase price by the full amount of any per-unit tax, such as a per-unit pollution charge. T F

10. A firm operating under conditions of pure competition will not be able to pass on any of a per-unit pollution tax and must therefore pay the whole tax out of reduced profits. T F

SUPPLEMENTARY EXERCISES

1. The demand curve for the problem in the Basic Exercise is

$$Q = 59.5 - .005P.$$

In Question 1 of the Basic Exercise, the total cost curve is

$$TC = 52,416 + 225Q^2.$$

a. Derive mathematical expressions for total revenue, marginal revenue, average cost, and marginal cost.
b. Use a piece of graph paper to plot the demand, marginal revenue, and marginal cost curves.
c. Use your expressions for marginal revenue and marginal cost to solve for the profit-maximizing level of output. Is your answer consistent with your graph in part b and your answer to the Basic Exercise?
d. What is the impact of the per-unit pollution tax and the fixed-charge pollution tax on your expressions for total, average, and marginal cost? Do differences here help explain the impact of these taxes on the profit-maximizing level of output?
2. Why is (a) the correct answer to question 10 in Test A? (You might want to refer back to Chapter 24.)

28

Between Competition and Monopoly

LEARNING OBJECTIVES

After completing the material in this chapter you should be able to:

- define, understand, and use correctly the terms and concepts listed below.
- compare the four conditions that define monopolistic competition with those of perfect competition.
- explain why and how the long-run equilibrium of a firm under monopolistic competition differs from that of a firm under pure competition.
- explain why monopolistic competitors are said to have excess capacity.
- explain why it is so difficult to make a formal analysis of an oligopolistic market structure.
- describe briefly the alternative approaches to modeling oligopolistic behavior.
- explain why most economists believe that it is difficult to maintain the discipline necessary to sustain a cartel.
- use marginal cost and marginal revenue curves to derive the implications for price and quantity of sales maximization as opposed to profit maximization.

- use the maximin criterion to determine the final outcome in a game-theory setting.
- use marginal cost and marginal revenue curves to explain how a kinked demand curve can imply sticky prices.
- explain how the concept of contestable markets means that even in an industry with few firms, no firm will earn long-run profits in excess of the opportunity cost of capital and inefficient firms will not survive.

IMPORTANT TERMS AND CONCEPTS

Monopolistic competition
Excess capacity theorem
Oligopoly
Oligopolistic interdependence
Cartel
Price leadership
Sales maximization
Game theory
Maximin criterion
Kinked demand curve
Sticky price
Perfectly contestable markets

CHAPTER REVIEW

Pure competition and pure monopoly are the polar examples of market structure most easily analyzed in textbooks. Actual markets tend more toward what economists call *monopolistic competition* and *oligopoly*, which are the subjects of this chapter. It is harder to model firm behavior in these market structures, especially in the case of oligopoly. However, you should not lose sight of the notion that profit maximization is still a dominant characteristic of most firms and that marginal cost and marginal revenue curves remain the important tools to help determine which decisions will maximize profits.

A market structure in which there are numerous participants, freedom of entry and exit, perfect informa-

(1) tion, and product heterogeneity is referred to as a situation of _____ competition. Because each seller is able to partially differentiate his product, individual firms will face a demand curve with a (negative/positive/zero) slope. At each point in time, profit-maximizing firms will try to produce at

the level of output where _____ _____ equals _____

_____. The assumption of freedom of entry and exit implies that in the long run under monopolistic competition firms will earn (negative/positive/zero) economic profit. If an individual firm is earning positive economic profits, the (entry/exit) of new firms will shift the demand curve down (and may raise costs) until the demand curve is just tangent to the (average/marginal) cost curve.

A market structure with only a few firms producing a similar or identical product, and in which some

(2) firms are very large, is called a(n) _____. Formal analysis of such market structures is difficult because when considering the decisions of one firm, one must take into account the possible reactions of competitors. No single model describes all the possible outcomes under oligopoly, and economists have found it useful to consider a number of possible models and outcomes. If firms in an oligopolistic market band together and act like a single profit-maximizing monopolist, the resulting group is

called a _____. If most firms look to pricing decisions made by a dominant

firm, economists refer to the outcome as one of _____ _____.

Oligopolistic firms tend to be large corporations with professional managers. Some argue that managers are likely to be more interested in maximizing total revenue than in maximizing profits. This outcome is more likely if the salary of managers depends more upon the size of the firm than upon its profitability. A firm

(3) interested in maximizing sales revenue will increase output until marginal revenue equals _____.

Compared with profit maximization, sales maximization will mean a (higher/lower) price and a _____ quantity.

Game theory has been fruitfully used in the study of oligopolistic behavior by a number of economists. Game theory involves listing the possible outcomes of your moves and your opponents' countermoves in a(n)

(4) _____ matrix and then choosing an appropriate _____.

Another traditional element of the analysis of oligopoly is the concept of a kinked demand curve. Such a

(5) demand curve comes from assuming that your competitors (will/will not) match any decrease in your price but (will/will not) match any increase in your price. As a result, there is a gap in the (marginal/average) revenue curve, and profit-maximizing prices may not change unless there is a significant shift in the

marginal _____ curve.

The concept of perfectly contestable markets suggests that even oligopolists may be limited in their ability

(6) to earn monopolistic profits. The crucial condition for perfect contestability is that _____

and _____ are costless and unimpeded. In such a case, competitors could and

would get into and out of the market whenever profits exceeded the _____

_____ of _____. While no market may be perfectly contestable, the notion of contestability clearly can limit the ability of firms to charge monopolistic prices.

DEFINITION QUIZ

Choose the letter that is the most appropriate definition for each of the following terms.

1. _____ Monopolistic competition

2. _____ Excess capacity theorem

3. _____ Oligopoly

4. _____ Cartel

5. _____ Price leadership

6. _____ Game theory

7. _____ Maximin criterion

8. _____ Perfectly contestable markets

a. Group of sellers who join together to control production, sales, and price.
b. Industry with a single purchaser.
c. Notion that under monopolistic competition firms will tend to produce at less than capacity, i.e., minimum average cost.
d. Market in which entry and exit are costless and unimpeded.
e. Mathematical analysis of the behavior of competing firms.
f. Industry composed of a few large rival firms.
g. Many firms selling slightly differentiated products.
h. Selecting the strategy that yields the maximum profit, assuming opponent tries to damage you as much as possible.
i. Situation where one firm sets the price and other firms follow.

BASIC EXERCISES

These problems explore several important issues in the analysis of monopolistic competition and oligopoly.

1. Our discussion of monopolistic competition argued that long-run equilibrium implies that the firm's demand curve will be tangent to its average cost curve. We have also argued that profit maximization requires that marginal revenue equal marginal cost (or, alternatively, that firms should expand output as long as marginal revenue exceeds marginal cost). How do we know that marginal revenue equals marginal cost at the quantity given by the tangency between the demand curve and the average cost curve?
   a. Table 28–1 contains data on weekly costs and revenue for Gretchen's restaurant. Average

revenue and average cost are plotted in Figure 28–1. Note that the demand curve is tangent to the average cost curve. Plot total profits in the left half of Figure 28–1. What output level maximizes profits?
   b. Use your results in Table 28–1 to compute marginal revenue and marginal cost in Table 28–2. According to Table 28–2, what level of output maximizes profits? Why?
2. Figure 28–2 shows the kinked demand curve for a profit-maximizing firm that produces TV sets in an oligopolistic situation.
   a. What is the profit-maximizing level of output and the corresponding price if TVs can be produced at a marginal cost of $100?

   Quantity _____

   Price _____
   b. Assume now that marginal cost increases by 40 percent to $140 per TV. Describe what

TABLE 28–1

Quantity	Average Revenue	Average Cost	Total Revenue	Total Cost	Total Profit
600	$19	$21.67	$11.400	$13,002	$ − 1,602
800	17	17.50	13,600	14,000	− 400
1000	15	15.00	15,000	15,000	0
1200	13	13.33	15,600	15,996	− 396
1400	11	12.14	15,400	16,996	− 1,596

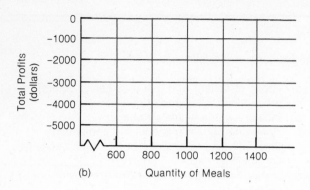

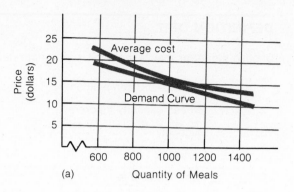

FIGURE 28-1

TABLE 28-2

Quantity	Marginal Revenue	Marginal Cost
600		
800	﹥	—
1000	﹥	
1200	﹥	
1400	﹥	

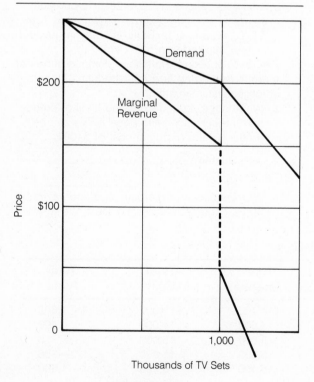

FIGURE 28-2

happens to the profit-maximizing levels of price and quantity following this increase in marginal cost.

_____

_____

c. What increase in marginal cost is necessary to induce a change in behavior on the part of this oligopolist and why?

_____

_____

d. What decrease in marginal cost is necessary to induce a change in behavior on the part of this oligopolist and why?

_____

_____

SELF-TESTS FOR UNDERSTANDING

Test A

Circle the correct answer.

1. Which of the following is the important difference between perfect and monopolistic competition?
   a. Few sellers rather than many.
   b. Heterogeneous rather than homogeneous product.
   c. Barriers to rather than freedom of entry.
   d. Long-run positive economic profits rather than zero economic profits.
2. Which of the following characterizes a firm's long-run equilibrium position under monopolistic competition?
   a. Marginal cost equals price.
   b. Production at minimum average cost.

c. A horizontal demand curve.

d. Zero economic profits.

3. Under monopolistic competition the heterogeneity of output implies that
   a. individual firms face downward-sloping demand curves.
   b. both marginal cost and marginal revenue will increase with additional units of output.
   c. individual firms can make positive economic profits even in the long run.
   d. in the long run, individual firms will produce at minimum average cost.

4. Oligopoly may be associated with all but which one of the following?
   a. Price leadership.
   b. Collusive behavior.
   c. Advertising.
   d. Lots of firms.

5. If oligopolistic firms get together to carve up the market and act like a monopolist, the result is called a
   a. cabal.
   b. contestable market.
   c. cartel.
   d. natural monopoly.

6. A firm interested in maximizing sales revenue will produce at a point where
   a. marginal revenue equals marginal cost.
   b. average cost is minimized.
   c. marginal revenue equals zero.
   d. average revenue equals average cost.

7. A firm that maximizes sales revenues instead of profits will charge
   a. a higher price.
   b. a lower price.
   c. the same price but will advertise more.

8. Game theory may be especially useful in analyzing a firm's behavior under conditions of
   a. pure competition.
   b. monopolistic competition.
   c. oligopoly.
   d. pure monopoly.

9. The term *kinked demand curve* refers to
   a. economists' inability to draw straight lines.
   b. the demand for X-rated movies.
   c. a situation where competitors match price decreases but not price increases.
   d. industries with substantial economies of scale.

10. Markets can be perfectly contestable if
    a. products are identical.
    b. entry and exit is free and easy.
    c. only two firms are bidding against each other.
    d. long-run economic profits are zero.

Test B

Circle T or F for True or False as appropriate.

1. Firms that operate under conditions of oligopoly are likely to engage in lots of advertising. T F

2. Heterogeneity of output is an important feature of monopolistic competition. T F

3. Under monopolistic competition, freedom of entry and exit will guarantee that a firm always earns a zero economic profit, in both the short run and the long run. T F

4. Under monopolistic competition, marginal revenue equals marginal cost in the short run but not in the long run. T F

5. There would be an unambiguous social gain if some firms in a market with monopolistic competition were forced by regulation to stop producing. T F

6. Oligopoly is characterized by a small number of firms, some very large, producing an identical or similar product. T F

7. Arrangements, such as price leadership and tacit collusion, are common in oligopolistic markets. T F

8. A firm that maximizes sales revenue will typically charge a higher price than a firm that maximizes profits. T F

9. An oligopolist facing a kinked demand curve will see a more elastic demand curve for price increases than for price decreases. T F

10. Perfectly contestable markets are only possible when there are a large number of competing firms. T F

SUPPLEMENTARY EXERCISE

The equations below for demand and total cost underlie the first problem in the Basic Exercises. Use these equations to derive explicit expressions for marginal cost, marginal revenue, and average cost. Now solve for the level of output that maximizes profits. Compare your answer with the results you obtained in the Basic Exercises.

$$Q = 2500 - 100\,P$$
(demand curve)
$$TC = 10{,}000 + 5\,Q$$
(total cost curve)

where Q = total quantity, P = price, and TC = total cost.

29

The Market Mechanism: Shortcomings and Remedies

LEARNING OBJECTIVES

After completing the material in this chapter you should be able to:

- define, understand, and use correctly the terms and concepts listed below.
- list the major shortcomings of free markets.
- explain why the existence of externalities, whether beneficial or detrimental, will result in an inefficient allocation of resources.
- explain why detrimental externalities mean that marginal private costs will understate marginal social costs.
- describe the important characteristics of public goods.
- explain why these characteristics mean that private profit-maximizing firms will not supply public goods.
- explain why some people believe that free markets are unlikely to result in an appropriate allocation of resources between the present and the future.
- explain how uneven productivity growth results in the cost disease of personal services.

IMPORTANT TERMS AND CONCEPTS

Opportunity cost
Resource misallocation
Production possibilities frontier
Price above and below marginal cost
Externalities (detrimental and beneficial)
Marginal social cost and marginal private cost
Public goods
Private goods
Excludability
Depletability
Irreversible decisions
Asymmetric information
Principals
Agents
Rent seeking
Moral hazard
Cost disease of the personal services

CHAPTER REVIEW

This chapter lists seven major shortcomings of unregulated markets. Some of these shortcomings have been discussed in previous chapters, and several others will receive a more complete treatment in later chapters. The discussion here focuses on four of the seven: externalities, public goods, the trade-off between present and future consumption, and the cost disease of personal services.

The material in Chapter 3 introduced the concept of an economy's *production possibilities frontier*. At that time we saw that the slope of the frontier measured how much the output of one commodity must be decreased in order to increase the production of another commodity. In other words, the slope of the

(1) production possibilities frontier measures the _____ cost of increasing the output of any one commodity.

Chapter 26 explained how a market economy can lead to an *efficient allocation of resources*; that is, one where marginal utilities and marginal costs are equal. If the utility of an increase in the output of some good is less than the marginal cost of producing that output, the result is a *misallocation of resources*. The

(2) virtue of competitive markets is that firms maximize profits by producing where price equals _____

_____ and individuals maximize by consuming where price equals _____

_____. Thus, our condition for an efficient allocation is automatically satisfied. An economy that satisfies all the assumptions necessary for perfect competition will automatically result in an efficient allocation of resources. The economy will operate (on/inside) the production possibilities frontier.

Many of the reasons mentioned at the beginning of the chapter may imply that an economy does not satisfy the conditions for perfect competition. In this case the wrong prices may get established, leading to an inefficient allocation of resources. If price is greater than marginal cost, the economy will tend to produce too

(3) (much/little) of a good to maximize consumer benefits. There may be a case for government intervention to allocate resources directly or, preferably, to help establish prices that will lead to an efficient allocation.

Externalities

Many economic activities impose incidental burdens or benefits on other individuals for which there is no com-

(4) pensation. These sorts of activities are said to involve _____. If an activity, such

as pollution, harms others and there is no compensation, one says that there are _____ externalities. If an activity benefits others who do not pay for the benefits they receive, one says that there are

_____ _____.

Externalities are important for questions of resource allocation because they imply that many activities are likely to have private benefits and costs that are different from social benefits and costs. In the case of detri-

(5) mental externalities, social costs will be (higher/lower) than private costs, while in the case of beneficial

externalities, social benefits will be _____ than private benefits.

(6) Private profit-maximizing firms will base their production decisions on (private/social) costs. If there are detrimental externalities, the result will be an (efficient/inefficient) use of resources. From a social viewpoint, too (much/little) of the commodity in question will be produced. In the case of beneficial externalities, unregulated markets are likely to produce (less/more) output than is socially desirable. Schemes for taxes and subsidies are, in principle, capable of adjusting private costs and benefits to more adequately reflect social costs and benefits.

Public Goods

Most goods provided by private profit-maximizing firms have two primary characteristics. The first is that the more of a good you use, the less there is for someone else. This characteristic is called

(7) _____. The second is that you must pay for them to be able to use them. This

characteristic is called _____. Goods that have neither of these characteristics are called _____ goods. Things like national defense, police protection, beautiful parks, and clean streets are examples of such goods.

(8)   Once public goods are provided to one individual, their benefits cannot easily be restricted to just a few people. It is (difficult/easy) to exclude nonpayers. As a result it is difficult to get individuals to make voluntary contributions to pay for the goods they can enjoy by reason of someone else's paying for them.

This is sometimes referred to as the free-_____ problem.

Besides the problem of lack of excludability, one person's use of public goods, such as enjoying a beautiful park, does not usually deplete the supply for others. In technical language, the marginal cost of

(9)   serving additional users is _____. This is to be contrasted to the case of private goods, where providing additional units of output does require additional resources and does entail a positive marginal cost. An efficient allocation of resources requires that price equal marginal social cost. The clear implication is that from an efficiency standpoint, the use of public goods should be priced at

_____ and one should not be surprised if profit-maximizing firms fail to provide public goods.

Present and Future Consumption

The productive use of resources is time-specific. Loafing today will not make tomorrow twice as long. A machine that is idle one day does not mean that there will be twice as many machine hours available the next day. While the use of resources is time-specific, the consumption of output is not. Output can be saved, either directly by adding to inventories in warehouses or indirectly by building plants and machines. Thus, an economy does have the ability to transfer consumption through time by acts of saving and investment.

The rate of interest is an important determinant of how much investment will actually take place. A number of observers have questioned whether the private economy will result in interest rates and investment spending that are socially optimal. In the real world, monetary and fiscal policies can be used to manipulate interest rates and hence to influence investment for many different purposes. Some, such as the English economist A. G. Pigou, have argued that people are simply shortsighted when it comes to saving for the future.

(10)   Individual investment projects often entail great risk for the individual investors, but little risk for society. Bankruptcy may wipe out an investor's financial investment, but it (does/does not) destroy buildings and machines. These capital goods will still be around for others to use. It has been argued that the high individual risk will result in a level of investment that is (less/more) than socially optimal.

(11)   Many decisions, such as damming a canyon, are essentially _____, and some people are concerned that unregulated market decisions in these cases do not adequately represent the interests of future generations. All these arguments suggest that even competitive markets are likely to result in inappropriate decisions about saving and investments.

Cost Disease of Personal Services

Many services—doctor visits, education, police protection—require mainly labor input and offer

(12)   (limited/substantial) opportunities for increases in labor productivity. By contrast, increasing mechanization and technological innovations have resulted in substantial increases in labor productivity in the production of many commodities. Increased labor productivity has led to higher wages for workers in these industries. Since workers can move between occupations, the wages of teachers and police, for example, have had to increase to remain competitive with opportunities in other jobs. In manufacturing industries, increased labor productivity helps to offset the cost pressures from higher wages. In service industries there are little or no increases in labor productivity to help contain cost pressures. The result is that many personal services have become more expensive over time because of the uneven pattern of increases in labor productivity. Increases in productivity always make an economy better off in the sense that the economy can now produce more of all goods, including personal services. But at the same time, society will find that lagging productivity in service industries means that the cost of these services has increased. Concerns about controlling costs may be misdirected if the major problem is the natural market response to differential productivity growth.

DEFINITION QUIZ

Choose the letter that is the most appropriate definition for each of the following terms.

1. _____ Opportunity cost
2. _____ Resource misallocation
3. _____ Production possibilities frontier
4. _____ Externalities
5. _____ Marginal private cost
6. _____ Marginal social cost
7. _____ Excludability
8. _____ Depletability
9. _____ Public good
10. _____ Private good
11. _____ Asymmetric information
12. _____ Principals
13. _____ Agents
14. _____ Rent seeking
15. _____ Moral hazard
16. _____ Cost disease of personal services

a. Tendency of clients who have the lowest risks to be the most likely insurance customers.
b. Results of activities that affect other people, without corresponding compensation.
c. Tendency of cost of services to rise more rapidly than inflation because of difficulty of increasing productivity.
d. Decision-makers who delegate their power to others.
e. Graph depicting the different combinations of various goods that can be produced with available resources and existing technology.
f. Commodity or service whose benefits are not depleted by an additional user and for which it is difficult to exclude people from enjoying its benefits.
g. Unproductive activity in pursuit of profit.
h. Utility of an increase in output differs from its opportunity cost.
i. Parties to a transaction know different things about the item to be exchanged.
j. Marginal private cost plus costs imposed on others.
k. Commodity or service whose benefits are depleted by an additional user and for which people are excluded from its benefits unless they pay.
l. The ability to keep someone who does not pay from enjoying a commodity.
m. Tendency of insurance to encourage risk taking.
n. Share of marginal cost for an activity that those who engage in the activity pay.
o. Those to whom decision-making authority is delegated.
p. Commodity is used up when consumed.
q. Foregone value of next best alternative that is not chosen.

BASIC EXERCISE

This exercise is designed to illustrate the cost disease of personal services.

Table 29–1 has spaces to compute the costs of producing both widgets and police services; both are assumed to be produced with only labor input. (Wages for police officers and for workers in the widget factory are assumed to be equal, as individuals can choose between these occupations.)

1. Fill in the missing spaces in the first column to determine the cost per widget of producing 240,000 widgets and the cost per hour of 200,000 hours of police services.

2. The first entry in the second column assumes that labor productivity in the production of widgets has risen by 4.17 percent. The earnings of both widget workers and police officers are assumed to increase by the same percentage as productivity. Now fill in the rest of the second column. What has happened to the average cost of producing one widget? What about the cost of producing one hour of police services?

3. The first entry in column 3 assumes that the growth in average labor productivity continues

TABLE 29-1
COSTS OF PRODUCING 240,000 WIDGETS

	(1)	(2)	(3)
Widgets per worker	1920	2000	3000
Number of workers[a]			
Annual earnings per worker	$21,120	$22,000	$33,000
Total labor costs (total cost)			
Cost per widget			

COSTS OF PRODUCING 200,000 HOURS OF POLICE SERVICES

Hours per police officer	2000	2000	2000
Number of police officers[b]			
Annual earnings per police officer	$21,120	$22,000	$33,000
Total labor cost (total cost)			
Cost per hour of police services			

[a]240,000 ÷ widgets per worker
[b]200,000 ÷ hours per police officer

for another 10 years. Again, the growth in earnings is assumed to match the growth in productivity. Fill in the rest of column 3. What is the increase in the cost of producing one widget?

_____

What about the cost of one hour of police

services? _____

4. One way to hold the line on police costs is to refuse to increase salaries for police officers. Another way is to reduce the number of police officers. What are the long-run implications of both these policies?

SELF-TESTS FOR UNDERSTANDING

Test A

Circle the correct answer.

1. Which of the following is a clear indicator of a misallocation of resources?
   a. Barney and Michelle, who subscribe to *Gourmet* magazine, despair over the increasing number of fast-food outlets.
   b. In the long run, Farmer Fran makes zero economic profit.
   c. After careful study, economists have concluded that the economy of Arcadia is operating at a

point inside its production possibilities frontier.
   d. The latest census survey indicates that the top 10 percent of the income distribution has an average income that is over 12 times that of the bottom 10 percent.

2. Which of the following is an externality?
   a. Imperfect information.
   b. Your pride in the new stereo system you just purchased at a bargain price.
   c. Natural monopolies, such as the local electric utility.
   d. The new road that was built for the NASA tracking station that has substantially reduced transportation costs for local farmers.

3. Detrimental externalities imply all but which one of the following?
   a. The marginal social cost of an increase in output will exceed marginal private cost.
   b. A misallocation of resources will result from the private market supplying less output than is socially desirable.
   c. Private firms will concentrate on private costs, ignoring the cost burden they are imposing on others.
   d. Taxes that impose additional private costs on those causing the externalities are, in principle, capable of correcting the misallocation.

4. If the production of gizmos involves beneficial externalities, then it is likely that
   a. marginal private benefits are less than marginal social benefits.

b. a free market will produce too many gizmos.

c. a tax on the production of gizmos will lead to a more efficient allocation.

d. the use of gizmos does not involve depletion.

5. Which of the following is not true?

a. Public goods are all things the government spends money on.

b. Public goods are unlikely to be supplied by profit-maximizing firms.

c. Public goods are defined as goods and services that many people can enjoy at the same time and from which it is difficult to exclude potential customers who do not want to pay.

d. Public goods have a zero marginal cost of serving additional users.

6. Which of the following does not have the characteristics of a public good?

a. Clean rivers.

b. Gasoline.

c. Police and fire protection.

d. Unscrambled radio and television signals.

7. The "free-rider" problem refers to

a. the difficulty of stopping kids from sneaking onto the local merry-go-round.

b. the difficulty of getting people to voluntarily contribute to pay for public goods.

c. the use of subsidies to encourage the production of goods with beneficial externalities.

d. increasing problems with hitchhikers on the interstate highways.

8. Which of the following explains the cost disease of personal services?

a. The supply effects of price controls, such as rent control.

b. The existence of monopoly elements in the economy.

c. Detrimental externalities.

d. The uneven prospects for improved labor productivity in different sectors of the economy.

9. Which of the following is *not* likely to suffer from the cost disease of personal services?

a. Individual piano lessons.

b. The production of television sets.

c. Small liberal arts colleges that maintain an unchanged student-faculty ratio.

d. Orchestras and symphonies.

10. Which of the following is *not* an argument that free markets will result in an inappropriate amount of saving and investment?

a. Investment projects are often riskier to individuals than to the community.

b. During periods of inflation, nominal interest rates will rise to incorporate expectations of continuing inflations.

c. Due to "defective telescopic faculties," people do not give enough consideration to the future.

d. Many decisions concerning natural resources are made without enough consideration given to their irreversible consequences.

Test B

Circle T or F for True or False as appropriate.

1. An unregulated market economy would never have business cycles.   T F

2. Externalities, whether beneficial or detrimental, imply that marginal social cost is always less than marginal private cost.   T F

3. An activity that causes damage to someone else and for which there is no compensation is said to involve a detrimental externality.   T F

4. A beneficial externality is likely to result in marginal private benefits exceeding marginal social benefits.   T F

5. Economists define public goods as anything for which the government spends money.   T F

6. The fact that it is difficult to restrict the use of public goods to those who are willing to pay is the problem of depletability.   T F

7. The provision of public goods is complicated by the "free-rider" problem.   T F

8. The fact that public goods are not depleted by use implies that the marginal cost of providing the goods to one more consumer is zero.   T F

9. The rate of interest plays an important role in the allocation of resources between the present and the future, because it affects the profitability of investment projects.   T F

10. Many investment projects will entail less risk for the individual investor than for the community as a whole.   T F

SUPPLEMENTARY EXERCISES

1. Consider the economy of Beethovia, which produces two goods: widgets and music recitals. Widgets are manufactured with capital and labor according to the following production function:

$$W = 60\, L^{\frac{1}{2}}\, K^{\frac{1}{2}},$$

where L = number of workers producing widgets and K = number of machines.

Music recitals are labor intensive and produced according to the following production function:

$$M = 50 \times L.$$

Initially there are 10,000 workers in Beethovia, meaning that the sum of labor allocated to the production of widgets or recitals cannot exceed 10,000. Initially, there are also 10,000 machines, or $K = 10,000$.

a. Draw the production possibilities frontier for Beethovia showing the trade-off between the production of widgets and recitals. (It is probably easiest to arbitrarily fix the number of recitals and then calculate the maximum production of widgets with the remaining labor and all the machines.)

b. Competitive markets have resulted in 9409 widget workers and 591 musicians. At this allocation, what is the marginal product and average product of labor in the production of widgets? In the production of recitals?

c. With the passage of time, saving and investment by the people of Beethovia have increased the number of machines to 12,100. At the initial allocation of labor, but with the new number of machines, what is the

marginal and average product of labor in the production of widgets? What has happened to the productivity of workers in the production of recitals?

d. What has happened to the opportunity cost of music recitals; that is, what is the new slope of the production possibilities frontier at the allocation specified in Question b? To answer this question either draw a new production possibilities frontier or derive a mathematical expression for the slope of the frontier.

e. If you have answered Question d correctly you should have determined that the cost of recitals has increased. Recitals suffer from the cost disease of personal services. At the same time, how can you show that the increase in productivity has made Beethovia unambiguously richer?

2. Go to the library or bookstore and get a copy of *Encounters with the Archdruid* by John McPhee. The book reports on three encounters between David Brower, who was president of the Sierra Club, and other individuals who want to dam the Colorado River, build a copper mine in the Cascades, and develop Hilton Head Island. Many think that McPhee's description of the raft trip down the Colorado River with Brower and Floyd Dominy, who was head of the Bureau of Reclamation, is especially good.

Whose position do you favor?

Is Brower always right? Is he ever right?

30

Real Firms and Their Financing: Stocks and Bonds

LEARNING OBJECTIVES

After completing the material in this chapter you should be able to:

- define, understand, and use correctly the terms and concepts listed below.
- explain the major advantages and disadvantages of alternative forms of business organization.
- explain why investors in common stock are not penalized in the form of lower rates of return from the double taxation of corporate dividends.
- explain how double taxation can affect the business investment decisions of corporations and may lead to inefficiency in resource allocation.
- explain the advantages of plowback as a source of funds to a corporation.
- explain why bond prices fall when interest rates go up and vice versa.
- explain how the use of stocks or bonds shifts risk between a corporation and financial investors.
- describe how portfolio diversification can reduce the risk faced by a financial investor.
- explain why the stock market is of critical importance to the financing of corporations even though new stock issues account for only a very small proportion of new funds raised by corporations.
- discuss the advantages and disadvantages of corporate takeovers.
- discuss the role of speculation both in the economy in general and in the securities markets in particular.

IMPORTANT TERMS AND CONCEPTS

Proprietorship
Unlimited liability
Partnership
Corporation
Limited liability
Double taxation
Limited partnership
Plowback or retained earnings
Common stock
Bond
Portfolio diversification
Stock exchanges
Takeovers
Speculation
Random walk

CHAPTER REVIEW

The purpose of this chapter is to explore the advantages and disadvantages of alternative legal forms of business organization. Special attention is given to the different ways in which corporations can raise funds and to the markets on which corporate securities are traded.

(1)   A business that is owned and operated by a single individual is called a _____.
This is by far the most common form of business organization in the United States. When, instead a firm's ownership and decision making are shared by a fixed number of individuals, the business is called a

_____. Another form of business organization is one in which the firm has the legal status of a fictional individual and is owned by a large number of stockholders and run by an elected

board of directors and officers. This form of organization is called a _____. A major advantage of the latter form of organization is that stockholders, the legal owners of the business, are

not liable for the firm's debts. The fact that corporations have _____ liability has made it possible for corporations to raise very large sums of money in the pursuit of profits.

(2)   Corporations raise funds in several ways. A corporation that raises funds by selling shares of ownership and offering a stake in future profits is issuing (stock/bonds). If a corporation issues securities that

promise to pay fixed sums of money as interest and principal, it is issuing _____.
Corporations can also borrow directly from large financial institutions, such as banks or insurance companies. The most common way of raising funds is to directly reinvest part of a corporation's profits. This

method of raising funds is called _____. Corporations typically prefer to use plowback to finance corporate investments as it avoids the cost and scrutiny that accompany new issues of stocks and bonds.

(3)   Assuming a firm does not become bankrupt, a bond that is held to maturity offers the bondholder a fixed and known stream of payments. Investing in stock promises future dividend payments and stock prices that (are/are not) known at the time of purchase. The greater uncertainty of future dividends and stock prices as compared to bond payments leads economists to conclude that from the viewpoint of individual investors, stocks are (more/less) risky than bonds. From the viewpoint of a firm (bonds/stocks) are more risky, because a failure to (meet bond payments/pay dividends) can force a firm into bankruptcy.

(4)   However, this comparison understates the riskiness to individual investors of investing in bonds. If a bond must be sold before maturity, and interest rates have changed, the market price of the bond will also change. If interest rates have risen, existing bonds with low coupon payments will look less attractive unless their price (rises/falls). Holders of these bonds will suffer a (gain/loss). Conversely, if interest rates have fallen, competition for existing bonds with high coupon payments will (increase/decrease) the price of existing bonds.

Shares of stock offer investors returns in the form of dividend payments and/or changes in the stock price. Investors have the option of buying shares of only one company or shares of several companies.

(5)   Buying shares of several companies is an example of _____. Institutional

investors who use computers to make automatic trading decisions are engaging in _____ trading. One assumes control of an existing corporation by buying a sufficient number of current shares of

stock. When such an action is contested it is called a _____ battle and can be an effective way to remove incompetent management. There is concern that these struggles lead to wasteful and costly actions on both sides of the battle.

(6)   Stocks and bonds are traded in markets that sometimes have a specific location, such as the New York Stock Exchange, but are also traded by dealers and brokers who keep track, by telephone or computer, of the latest price changes. New stock issues (are/are not) usually sold through established exchanges. Two

important functions served by established exchanges include (1) reducing the _____ of stock ownership by providing a secondary market in existing shares and (2) determining the current price of a company's stock. In the latter role, established exchanges help to allocate the economy's resources to those firms that, in the market's judgment, are expected to make the most profitable use of those resources.

Speculators are not much different from most investors who hope to profit from increases in stock prices. From a general perspective, speculation serves two important functions. First, it can help to decrease price fluctuations. Buying now at low prices in anticipation of being able to sell next year at high prices will,

(7) in fact, make prices today (higher/lower) than they otherwise would be and will also make prices next year

_____ than they otherwise would be. The second function of speculation is that

it can work to provide _____ for those who want to avoid taking risks. Commodity speculators will agree now on a price to be paid for buying crops next year, thus insuring a farmer against the adverse effects of a decrease in price. Other speculators may agree now on a price at which to sell crops next year to a milling company, thus insuring the miller against the adverse effects of an increase in price.

The behavior of individual stock prices has long fascinated many investors. Much time and effort is spent trying to forecast the movement of stock prices. Some investors look at things like a firm's earnings and its current stock price; others plot recent stock prices and try to discover laws of motion in their graphs. Economists have also studied the changes in individual stock prices. Much of this research supports the conclusion that changes in stock prices are essentially unpredictable, that is they look like a

(8) _____ _____. Such a result could arise because of essentially random waves of buying and selling as investors try to outguess each other. It could also arise from investors' careful study and analysis of individual companies, study that is so complete that all anticipated future events are fully reflected in current stock prices. The expectation today of higher profits tomorrow raises stock prices (today/tomorrow). In this view, changes in stock prices can only reflect currently unanticipated events, events that will likely look like random events. This viewpoint has been formalized in the hypothesis of "efficient markets." Much advanced research in financial economics is concerned with testing this hypothesis.

DEFINITION QUIZ

Choose the letter that is the most appropriate definition for each of the following terms.

1. _____ Proprietorship
2. _____ Unlimited liability
3. _____ Partnership
4. _____ Corporation
5. _____ Limited liability
6. _____ Double taxation
7. _____ Limited partnership
8. _____ Retained earnings (plowback)
9. _____ Common stock
10. _____ Bond
11. _____ Portfolio diversification
12. _____ Takeovers
13. _____ Speculation
14. _____ Random walk
15. _____ Stock exchange

a. Change in variable is completely unpredictable.
b. Legal obligation to repay company debts only with money owners have already invested in the firm.
c. Purchase of risky assets in anticipation of favorable price changes.
d. Corporation's promise to pay a fixed sum at maturity plus annual interest.
e. Firm owned by a single individual.
f. Portion of a corporation's profits that management returns to shareholders.
g. Holding a number and variety of stocks, bonds, and other assets in an attempt to find offsetting risks.
h. A group of individuals not currently in control of a firm buys enough stock to gain control.
i. Legal obligation to repay company's debts with whatever resources owners may have.
j. Piece of paper that gives holder a share of ownership in a company.
k. Firm that is organized as a partnership but gives some partners the legal protection of limited liability.
l. Firm owned by a fixed number of individuals.
m. Portion of a corporation's profits that management decides to keep and reinvest.
n. Firm with the legal status of a fictitious individual, owned by stockholders.
o. Taxes on corporate profits before distribution to shareholders and taxes on dividends received by shareholders.
p. Organized market for trading corporate shares.

BASIC EXERCISE

This exercise is designed to illustrate how the prices of stocks are adjusted by market forces to reflect alternative yields that are available to investors and to insure that the returns to shareholders are not reduced by the double taxation of corporate profits.

The XYZ corporation earns $80 million in profits a year and pays $28 million in profits tax to the government, leaving $52 million that is paid out as a $4 dividend on each of 13 million shares of stock. (XYZ does not plow back any of its after-tax profits.) Investors in XYZ stock have the option of investing in corporate bonds and earning a return of 10 percent on which they will have to pay income taxes, just as they must pay taxes on dividend income.

Stock Price	Dividend Before Taxes	Dividend Yield (col. 2 ÷ col. 1)
$ 25	$4	_____
40	4	_____
64	4	_____
100	4	_____

1. Fill in the blank column to compute the dividend yield on a share of XYZ stock at various prices.
2. Assume that the XYZ dividend has always been $4 and is expected to remain $4 in the future. Further, since XYZ does not plow back any of its after-tax profits, the price of XYZ stock is not expected to change. If investors require the same return on shares of XYZ stock as they do on corporate bonds, what will be the price of

   XYZ stock? _____
   Do investors in XYZ stock receive a lower rate of return because of the double taxation of corporate income—once as corporate profits and then again as dividends? Why or why not?
3. What is likely to happen to the price of XYZ stock if the interest rate of government bonds rises to 16 percent? Falls to 6.25 percent?
4. Suddenly and unexpectedly, the president of XYZ announces that oil has been discovered on company property. The revenues from this discovery will double profits for the foreseeable future. Furthermore, XYZ announces that starting next year and continuing into the future, the dividend per share will also be doubled to $8. Why will the price of XYZ stock rise immediately rather than waiting until next year when higher dividend payments start?

5. If everyone believes that dividends on XYZ stock will double beginning next year and if alternative investments continue to yield 10 percent, what is the likely new stock price? Why?

SELF-TESTS FOR UNDERSTANDING

Test A

Circle the correct answer.

1. Which one of the following is *not* true of proprietorships?
   a. The proprietor has complete and full personal control of the business.
   b. Limited liability on the part of the proprietor for the debts of the business.
   c. Income is only taxed once.
   d. Few legal complications.
2. In which form of business is income subject to double taxation?
   a. Proprietorship.
   b. Partnership.
   c. Corporation.
3. Ways in which corporations can raise money include all but which one of the following?
   a. Issuing shares of stock.
   b. Borrowing money in the form of bonds.
   c. The reinvestment, or plowback, of profits.
   d. Paying dividends.
4. Which of the following is the most important source of new funds for corporations?
   a. New stock issues.
   b. Corporate bonds.
   c. Retained earnings.
   d. Bank loans.
5. A decrease in the general level of interest rates will tend to
   a. increase bond prices.
   b. lower bond prices.
   c. have no effect on bond prices.
6. Emerson purchased a newly issued General Electric bond last year with coupon payments offering an interest rate of 10 percent. Since then, market interest rates on similar bonds have risen to 12 percent. Which of the following is true?
   a. The market value of the bonds that Emerson bought will have increased from the price he paid.
   b. If held to maturity, and General Electric does not default, Emerson will earn 12 percent on his original investment.

c. Anyone purchasing such bonds today, at their current market price and holding them to maturity, can expect to earn only 10 percent on the investment.

d. If Emerson sold his bonds today, at their current market price, he would have to sell the bonds for less than he paid.

7. There are 5 million outstanding shares of stock in the XYZ corporation. If the price of XYZ stock rises by $1, then

a. the XYZ corporation will have $5 million more to invest or use to pay higher dividends.

b. existing shareholders will benefit by $1 a share.

c. investors who hold XYZ bonds will have suffered a capital loss.

d. the XYZ corporation will owe federal tax on the increased stock price.

8. Which of the following $100,000 investments offers the most diversification?

a. $100,000 of Boeing stock.

b. $100,000 of New York City bonds.

c. $100,000 of gold.

d. $25,000 invested in each of the following: Kodak, Sears, DuPont, and Shell Oil.

9. The important economic functions of organized stock exchanges include all but which one of the following?

a. Offering investors insurance against the risk of changes in stock prices.

b. Reducing the risk of purchasing stock by offering investors a place to sell their shares should they need the funds for some other purpose.

c. Helping to allocate the economy's resources, since companies with high current stock prices will find it easier to raise additional funds to pursue investment opportunities.

10. If Maxine is to be a successful speculator she must

a. buy during a period of excess supply and sell during a period of excess supply.

b. buy during a period of excess supply and sell during a period of excess demand.

c. buy during a period of excess demand and sell during a period of excess demand.

d. buy during a period of excess demand and sell during a period of excess supply.

Test B

Circle T or F for True or False as appropriate.

1. Corporations, while constituting a minority of the *number* of business organizations, are the most

important form of organization when measured by total *sales*. **T F**

2. When measured by the number of firms, proprietorships are the most common form of business organization in the United States. **T F**

3. The double taxation of corporate income— once as corporate profits and then again as dividends—means that investors in the stock market must settle for a lower rate of return on stocks. **T F**

4. Assuming no bankruptcy, a corporate bond is a riskless investment even if the bond must be sold before maturity. **T F**

5. Any individual who wants to buy or sell shares of stock can do so by walking onto the floor of the New York Stock Exchange and announcing her intentions.

6. Whenever a share of Xerox stock is sold on the New York Stock Exchange, Xerox gets the proceeds. **T F**

7. If a corporation decides to issue new stock, it will typically offer these shares initially through one of the regional stock exchanges. **T F**

8. Established stock exchanges, such as the New York Stock Exchange, are really just a form of legalized gambling and serve no useful social function. **T F**

9. The finding that stock prices follow a random walk implies that investing in stocks is essentially a pure gamble. **T F**

10. Profitable speculation involves buying high and selling low. **T F**

SUPPLEMENTARY EXERCISES

1. **Stocks and Bonds**

Get a copy of *The Wall Street Journal*. Turn to the bond page, which is toward the back. (Actually the financial page of any newspaper that lists bonds will do.) Find the listing for several regular bonds of different corporations with a similiar maturity date that is sometime past 2000. Write down their coupon rate, current yield, and market price. Also note stock prices for the same companies. After three months, look up the stock prices and the current yield and price of the bonds again. Check to see that any increase (or decrease) in the current yield is matched by an opposite movement in the bond

TABLE 30-1

(1) Company	(2) Number of Shares if Investing $1000	(3) Number of Shares if Investing $10,000	(4) Stock Price in 3 Months	(5) Value of $1000 Investment[a]	(6) Value of $10,000 Investment[b]
1. AT&T	32.52	325.20			
2. Boeing	21.68	216.80			
3. Citicorp	57.97	579.71			
4. Disney	10.57	105.68			
5. du Pont	28.47	284.70			
6. Exxon	19.46	194.65			
7. IBM	9.58	95.81			
8. Maytag	76.19	761.90			
9. Reebock	82.47	824.74			
10. Xerox	25.40	253.97			

Value of portfolio[c] _____

[a](5) = (2) × (4).   [b](6) = (3) × (4).   [c]Sum the 10 entries in (5).

price. Had you actually bought these bonds, would you now have a gain or loss? What if you had bought shares of stock? Have all or most of the bond prices moved together? Have all the stock prices moved together? (It would not be surprising if the prices of bonds of different corporations rose or fell together. Stock prices are much less likely to change together. Can you explain why?)

2. Portfolio Diversification

Assume you invested $10,000 in the ten stocks listed in Table 30-1 on September 14, 1990. Use the financial section of your local newspaper or *The Wall Street Journal* to complete the table from current prices on the New York Stock Exchange. The sum of the entries in column (5) will show you the return on a diversified portfolio that invested $1,000 in each company. Column (6) will show you possible gains and losses had you put all your eggs in one basket. It is easy to pick the winners after the fact, but in reality you must choose without knowing the future stock prices. How do your results illustrate the link between portfolio diversification and risk?

3. Bond Prices and Interest Rates

As seen in Chapter 14, the market price of a $1,000 bond paying interest once a year can be calculated by computing the present value of future payments as shown below:

$$\text{Price} = \sum_{t=1}^{N} \frac{\text{INT}}{(1 + i)^t} + \frac{1,000}{(1 + i)^N}$$

Where Price = market price, i = market interest rate, N = number of years to maturity, and INT = interest payment.

It may be easiest to complete the following exercises if you have access to a microcomputer or sophisticated hand calculator.

a. Show that if INT = $90 and i = .09 that the market price of this bond will be $1,000 for all values of N.

b. Now vary i, holding INT constant at $90 and N constant at 25 years. Note how the price of a bond issued with a coupon payment of $90 changes as market interest rates change. You should find that price is less than $1,000 when i is greater than .09 and price is greater than $1,000 when i is less than .09.

c. Choose a particular value for i, say .08, and see how the difference in price from the original $1,000 varies as N varies from 1 year to 25 years. You should find that the change in price is greater as N gets larger; that is, longer term bonds show a greater change in price for a given change in interest rates.

PART 7

THE GOVERN-MENT AND THE ECONOMY

31

Limiting Market Power: Regulation of Industry

LEARNING OBJECTIVES

After completing the material in this chapter you should be able to:

- define, understand, and use correctly the terms and concepts listed below.
- describe the two major purposes of regulation.
- identify the major regulatory agencies and the industries they regulate.
- critically evaluate each of the arguments given in favor of regulation.
- explain why regulators often raise prices.
- discuss the implications of "fully distributed costs" as a basis for price floors.
- explain why marginal cost pricing may be infeasible in an industry with significant economies of scale.
- explain why allowing a firm to earn profits equal to the opportunity cost of its capital provides little incentive for increased efficiency.
- evaluate the alternatives suggested for present regulatory practices.

- summarize recent experience under deregulation of several industries.
- discuss the experience of nationalized and regulated industries.

IMPORTANT TERMS AND CONCEPTS

Nationalization
Price floor
Price ceiling
Natural monopoly
Economies of scale
Economies of scope
Cross-subsidization
Self-destructive competition
Fully distributed cost
Marginal cost pricing
Ramsey Pricing Rule
Price caps
Regulatory lag
Stand-alone cost

CHAPTER REVIEW

(1) By and large the United States has chosen to (regulate/nationalize) rather than to _____ industries where there is concern about the exploitation of excessive market power. This chapter discusses a number of the controversies about current regulatory practices and the roles played by the regulatory agencies.

Regulatory procedures have been adopted basically for four reasons:

(2) 1. To regulate the actions of natural monopolies in industries where economies of _____ and economies of _____ mean that the free competition between a large number of suppliers (is/is not) sustainable.

2. To ensure service at reasonable prices to isolated areas of the country. It is argued that regulation is necessary in this case so that suppliers can offset (above/below)-cost prices in isolated areas with (above/below)-cost prices elsewhere and thus be protected from competitors who concentrate only on the profitable markets.

3. To avoid self-destructive competition among firms in industries with high (fixed/marginal) costs and low short-run _____ costs.

4. To protect consumers, employees, and the environment from unscrupulous business practices.

The first three justifications for regulation often lead to direct regulation of prices and/or earnings. The last reason, concerning consumer, employee, and environmental protection, usually does not involve the direct regulation of prices, although compliance can impose substantial costs on firms.

Regulation of prices has turned out to be a very complicated undertaking. Established to prevent abuses of monopoly power such as charging prices that are "too high," the regulatory agencies have, in many cases, actually raised prices. In these cases, regulation preserves the shadow of competition only by (3) protecting (high/low)-cost, inefficient firms.

Several criteria have been proposed to evaluate whether prices are "fair." One method looks at all costs related to a given line of business as well as some portion of shared overhead costs. This method (4) leads to what is called _____ _____ costs. Economists typically argue for the use of _____ cost as a more appropriate basis for price floors. One can conceive of cases, often in connection with regulated earnings, where any price above long-run marginal cost yet below fully distributed costs will allow (higher/lower) prices for all of a firm's customers.

The application of marginal cost pricing is difficult in an industry with significant economies of scale. In this case, average cost will be declining as output increases. When average cost declines, marginal cost is (5) (greater/less) than average cost. Economists and some regulators have urged the use of the Ramsey Pricing Rule, under which the excess of price over marginal cost depends upon the elasticity of _____. Difficulties with implementing the Ramsey Pricing Rule have led to interest in the concept of stand-alone cost. Under this approach, regulators would not set price, but rather floors and ceilings within which prices could vary. Price floors would reflect minimal competitive prices, or (marginal/average) cost. Price ceilings would reflect the competitive costs of providing the service or good in question, or _____ _____ cost.

A number of alternatives to the present system of regulation have been considered. In some markets it (6) appears that viable competition is now possible. In these cases, many observers have argued for (more/less) regulation. Recently there has been significant deregulation of airlines, trucking, railroads, telecommunications, and banking. In other cases, the problem of incentives for efficiency might be addressed by the use of explicit _____ criteria, which would reward firms for measurable increased efficiency.

The term regulatory lag has been coined to describe the long and drawn-out regulatory process. Some suggest that this process itself offers one of the few incentives for efficiency and innovation, since it

(7)   actually builds in some penalty for (efficiency/inefficiency) and some reward for _____.
A variant of this notion would predetermine price ceilings or caps and leave firms free to earn higher profits through even greater efficiency.

   Experience with deregulation, especially in airline, transportation, and telephone service, is now over a decade old. While it is still too early for a definitive evaluation, a number of trends have emerged.

1. Prices have generally declined.
2. Local airline service has not suffered as was feared due to the establishment of specialized commuter airlines.
3. New firms have entered previously regulated industries.
4. Unions in previously regulated industries have been under significant pressure to reduce wages and adjust work rules.
5. Mergers have increased the average size of the largest firms.

Items 4 and 5 need careful interpretation. To the extent that regulation allowed firms to easily pass on increased labor costs, unions will find the bargaining position of firms now subject to competitive market pressures much tougher. Mergers are understandable if regulation was originally concentrated on industries with economies of scale. We now need to balance the potential cost savings from larger firms against the potential of monopoly abuses.

DEFINITION QUIZ

Choose the letter that is the most appropriate definition for each of the following terms.

1. _____ Nationalization
2. _____ Price floor
3. _____ Price ceiling
4. _____ Natural monopoly
5. _____ Economies of scale
6. _____ Economies of scope
7. _____ Cross-subsidization
8. _____ Ramsey Pricing Rule
9. _____ Fully distributed cost
10. _____ Stand-alone cost
11. _____ Regulatory lag

a. Losses on one product balanced by profits on another.
b. Principle that, in a multiproduct, regulated firm where price must exceed marginal cost for the firm to break even, the ratio of price to marginal cost should be highest for the products with the lowest demand elasticities.
c. Legal maximum price.
d. Fair share of a firm's total cost as determined by accounting conventions.
e. Industry in which a single firm is able to supply the market output at lower average cost than a number of smaller firms could.
f. Savings acquired through simultaneous production of different products.
g. Government ownership and operation of a business firm.
h. Hypothetical cost for efficient firm to supply particular service.
i. Sale of government agency to private concern.
j. Delays in considering requests for price changes.
k. Legal minimum price.
l. Savings acquired through increases in quantities produced.

BASIC EXERCISE

This exercise illustrates the difficulty of marginal cost pricing when average cost is declining.

Imagine that the efficient provision of telephone calls in a medium-sized city involves an initial investment of $75 million financed by borrowing at 9 percent and variable cost of 5 cents a phone call. The phone company's annual fixed cost would be $6.75 million (9 percent of $75 million).

1. Use this information about costs to plot marginal cost and average total cost in Figure 31–1. (Use the $6.75 million figure for annual fixed cost.)
2. Assume that regulators set price at 5 cents, the level of marginal cost. What is the firm's profit position if 30 million calls a year are demanded at that price? 60 million? 120 million?
3. Is setting price equal to marginal cost a viable option in this case? Why or why not?

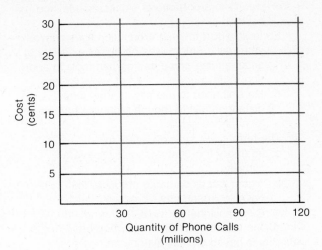

FIGURE 31–1

SELF-TESTS FOR UNDERSTANDING

Test A

Circle the correct answer.

1. Match each of these regulatory agencies with the appropriate industries from the list below.
   Interstate Commerce Commission (ICC)

   _____

   Federal Communications Commission (FCC)

   _____

   Federal Energy Regulatory Commission (FERC)

   _____

   Federal Reserve

   _____

   Securities and Exchange Commission (SEC)

   _____

   a. Banking
   b. Automobile manufacturers
   c. Broadcasting and telecommunications
   d. Railroads, barges, pipelines, and some trucking
   e. Telephone
   f. Securities (stock and bonds)
   g. Interstate transmission of electric power and sales of natural gas
   h. Pharmaceuticals
2. Proponents of regulation would disagree with which one of the following?
   a. The public needs to be protected from the potential abuses of natural monopolies.
   b. Destructive competition may benefit consumers in the short run, but will leave them open to monopoly abuses in the long run.
   c. "Caveat emptor" is an appropriate principle for the marketplace.
   d. In the absence of regulation many isolated communities might find themselves without vital services.
3. Which of the following is an example of economies of scale?
   a. Anna finds her costs increasing as she tries to increase the production of her custom-designed clothes.
   b. Jim discovers that a 15 percent reduction in price leads to a 30 percent increase in sales.
   c. Sarah realizes that the expertise and experience of her firm in producing specialized medical equipment will be useful in the production of testing equipment for physicists.
   d. IBM is able to reduce unit costs when it doubles the production of the IBM PC.
4. Which of the following is an example of economies of scope?
   a. An increase in circulation for the *Daily Planet* would involve only printing costs and require no increase in the editorial staff.

235

b. Ramona and Ricardo have invested their wealth in a portfolio of stocks, bonds, and real estate.

c. In an effort to keep production lines busy all year, Artic Enterprises produces a variety of small-engine home and garden tools in addition to its successful line of snowblowers.

d. Ma Bell used to use profits from long-distance calls to reduce monthly charges for local phone service.

5. The term *cross subsidy* refers to
   a. an angry firm that does not receive a subsidy.
   b. higher prices on some products that help to cover costs on other products.
   c. Congressional subsidies for agriculture.
   d. the financing of Christian churches.

6. Prices based on fully distributed costs
   a. would be identical to those based on long-run marginal costs.
   b. would be identical to Ramsey prices.
   c. have been proposed as a way of ensuring that prices on all lines of business are fair to both customers and competitors.
   d. provide strong incentives for increased efficiency.

7. Which one of the following is not among the alternatives that have been proposed to the present system of regulation?
   a. Deregulation of industries where there appears to be sufficient competition.
   b. The use of explicit performance criteria where feasible.
   c. An institutionalized regulatory lag in an effort to promote efficiency.
   d. More extensive use of fully distributed costs.

8. The term *regulatory lag* refers to
   a. the time it takes people to respond to a change in prices.
   b. the long time it may take for a change in regulated prices to be approved.
   c. the slowness of moves to deregulation.
   d. the delay that occurs on many long-distance phone calls.

9. Which of the following does *not* provide a strong incentive for increased efficiency on the part of regulated firms?
   a. Regulating profits so they equal the opportunity cost of capital.
   b. Deregulation.
   c. Performance criteria.
   d. Regulatory lag.

10. In the United States natural monopolies tend to be regulated while in Europe they tend to be
    a. nationalized.   c. revitalized.
    b. privatized.   d. capitalized.

Test B

Circle T or F for True or False as appropriate.

1. Regulators are exclusively concerned with getting regulated industries to lower prices. T F

2. The term *economies of scope* refers to the reduction in average costs that result from large-scale production. T F

3. Fair-rate-of-return regulations—that is, price controls that allow firms in an industry to earn profits sufficient to cover the opportunity cost of their capital—offer strong incentives for efficiency and innovation. T F

4. The term *regulatory lag* refers to the lag between actual regulatory practice and the conventional wisdom as to the best practice. T F

5. In the absence of regulation, firms that are required to provide service to isolated communities at high cost might find their more profitable low cost markets taken over by competitors through a process called cream-skimming. T F

6. Self-destructive competition is often used as an argument in favor of regulation. T F

7. Stand alone cost, based on the idea of contestable markets, has been proposed as an alternative to direct regulation of prices. T F

8. Noneconomists who talk about fully distributed costs and economists who talk about long-run marginal costs are using different language to describe the same thing. T F

9. A limitation of nationalization as a solution to the problem of natural monopolies is that there are few systematic mechanisms to promote efficiency in nationalized industries. T F

10. Nationalized industries in all countries are terribly inefficient. T F

SUPPLEMENTARY EXERCISE

Pick your favorite regulatory agency, then go to the library and look up the appropriate annual reports to find out who has served on the regulatory commission recently. Use biographical information, such as is found in *Who's Who in America*, to trace the careers of these individuals. Did these commissioners come from the industry they regulated? After leaving the government did they take a job with the industry they regulated? Who is regulating whom?

32

Limiting Market Power: Antitrust Policy

LEARNING OBJECTIVES

After completing the material in this chapter you should be able to:

- define, understand, and use correctly the terms and concepts listed below.
- explain the major features of each of the five basic antitrust laws.
- describe the shift in judicial emphasis from conduct to structure as grounds for identifying illegal monopolies.
- describe the evidence about changes in concentration in the United States.
- explain the differences between vertical, horizontal, and conglomerate mergers.
- discuss the major arguments in favor of and opposed to bigness per se.
- describe how concentration may or may not be related to market power.
- evaluate arguments in favor of price discrimination.

IMPORTANT TERMS AND CONCEPTS

Antitrust policy
Sherman Act
Clayton Act
Price discrimination
Celler-Kefauver Antimerger Act
Federal Trade Commission Act
Robinson-Patman Act
Rule of reason
Structure versus conduct
Horizontal merger
Vertical merger
Conglomerate merger
Concentration of industry
Concentration ratio
Patent
Market power

CHAPTER REVIEW

This chapter discusses antitrust policy, which is designed to control the growth of monopolies and prevent undesirable behavior on the part of powerful firms. The history of antitrust legislation in the United States

(1)   starts with the _____ Act, passed in 1890. This act declared illegal any actions in restraint of trade and any attempts to monopolize trade. Vigorous antitrust legal action (was/was not) immediately adopted.

The next important pieces of legislation were both passed in 1914. The Federal Trade Commission Act

(2)   established the Federal Trade Commission, and the _____ Act prohibited a number of practices, including the following: preferential prices to some buyers that were not based on cost

differences, known as _____ _____; requirements that buyers purchase

not only what they want but also other goods exclusively from the same seller, called _____
contracts; the practice of having the same individuals serve as directors of two or more competing firms, or

_____ _____; and the purchasing of a competitor's
stock if that acquisition tended to reduce competition.

(3)   At this time, court decisions in antitrust cases were based on the rule of _____,

which said that size per se (is/is not) illegal; rather the focus was on firm _____.
In the Alcoa case, decided in 1945, the Supreme Court ruled that in addition to illegal conduct, size per se (was/was not) sufficient grounds for antitrust actions.

A firm can grow bigger by expanding its own factories or building new ones. A firm can also become

(4)   bigger by buying up other firms. The combination of two firms into one is a _____.
When two companies, one of which sells inputs to the other, merge it is called a (vertical/horizontal) merger.

Mergers between competitors are called _____ mergers. The merger of two

unrelated firms is called a _____ merger.
Economists and others have long argued the question of whether bigness per se is good or bad. Opponents of bigness argue that the flow of wealth to firms with significant market power is socially

(5)   undesirable and should be restrained; profit-maximizing monopolists are likely to produce (more/less) output than is socially desirable; and large firms with significant market power have little inducement for

_____.

Those in favor of bigness argue that large firms are necessary for successful innovation. Further, they

(6)   maintain that many big firms, because of (increasing/decreasing) returns to scale, can yield benefits to the public as a result of the associated (reduction/increase) in unit cost that goes along with large-scale production. To break up these firms into smaller units would (increase/decrease) costs.

There is no perfect measure of how concentrated an industry is. One widely used measure looks at the percent of industry output accounted for by the four largest firms. This measure is called a four-firm

(7)   _____ ratio. In this century, concentration ratios in the United States have shown (much/little) change.

DEFINITION QUIZ

Choose the letter that is the most appropriate definition for each of the following terms.

1. _____ Antitrust policy

2. _____ Price discrimination

3. _____ Horizontal merger

4. _____ Vertical merger

5. _____ Conglomerate merger

6. _____ Concentration ratio

7. _____ Patent

8. _____ Market power

a. Temporary grant of monopoly rights over an invention.
b. Joining firms that produce similar products into a single firm.
c. Ability of a firm to affect the price of its output for its own benefit.
d. Programs designed to control growth of monopoly and to prevent powerful firms from engaging in "undesirable" practices.
e. Temporary grant of monopoly rights over a publication.
f. Charging different buyers different prices for the same product.
g. Combining two unrelated firms into a single firm.
h. Percentage of an industry's output produced by its four largest firms.
i. Joining firms, one of which supplies input(s) to the other, into a single firm.

BASIC EXERCISE

This exercise illustrates how a monopolist may be able to increase her profits by engaging in price discrimination. Table 32–1 contains data on the demand for snow tires in two cities, Centerville and Middletown. Centerville does not get much snow, and the demand for snow tires is quite elastic. Middletown is smaller. And, since it gets more snow, it should not be surprising that the demand for snow tires in Middletown is less elastic than is the demand in Centerville. Snow tires are supplied to both Centerville and Middletown by a monopolist who can produce tires with a fixed cost of $2,500,000 and a constant marginal cost of $10 a tire.

1. Assume that the monopolist charges the same price in both towns. Use the data on total demand to compute the monopolist's profit-maximizing level of output and price. First compute total revenue in order to compute marginal revenue per tire by dividing the change in total revenue by the change in output. Then compare marginal revenue to the monopolist's marginal cost of $10 to determine the profit-maximizing level of output.

TABLE 32–1

Price	Quantity Demanded Centerville	Quantity Demanded Middletown	Total Demand	Total Revenue	Marginal Revenue
48	10,000	40,000	50,000	_____	
45	25,000	43,750	68,750	_____	_____
42	40,000	47,500	87,500	_____	_____
39	55,000	51,250	106,250	_____	_____
36	70,000	55,000	125,000	_____	_____
33	85,000	58,750	143,750	_____	_____
30	100,000	62,500	162,500	_____	_____
27	115,000	66,250	181,250	_____	_____

TABLE 32-2

| | Centerville | | Middletown | |
Price	Total Revenue	Marginal Revenue	Total Revenue	Marginal Revenue
48	_____		_____	
45	_____	_____	_____	_____
42	_____	_____	_____	_____
39	_____	_____	_____	_____
36	_____	_____	_____	_____
33	_____	_____	_____	_____
30	_____	_____	_____	_____
27	_____	_____	_____	_____

Price? $_____

Output? _____

Profits? $_____

2. Assume now that the monopolist can charge different prices in the two towns; that is, the monopolist is a price discriminator. Can the monopolist increase her profits by charging different prices? Complete Table 32–2 to answer this question.

Profit-maximizing price in Centerville: $_____

Profit-maximizing price in Middletown: $_____

Quantity of snow tires in Centerville: _____

Quantity of snow tires in Middletown: _____

Total Profits: $_____

3. In which town did the monopolist raise the price? In which town did she lower the price? The monopolist should charge a higher price in the town with the lower elasticity of demand. Can you explain why? Is that the case here?

SELF-TESTS FOR UNDERSTANDING

Test A

Circle the correct answer.

1. In regard to the Sherman Act, which of the following is *not* true?
   a. It prohibited contracts, combinations, and conspiracies in restraint of trade.
   b. It prohibited acts that attempt monopolization of trade.
   c. It declared any firm with 50 percent of an industry's output to be an illegal monopoly.
   d. It contained no mechanism for enforcement.

2. The Clayton Act prohibits all but which one of the following?
   a. The direct purchase of a competitor's assets.
   b. Tying contracts.
   c. Price discrimination.
   d. Interlocking directorates.

3. Which of the following cases is an example of an interlocking directorate?
   a. Abby Aldrich serves as a director of Alcoa and of Shell Oil.
   b. Franklin Fish serves as a director of Pillsbury and of United Airlines.
   c. Carlos Calvo serves as a director of Bank of America and of General Motors.
   d. Brenda Buchanan serves as a director of IBM and Apple Computer.

4. Which of the following indicates that structure per se, rather than conduct, may be used as evidence of an illegal monopoly?
   a. The Clayton Act.
   b. The Celler-Kefauver Act.
   c. The Alcoa case.
   d. The General Electric-Westinghouse price-fixing case.

5. Which of the following would constitute a vertical merger?
   a. A grocery chain merges with the bakery that supplies it with bread.
   b. Two television manufacturers merge.
   c. Mobil Oil buys Montgomery Ward.
   d. U.S. Steel buys Marathon Oil.
6. Which of the following would be a horizontal merger?
   a. DuPont buys Texaco.
   b. General Electric merges with *The New York Times.*
   c. Ford Motor Company merges with Goodyear Tire.
   d. TWA merges with United Airlines.
7. Which of the following would be a conglomerate merger?
   a. Ford merges with Goodyear.
   b. General Electric merges with *The New York Times.*
   c. TWA merges with United.
   d. Apple buys IBM.
8. If an industry is composed of 10 firms, each the same size, then the 4-firm concentration ratio would be
   a. 4
   b. 10
   c. 40
   d. 100
9. Data for the United States suggest that industrial concentration
   a. has declined significantly since the passage of the Clayton Act.
   b. has shown little trend during the past 90 years.
   c. has increased dramatically since World War II.
10. Proponents of vigorous antitrust policy argue that bigness per se is bad for all but which one of the following reasons?
   a. Bigness may lead to undesirable concentrations of political and economic power.
   b. Monopolies may not feel competitive pressures to be innovative.
   c. Monopolies, in the pursuit of maximum profits, will usually restrict output below socially desirable levels.
   d. Large-scale firms may imply significant economies of scale.

Test B

Circle T or F for True or False as appropriate.

1. A government antitrust case always imposes a large financial burden on a company whether it has engaged in illegal actions or not.   T F

2. The Sherman Act outlawed actions in restraint of trade and monopolization of trade.   T F

3. The Clayton Act established the Federal Trade Commission.   T F

4. If a manufacturing firm merges with its supplier, it is engaging in a horizontal merger.   T F

5. A four-firm concentration ratio is the percentage of industry output produced by the four largest firms.   T F

6. Experience clearly shows that any increase in concentration leads to an increase in market power.   T F

7. Actual evidence on four-firm concentration ratios indicates a significant increase in concentration of American business over the last 80 years.   T F

8. A technological innovation that favors large-scale production will always increase concentration in an industry.   T F

9. Research by economists suggests that only the largest firms can afford to engage in research and development.   T F

10. Price discrimination is always unfair.   T F

SUPPLEMENTARY EXERCISE

The two lists in Table 32–3 identify the 25 largest industrial firms in the United States in 1929 and 1955, ranked by assets. The list for 1955 comes from the first *Fortune*[1] list of the 500 largest industrial companies. The list for 1929 comes from work by two economists, Norman Collins and Lee Preston.[2]

See if you can list the largest industrial firms today. Then go to the library and look up the most recent list of the *Fortune* 500. It is usually in the May issue. How many of these corporations are still in the top 25? How many corporations have slipped in ranking? How many have gained?

[1]*Fortune*, July 1956, Supplement, page 2. Reprinted with permission.

[2]Norman R. Collins and Lee E. Preston, "The Size Structure of the Largest Industrial Firms, 1901–1958", *American Economic Review*, vol. 51, Number 5, December 1961, pages 986–1011.

In 1955 these companies had sales that totaled $46.8 billion. Their sales equaled 12 percent of GNP. What are comparable figures today?

Fortune ranks firms by sales and assets. How do these rankings compare?

Fortune also publishes a list of the 500 largest industrial firms in the world. How big are the biggest American firms when compared to their international competition?

TABLE 32-3

1929	Rank	1955
U.S. Steel	1	Standard Oil (N.J.)
Standard Oil (N.J.)	2	General Motors
General Motors	3	U.S. Steel
Bethlehem Steel	4	DuPont
Anaconda	5	Mobil Oil
Ford Motor Company	6	Standard Oil (Ind.)
Mobil Oil	7	Gulf Oil
Standard Oil (Ind.)	8	Texaco
Gulf Oil	9	General Electric
Shell Oil	10	Standard Oil (Cal.)
Texaco	11	Bethlehem Steel
Standard Oil (Cal.)	12	Westinghouse
DuPont	13	Union Carbide
General Electric	14	Sinclair Oil
Armour	15	Phillips Petroleum
Sinclair Oil	16	Western Electric
Allied Chemical	17	Cities Service
International Harvester	18	Shell Oil
Western Electric	19	Chrysler
Union Oil	20	International Harvester
Union Carbide	21	Alcoa
Swift	22	Anaconda
Kennecott Copper	23	American Tobacco
International Paper	24	Republic Steel
Republic Steel	25	Kennecott Copper

33

Taxation, Government Spending, and Resource Allocation

LEARNING OBJECTIVES

After completing the material in this chapter you should be able to:

- define, understand, and use correctly the terms and concepts listed below.
- distinguish between progressive, proportional and regressive tax systems.
- describe the major taxes levied by the federal, state, and local governments and identify which are direct taxes and which are indirect taxes.
- explain why the payroll tax is regressive.
- explain what issues make the social security system controversial.
- explain the concept of fiscal federalism.
- contrast various concepts of fair or equitable taxation.
- explain the difference between the burden and the excess burden of a tax.
- explain how changes in economic behavior can enable individuals to shift the burden of a tax; that is, explain what is wrong with the flypaper theory of tax incidence.
- explain what factors influence how the burden of a tax will be shared by consumers and suppliers.

IMPORTANT TERMS AND CONCEPTS

Progressive, proportional, and regressive taxes
Average and marginal tax rates
Direct and indirect taxes
Personal income tax
Payroll tax
Corporate income tax
Excise tax
Tax loopholes
Tax Reform Act of 1986
Social security system
Property tax
Fiscal federalism
Horizontal and vertical equity
Ability-to-pay principle
Benefits principle of taxation
Economic efficiency
Burden of a tax
Excess burden
Incidence of a tax
Flypaper theory of incidence
Tax shifting

CHAPTER REVIEW

This chapter concentrates on taxes: What sorts of taxes are collected in America and what economic effects they have. Few people like paying taxes. In fact, many people make adjustments in their behavior to reduce the taxes they must pay. It is these adjustments that are the important measure of the economic effects of taxes, a part that is often overlooked in popular discussions.

Taxes are levied by federal, state, and local units of government. For the most part, federal taxes tend to

(1) be (direct/indirect) taxes, while state and local governments rely more on _____

taxes. The largest revenue raiser for the federal government is the _____ _____

tax. Next in line in terms of revenue raised is the _____ tax. Other important

federal taxes include the _____ income tax and excise taxes.

When talking about income tax systems it is important to distinguish between *average* and *marginal* tax

(2) rates. The fraction of total income paid as income taxes is the (average/marginal) tax rate, while the fraction of

each additional dollar of income paid as taxes is the _____ tax rate. If the

average tax rate increases with income, the tax system is called _____. If the

average tax rate is constant for all levels of income, the tax system is said to be _____,

while if the average tax rate falls as income increases, the result is a _____ tax
system. Changes under the Tax Reform Act of 1986 have reduced marginal income tax rates and enhanced
the efficiency of the U.S. federal personal income tax by closing a number of loopholes.

(3) The social security system is financed by (income/payroll) taxes. These taxes are considered
(regressive/progressive) because they (do/do not) apply to all sources of income and because after a certain

level of income the marginal tax rate becomes _____. Social security benefits do
not work like private pension funds, because benefits are not limited by individual contributions.

The social security system has been able to offer retired people good benefits for two reasons: (1) Real
wages and incomes of those currently employed have shown substantial growth; and (2) the number of working
people has been large relative to the number of retired individuals. The continued operation of both these
factors has recently been called into question by the slowdown in the growth of real wages and the population.
Recent adjustments in both taxes and benefits have attempted to solve the problem by accumulating a
surplus in the social security trust fund to pay future benefits.

(4) The major state and local taxes, _____ taxes and _____
taxes, are indirect taxes. In the aggregate, state income taxes raise a smaller percentage of state revenues, but
their importance is growing. Property taxes are usually levied as a percent of (assessed/market) value rather

than _____ value. Numerous inequities arise as market values change almost
continuously, while assessments for tax purposes are made only infrequently. There (is/is not) general
agreement about the progressivity or regressivity of the property tax. In addition to the taxes raised by state
governments, there is a system of transfers from the federal to state governments called fiscal

_____.

Economists use their dual criteria of equity and efficiency to judge taxes. When talking about the fairness

(5) of a particular tax, one is talking about _____. Various criteria have been
advanced to judge the fairness of a particular tax. The principle that equally situated individuals should pay

equal taxes is referred to as _____ _____. The principle that differentially
situated individuals should be taxed in ways that society deems fair is referred to as _____

_____. The ability-to-pay principle is an example of _____
equity. Rather than looking at the income and wealth of families, there is an alternative approach to taxation
that says people should pay in proportion to what they get from public services. This principle for taxation is

called the _____ principle. User fees for a variety of public services, such as

garbage collection, the use of parks, street cleaning, and so on, are an example of the _____
principle.

Efficiency is the other criterion that economists use to judge taxes. Almost all taxes cause some inefficiency. The amount of money that would make an individual as well off with a tax as she was without the

(6) tax is called the _____ of the tax. Sometimes it is just equal to the tax payment an
individual makes, but more generally it is (greater/less) than an individual's tax payment. The difference between

the total burden and tax payments is called the _____ _____. The reason
that tax payments typically understate the total burden of a tax is that the existence of the tax will often induce
a change in behavior. Measuring only the taxes paid (does/does not) take account of the loss of satisfaction
resulting from the induced change in behavior. The excess burden is the measure of the inefficiency of a
particular tax. Thus the principle of efficiency in taxation calls for using taxes that raise the same revenue
but with the (largest/smallest) excess burden. That is, the principle of efficiency calls for using taxes that
induce the smallest changes in behavior.

Often taxes will affect even those people who do not pay the tax. Imagine, for example, that the government imposes a $50 excise tax on bicycles, paid for by consumers at the time of purchase. Even though paid
for by consumers, it may be easiest to examine the impact of this tax by viewing it as a shift in the supply
curve, as illustrated in Figure 33–1. Consumers do not care why the price of bicycles has increased; there is
no reason for their demand curve to shift. Suppliers collect the tax for the government and are concerned with
what is left over after taxes in order to pay their suppliers and cover both their labor cost and the opportunity
cost of their capital. How suppliers will respond to the after-tax price is given by the original supply curve. The
before-tax supply curve comes from adding the excise tax onto the original supply curve and is given by the
dashed line in Figure 33–1.

Looking at Figure 33–1 we see that compared with the original equilibrium, the new equilibrium involves a
(7) (higher/lower) price to consumers, a (higher/lower) price to suppliers, and a (larger/smaller) quantity of bicycles

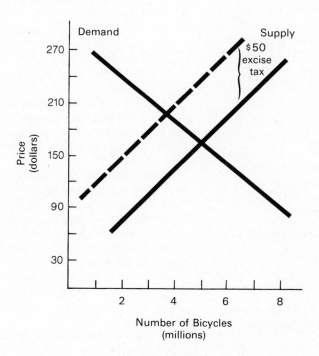

FIGURE 33–1

DEMAND FOR AND SUPPLY OF BICYCLES

produced. It would not be surprising if the change in supply resulted in some or all of the following: some unemployed bicycle workers, lower wages for employed bicycle workers, and fewer bicyle firms. None of these workers or firms paid the tax, yet all were affected by it.

In the bicycle example, as consumers adjusted to the new tax, they shifted part of the burden of the tax onto others. The question of how the burden of taxes is divided up among different groups is the question of tax

(8) _____. At first glance it might appear that the burden of the tax is borne entirely by consumers who pay the tax at the time of sale. The notion that the burden of the tax rests with those who

pay the tax is called the _____ theory of tax incidence. As the bicycle example makes clear, if consumers change their behavior as a result of the tax, they may succeed in _____ part of the burden of the tax.

The study of tax incidence suggests that the incidence of excise or sales taxes depends on the slopes of

(9) both the _____ and _____ curves. Payroll taxes, such as social security taxes, are like an excise tax on labor services. Statistical work suggests that for most workers the supply of labor services is relatively (elastic/inelastic) with respect to wage rates, which in turn

suggests that (workers/firms) rather than _____ bear most of the burden of the payroll tax.

DEFINITION QUIZ

Choose the letter that is the most appropriate definition for each of the following terms.

1. _____ Progressive tax

2. _____ Proportional tax

3. _____ Regressive tax

4. _____ Average tax rate

5. _____ Marginal tax rate

6. _____ Direct taxes

7. _____ Indirect taxes

8. _____ Excise tax

9. _____ Tax loophole

10. _____ Fiscal federalism

11. _____ Horizontal equity

12. _____ Vertical equity

13. _____ Ability-to-pay principle

14. _____ Benefits principle of taxation

15. _____ Burden of a tax

16. _____ Excess burden

17. _____ Incidence of a tax

18. _____ Flypaper theory of incidence

19. _____ Tax shifting

a. Provision in tax code that reduces taxes below statutory rates if certain conditions are met.
b. Average tax rate increases with income.
c. People who derive benefits from a government-provided service should pay the taxes to support it.
d. Amount an individual would have to be given to make her just as well off with the tax as she was without it.
e. Allocation of the burden of a tax to specific groups.
f. Notion that the burden of a tax is borne by those who pay the tax.
g. Taxes levied on people.
h. Equally situated individuals ought to be taxed equally.
i. Average tax rate falls as income rises.
j. Frequency with which a tax is levied.
k. Sales tax on a specific commodity.
l. Situation where economic reactions to a tax mean others bear part of the burden of the tax.
m. System of grants from one level of government to the next.
n. Ratio of taxes to income.
o. Wealthier people should pay higher taxes.
p. Average tax rate is the same at all income levels.
q. Amount by which the burden of a tax exceeds the tax paid.
r. Fraction of each additional dollar of income that is paid in taxes.
s. Taxes levied on specific economic activities.
t. Differently situated individuals should be taxed differently in accordance with social norms.

BASIC EXERCISE

This exercise is designed to illustrate how the incidence of an excise tax depends on the elasticity (slope) of the demand and supply curves.

1. Table 33–1 has data on the demand and supply of running shoes. Plot the demand curve from column 1 and the supply curve from column 3 in Figure 33–2.
2. Determine the initial equilibrium price and quantity of running shoes.

    Price $ _____

    Quantity _____

3. Now assume that in a fit of pique, non-running legislators impose a fitness tax of $10 on each pair of shoes. Draw the new supply curve by shifting the original supply curve by the magnitude of the excise tax. The new equilibrium price

    is $_____, and the new

    equilibrium quantity is _____.
4. How much more do consumers, who continue to

    buy running shoes, pay? $_____
    How does this increase in price compare with the excise tax of $10?

5. What is likely to happen to employment, wages, and profits in the running-shoe industry?
6. On Figure 33–3, plot the demand curve from column 2 and supply curve from column 3 of Table 33–1. Comparing Figures 33–2 and 33–3, we have the same supply curve but different demand curves. Both figures should show the same initial equilibrium price and quantity.
7. At the initial equilibrium price and quantity, which

    demand curve is more elastic? _____
    (Review the appropriate material in Chapter 22 if you do not remember how to compute the price elasticity of a demand curve.) Remember this distinction when it comes to comparing results.
8. Now analyze the impact of the imposition of the same excise tax of $10 per pair of running shoes using Figure 33–3. The new equilibrium price is

    $_____ and the new equilibrium

    quantity is _____. In which case, Figure 33–2 or Figure 33–3, does the equilibrium price of running shoes rise the most?

    _____. In which case are the volume of employment and the level of wages

    likely to fall the least? _____
    From this comparison we can conclude that the

TABLE 33–1

DEMAND FOR AND SUPPLY OF RUNNING SHOES

(1) Demand (millions of pairs)	(2) Price (dollars)		(3)	(4) Supply (millions of pairs)
68	53.0	30	38	48.00
65	52.5	32	40	48.33
62	52.0	34	42	48.67
59	51.5	36	44	49.00
56	51.0	38	46	49.33
53	50.5	40	48	49.67
50	50.0	42	50	50.00
47	49.5	44	52	50.33
44	49.0	46	54	50.67
41	48.5	48	56	51.00
38	48.0	50	58	51.33
35	47.5	52	60	51.67
32	47.0	54	62	52.00

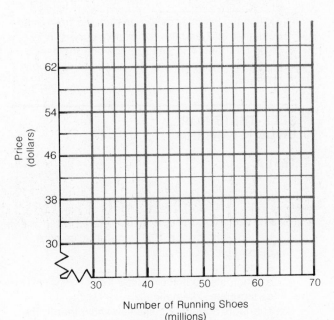

Number of Running Shoes
(millions)

FIGURE 33–2

DEMAND FOR AND SUPPLY OF RUNNING SHOES

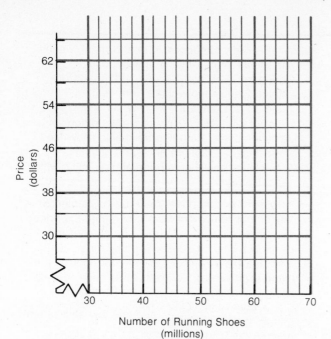

FIGURE 33-3

DEMAND FOR AND SUPPLY OF RUNNING SHOES

more inelastic the demand curve, the more the burden of an excise tax will be borne by

_____.

9. (Optional) Use information on demand from either column 1 or 2 and the two supply curves in columns 3 and 4 to analyze how the incidence of the tax is affected as the elasticity of supply changes.

SELF-TESTS FOR UNDERSTANDING

Test A

Circle the correct answer.

1. The facts about tax collection show that in the United States since 1950 federal taxes as a proportion of GNP have
   a. declined.
   b. fluctuated but shown little trend.
   c. increased dramatically.
2. The facts about tax collection show that in the United States state and local taxes as a percentage of GNP have
   a. declined since 1960.
   b. shown virtually no change over the last 60 years.

   c. increased from 1945 to the early 1970s and shown little trend since then.
3. The facts about tax collection show that as compared with other industrialized countries, total tax collections in the United States are
   a. higher than in any other country.
   b. lower than in many other countries.
   c. no different from those in other countries.
4. Which of the following is an example of an indirect tax?
   a. Income taxes.
   b. Inheritance taxes.
   c. Head taxes.
   d. Sales taxes.
5. The Abbotts have an income of $20,000 a year and pay $2000 a year in income taxes. The Beards have an income of $40,000 a year and pay $5000 a year in income taxes. From this information we can conclude that this tax system
   a. is regressive.
   b. is proportional.
   c. is progressive.
   d. satisfies the benefits principle of taxation.
6. The ability-to-pay principle of taxation is an example of
   a. horizontal equity.
   b. vertical equity.
   c. the benefits principle.
   d. fiscal federalism.
7. If two families are identical in all respects, the principle of horizontal equity says that
   a. both families should pay more income taxes than other families with less income.
   b. both families should pay the same income tax.
   c. both families should have a lower average tax rate than a richer family.
   d. income taxes are, from a social viewpoint, a more appropriate form of taxation than are payroll taxes.
8. Which of the following is an example of the benefits principle of taxation?
   a. Excise taxes on cigarettes.
   b. Higher property taxes as a percent of market value for more expensive homes.
   c. Special assessments on homeowners in proportion to their street frontage to help pay for repairs to curbs and gutters.
   d. Social security taxes.
9. A sales tax on which of the following will involve a small excess burden?
   a. A tax on a commodity with a zero price elasticity of demand.
   b. A tax on a commodity with a very high elasticity of demand.

c. A tax on a commodity that is consumed primarily by poor families.

d. A tax on a commodity that is consumed primarily by rich families.

10. The flypaper theory of tax incidence
   a. is a shorthand reference to such sticky issues as the appropriate degree of progressivity in the personal income tax.
   b. implies that if a tax induces changes in economic behavior, part of the burden of the tax may be shifted to other economic agents.
   c. is usually right regarding who bears the burden of a tax.
   d. says that the burden of a tax is borne by those who pay the tax.

Test B

Circle T or F for True or False as appropriate.

1. Over the past 35 years federal government taxes have been taking an ever-increasing share of the GNP. T F

2. Federal payroll taxes are a less important source of revenue than either the federal personal income tax or the federal corporate income tax. T F

3. State personal income taxes are an example of a direct, as opposed to indirect, tax. T F

4. State taxes are primarily indirect taxes. T F

5. The principle of horizontal equity says that equally situated individuals should be taxed equally. T F

6. The ability-to-pay principle says that people who derive benefits from a particular public service should pay the taxes to finance it. T F

7. The burden of a tax is normally less than the revenue raised by the tax. T F

8. If a tax does not induce a change in economic behavior, then there is no excess burden. T F

9. The flypaper theory of incidence is correct in regards to social security taxes. T F

10. The concept of excess burden proves that taxes can never improve efficiency. T F

SUPPLEMENTARY EXERCISE

The proposal by President Bush to eliminate the deductibility of state income taxes on federal income tax returns focused attention on the issue of double deductibility.

Jules has a statutory marginal federal income tax rate of 15 percent. Julia has a statutory marginal federal income tax rate of 28 percent. Their state has just enacted a state income tax equal to 6 percent of taxable income at all levels of income. Both Jules and Julia itemize deductions and can thus subtract any state taxes paid from their income before figuring their federal income tax. The state tax law also allows them to subtract their federal income tax payments when computing taxable income. Allowing for the double deductibility, have effective marginal income tax rates gone up by 6 percentage points for both Jules and Julia?

34

Environmental Protection and Resource Conservation

LEARNING OBJECTIVES

After completing the material in this chapter you should be able to:

- define, understand, and use correctly the terms and concepts listed below.
- explain why, in most cases, it is undesirable to reduce pollution to zero.
- explain why it is unlikely that profit-maximizing private firms can be expected to clean up the environment.
- describe the major approaches to limiting pollution.
- compare the advantages and disadvantages of using taxes and permits to control pollution.
- explain why, under perfect competition and in the absence of any change in the cost of extraction, the price of depletable resources would be expected to rise at the rate of interest.

- explain how and why actual prices of depletable resources have behaved differently over most of the twentieth century.
- describe the three virtues of rising prices for scarce resources.
- explain why known reserves for many resources have not tended to fall over time.

IMPORTANT TERMS AND CONCEPTS

Externality
Direct controls
Pollution charges (taxes on emissions)
Subsidies for reduced emissions
Emissions permits
Known reserves
Organization of Petroleum Exporting Countries (OPEC)
Rationing
Paradox of growing reserves of finite resources

CHAPTER REVIEW

This chapter explores the economics of environmental protection and resource conservation, with special emphasis on the strengths and weaknesses of a market economy in dealing with both issues.

Environmental Protection

Pollution is one example of instances in which unregulated markets will fail to achieve an efficient allocation of resources. Typically, pollution imposes little or no cost on the polluter, yet it imposes costs on

(1) others. In the language of economists, pollution is an example of a detrimental _____. Pollution happens because individuals, firms, and government agencies use the air, land, and waterways as free dumping grounds for their waste products. Economists believe that if there is a high cost to using these public resources, then the volume of pollution will (increase/decrease) because people will be more careful about producing wastes and/or choose less costly alternatives for waste disposal. One way to make the use of public resources costly is to impose (taxes/subsidies) in direct proportion to the volume of pollution emitted. This is an example of using the price system to clean up the environment.

(2) However, many government policies have relied on voluntarism and direct _____. Both of these policies have their place in a coordinated attempt to clean up the environment. Economists, though, are skeptical of relying on voluntary cooperation as a general long-range solution. Cleaning up the environment is costly, and firms that voluntarily incur these costs are likely to be undersold by less public-spirited competitors.

A government ruling that mandates an equal percentage reduction in pollution activity by all polluters is an example of a direct control. Economists argue that since the costs of reducing pollution are apt to vary among

(3) polluters, an equal percentage reduction by all polluters is likely to be (efficient/inefficient) compared with other alternatives, such as emissions taxes. From a social viewpoint, unequal reductions in pollution will be more

_____, as it is likely to cost less for some firms to reduce pollution. Faced with an emissions tax, firms will reduce pollution until the (marginal/average) cost of further reductions exceeds the tax. Firms that continue to pollute will pay the tax; other firms will pay for pollution-control devices. All firms will choose the least costly alternative.

Resource Conservation

Some resources, such as trees and fish, are called renewable resources. As long as breeding stocks are not destroyed, these resources will replenish themselves. The rest of this chapter concentrates on nonrenewable or depletable resources such as minerals and oil. In this case there is no reproduction, although in some cases there may be recycling.

Many observers have voiced concern that the world is running out of natural resources. They allege that soon the quantity of resources supplied will not be able to keep up with the quantity of resources demanded and that the result will be massive shortages and chaos. Yet, in a free market we know that the quantity

(4) demanded (can/can never) exceed the quantity supplied, because demand and supply will always be brought into equilibrium by adjustments in _____. This fundamental mechanism of free markets, first discussed in Chapter 4, is as applicable to the supply and demand of scarce resources as it is to any other commodity.

Harold Hotelling first described the special behavior of the prices of depletable resources in free markets. He discovered that if the costs of extraction are constant, the price of depletable resources must

(5) rise at a rate equal to the rate of _____. This result follows from relatively simple considerations. Assets held in the form of bank deposits or bonds earn interest for their owners. Owners of natural resource reserves expect their asset—the reserves—to earn a similar risk-adjusted return. If increases in the price of future resources offer a less attractive return than do interest rates, resource owners will sell their resources and put the money in the bank. This action decreases the current

price of resources. There will be a continuing incentive to sell, with downward pressure on current resource prices, until the return from holding resources again provides a return competitive with interest rates. Similarly, if the future return from holding resources is expected to be extremely high, more investors will want to buy resource inventories, _____ current prices. These pressures will continue until holding resource inventories again offers a risk-adjusted return comparable to that of investments in the bank.

The theory sketched above suggests that the prices of depletable resources should show a rising trend

(6) at a rate equal to the rate of _____. The unexpected discovery of resource reserves that were previously not known, technological progress that reduces the cost of extraction, and government attempts at price controls can all make prices behave differently. Data on known reserves, rather than declining as implied in the literal interpretation of a nonrenewable resource, have typically shown slight increases. These increases in reserves reflect the workings of the price system as the pressure for higher prices has induced new exploration. It is the results of new exploration that help to explain actual price behavior. It is less clear how long one can expect continuing new discoveries. At some time market pressures for increasing resource prices must prevail. However, it is important to remember that this pressure for higher prices is what equates demand and supply, avoids chaos, and facilitates the adjustment to alternative technologies.

Many economists see increasing prices for depletable resources as an important virtue of free markets. Increasing prices help to deal with the problem of declining reserves in three important ways:

(7) 1. Increasing prices (encourage/discourage) consumption and waste and provide a(n) (disincentive/incentive) for conservation on the part of consumers.

2. Increasing prices (encourage/discourage) more efficient use of scarce resources in the production of commodities.

3. Increasing prices provide a(n) (disincentive/incentive) for technological innovation and the use of substitutes as well as (encouraging/discouraging) additional exploration and the exploitation of high-cost sources of supply.

DEFINITION QUIZ

Choose the letter that is the most appropriate definition for each of the following terms.

1. _____ Externality

2. _____ Direct controls

3. _____ Pollution charges

4. _____ Emissions permit

5. _____ Known reserves

6. _____ Organization of Petroleum Exporting Countries

7. _____ Rationing

a. Cartel of oil-rich nations which has attempted to control oil market.

b. Monetary incentives and penalties used to make polluting financially unattractive.

c. Fees paid to polluting firms in exchange for reductions in pollution.

d. Result of activities that affect other people, without corresponding compensation.

e. Authorization to pollute up to some specified level.

f. Legal limits on pollution emissions or performance specifications for polluting activities.

g. Nonprice methods of distributing scarce supplies.

h. Amount of a resource available if one relies solely on existing technology and already discovered sources.

BASIC EXERCISES

1. This exercise examines the implications of alternative pollution taxes.

Assume that plastic trash bags are produced in a market that is best characterized as one of perfect competition. All manufacturers have long used local rivers as convenient, free dumping grounds for their

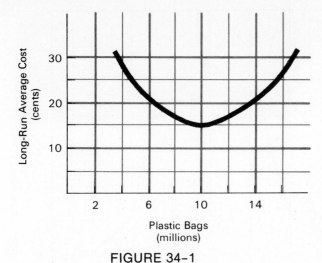

FIGURE 34-1

industrial wastes. Figure 34-1 plots the average cost of producing trash bags. These data are applicable for each firm.

a. In the absence of any pollution-control measures, what is the long-run equilibrium price of plastic

bags? $_____. What is the long-run equilibrium level of output for each firm?

_____ (To answer this question you may want to review the material in Chapter 25 about long-run equilibrium under perfect competition.)

b. The amount of pollution discharge is directly proportional to the number of bags produced. Assume that the government imposes a pollution charge of 5 cents per bag. Draw in the new average cost curve on Figure 34-1. Will there be an increase, a decrease, or no change in each of the following as a result of the pollution charge? (Assume for now that there is no pollution-control technology, that each firm must pay the tax, and that the demand for plastic bags declines as price rises.)

Industry output	_____
Price	_____
Number of firms in industry	_____
Average cost curve for each firm	_____
Output level of each firm	_____
Total pollution	_____

c. Assume now that pollution-control equipment becomes available. This equipment will eliminate

TABLE 34-1

Year	Real GNP (billions of 1982 $)	Energy Consumption (quadrillion BTUs)	Energy Consumption per $1000 GNP (thousands of BTUs)
1970	2416.2	66.4	_____
1971	2484.8	67.9	_____
1972	2608.5	71.3	_____
1973	2744.1	74.3	_____
1974	2729.3	72.5	_____
1975	2695.0	70.5	_____
1976	2826.7	74.4	_____
1977	2958.6	76.3	_____
1978	3115.2	78.1	_____
1979	3192.4	78.9	_____
1980	3187.1	76.0	_____
1981	3248.8	74.0	_____
1982	3166.0	70.8	_____
1983	3279.1	70.5	_____
1984	3501.4	74.1	_____
1985	3618.7	74.0	_____
1986	3717.9	74.2	_____
1987	3853.7	76.8	_____
1988	4024.4	80.2	_____
1989	4142.6	81.3	_____

Source: GNP: *Economic Report of the President*, 1989, Table B-2; Energy: *Statistical Abstract of the United States*, 1990, Table 940; and *Monthly Energy Review*, January 1990, Table 1.4.

75 percent of pollution at an average cost of 4 cents per bag. Explain why no firm will adopt the pollution-control equipment if the pollution charge is unchanged at 5 cents a bag. (Assume that the cost of the control equipment is all variable cost at 4 cents per bag and that there is no fixed-cost component.)

d. Assume now that the tax is shifted to the volume of emissions, not to the number of bags produced, and that it is equivalent to 5 cents a bag if no pollution-control equipment is installed. Will any firm purchase the pollution-control equipment?

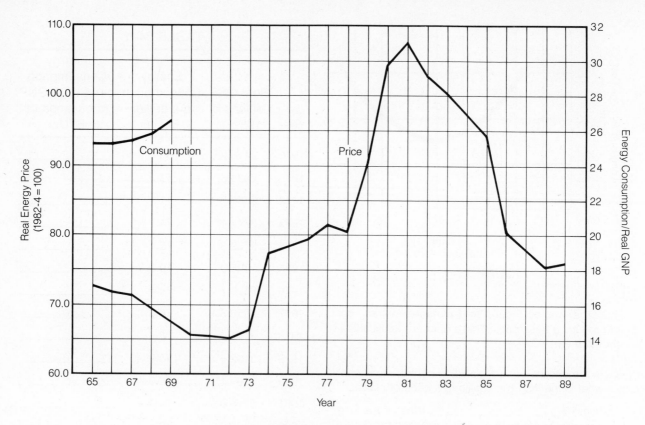

FIGURE 34-2

ENERGY PRICES AND CONSUMPTION

e. With the emissions tax at a rate of 5 cents per bag, to what rate must the cost of pollution control decline before firms will use it? If the cost of pollution control is constant at 4 cents, to what rate must the tax increase to induce firms to install the pollution-control equipment?

f. (Optional) Assume now that the costs of reducing pollution are not identical for all firms. For simplicity, assume that there are two types of firms, low-cost pollution-control firms and high-cost pollution-control firms. The low-cost firms can eliminate pollution at costs lower than the emissions tax but the high-cost firms cannot. What is the result of the imposition of an emissions tax? What will happen to total industry output? Will any firms leave the industry? If so, which ones, the high-cost or the low-cost firms? Why?

2. a. Table 34-1 contains data on real output and energy consumption for the U.S. economy. Use these data to compute the use of energy per thousand dollars of GNP.

b. Figure 34-2 shows real energy prices, i.e.,

energy prices divided by the consumer price index. Complete Figure 34-2 by plotting the data on energy consumption per thousand dollars of GNP. Use this graph to discuss the pattern of energy consumption over the last 25 years.

SELF-TESTS FOR UNDERSTANDING

Test A

Circle the correct answer.

1. Which of the following suggests that, except for recycling, all economic activity results in a disposal problem?
   a. The edifice complex.
   b. The law of conservation of energy and matter.
   c. Emissions permits.
   d. Externalities.

2. The fact that pollution is often a detrimental externality suggests that
   a. cleaning up the environment must be done by direct government expenditures.
   b. without government intervention, profit-maximizing private firms cannot be expected to clean up the environment.
   c. public agencies have been responsible for most pollution.
   d. direct controls are superior to other forms of government intervention.

3. Which of the following is not an example of using financial incentives to clean up the environment?
   a. Mandated pollution-control equipment in an attempt to reduce automobile emissions.
   b. A graduated tax that increases with the polluting characteristics of each automobile engine.
   c. The sale of a limited number of permits to control emissions into Lake Erie.
   d. Allowing firms to buy and sell emission rights originally assigned under a program of direct controls.

4. The use of pollution charges as a means of cleaning up the environment
   a. is the predominant form of pollution control in the United States.
   b. is likely to be more efficient than a system of direct controls.
   c. would be most appropriate in situations calling for sudden action, such as a serious smog condition.
   d. would have exactly the same effects on the volume of pollution as do subsidies for pollution-control equipment.

5. Compared with a system of direct controls, pollution charges
   a. are basically a ''carrot'' approach, relying on everyone's voluntary cooperation.
   b. are likely to lead to an equal percentage reduction in emissions from all pollution sources.
   c. will not reduce pollution, as firms will simply pass on these costs to their consumers with no impact on output levels.
   d. offer an incentive for continually reducing emissions, rather than reducing them just to some mandated level.

6. Harold Hotelling argued that, in competitive markets, even if extraction costs are constant the price of depletable resources will rise at a rate equal to the rate of
   a. inflation.
   b. unemployment.
   c. interest.
   d. growth of real income

7. Which one of the following would be expected to reduce the price of a natural resource?
   a. The establishment of an effective producer cartel.
   b. The discovery of previously unknown reserves.
   c. An increase in the rate of inflation.
   d. An increase in GNP.

8. Rising resource prices can be a virtue as they lead to all but which one of the following?
   a. Increased conservation.
   b. Increased use of substitutes.
   c. Increased waste.
   d. Increased innovation.

9. Data for the period 1950–1980 suggest that, when measured in relation to current consumption, the known reserves of some natural resources
   a. have declined.
   b. have remained roughly constant.
   c. have increased.

10. Effective price ceilings for natural resources are likely to
    a. provide an increased incentive for further exploration.
    b. shift the demand curve to the left.
    c. induce consumers to conserve.
    d. lead to resource shortages.

Test B

Circle T or F for True or False as appropriate.

1. Pollution has become a serious problem only since World War II.   T F

2. Only capitalist economies suffer from extensive pollution.   T F

3. When considering public policies to limit discharges of wastes into a river basin, an equal percentage reduction by all polluters is likely to be the most economically efficient policy.   T F

4. Pollution charges imposed on monopolist firms will have no effect on the volume of their polluting activity, because they will simply pass on the higher costs in the form of higher prices.   T F

5. Efficiency considerations strongly suggest that society should spend enough to reduce all pollution to zero.   T F

6. If left unchecked, the free-market mechanism will cause the demand for natural resources to exceed supply.   T F

7. For much of the twentieth century the relative prices of most natural resources have shown dramatic increases.   T F

8. Hotelling argued that, in free markets and with constant extraction costs, the price of natural resources will rise at the rate of inflation.   T F

9. The unexpected discovery of new resource deposits would reduce prices and delay the onset of the Hotelling pricing principle.   T F

10. Rising prices can help control resource depletion as they induce firms and households to conserve.   T F

SUPPLEMENTARY EXERCISES

1. The Great California Drought

During 1976 and 1977, northern California suffered from below-normal rainfall. The effects of the water shortage became progressively more severe, leading to the widespread adoption of various schemes for water rationing.

Throughout 1976 many public and private agencies joined together in a campaign to encourage voluntary reduction in water usage. As the drought persisted, many areas established quotas for water usage, based usually on family size, with stiff increases in price for water consumption in excess of the quota. (The dashed line in Figure 34–3 illustrates such a quota–high-price scheme. The dashed line indicates the total water bill. The price per gallon is given by the slope of the line.)

a. The quota–high-price scheme offers a strong incentive to limit water consumption to the basic quota, but there is little monetary incentive to reduce water consumption below the quota. Economist Milton Friedman suggested that rather than impose quotas with high prices for excess consumption, water districts should charge a very high price for *all* water consumption, with a rebate to consumers with especially low water consumption. (See *Newsweek*, March 21, 1977.) The solid line in Figure 34–3 illustrates a possible high-price-rebate scheme. To ensure that a water district has enough money to cover its fixed costs, the position and/or slope of the solid line could be adjusted. Parallel shifts of the solid line would affect the maximum rebate and the no-charge point, but not the price of a gallon of water. Shifts in the slope would change the

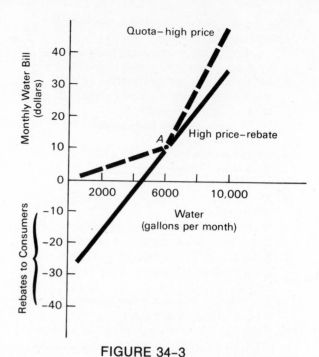

FIGURE 34–3

price. For example, pivoting the solid line on point A would change both the price and the maximum rebate, while leaving the cost of the basic quota unchanged.

Which pricing scheme has the greater incentive for conserving water? Which scheme is the most equitable?

b. Ross and Judy live in San Francisco. During 1976, in response to the growing concern about water conservation, they voluntarily cut their water consumption significantly below the quotas established by other water districts. The San Francisco rationing scheme, adopted in early 1977, mandated that all San Francisco residents reduce their consumption below 1976 levels by the same percentage. How equitable is such a system? What incentives do Ross and Judy have for future voluntary cooperation?

c. In 1965, New York City suffered from a severe drought. Residents of New York City pay for water through city taxes. Usage has not been metered. What options would be available to reduce water usage in a city like New York that does not meter individual usage? How effective are these options likely to be compared with the options available to a city that does meter water usage?

2. Pollution and Prices

Can a producer simply pass on to her customers any pollution charge imposed on her? This numerical example expands upon the problem in the Basic Exercise.

Consider the production of plastic bags, which cause pollution in direct proportion to the volume of production. The demand for bags is given by

$$Q = 2600 - 40P$$

where Q is measured in millions of bags.

a. Assume that plastic bags are produced by a monopolist at a cost of 15¢ a bag; that is,

$$TC = 15 \times Q.$$

Plot the demand, marginal revenue, average cost, and marginal cost curves on a piece of graph paper. What is the monopolist's profit maximizing level of output, the associated price, and her profits?

b. The government now imposes a pollution tax of 5¢ a bag, that is, $TC = 20 \times Q$. What happens to output, prices, and profits if the monopolist simply raises her price by 5¢? Can she do better by charging a different price? If so, what is that price, the associated quantity, and the new level of profits?

c. Assume now that bags are produced by identical small firms under conditions of perfect competition. Each firm produces bags with average cost given by

$$AC = .4(Q - 10)^2 + 15.$$

What is the long-run market equilibrium price and quantity? How many firms are in the industry? How many bags does each firm produce?

d. Again the government imposes a pollution tax of 5¢ a bag on each producer. What happens in the short run when there are still the same number of bag producers? What about the long run? How many firms will produce how many bags at what price?

3. You might enjoy reading Robert M. Solow, "The Economics of Resources or the Resources of Economics," *American Economic Review*, May 1974, pages 1–14, for a nontechnical discussion of the implications of the Hotelling pricing principle.

You might enjoy the following exchange about limits to growth:

Council on Environmental Quality and the Department of State (Gerald O. Barney, study director), *Global 2000 Report to the President of the U.S., Entering the 21st Century* (U.S. GPO, 1980–1981); also (Pergamon Press, 1980–1981).

Herman Kahn and Julian L. Simon, editors, *The Resourceful Earth: A Response to 'Global 2000'*, (Basil Blackwell, 1984).

PART
8

THE DISTRI- BUTION OF INCOME

35

Pricing the Factors of Production

LEARNING OBJECTIVES

After completing the material in this chapter you should be able to:

- define, understand, and use correctly the terms and concepts listed below.
- explain why the demand curve for a factor of production is the downward sloping portion of its marginal revenue product curve.
- explain why the demand for inputs is a derived demand.
- distinguish between investment and capital.
- explain how changes in interest rates may affect the profitability of specific investment decisions and hence the demand for funds.
- explain who gains and who loses, and why, under an effective usury ceiling.
- distinguish between land rents and economic rents.
- identify input units that receive economic rent, given supply curves of various slopes.
- explain why the fact that apartment buildings need to be maintained and that they can be reproduced at close to constant cost implies that, in the long run, rent control measures will be self-defeating.

- explain why, in the real world, profits are likely to offer returns in excess of the rate of interest.
- explain how the concept of economic rent is relevant to issues concerning the taxation of profits.

IMPORTANT TERMS AND CONCEPTS

Factors of production
Entrepreneurship
Marginal productivity principle
Marginal physical product
Marginal revenue product
Derived demand
Usury laws
Investment
Capital
Interest
Discounting
Marginal land
Economic rent
Entrepreneurs
Risk bearing
Invention versus innovation

CHAPTER REVIEW

The material in this chapter initiates the discussion of input prices by considering what determines the rental price of money, the rental price of land, and the income of entrepreneurs. If this material is combined with the material in Chapter 36 on wages—or the rental price for labor services—and material in Chapter 34 on the price of natural resources, one has a complete theory of income distribution based on

(1) marginal _____. The material in this chapter and in Chapter 36 builds upon our earlier discussion of optimal input use by firms. In Chapter 23 we saw that the demand for factors of production can be derived from profit-maximizing considerations. A firm is willing to pay for labor, land, natural resources, and so forth because it can use these factors to produce and sell output. In Chapter 23 we also learned that the demand curve for a particular factor of production is simply the downward-sloping portion

of the marginal _____ product curve.

Interest rates adjust to balance the demand for funds by borrowers and the supply of funds from lenders.

(2) The demand curve for funds has a (negative/positive) slope, indicating that at a lower rate of interest people will want to borrow (less/more). The supply curve of funds will have a (negative/positive) slope, indicating that a (higher/lower) interest rate is necessary to induce lenders to increase the supply of loans. An effective usury ceiling would impose an interest rate (above/below) the market clearing rate as determined by the

_____ of the demand and supply curves.

The demand for funds for business borrowing derives from a consideration of the profitability of investment projects. In earlier chapters we talked about capital and labor as factors of production. Investment projects add to the stock of capital. The profitability of investment projects is another way of referring to the marginal revenue product of more capital. The profitability of investment projects is complicated because most projects require dollar outlays immediately while offering returns sometime in the future. To evaluate the profitability of an investment project we need some way of comparing dollars now with dollars in the future. Economists and

(3) business people compare future and present dollars through a process called _____. As explained in an appendix to this chapter, this process relies on interest rate calculations. Higher interest rates will mean that (fewer/more) investment projects will be profitable. Thus higher interest rates will be associated with a (higher/lower) quantity of funds demanded and imply a (negatively/positively) sloped demand curve for business borrowing. (Remember the distinction between real and nominal interest rates first introduced in Chapter 6. Conclusions here about the impact of interest rates on the demand for funds refer to the impact of real interest rates.)

The first thing to remember when considering the notion of *rent* is that economists use this term in a very special way that is different from everyday usage. Most of the rent that you may pay for an apartment

(4) (is/is not) economic rent. Economic rent refers to the earnings of a factor of production that exceed the minimum amount necessary to keep that factor in its current employment.

If the supply curve of some factor, like land, is really vertical, it means that the factor would be willing to work for as little as nothing. It also means that it is impossible to duplicate this factor at any cost; otherwise a high enough price would induce an increase in supply and the supply curve would not be vertical. In the case

(5) of a vertical supply curve, (some/all) of any market price would be economic rent. If the supply curve of some factor is a horizontal line, the market price will reflect exactly what is necessary to induce any supply. In

this case an economist would say that the factor receives _____ economic rent.

An upward-sloping supply curve means that higher prices will induce an increase in supply, but there will

(6) be some units of supply that would have been present at lower prices. In this case (most/all) units of the factor will receive economic rent. In fact, it is only the marginal unit, the unit on the supply curve at the market equilibrium price, that earns no economic rent. The market price is as high as it is to induce this last unit to supply itself. All other units would have been available at a lower price and thus (part/all) of their earnings are economic rent. Land is a traditional input to use when talking about rent, but remember that land is not the only factor to earn economic rent. Anyone who would stay in a particular job for less pay, because he or she likes the work or the location, or for any other reason, (is/is not) earning some economic rent.

When considering land rentals it is clear that not all land is the same: some parcels are more productive or better located than others. Economists would expect that land rentals, the price for using a piece of land for a period of time, will adjust to reflect these differences. More productive land that produces the same

(7)   output at lower cost will receive a (higher/lower) land rent. In equilibrium, rents should adjust so that the total cost of producing the same quantity of output, including land rents, will be _____ on all parcels of land. If not, there is a clear incentive to use the land with lower total cost. This incentive to switch parcels increases the rent on the originally (low/high)-cost piece of land and decreases rent on the other pieces of land. The process stops only when land rentals have adjusted to again equate total cost.

(8)   As with any other productive factor, an increase in the demand for goods produced with land will (decrease/increase) the demand for land. Poor quality land, whose use was unprofitable at lower output prices, will now become profitable to use. Thus, more land will be used, and land rents will again adjust to equalize the costs of production on all parcels. As a result, the rent on previously used, higher quality land will (increase/decrease). An additional part of the response to an increased demand for land is likely to be (more/less) intensive use of existing land.

        Profits are a residual item after revenues have been used to pay other costs: labor, material inputs, interest on borrowed funds, and taxes. Profits also represent the return on equity investments in a firm.[1] In a world of perfect certainty, capitalists should expect that the profits on their investments will offer them a return that is just equal to the rate of interest. The rate of interest would be the opportunity cost of their equity investment in the firm. Any higher return would be competed away. Any lower return would lead some funds to be invested elsewhere in the pursuit of returns at least equal to the rate of interest. (Remember that in competitive markets, economic profits are equal to zero in long-run equilibrium.)

        In the real world, investments are not certain. Many business investments look like uncertain gambles. If entrepreneurs dislike taking risks, then profits will have to offer them the expectation of returns that are
(9)   (greater/less) than the rate of interest. Profits that are the result of monopoly power would be (greater/less) than the rate of interest. Finally, successful (innovation/invention) will often give an entrepreneur temporary monopoly profits and will also lead to a rate of profit that is (greater/less) than the rate of interest. The effects of taxing profits will depend upon whether profits are mostly economic rents or mostly a necessary return to attract entrepreneurial talent.

DEFINITION QUIZ

Choose the letter that is the most appropriate definition for each of the following terms.

1. _____ Factors of production

2. _____ Entrepreneurship

3. _____ Marginal productivity principle

4. _____ Marginal physical product

5. _____ Marginal revenue product

6. _____ Usury law

7. _____ Investment

8. _____ Capital

9. _____ Interest

10. _____ Discounting

11. _____ Marginal land

12. _____ Economic rent

13. _____ Invention

14. _____ Innovation

a. Payment to a factor of production in excess of the minimum amount necessary to keep the factor in its present employment.

b. Additional units of a given input add diminishing amounts to total output.

c. Starting new firms, introducing innovations, and taking the necessary risks in seeking business opportunities.

d. The change in sales revenue from selling the marginal physical product of a given input.

e. Flow of resources into the production of new capital.

f. Stock of plant, equipment, and other productive resources.

g. Inputs used in production process.

h. Act of putting a new idea into practical use.

i. Land on the borderline of being used.

j. Profit-maximizing firm should hire that quantity of an input at which marginal revenue product equals the price of the input.

k. Using interest rates to determine the present worth of a sum of money receivable or payable at some future date.

l. Payment for the use of funds.

m. Increase in output resulting from a one-unit increase in a given input.

n. Act of generating a new idea.

o. Maximum legally permissible interest rate.

[1]Equity refers here to the amount of their own money the owners have tied up in the firm. Specifically, if they sold the firm and paid off their creditors, the amount left over is their equity.

BASIC EXERCISE

This exercise is designed to illustrate how differences in land rents reflect differences in land productivity.

Dionne is considering her summer employment opportunities. She can work as a checker at the local grocery store for as many hours as she wants, earning $8 an hour.

Dionne is also considering raising flowers for sale on one of two plots of land. One plot, the sunny plot, has good soil and Dionne estimates that if she worked 40 hours a week she could earn $400 a week raising flowers on this land. The second plot is marginal land. It would require the use of fertilizer and special mulches in order to raise the same quantity of flowers. Dionne estimates that these extra costs would total $30 a week.

1. Calculate Dionne's profit from using the marginal plot of land on the assumption that it is available for free; that is, at a rent of zero. Do not forget to include the opportunity cost of Dionne's own work as an element of cost.
2. If Dionne's estimate of the increased cost of using the marginal land is typical of other uses, what market rent would you expect will be charged for the use of the sunny plot and why?
3. Explain why the profit that Dionne could earn from using the marginal plot of land limits the rent the owner of the sunny plot will be able to charge.

SELF-TESTS FOR UNDERSTANDING

Test A

Circle the correct answer.

1. The demand curve for productive factors is the downward-sloping portion of the relevant
   a. marginal physical product curve.
   b. marginal cost curve.
   c. marginal revenue product curve.
   d. average cost curve.
2. Profit-maximizing firms will use more of a productive factor as long as the price of the factor is less than its
   a. marginal physical product.
   b. marginal cost.
   c. marginal revenue product.
   d. average product.
3. The concept of discounting suggests that when compared with a dollar next year, a dollar today is worth
   a. less.
   b. more.
   c. the same.
4. Which of the following is an example of investment as opposed to capital?
   a. The fleet of 747s owned by American Airlines.
   b. Julia's purchase of 100 shares of Xerox stock.
   c. The five apartment buildings owned by Ralph.
   d. The expanded warehouse facilities that Norma will have built this year.
5. Parcel of land B can be used to raise corn at a cost of $50,000. The same amount of corn can be raised on parcel P for $75,000. An economist would expect the rent on parcel B to exceed that on parcel P by
   a. $25,000.
   b. $50,000.
   c. $75,000.
   d. $125,000.
6. Marginal land refers to land that
   a. is most productive for growing any given crop.
   b. is on the borderline of being used in productive activity.
   c. earns economic rent.
   d. borders interstate highways in rural areas.
7. An input will earn pure economic rent if the supply curve for the input is
   a. horizontal.
   b. upward sloping.
   c. vertical.
8. Which of the following individuals are earning economic rent?
   a. Ruth, who says, "If this job paid any less I'd quit; it wouldn't be worth the hassle."
   b. Sergio, who says, "This job is so interesting I'd work here even for a lot less."
   c. Nick, whose purchase of an apartment building should bring him a return equal to the rate of interest.
   d. Sophia, who is expecting a substantial profit from her investment in the manufacture of solar energy panels to compensate her for the risks she is taking.
9. Which of the following is not a reason why, in the long run, profits might be greater than the rate of interest?
   a. Monopolies will earn profits in excess of the opportunity cost of capital.
   b. Nominal profits must be greater than the nominal rate of interest to allow for the loss of purchasing power from inflation.

c. Risk-bearing, safety-conscious entrepreneurs often demand that they earn profits greater than what they could get from relatively safe investments at the rate of interest.

d. Innovation is a relatively risky undertaking and, if successful, often results in a temporary period of monopoly power.

10. Higher taxes on profits will have little impact if
a. profits are mostly economic rent.
b. profits are equal to nominal interest rates.
c. profits are growing.
d. the supply curve for entrepreneurial talent is horizontal.

Test B

Circle T or F for True or False as appropriate.

1. The demand curve for a factor of production is identical to its curve of marginal physical productivity.   T F

2. Interest rates represent the market price for the use of funds.   T F

3. Discounting means using the rate of interest to compare future and present dollars.   T F

4. The factories that the Ford Motor Company uses to produce cars are an example of investment rather than capital.   T F

5. According to economists, only land earns economic rent.   T F

6. Inputs available in perfectly elastic supply will earn no economic rent.   T F

7. The rent on any piece of land will equal the difference between production costs on that piece of land and production costs on the next-best available piece of land.   T F

8. The law of diminishing returns implies that an increase in the demand for land will actually reduce the rent paid on most parcels of land.   T F

9. The reason that most rent-control laws have adverse effects in the long run is that the long-run supply of structures, as opposed to land, is likely to be quite elastic.   T F

10. Economic theory proves that the rate of profits must equal the rate of interest.   T F

Appendix A: Discounting and Present Value

calculations can help when considering investment decisions.

LEARNING OBJECTIVE

After completing this exercise you should be able to appreciate how discounting, or present value,

IMPORTANT TERMS AND CONCEPTS

Discounting
Present value

DEFINITION QUIZ

Choose the letter that is the most appropriate definition for each of the following terms.

1. _____ Present value

a. Using interest rates to determine the current value of dollars to be received or paid at various dates in the future.
b. Future worth of a sum of money receivable or payable at the present date.

BASIC EXERCISE

Eric has an opportunity to purchase a machine to make gyros. The machine costs $4000 now and is expected to last for two years. After other expenses, Eric expects to net $2000 next year and $2500 in two years. Assume that Eric has the $4000 to buy the machine now. Is it a good investment?

1. Fill in the column of Table 35–1 to compute the present value of costs and returns on the assumption that the rate of interest is 10 percent.
2. Add up the present value of the returns and compare this sum with the present value of the

   cost. Which is greater? _____.
   Should Eric purchase the machine?

   _____

3. Assume now that the rate of interest is 5 percent. Fill in the relevant column of the table to compute the present value of the returns at a rate of interest of 5 percent.
4. Sum the present value of the returns and compare this sum with the present value of the cost. Which

   is greater? _____ Should Eric

   purchase the machine? _____
5. The decision rule discussed in the text, and the one you should have used when answering questions 2 and 4, compares the present value of future returns to the present value of costs. If the present value of the returns exceeds the present value of the cost, it means that Eric can do better by undertaking the investment than by investing in financial assets that yield the rate of

interest we used to compute the present values. If the present value of the returns is less than the present value of the cost, it means that Eric would do better with a financial investment. You can verify that this is the case by filling in the missing parts of Table 35–2 for interest rates of 5 and 10 percent.

6. What if Eric had to borrow the money? Would the same sorts of calculations be sufficient to help you decide whether or not he should borrow the money? The answer is yes. The reason is that while figuring the present value of the returns, you are accounting for interest payments whether Eric has the money or not. If Eric does not have the money, he will need to pay a lender. Even if he does have the money he will need to "pay" himself as much as he might have earned in some other investment. That is, he will need to meet the opportunity cost of his own money. Fill in the missing parts of Table 35–3, which has been constructed to illustrate just this point.

To summarize

a. Present value calculations use interest rates to transform dollars in the future into their equivalent today.
b. Comparing the present value of returns and cost is a good way to evaluate investment opportunities.
c. Comparing present value of returns and cost is a good procedure whether you have to borrow the money or not, assuming that you can borrow or lend at the same rate of interest you are using in your present value calculations.

TABLE 35–1
ERIC'S GYRO MACHINE

Time	Item	Amount	Present Value* $i = 5$ percent	Present Value* $i = 10$ percent
Now	Cost	$4000	_____	_____
One year	Return	2000	_____	_____
Two years	Return	2500	_____	_____
	Present value of all returns		_____	_____
	Net present value of project		_____	_____

*Present value $= \dfrac{\text{dollars in } n \text{ years}}{(1 + i)^n}$

$=$ (dollars in the nth year) divided by (1 plus the rate of interest multiplied by itself n times)

TABLE 35-2

CAN ERIC DO AS WELL BY INVESTING $4000 AT THE RATE OF INTEREST?

	Interest Rate	
	5 percent	10 percent
1. Initial deposit	$4000	$4000
2. Interest after one year (5 percent and 10 percent of line 1)	_____	_____
3. Balance after one year (line 1 plus line 2)	_____	_____
4. Withdrawal after one year*	$2000	$2000
5. New balance (line 3 minus line 4)	_____	_____
6. Interest during second year (5 percent and 10 percent of line 5)	_____	_____
7. Balance after second year (line 5 plus line 6)	_____	_____

Compare line 7 with the $2500 Eric would have received in the second year if he had bought the gyro machine. Line 7 should be greater (less) if the net present value of the project in Table 35–1 is negative (positive). That is, if the net present value of the project is negative (positive), Eric will do better (worse) by making a financial investment at the given rate of interest.

*This $2000 matches the return after one year from the gyro investment.

TABLE 35-3

WHAT IF ERIC HAD TO BORROW THE $4000?

	Interest Rate	
	5 percent	10 percent
1. Amount borrowed	$4000	$4000
2. Interest due at end of first year	$ 200	$ 400
3. Cash flow from investment	$2000	$2000
4. Net cash flow after interest payment (line 3 minus line 2)	_____	_____
5. Interest earned during second year by investing net cash flow (5 percent and 10 percent of line 4)	_____	_____
6. Cash flow from investment	$2500	$2500
7. Total at end of second year (line 4 plus line 5 plus line 6)	_____	_____
8. Interest due at end of second year	$ 200	$ 400
9. Loan repayment	$4000	$4000
10. Net (line 7 minus line 8 and line 9)	_____	_____

The crucial question is whether the gyro investment offers any return after paying back the loan with interest. Any dollars left over are pure profit for Eric since he did not invest any of his own money. It should be true that Eric will have a positive (negative) net if the present value of returns is greater (less) than the present value of costs. Is it?

(The entries on line 10 are dollars in the second year. What is the present value of these dollars? How do these present values compare with the net present values calculated in Table 35–1 above?)

d. If the present value of returns equals the present value of cost, an investment opportunity offers the same return as investing at the rate of interest.

e. If the present value of returns exceeds the present value of costs, an investment opportunity offers a greater return than investing at the rate of interest.

f. If the present value of returns is less than the present value of costs, an investment opportunity offers a worse return than investing at the rate of interest.

SUPPLEMENTARY EXERCISE

Can You Share in Monopoly Profits?

Assume for the moment that the major oil companies are able to exercise considerable monopoly power and, as a result, earn substantial monopoly profits on their investments, far in excess of the rate of interest. Can you share these profits and earn the same high rate of return by buying oil company stocks?

What determines the price of oil company stocks? An economist would expect the market price to be close to the present value of the future returns from owning the stock, that is, close to the present value of expected future dividends and capital gains. Thus if dividends are high because of huge monopoly profits, the price of the stock will be

_____. If huge monopoly profits and the resulting future dividends were known for sure, what rate of return do you think you could earn by buying oil company stocks? Just who does earn those monopoly profits?

36

Labor: The Human Input

LEARNING OBJECTIVES

After completing the material in this chapter you should be able to:

- define, understand, and use correctly the terms and concepts listed below.
- explain how income and substitution effects influence the slope of the supply curve of labor.
- explain how the demand for labor is derived from a firm's profit-maximizing decisions about the use of factors of production.
- use demand and supply curves to determine the equilibrium wage and employment in a competitive labor market.
- explain why wages for some individuals contain substantial economic rent.
- discuss how human capital theory explains the observed correlation between more education and higher wages.
- discuss some of the alternative views of the role of education.
- use demand and supply curves to analyze the impact of minimum wage legislation.
- describe the history of unions and major labor legislation in the United States.
- use demand and supply curves to describe the alternative goals that labor unions might follow.

- describe the alternative strategies that a union might follow in an effort to increase wages.
- distinguish between a monopsonist and a monopolist.
- describe the differences between arbitration and mediation.

IMPORTANT TERMS AND CONCEPTS

Minimum wage law
Income and substitution effects
Backward-bending supply curve
Economic rent
Investments in human capital
Human capital theory
Dual labor markets
Union
Industrial and craft unions
Taft-Hartley Act (1947)
Closed shop
Union shop
Seniority rules
Monopsony
Bilateral monopoly
Collective bargaining
Mediation
Arbitration

CHAPTER REVIEW

In a competitive market without minimum wages or unions, wages and employment—the price and quantity of labor services—will be determined by the interaction of the demand for and the supply of labor services and can be analyzed with tools that should now be familiar—demand and supply curves.

The supply of labor comes from individual decisions to work. Individual decisions to supply work are simultaneously decisions to forgo leisure. Thus, a decision to supply less labor is simultaneously a decision to

(1) demand _____. At higher wages, the same number of working hours will mean a larger income. If leisure is not an inferior good, people are apt to demand (more/less) leisure as their income increases. This suggests that the supply of labor might (increase/decrease) as wages increase. This is called the (income/substitution) effect of higher wages but it is only part of the story.

Higher wages also increase the opportunity cost of an hour of leisure. As a result we expect that as

(2) wages increase the substitution effect will lead people to work (more/less). The ultimate effect of increased wages comes from the sum of the income and substitution effects. Statistical evidence suggests that at low wages the _____ effect predominates and labor supply (increases/decreases) with an increase in wages, while at high wages the two effects tend to (enhance/offset) each other. The response of individuals to a change in wages, the income and substitution effects, helps to determine the (slope/position) of the supply curve of labor. Other factors such as the size of the available working popula-tion and nonmonetary aspects of many jobs help to determine the _____ of the labor supply curve. The strength of the (income/substitution) effect is important for an understanding of the historical evidence on real wages and average weekly hours in the United States.

The demand for labor comes from the decisions of firms to use labor as one of many factors of pro-duction. Labor services are valuable to a firm because they add to output and, it is hoped, to profits. Thus the demand for labor is a derived demand. The discussion in Chapters 23 and 35 of how a profit maximizing firm makes optimal decisions about the use of factors of production showed us that a firm should use more of any factor as long as the addition to revenue exceeds the addition to cost or, in technical terms, as long as the marginal revenue product of the factor is greater than the marginal cost of the factor. The demand curve for labor is determined by the marginal revenue product curve. The curve has a negative slope because of the law of diminishing marginal returns.

In competitive markets, equilibrium wages and employment are determined by the intersection of the market demand and supply curves, which come from the horizontal summation of firms' demand curves and individuals' supply curves. Any factor that causes a shift in either curve will change equilibrium wages and employment. For example, an increase in the demand for a firm's output or a technological innovation that

(3) increases the productivity of labor will shift the (demand/supply) curve and lead to (higher/lower) wages, employment, or both.

Wages will differ for a number of reasons. Differences in abilities and work effort will affect individual wages. Differing amounts of other factors of production would also be expected to affect the marginal physical product of labor and hence wages. If individual skills are not easily duplicated, as may be the case for star athletes or performers, wages will be high as they contain significant economic rents. If skills are easily duplicated, one would expect that competition in the form of entry would work to keep wages in line with the costs of acquiring skills.

Education and wages are positively correlated. That is, people with more education typically earn higher wages. Human capital theory views these higher wages as the return to higher productivity from investments in human capital—that is, the time, money, and effort spent on schooling and training. Other theories of the effects of education on earnings offer alternative viewpoints to explain the correlation of education and earnings. Some observers argue that rather than enhancing skills schooling only sorts workers by their innate abilities, helping employers to identify those who will be most productive on the job. Radical critics charge that schooling only sustains existing class differences by teaching discipline and obedience. Theories of dual labor markets combine alternative approaches arguing that schooling sorts workers into

(4) good and bad jobs. In the primary labor market with good jobs, education (does/does not) enhance the skills and wages of workers. In the secondary labor market, workers (do/do not) have an incentive to invest in their own skills.

In some cases the market determination of wages and employment is affected by a legal floor on

(5) wages rates, or a(n) _____ wage. Chapter 4 discussed the effects of price

floors. One should expect similar results from minimum wages. To be effective the minimum wage must be (higher/lower) than the market wage. The imposition of a minimum wage will (increase/decrease) the volume of employment as firms move backward and to the left along their demand curves for labor. At the same time the promise of higher wages is apt to increase the (demand/supply) of labor. The net result will be higher wages and income for those lucky enough to have jobs, but only frustration for many others who are seeking work.

(6)   Minimum wage laws affect primarily (skilled/unskilled) labor markets. A major noncompetitive feature in

many skilled labor markets is the existence of labor _____. Currently, about a sixth of American workers belong to a union. The development of unions in America can be traced back about 100 years. Significant union gains were made during the 1930s with the passage of the Wagner, or

_____ _____ _____ Act, which guaranteed workers the right to form unions and established the National Labor Relations Board to see that these rights were not

violated. Some union practices were declared illegal by the _____-_____ Act, passed in 1947.

           In some labor markets, unions are the only supplier of labor services; that is, they are a

(7)   (monopolist/monopsonist). As such, they face a trade-off between wages and employment just as a monopoly supplier of widgets faces a trade-off betwen price and output. Geometrically, a union, as a monopolist, can

choose any point on the relevant _____ curve for labor. The trade-off between wages and employment comes because the demand curve for labor has a negative slope. A union might be able to raise both wages and employment if it can shift the demand curve for labor to the (right/left). Increasing the demand for union made products or featherbedding and other restrictive work practices will have the desired impact on the demand for union labor. (In terms of efforts to increase wages and income, do not limit your conception of unions to the AFL-CIO or to the Teamsters. Many professional organizations, such as the American Medical Association, also attempt to limit supply. When effective, these organizations will raise the wages and incomes of their members.) Efforts to increase productivity are an alternative way to increase the demand for labor.

           Sometimes a union, as a monopolistic supplier of labor, faces a single buyer of labor services. When

(8)   one buyer constitutes the entire market demand, the buyer is called a _____. Both monopolists and monopsonists realize that their decisions about quantity of labor must at the same time

affect _____. Monopolists who want to sell more must accept a (higher/lower)

price and monopsonists who want to buy more must pay a _____ price. If a

monopsonist faces a monopolist, then the whole market has only _____ participants.

The technical term for this situation is _____ monopoly. Each will consider the actions of the other, and, as for oligopoly, the outcome is difficult to predict.

           When union and management sit down to decide on the terms and conditions of employment, they are

(9)   engaging in _____ _____. This process will decide not only wages but also fringe benefits, overtime premiums, grievance procedures, and a host of other details. If both sides cannot come to an agreement and wish to avoid a strike they may agree to

_____ or _____. If the middleman only helps labor and management to reach an agreement but has no power to enforce a settlement, he is called a(n)

_____. If the middleman listens to the arguments of both sides and then also

makes the final decisions, he is called a(n) _____.

DEFINITION QUIZ

Choose the letter that is the most appropriate definition for each of the following terms.

1. _____ Minimum wage law
2. _____ Income effect (of higher wages)
3. _____ Substitution effect (of higher wages)
4. _____ Backward-bending supply curve of labor
5. _____ Human capital theory
6. _____ Dual labor markets
7. _____ Industrial union
8. _____ Craft union
9. _____ Closed shop
10. _____ Union shop
11. _____ Seniority rules
12. _____ Monopsony
13. _____ Bilateral monopoly
14. _____ Collective bargaining
15. _____ Mediation
16. _____ Arbitration

a. All workers must join the union.
b. Reduction in supply of labor as wages increase.
c. Legal floor on wages for all workers.
d. Viewing education as an investment in a person's earning potential.
e. Market composed of a single seller and a single buyer.
f. Group representing similar skilled workers in all industries.
g. Market situation in which there is only one producer.
h. Impact on demand for increased leisure from higher income when wages increase.
i. Intervention of an impartial individual who is empowered to impose binding decisions on unresolved issues.
j. Market situation in which there is only one buyer.
k. Group representing all types of workers in a single industry.
l. Increased opportunity cost of leisure as wages increase.
m. Hiring only union members.
n. Discussions between labor and management to determine wages and conditions of employment.
o. Intervention of an impartial observer who attempts to hasten the bargaining process.
p. Substitution effect of higher wages outweighs income effect.
q. Notion that there are mainly two types of jobs: those offering opportunities for acquisition of skills and promotions, and "dead-end jobs."
r. Job-related advantages to workers who have held their jobs longest.

BASIC EXERCISE

This problem illustrates the determination of wages and employment in both a competitive market and a market monopolized by a labor union.

Tony runs a small company, Bearpaw Boots, that manufactures hiking boots. Table 36–1 shows the total output of boots per month for different quantities of labor.

1. Fill in the third column by using the data in the second column to compute the marginal physical product of each additional worker.
2. Tony can sell boots for $60 a pair. Each boot contains $20 worth of leather, leaving $40 for wages or profits. As Tony has a small firm, the prices of boots is unaffected by the quantity that he sells. Fill in the fourth column by computing the marginal revenue product of each worker. Be sure to use the $40 net figure rather than the $60 gross.
3. Tony is interested in maximizing profits. How many workers should he employ if monthly wages are $1100? _____
4. Show that your answer to Question 3 maximizes profits by computing total profits for one more and for one less worker.

TABLE 36-1
OUTPUT FIGURES FOR BEARPAW BOOTS

Number of Bootmakers	Total Number of Pairs of Boots per Month	Marginal Physical Product (boots)	Marginal Revenue Product (dollars)
1	60	____	____
2	115	____	____
3	165	____	____
4	210	____	____
5	250	____	____
6	285	____	____
7	315	____	____
8	340	____	____
9	360	____	____
10	375	____	____

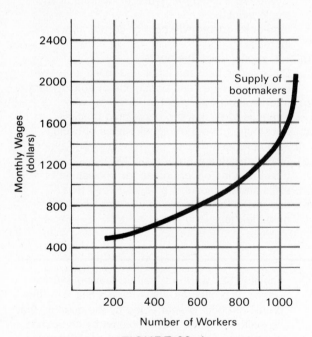

FIGURE 36-1

INDUSTRY DEMAND FOR AND SUPPLY OF BOOTMAKERS

5. Figure 36-1 shows the supply of bootmakers for the entire industry. Assume that there are 100 competitive firms just like Tony's. Using your data on the marginal revenue product for a typical firm, plot the market demand for boot-makers. What is the equilibrium market wage and employment? $_____ and _____.
At the equilibrium market wage, how many workers should Tony employ? _____
What are Tony's profits? _____

6. Assume now that the International Association of Bootmakers has been successful in unionizing all bootmakers. In order to evaluate possible alternative goals, the union has asked you to use your knowledge of the industry demand curve to answer the following questions:
   a. If union membership is limited to 400 persons, what is the maximum monthly wage the union can get from employers? _____
   b. If the union wage is set at $700 a month, what is the maximum amount of employment?

   _____
   c. (Harder) What wage and employment combination will maximize total wage payments?

   _____

SELF-TESTS FOR UNDERSTANDING

Test A

Circle the correct answer.

1. A change in which of the following will affect the slope of the labor supply curve?
   a. An increase in the working age population.
   b. A technological innovation that increases labor productivity.
   c. An increase in the price of a competitive firm's output.
   d. An increase in the willingness of people to trade higher money incomes for more leisure.
2. A change in which of the following will affect the demand for labor by affecting the marginal physical product of labor?
   a. The demand for a firm's output.
   b. The amount of other factors of production per worker.
   c. The supply of labor.
   d. The minimum wage.
3. A change in which of the following will affect the demand for labor by affecting the marginal revenue product of labor?
   a. The demand for a firm's output.
   b. Union militancy.
   c. The supply of labor.
   d. The minimum wage.

4. Historical data that show a declining work week along with rising real wages are probably reflecting
   a. minimum wage laws.
   b. the income effect of higher wages.
   c. the substitution effect of higher wages.
   d. the Taft-Hartley Act.

5. The supply curve for schmoos is upward sloping. An increase in the demand for schmoos (the demand curve shifts to the right) will lead to all but which one of the following?
   a. The price of schmoos increases.
   b. The marginal physical product of labor schedule shifts upward.
   c. The marginal revenue product of labor schedule shifts upward.
   d. The demand curve for labor to produce schmoos shifts upward.
   e. More employment and/or higher wages in the schmoo industry.

6. The theory of human capital says that
   a. individuals can repair their own bodies with artificial parts, just like machines.
   b. soon all work will be done by computer-operated robots.
   c. Individual decisions to seek training and new skills can be modeled in the same way as ordinary investment decisions, involving present costs in the expectation of future returns.
   d. slavery in the United States was doomed to fail because it was uneconomical.

7. In contrast with unions in Europe and Japan, unions in America
   a. are much more political.
   b. have resulted in almost twice the level of strike activity found in any other country.
   c. currently involve a smaller percentage of the labor force than do most European unions.
   d. have been less adversarial than unions in Japan.

8. The Taft-Hartley Act
   a. permitted states to ban union shops.
   b. legalized closed shops.
   c. created the National Labor Relations Board.
   d. increased the minimum wage.

9. A single union that controls the supply of labor to many small firms is a
   a. socialist.
   b. monopsonist.
   c. oligopolist.
   d. monopolist.

10. Which of the following are examples of

    mediation   _____

    arbitration   _____

    strike   _____

    featherbedding   _____

    work slowdown   _____

    union shop   _____

    closed shop   _____

    a. Public school teachers and the local school board, who have been unable to reach agreement, agree to accept the determination of a three-person board.
    b. Plane schedules are delayed as air traffic controllers "do it by the book" in their handling of planes.
    c. Anyone may seek work at the local meat-packing plant, but once employed they must join the union.
    d. In an attempt to avert a steel strike, the Secretary of Labor helps the United Steelworkers and the steel companies to resolve their differences.
    e. The United Mine Workers start picketing after contract negotiations fail.
    f. none.

Test B

Circle T or F for True or False as appropriate.

1. Information on the marginal revenue product of labor can be used to derive a firm's demand for labor.   T F

2. The "law" of diminishing returns implies that the demand curve for labor will have a negative slope.   T F

3. The income effect of higher wages suggests that the supply of labor schedule may have a positively sloped portion.   T F

4. An increase in wages that increases the quantity of labor supplied is represented as a shift in the supply curve.   T F

5. Raising the minimum wage will raise the income of all people currently earning less than the minimum wage.   T F

6. If a labor union has complete control over the supply of a particular type of labor, it is a monopsonist.   T F

7. A market with a single buyer and a single seller is called an oligopoly.   T F

8. In general there is no conflict between union attempts to maximize wages for current union members and attempts to provide employment for the largest possible number of workers. T F

9. Statistical evidence suggests that unions have been successful in raising wages by 50 to 100 percent above their competitive level. T F

10. If a union and employer, unable to reach agreement on a new contract, agree to accept the decision of an impartial third party, they have agreed to settle their differences by arbitration. T F

Appendix: The Effects of Union and Minimum Wages Under Monopsony

LEARNING OBJECTIVE

The exercise below is designed to increase your understanding of the material in the appendix to Chapter 36.

IMPORTANT TERMS AND CONCEPTS

Marginal labor costs

DEFINITION QUIZ

Choose the letter that is the most appropriate definition for the following term.

1. _____ Marginal labor cost

   a. Wage rate.
   b. Change in total wages paid as employment increases.
   c. Change in total wages as percent of change in total cost.

BASIC EXERCISE

This problem illustrates what can happen when unorganized workers face a monopsonistic employer.

Assume that Bearpaw Boots (the subject of the Basic Exercise for the chapter) is located in a small, isolated town in northern Maine and is the sole employer of bootmakers. Tony still sells his boots in a competitive market for a net price of $40. Table 36–2 contains data on what wages Tony must pay to get various numbers of employees.

1. Use the data in the first two columns of Table 36–2 to plot the supply curve of labor in Figure 36–2. Use the data on the marginal revenue product computed in Table 36–1 to plot the demand curve for labor in Figure 36–2. These curves

   intersect where wages are $_____

   and the number of employees is _____.
   Will Tony pay this wage and employ this many workers? (yes/no) Why?

2. Remember, Tony is the only employer of boot-

TABLE 36–2

SUPPLY OF BOOTMAKERS IN A SMALL ISOLATED TOWN

Number of Bootmakers	Monthly Wage (dollars)	Total Labor Cost (dollars)	Marginal Labor Costs (dollars)
1	300	_____	_____
2	400	_____	_____
3	500	_____	_____
4	600	_____	_____
5	700	_____	_____
6	800	_____	_____
7	900	_____	_____
8	1000	_____	_____
9	1100	_____	_____
10	1200	_____	_____

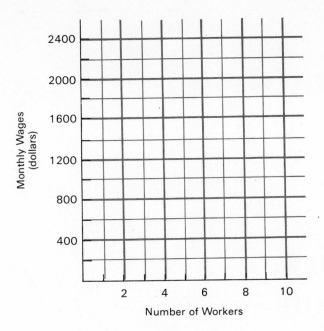

FIGURE 36–2
DEMAND FOR AND SUPPLY OF
BOOTMAKERS

makers in town. As he employs additional
workers, he must pay a higher wage not only to
each new employee but also to all existing
employees. Thus the marginal labor cost of an
additional worker is (greater/less) than the wage.
Fill in the remaining columns of Table 36–2 to
compute Tony's marginal labor costs.

3. Plot the figures on marginal labor costs in
   Figure 36–2.
4. Tony's profit-maximizing level of employment is

   _____ workers.
5. What is the lowest wage that Tony must offer in
   order to attract the profit-maximizing number of

   workers? $_____
6. What are Tony's profits (net revenue minus total

   wages?) $_____
7. If Tony were forced to pay a minimum wage of
   $1100 a month, what would happen to wages
   and employment as compared with your answers
   to Questions 4 and 5? _____
8. Would a union necessarily force the minimum
   wage solution to Question 7 on Tony? Why or
   why not?

SUPPLEMENTARY EXERCISE

Does College Pay?
Data on income distribution for 1985 reports an
average income of $27,319 for heads of households

completing four years of high school and an income
of $46,387 for those who have completed four or
more years of college. If we assume that on average
a college graduate will earn the $19,068 difference
every year she works, is college a good financial
investment?

To answer this question you will need to compare the present value of the cost of college to the
present value of the earnings differential. Remember
from the Supplementary Exercise to Chapter 3 that
the cost of college includes the opportunity cost of
lost wages from not working, spending on tuition,
fees, and books, and any differential living expenses.
Basic room and board should not be included as
one would incur those expenses whether going to
school or not. Table 36–3 contains an illustrative
calculation on the assumption that one spends four
years in college from age 19 to 22 and then works
for 43 years until age 65. An interest rate of 10
percent has been used to calculate present values.
What would such a calculation show for you? How
would a change in the rate of interest affect the net
present value? Why might someone value a college
education even if it did not promise a financial
return?

The calculations in Table 36–3 are meant to be
illustrative not definitive. The $27,319 income figure
is an average for all high school graduates. One would
expect that recent graduates would earn less, lowering the cost of college. Similarly, the income differential between college and high school graduates
is likely to be small at first and grow over time.

TABLE 36–3

	Public	Private
Cost of college for each of four years		
Lost wages	$27,319	$27,319
Tuition fees (Table 2–3)	$1,536	$7,374
Books & incidentals	$1,500	$1,500
Present value at age 19 of costs[1]	$105,843	$126,120
Present value at age 19 of returns[2]	$140,882	$140,882
Net present value	$35,039	$14,762

1. $PV = \sum_{t=0}^{3} \frac{\text{Total Cost}}{(1.1)^t}$

All costs are assumed to be paid at the beginning of the year.

2. $PV = \sum_{t=23}^{65} \frac{\text{Income Differential}}{(1.1)^{t-19}} = \sum_{t=23}^{65} \frac{\$19,068}{(1.1)^{t-19}}$

All income is assumed to be earned at the end of the year.

Poverty, Inequality, and Discrimination

LEARNING OBJECTIVES

After completing the material in this chapter you should be able to:

- define, understand, and use correctly the terms and concepts listed below.
- discuss some of the facts of poverty and income distribution.
- describe the implications of the use of absolute or relative concepts of poverty.
- explain what a Lorenz curve is.
- draw a Lorenz curve, given appropriate data on population and income.
- describe what factors account for differences in incomes, how some of these factors reflect voluntary choices, and why these factors make the identification of economic discrimination so difficult.
- explain how competition can work to minimize some forms of discrimination by employers.
- explain why the trade-off between equality and efficiency implies that the optimal distribution of income will involve some inequality.

- explain the concept of a negative income tax and how it affects work incentives.
- describe the controversy surrounding programs for affirmative action and comparable worth.

IMPORTANT TERMS AND CONCEPTS

Poverty line
Absolute and relative concepts of poverty
Lorenz curve
Economic discrimination
Statistical discrimination
Optimal amount of inequality
Trade-off between equality and efficiency
Aid to Families with Dependent Children (AFDC)
Food stamps
Negative income tax (NIT)
Civil Rights Act
Equal Employment Opportunities Commission (EEOC)
Affirmative action
Comparable worth

CHAPTER REVIEW

The material in this chapter discusses a number of topics concerned with the distribution of income: poverty, inequality in the distribution of income, and discrimination, as it contributes to poverty and inequality.

Discussions of poverty in America usually focus on the number of families below the *poverty line*. In

(1) 1989 this dividing line was about $_____ a year for a family of four. It is adjusted every year for changes in prices. Since the yearly adjustment reflects only prices and not general increases in real income,

the poverty line is a(n) (absolute/relative) concept of poverty rather than a(n) _____ concept.

The facts about the distribution of income can be presented in a number of different ways. Economists

(2) often use a particular form of graphical representation called a(n) _____ curve. To construct such a curve, one first orders families or individuals by income, lowest to highest. Then the cumulative percentage of total income is plotted against the cumulative percentage of families (or

individuals). The Lorenz curve starts at the origin, where zero percent of families have _____ percent of income. Perfect equality in the distribution of income would result in a Lorenz curve that coincided

with the _____ line. In real economies, with inequality in the distribution of income, the Lorenz curve

has a _____ slope and lies (above/below) the 45° line. (Can you convince yourself why the Lorenz curve never has a negative slope and why it never crosses the 45° line?) In fact, some researchers measure the degree of inequality by the area between the Lorenz curve and the 45° line as a proportion of the total area under the 45° line. Over the last 30 years this measure shows (no/very little/significant) change in inequality of the distribution of income in the United States.

U.S. income data show that in 1988, families with incomes above $58,500 were in the top 20 percent of the income distribution, while families with incomes below approximately $15,250 were in the bottom 20

(3) percent. The top 20 percent of families received _____ percent of income while the bottom 20

percent received _____ percent.

Why do incomes differ? The list of reasons is long and includes differences in abilities, intensity of work, risk taking, wage differentials for unpleasant or hazardous work, schooling and training, work experience, inherited wealth, luck, and discrimination. Some of the reasons for differences in incomes represent voluntary choices by individuals to work harder, take more risks, or accept unpleasant work in order to earn higher incomes. Measures to equalize incomes may adversely affect the work effort of these individuals. In more tech-

(4) nical terms, efforts for greater equality may mean reduced _____. This important trade-off does not mean that all efforts to increase equality should be abandoned. It does mean that efforts to increase equality have a price and should not be pushed beyond the point where the marginal gains from further equality are worth less than the marginal loss from reduced efficiency. Exactly where this point is reached is the subject of controversy and continuing political debate.

The trade-off between equality and efficiency also suggests that in the fight for greater equality one should choose policies with small rather than large effects on efficiency. Economists would argue that many current welfare programs are inefficient. One important reason is the relatively large reduction in benefits for

(5) each additional dollar of earned income. These high implicit (marginal/average) tax rates (increase/decrease) the incentive for increased work effort on the part of welfare recipients who are able to work.

Many economists favor replacing the current welfare system with a negative income tax, that is, a system of direct cash grants tied to income levels and linked to the tax system. These schemes usually start

(6) with a minimum guaranteed level of income and a tax rate that specifies the (increase/decrease) in the cash grant for every dollar increase in income. A low tax rate will retain significant work incentives; however, a low tax rate also means that grants continue until income is quite high. The point where payments from the

government stop and payments to the government start is called the _____-

_____ level of income. A negative income tax with a low marginal tax rate can offer significantly better work incentives to those currently receiving welfare, but there will be (positive/negative) work incentives for those not now on welfare. Recent negative income tax experiments have investigated the size of these negative work incentives and found them to be (large/small).

Economic discrimination is defined as a situation in which equal factors of production receive

(7) _____ payments for equal contributions to output. Average differences in income between large social groups, such as men and women or blacks and whites, (are/are not) sufficient proof of economic discrimination. These average differences tend to (overstate/understate) the amount of economic discrimination. To accurately measure the impact of possible discrimination, one needs first to correct for the factors listed above that could create differences in income without implying economic discrimination. Some factors, such as schooling, are tricky to handle. For instance, differences in wages associated with differences in schooling would not imply any discrimination if everyone has had an equal opportunity for the same amount of schooling. But it is unclear whether observed differences in schooling represent voluntary choices or another form of discrimination. Public policy makes it illegal to discriminate, but the evidence as to what constitutes discrimination is often subject to much dispute. Competitive markets can work to decrease some forms of discrimination, especially discrimination by (employers/employees). Dissatisfaction with apparent continuing discrimination has led to the adoption of policies for affirmative action and comparable worth adjustments in wages.

DEFINITION QUIZ

Choose the letter that is the most appropriate definition for each of the following terms.

1. _____ Poverty line

2. _____ Lorenz curve

3. _____ Economic discrimination

4. _____ Statistical discrimination

5. _____ Affirmative action

6. _____ Comparable worth

7. _____ AFDC

8. _____ Negative income tax

9. _____ Food stamps

a. Amount of income below which a family is considered "poor."
b. Active efforts to recruit and hire members of underrepresented groups.
c. Graph depicting the distribution of income.
d. Income share of poorest quartile of income distribution.
e. Public assistance to families with children but no working parent.
f. Pay standards that assign equal wages to jobs deemed "comparable."
g. Estimating a particular worker's productivity as low solely because that worker belongs to some group.
h. Stamps that allow families to buy food at subsidized prices.
i. Paying different amounts to equivalent factors of production for equal contributions to output.
j. Income conditioned cash grants available to all families as an entitlement.

BASIC EXERCISE

This problem illustrates the high marginal tax rates that often result from combining many welfare programs. The numbers in this problem do not come from any specific welfare program but are illustrative of many.

Imagine a welfare system that offers a family of four the following forms of public support.

- *General assistance* in the form of a basic grant of $300 a month. The first $50 of earned income every month is assumed to be for work-related expenses and does not reduce benefits. After

that, benefits are reduced by 50 cents for every dollar of earned income.

- *Food stamps* that offer the family $2,500 a year but require payments equal to 25 percent of gross wage earnings.

- *Medicaid benefits* of $1,500 a year. The family is assumed to receive these benefits as long as it is eligible for general assistance.

- *Housing subsidy* that gives the family an apartment worth $4,800 a year in rent. The family must pay rent equal to 25 percent of its net income, which is determined as gross wage earnings plus general assistance minus $500 for each dependent.

TABLE 37-1
(dollars)

(1) Earned Income	(2) Social Security and Income Taxes*	(3) General Assistance	(4) Food Stamps	(5) Medicaid Subsidy	(6) Housing Subsidy	(7) Net Income (1) + (2) + (3) + (4) + (5) + (6)
0	0	3,600	2,500	1,500	4,400	_____
600**	39	3,600	2,350	1,500	4,250	_____
6,500	422	650	875	1,500	3,513	_____
7,799	324	1	550	1,500	3,350	_____
7,800	324	0	550	0	3,350	_____
10,000	159	0	0	0	2,800	_____
10,250	140	0	0	0	2,738	_____
13,200	− 376	0	0	0	2,000	_____
19,350	− 2,376	0	0	0	463	_____
21,200	− 2,792	0	0	0	0	_____

*Income taxes include earned income credit at low levels of income and are based on 1989 tax rates.

**Assumed to be $50 a month.

1. Fill in column 7 of Table 37-1 by computing net income after taxes and after welfare payments for the different levels of earned income.
2. Use the data in columns 1 and 7 to plot net income against earned income in Figure 37-1. Plot each pair of points and then connect successive pairs with a straight line. What does the graph suggest about work incentives under these programs?
3. Use the data in Table 37-1 to complete Table 37-2, computing the implicit marginal tax rates that this family faces as it earns income. What is the relationship between the implicit marginal tax rates you computed in Table 37-2 and the slope of the graph in Figure 37-1? (How do these marginal rates compare with marginal rates under the positive portion of federal income taxes of 15, 28, and 33 percent?)
4. (Optional) One could reduce the implicit marginal tax rate by lowering the rate at which benefits are reduced under any of the programs. To investigate the impact of such reductions, construct a new version of Table 37-1 in which general assistance payments are reduced by only 25 cents for every dollar reduction in income, and the food

stamp subsidy is reduced by only 10 cents. What happens to the magnitude of the subsidy payments at each level of income? What happens to the break-even levels of income for each program, that is, to the level of income when a family is no longer eligible? What would happen to total public outlays for these programs?

SELF-TESTS FOR UNDERSTANDING

Test A

Circle the correct answer.

1. Defining poor people as those who fall in the bottom 20 percent of the income distribution
   a. is an absolute concept of poverty.
   b. is a relative concept of poverty.
   c. means that continued economic growth will eliminate poverty.
   d. implies that the Lorenz curve is a straight line.

TABLE 37–2

(1) Earned Income (dollars)	(2) Change in Earned Income (dollars)	(3) Net Income (Table 37–1, column 7) (dollars)	(4) Change in Net Income (dollars)	(5) "Implicit Taxes" (2) − (4) (dollars)	(6) Implicit Marginal Tax Rate (5) ÷ (2) (percent)
0					
	600				
600					
	5,900				
6,500					
	1,299				
7,799					
	1				
7,800					
	2,200				
10,000					
	250				
10,250					
	2,950				
13,200					
	6,150				
19,350					
	1,850				
21,200					

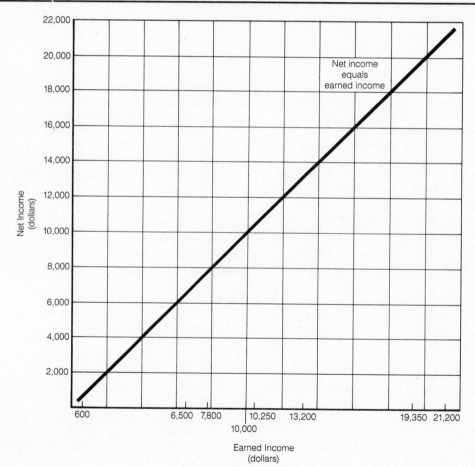

FIGURE 37–1

2. The facts on income distribution in the United States show
   a. a substantial move toward equality over the last 30 years.
   b. that the richest 20 percent of families receive about 80 percent of the total income.
   c. that the poorest 20 percent of families receive less than 2 percent of income.
   d. a Lorenz curve that sags below the 45° line.

3. Compared with other industrial countries, data on the distribution of income in the United States show
   a. more inequality than most other countries.
   b. about the same degree of inequality.
   c. much more equality.

4. Which of the following statements about the Lorenz curve is false?
   a. It is a graph of the cumulative percentage of families (or persons) and the associated cumulative percentage of total income they receive.
   b. It has a positive slope.
   c. It would be a straight line if there were no economic discrimination.
   d. For the United States it has not shifted much in the last 30 years.

5. Between 1983 and 1989, the proportion of families with incomes below the official poverty line
   a. decreased but remained above previous low values.
   b. stayed about the same.
   c. rose substantially.
   d. declined to its lowest point ever.

6. Consider a negative income tax scheme with a guaranteed minimum income level of $6,000 for a family of four and a tax rate of 50 percent. Which of the following statements is false?
   a. The break-even level of income will be $12,000.
   b. Reducing the tax rate below 50 percent will increase work incentives and increase the break-even level of income.
   c. Increasing the minimum guarantee without changing the tax rate increases the break-even level of income.
   d. If the Uptons earn 4,000 in wages, their total income (earnings plus negative tax payment) will be $10,000.

7. If a negative income tax system is to be financed within a given budget, then a reduction in the negative tax rate to increase work incentives
   a. must be offset by a reduction in the minimum guaranteed level of income.
   b. needs no change in the minimum guaranteed level of income.
   c. must be offset by an increase in the minimum guaranteed level of income.

8. Which of the following would be an example of economic discrimination?
   a. Census data showing that, on average, women earn less than men.
   b. Nurses earn less than doctors.
   c. Over the period 1980 to 1987, plumbers and electricians received larger percentage wage increases than did college professors.
   d. A careful study showing that among blacks and whites with identical education, work experience, productivity, and motivation, blacks earn less than whites.

9. All but which one of the following could give rise to differences in income without implying discrimination?
   a. Schooling.
   b. Ability.
   c. Compensating wage differential for night work.
   d. Intensity of work effort.

10. Competitive markets work to erode what type of discrimination?
    a. Discrimination by employees.
    b. Discrimination by employers.
    c. Statistical discrimination.

Test B

Circle T or F for True or False as appropriate.

1. Continued economic growth is capable of eliminating poverty as measured by an absolute standard, but not as measured by a relative standard.   T F

2. U.S. data show no change in poverty as measured by the number of families below the poverty line since 1960.   T F

3. In the United States, the 20 percent of families that are poorest receive about 20 percent of total income.   T F

4. Perfect equality in the distribution of income would result in a Lorenz curve that lies on the 45° line.   T F

5. Data for the last 30 years show little change in the Lorenz curve for the United States.   T F

6. The fact that women, white or black, have lower average incomes than men, is sufficient proof of economic discrimination.   T F

7. Competitive markets can help to eliminate discrimination by employers.   T F

8. In the absence of monopolies, unregulated markets would result in an equal distribution of income.   T F

9. Some differences in income reflect voluntary choices, such as decisions to work more hours or to take early retirement.   T F

10. The federal personal income tax system has substantially reduced the degree of income inequality in the United States.   T F

SUPPLEMENTARY EXERCISES

1. Table 37–3 shows data on the distribution of income for 12 Organization for Economic Cooperation and Development (OECD) countries. Which countries have the greatest equality in the distribution of income? You might try drawing a Lorenz curve for several countries to help you decide. For example, consider Japan and Sweden. Use one large piece of graph paper to draw a Lorenz curve for both countries. In which country is income distributed more equally?

   If you have access to a microcomputer, try writing a small program to compute the area between the line of equality and the Lorenz curve for each of the countries in Table 37–3.

   Compare these data on income distribution for industrialized countries with similar data for lower-income developing countries. *World Development Report*, published annually by the World Bank, reports data on income distribution for a large number of countries.

2. Following is a suggested list of additional readings on three important topics covered in this chapter.

   On the general issue of trade-offs between increased equality and reduced efficiency, read Arthur Okun's *Equality and Efficiency: The Big Trade-off*, published by the Brookings Institution, 1975. This important book is the source of the "leaky bucket" analogy used in the text.

   For an excellent discussion of how existing welfare schemes confront poor people with "economic choices no rational person would want to make," read *Why Is Welfare So Hard to Reform?* by Henry J. Aaron, published by the Brookings Institution, 1973. The book was written following the Nixon administration's attempt to implement a negative income tax scheme.

   Martin Anderson's book, *Welfare: The Political Economy of Welfare Reform in the United States*, Hoover Institution Press, 1978, argues that existing welfare programs have essentially eliminated poverty as a critical social issue. Anderson served for a while as one of President Reagan's White House aides for domestic policy. More recent data on the impact of noncash benefits can be found in *The Statistical Abstract of the United States*.

3. Women now account for over 45 percent of the American labor force. Economic issues concerning the role of women in the labor force are examined by Claudia Goldin in *Understanding the Gender Gap: An Economic History of American Women*, Oxford University Press, 1990.

4. Investigate the details of welfare programs in the city or county in which you live. Use this information to construct your own version of Table 37–1.

TABLE 37–3

PERCENTAGE OF POST-TAX INCOME RECEIVED BY POPULATION DECILES

		Population Deciles									
	Year	1	2	3	4	5	6	7	8	9	10
Australia	1966–67	2.1	4.5	6.2	7.3	8.3	9.5	10.9	12.5	15.1	23.7
Canada	1969	1.5	3.5	5.1	6.7	8.2	9.7	11.2	13.1	15.9	25.1
France	1970	1.4	2.9	4.2	5.6	7.4	8.9	9.7	13.0	16.5	30.4
Germany	1973	2.8	3.7	4.6	5.7	6.8	8.2	9.8	12.1	15.8	30.3
Italy	1969	1.7	3.4	4.7	5.8	7.0	9.2	9.8	11.9	15.6	30.9
Japan	1969	3.0	4.9	6.1	7.0	7.9	8.9	9.9	11.3	13.8	27.2
Netherlands	1967	2.6	3.9	5.2	6.4	7.6	8.8	10.3	12.4	15.2	27.7
Norway	1970	2.3	4.0	5.6	7.3	8.6	10.2	11.7	13.0	15.1	22.2
Spain	1973–74	2.1	3.9	5.3	6.5	7.8	9.1	10.6	12.5	15.6	26.7
Sweden	1972	2.2	4.4	5.9	7.2	8.5	10.0	11.5	13.3	15.7	21.3
United Kingdom	1973	2.5	3.8	5.5	7.1	8.5	9.9	11.1	12.8	15.2	23.5
United States	1972	1.5	3.0	4.5	6.2	7.8	9.5	11.3	13.4	16.3	26.5

Source: Malcolm Sawyer, "Income Distribution in OECD Countries," *OECD Occasional Studies*, July 1978, Table 4, page 14. Reprinted by permission.

PART
9

ALTERNATIVE ECONOMIC SYSTEMS

38

Growth in Developed and Developing Countries

LEARNING OBJECTIVES

After completing the material in this chapter you should be able to:

- define, understand, and use correctly the terms and concepts listed below.
- distinguish between growth in total GNP and GNP per capita.
- describe what exponential growth is and explain why it cannot continue forever.
- explain why the composition of aggregate demand is an important determinant of the rate of economic growth.
- describe other factors that are important in determining an economy's rate of growth.
- describe the arguments for and against continued growth.
- distinguish between embodied and disembodied growth.
- discuss some of the important factors that impede the growth of incomes in LDCs.
- discuss what things LDCs can do for themselves to increase their growth.

- describe what role developed countries can play in assisting LDCs.
- explain what the World Bank is and what it does.

IMPORTANT TERMS AND CONCEPTS

Output per capita
Exponential growth
Social infrastructure
Exchange between present and future consumption
Embodied growth
Disembodied growth
Less developed countries (LDCs)
Growth rate in GNP vs. per capita income
Multinational corporations
Disguised unemployment
Entrepreneurship
Brain drain
World Bank

CHAPTER REVIEW

This chapter discusses some of the general issues concerned with economic growth: Can it continue forever? Is it desirable? What actions can countries take to influence their rates of growth? Economics cannot always offer definitive answers to these questions, but it can help you to sort out and to think about the issues in a systematic fashion.

(1) Growth that occurs at a constant percentage rate for a number of years is called _____ growth. This "snowballing" effect, when projected into the future, seems to suggest doom for the human race. Simple extrapolations of population at current rates of growth lead to ridiculous conclusions. The clear implication is that growth cannot continue at current rates forever and that actual growth experience will be more a matter of economic choices than mechanical extrapolations.

Many factors are clearly important for growth that are not well understood by economists or by anyone

(2) else. Examples include _____, _____, and the

_____ _____. Other factors that influence growth rates, and that countries *can* do something about, include accumulating more capital by higher levels of

(consumption/investment) and devoting more resources to _____ and

_____. Some new ideas and inventions require new machines before they can help increase output. Growth from these sorts of inventions is called (disembodied/embodied) economic growth. If new ideas permit more output from existing resources, the resulting growth is called

_____ growth.

In a full-employment economy, more of anything, including investment spending or research and development, requires less of something else. This reduction, which is necessary to release resources for an

(3) increase in investment, is the _____ cost of increased investment. In a full-employment economy, resources for more investment would be available if it decided to decrease current

(consumption/savings) and increase the amount of _____.

The tools of economics cannot help you determine whether an economy should grow faster or slower; they can, however, identify the sources of growth and the consequences of more or less growth. In particular, a number of economists oppose zero economic growth on the grounds that a move in this direction would require extensive government controls and may seriously hamper efforts to eliminate poverty and to protect the environment. Solutions to these last two problems are likely to require more rather than fewer resources. Many feel that it is easier to reach a political agreement to devote resources to problems of poverty and the environment if total output is expanding rather than if it is not growing.

Concerns about economic growth are an everyday reality for citizens in developing countries. While one inevitably ends up making lists of "the problems" of developing countries, it is important to remember that there is much diversity among these countries and that their problems are not all alike. The growth and density of population show a wide diversity among LDCs, as do recent gains in per capita incomes.

Three-fourths of the world's population lives in countries with a per capita GNP of $2,000 or less per year. While income per capita increased in a number of developing countries during the 1970s, more recent developments have been less favorable, illustrating the fragility of recent growth trends. The world recession in the early 1980s had adverse impacts on a number of countries. High levels of external debt are a serious burden for some countries; there is evidence that recent growth has been accompanied by a worsening distribution of income; the rate of population growth remains high in many countries; and all LDCs have not shared equally in increases in per capita income.

As for narrowing the income gap with the developed countries, it should be remembered that growth in

(4) the developed countries (has/has not) stopped. Even if developed countries and LDCs show the same percentage growth in income, the absolute differences in incomes will (increase/decrease) due to the (higher/lower) base of the developed countries.

LDCs face many problems in their quest for higher incomes. A fundamental problem is the lack of physical capital. More capital would help to increase labor productivity. LDCs can accumulate more capital in either of two ways. They can try to get it either from domestic sources or from foreign sources. The first

(5) option, domestic sources, would require (more/less) consumption in order to increase savings and investment.[1] This option will be (easy/difficult) for many countries because of their current extremely low levels of income. The second option, foreign sources, is not without its own risks. Profit-maximizing private businesses will clearly want as good a deal for themselves as possible. Mutual gain is still possible, however, especially if the LDCs insist upon the training of native workers for positions of responsibility and the development of social infrastructures, such as transportation and communication systems.

(6)   Population growth continues to be high for many LDCs primarily because of recent dramatic declines in (birth/death) rates. These declines appear to be the result of relatively (inexpensive/expensive) public health measures rather than the result of advancements in medical technology. High rates of population growth result in tremendous demands on a country to ensure that people do not starve. The experience of advanced economies suggests that birthrates may (increase/decrease) as income rises. A lack of trained technical workers, extensive unemployment—especially disguised unemployment—a lack of entrepreneurship, and other social impediments to business activity, as well as extensive government interferences in markets, are additional problems facing LDCs.

        What can the advanced economies do for the LDCs? They can help them accumulate both technical skills and physical capital. Training individuals from LDCs will add to the pool of technical skills for these countries if those receiving education return to their native countries. The fact that many of these individuals

(7)   have not returned is referred to as the _____ _____. Aid in acquiring physical capital can be provided by long-term loans at preferential terms or by direct grants that never have to be repaid. Aid can be given by individual countries or through international organizations, drawing

on the resources of many countries, such as the _____ Bank.

DEFINITION QUIZ

Choose the letter that is the most appropriate definition for each of the following terms.

1. _____ Exponential growth

2. _____ Social infrastructure

3. _____ Embodied growth

4. _____ Disembodied growth

5. _____ Disguised unemployment

6. _____ Brain drain

7. _____ Multinational corporation

8. _____ Entrepreneurship

9. _____ World Bank

a. Educated individuals from developing countries who emigrate to wealthier countries.
b. Transportation network, telecommunications system, and schools.
c. Growth due to better ideas.
d. Companies with operations in many countries.
e. The excess of savings over investment.
f. International organization that makes loans to developing countries to finance investments in social infrastructure.
g. Situation where more people are employed than the most efficient number required.
h. Starting new firms, introducing innovations, and taking the necessary risks in seeking business opportunities.
i. Innovations that require new instruments before they can affect economic growth.
j. Growth at a constant percentage rate.

---

[1]We have seen earlier that $Y = C + I + G + X - IM$. If one wants to increase I and Y cannot be expanded, then reductions in C, G, or $(X - IM)$ will do. In an analysis of opportunities for growth, it is often useful to reclassify elements of G and X as either C or I. With respect to G, highways and dams would be _____, while bureaucrats and paper clips would be _____. With this reclassification, the only way to increase I is to reduce _____ or to get resources from abroad through an increase in _____.

BASIC EXERCISE

Complete Table 38–1 with your best estimate of GNP and GNP per capita for 1987 for each of the countries listed in terms of American dollars. Data for the United States is given as a starting point. Check the accuracy of your estimates in the answers section of the Study Guide.

TABLE 38–1

Country	GNP (billions of dollars)	GNP per capita (dollars)
United States	$4,518	$18,530
Brazil		
Canada		
China		
Egypt		
Great Britain		
Indonesia		
Japan		
Kenya		
Korea		
Mexico		
Norway		
Poland		
West Germany		

SELF-TESTS FOR UNDERSTANDING

Test A

Circle the correct answer.

1. If the objective of economic growth is an increase in individual material welfare, which of the following is an appropriate indicator?
   a. Growth in total output.
   b. Growth in inflation.
   c. Growth in inventiveness.
   d. Growth in output per capita.

2. Exponential growth
   a. in human population can be expected to continue at current rates forever.
   b. can prove that economic growth must come to an end within the next 200 years.
   c. means that the absolute amount of successive increases is the same, and thus the percentage increase becomes smaller over time.
   d. means that the percentage increase is the same, and thus the absolute increase becomes larger and larger.

3. Which of the following is not an example of investment in social infrastructure?
   a. The construction of the trans-Amazon highway in Brazil.
   b. Substantial investments in public education in the United States.
   c. The development of Indonesian oil fields by American oil companies.
   d. Investments in public health to reduce the incidence of infant mortality.

4. Which of the following is the appropriate measure of the opportunity cost of increased investment undertaken to raise the rate of growth?
   a. The resulting increase in future consumption.
   b. The rate of interest.
   c. The present consumption goods that could have been produced with the resources used to produce the investment goods.
   d. Zero, because economic growth is really costless.

5. Disembodied economic growth
   a. refers to increased output from better ways of using existing resources.
   b. has a zero opportunity cost because it requires only new ideas.
   c. has never been important in the real world.
   d. is likely to mean more resource depletion than embodied growth.

6. The recent record of economic growth in LDCs shows
   a. no growth in either GNP or GNP per capita.
   b. an increasing divergence of LDCs into relatively richer and relatively poorer groups.
   c. substantial increases in both GNP and GNP per capita for all LDCs.
   d. equal increases in GNP per capita for all LDCs.

7. High rates of population growth in many developing countries are the result of
   a. recent dramatic increases in birthrates.
   b. recent dramatic declines in death rates.
   c. the application of advanced medical technology.

   d. the success of compulsory programs of birth control.

8. Which of the following is *not* among the obstacles to high levels of income in the LDCs?
   a. Large rural–urban migration with dramatic increases in urban unemployment.
   b. Domestic savings rates that are so high they depress aggregate demand.
   c. A lack of entrepreneurial talent.
   d. Numerous well-intentioned government interventions that discourage the efficiency of private business.

9. Which one of the following is *not* likely to help LDCs achieve higher levels of income?
   a. Any increase in savings and investment that can be squeezed out of existing low levels of income.
   b. Expanded programs of technical trainings.
   c. Policies that discourage foreign investment.
   d. Removal of impediments to innovation and entrepreneurial talent.

10. Which one of the following has *not* been an important source of loans and grants for development projects in LDCs?
    a. The World Bank.
    b. The International Monetary Fund.
    c. The United States.
    d. The Soviet Union.

Test B

Circle T or F for True or False as appropriate.

1. GNP per capita will increase whenever total GNP increases.   T F

2. The fact that population growth has recently been exponential is a good reason to believe that it will continue that way forever.   T F

3. Zero economic growth would be easy to achieve and an unambiguous gain for the fight to clean up the environment.   T F

4. Increased investment spending leading to more capital accumulation is likely to increase the rate of economic growth.   T F

5. Embodied economic growth refers to ideas and inventions that require new machinery.   T F

6. Disembodied economic growth means that an economy can have higher rates of growth without having to sacrifice any current consumption.   T F

7. For any year that the growth rate of income per capita in the LDCs matches that of the developed countries, the absolute difference in income will decrease.   T F

8. Recently all LDCs have shared equally in increases in income per capita.   T F

9. Historical evidence refutes the Malthusian law of population growth.   T F

10. Research suggests that expenditures on technical training rather than general education are likely to have a greater impact on the rate of economic growth in LDCs.   T F

11. Disguised unemployment is only a problem for developed economies and has little relevance for LDCs.   T F

12. Unlike the United States, LDCs have not experienced any substantial rural–urban migration.   T F

13. The only real constraint to growth in the LDCs is a lack of entrepreneurship.   T F

14. In order to avoid the problem of default on loans, the World Bank makes loans only to developed countries, such as Britain and France.   T F

SUPPLEMENTARY EXERCISES

1. The total volume of U.S. aid to LDCs has dwarfed that from all other sources. However, the U.S. economy also dwarfs that of all other countries. How does the U.S. commitment to development assistance stack up when measured as a percent of GNP? Has the volume of aid from all developed economies, both in total and as a percent of GNP, been increasing or decreasing? What about OPEC countries? A good place to start to answer these questions is the library. *World Development Report* typically contains data on official development assistance from major industrialized countries and OPEC countries. *The United States Statistical Yearbook* is another source of data.

    Some observers argue that looking only at foreign aid is incomplete as a measure of a country's concern for others. These people suggest that in view of many multilateral defense agreements, one must also consider military expenditures. What do you think of the argument? What is its quantitative significance? What does it imply at a time when superpower military tensions appear to be diminishing dramatically? The *Statistical Abstract of the United States* is another place to start looking for data.

2. In 1950, the world's population was estimated to be 2.501 billion. From 1950 to 1990 it grew at an average annual rate of 1.905% to 5.320 billion. Assume that population has always grown at an annual rate of 1.905%. If we started with a population of two, how many years would it take for the world population to reach 5.320 billion? How long will it take for the world's population to double if it continues to grow at 1.905% per year?

39

The Economics
of Karl Marx

LEARNING OBJECTIVES

After completing the material in this chapter you should be able to:

- define, understand, and use correctly the terms and concepts listed below.
- explain what Marx meant by "historical materialism."
- describe Marxian value theory and explain how it differs from traditional price determination.
- explain the role of prices in the Marxian analysis.
- explain how in Marxian analysis the process of accumulation of wealth will undermine capitalism.

IMPORTANT TERMS
AND CONCEPTS

Historical materialism
Marxian "commodity"
Marxian "value"
Value of labor power
Surplus value
Marxian price–value analysis
Alienation
Underconsumption models
Marx's business-cycle analysis

CHAPTER REVIEW

The purpose of this chapter is to present an overview of Marxian economic analysis and to separate the facts from the myths about what Marx did and did not say in his writings on the subject. From the perspective of modern economics, elements of Marxian analysis are incomplete and misleading. At the same time many other aspects of Marx's writings continue to offer important insights.

Marx saw economic systems as evolving over time. Historically, capitalism supplanted feudalism and there is no reason to believe the process will stop. This emphasis on the historical perspective is referred to as

(1) _____ _____. In Marx's view, changes over time are strongly influenced but not uniquely determined by (economic/cultural) conditions.

(2)   Marx spent most of his time analyzing the nature of capitalism. As a result he (was/was not) very specific about the organization of a socialist economy. One thing that Marx did expect under socialism was a transformation of work from deadening, repetitive tasks associated with specialization to more stimulating and pleasant jobs allowing for the complete development of every individual. Marx (was/was not) explicit about how this change was to come about.

     Marx worked to understand the laws of motion of capitalism in a historical setting. According to Marx, the central purpose of capitalism is the accumulation of profits. This process explains both the expansion of capitalism and the increasing unhappiness of workers, which Marx expected would undermine the capitalistic system itself.

(3)   In Marxian terms, the value of a commodity is determined by the amount of _____

_____ necessary for its production. (The Marxian value (is/is not) always equal to a commodity's price.) Another Marxian concept is the *value of labor power*. The value of labor power is the labor time required to produce the commodities necessary for the maintenance of the laborer, or the minimum subsistence wage. The fact that the value of labor power is only a fraction of a day's work is what allows for profits and the accumulation of wealth that are basic to the evolution of capitalism. The difference

between a day's work and the value of labor power is called _____ _____.

It is this difference that is accumulated by capitalists. According to Marx, only _____ creates value.

(4)   When it came to determining prices and wages, Marx (adopted/rejected) the traditional analysis of price determination by demand and supply. In a long-run Marxian equilibrium, prices and outputs adjust so that all investors earn (the same/different) rate(s) of return. Prices adjust to redistribute the surplus values produced by the entire economy. In modern terms, firms in competitive industries will earn profits equal to the opportunity cost of capital, and price will equal (long/short)-run average cost. (If costs are primarily labor costs, our earlier analysis of a competitive long-run equilibrium showed that prices of different commodities would vary with the labor required for their production. This modern statement about implications of long-run equilibrium is very different from the Marxian definition of value.)

(5)   To summarize, Marxian value analysis states that all value is created by _____.

Because the value of labor power is a fraction of a day's work, labor also creates _____

_____, which in turn allows for the accumulation of more machines. It is the role of prices and profits to redistribute the wealth made possible by labor's production of surplus value in a process of "capitalist communism."

(6)   Marx analyzed capitalism in order to describe its inevitable collapse. He (did/did not) emphasize a single set of events leading to the collapse of capitalism. Rather there are a number of arguments, each one of which suggests the demise of capitalism. One strain of thought involves the increasing unhappiness of

workers and eventual revolution. Although somewhat ambiguous, the concept of _____ is important here. One interpretation of alienation stresses that factories and machines are originally produced by workers. Then, because of their importance to the capitalist production process, these creations of labor come to dominate workers. Automated factories and the repetitive detail of assembly techniques lead to

worker _____ and eventually to revolution born of class antagonisms.

(7)   Another Marxian source of the collapse of capitalism is successive business _____.
At the time Marx wrote, many economists denied the possibility of business cycles, believing that

"(Demand/Supply) creates its own _____." Marx denied _____
Law and was one of the first to undertake a serious study of business cycles.

DEFINITION QUIZ

Choose the letter that is the most appropriate definition for each of the following terms.

1. _____ Historical materialism
2. _____ Surplus value
3. _____ Alienation
4. _____ Value of labor power
5. _____ Marxian commodities
6. _____ Marxian value

a. View that workers' employment depends on the accumulated capital that workers previously produced themselves.
b. Goods produced in order to earn profits.
c. Difference between value to the consumer of the quantity purchased of a given commodity and the consumer's expenditure on that quantity.
d. Notion that an economy cannot be understood without recognizing its place in history.
e. Minimum subsistence wage.
f. Portion of output available for accumulation by capitalists.
g. Labor time necessary for production of a commodity.

SELF-TESTS FOR UNDERSTANDING

Test A

Circle the correct answer.

1. Historical materialism suggests that
   a. all social decisions are solely the result of economic factors.
   b. capitalism is the highest and final form of economic evolution.
   c. one should view economic systems and institutions in their historical context as part of an ongoing process of change and evolution.
   d. only material goods are important to the welfare of a country's citizens.
2. Which of the following is *not* an important part of the final socialist state as perceived by Marx?
   a. The abolition of the division of labor.
   b. Increasing specialization of labor for increased efficiency and maximum output.
   c. Common ownership of the means of production.
   d. Wages and incomes determined by individual need.
3. Marx was primarily interested in
   a. providing detailed guidance for the formation of a communist state.
   b. advancing mathematical economic analysis.
   c. the Soviet Union and China.
   d. a meticulous analysis and critique of capitalism.

4. Which of the following would *not* be a commodity as defined by Marx?
   a. A frozen TV dinner purchased in the grocery store.
   b. A Big Mac from McDonald's.
   c. A dinner prepared by a family from crops and livestock produced on its own farm.
   d. Dinner for two at the top of the World Trade Center in New York.
5. According to Marx, which of the following is an example of productive labor?
   a. The time spent by a professional painter painting his own house.
   b. The time you spend helping your friend paint her house.
   c. The time you spend sewing your own down jacket.
   d. The time of a paid seamstress who produces down jackets for a larger retailer.
6. According to Marx, the value of labor power is
   a. its ability to overthrow the ruling classes.
   b. determined by forces of supply and demand.
   c. what capitalists appropriate during the process of accumulation.
   d. the labor time necessary for workers to see to their own subsistence.
7. According to Marx, which of the following is responsible for the value of commodities?
   a. Workers.
   b. Capitalists.
   c. Landlords.
   d. Investors.
8. The purpose of Marxian value theory was to show that

a. capitalism is immoral.
b. labor is the source of all profits.
c. profits amounted to robbery of workers.
d. revolution in Russia was inevitable.

9. According to Marx, the prices of commodities
   a. will be equal to the value of commodities.
   b. are equal to the value of labor power used in their production.
   c. are determined by the forces of supply and demand.
   d. are artificially determined by capitalists in order to subjugate the working classes.

10. When discussing business cycles, Marx
    a. accepted Say's Law that "supply creates its own demand."
    b. clearly argued that capitalism must collapse from a series of increasingly severe business cycles.
    c. identified a number of possible causes, but without a systematic discussion of specific causes.

Test B

Circle T or F for True or False as appropriate.

1. Historical materialism asserts that all individuals, capitalists and laborers, make decisions solely on the basis of their own economic self interests.   T F

2. Marx agreed with Henry Ford that history is bunk.   T F

3. Marx was not very explicit about the collapse of capitalism or the organization of a communist society.   T F

4. According to Marx, the major purpose of the capitalist system is the accumulation of wealth.   T F

5. Like modern economists, Marx used the term *capital* to refer to buildings and machines used in productive processes.   T F

6. According to Marx, the price of a commodity is determined by the labor time necessary for its production.   T F

7. Marx accepted the analysis of price determination proposed by classical economists such as Adam Smith and David Ricardo.   T F

8. According to Marx, capitalists prosper by conspiring to keep wages at a subsistence level.   T F

9. Marx defined surplus value as the difference between a day's worth of labor time and the value of labor power.   T F

10. Marx accepted Say's Law as an explanation of business cycles.   T F

40

Comparative Economic Systems: What Are the Choices?

LEARNING OBJECTIVES

After completing the material in this chapter you should be able to:

- define, understand, and use correctly the terms and concepts listed below.
- describe how in theory and practice the decisions about economic coordination and ownership—markets or planning; capitalism or socialism—are distinct choices.
- evaluate the record of market and planned economies regarding
  - the choice of goods to produce
  - the efficiency of production
  - the distribution of income
  - economic growth
  - fluctuations in economic activity.
- describe the role of the "profit motive" in capitalism and the implications of its absence under socialism.
- briefly describe the choices as to ownership and coordination and the experiences with these choices in Yugoslavia, the Soviet Union, China, and Japan.

- explain why the Soviet Union was able to achieve high rates of economic growth in the face of substantial inefficiences of production.
- describe the Soviet planning process: who makes the decisions, the role of Five-Year and One-Year Plans, and the meaning of material balance.
- contrast Chinese and Soviet styles of planning.
- contrast the Japanese corporatist and American individualistic styles of doing business.

IMPORTANT TERMS AND CONCEPTS

Capitalism
Socialism
Planning
Free markets
Consumer sovereignty
Workers' management
Soviet Five-Year and One-Year Plans
Material balance
Material incentives
Great Leap Forward
Great Proletarian Cultural Revolution
Export-led growth
Industrial policy

CHAPTER REVIEW

Countries must make choices about how to organize their economies. The discussion in this chapter looks at two crucial decisions: How should economic activity be coordinated? And who should own the means of production? The alternatives are compared using indicators of both equity and efficiency, and the experiences of three countries—the Soviet Union, China, and Japan—are considered in terms of the above issues.

When considering how to coordinate economic activity, economies can choose to emphasize

(1) _____ or _____. These options are not simple all-or-nothing alternatives. For most countries the choice is a matter of emphasis and degree. That is, market economies allow for government intervention in many areas, and most planned economies rely on market forces in several areas.

When considering ownership of the means of production, economies can choose to emphasize private

(2) ownership, that is, _____, or public ownership, that is, _____. Again, most countries do not choose one to the exclusion of the other. Most countries have some of both.

Are socialism/planning and capitalism/markets the only feasible combinations? Both theory and real-world

(3) examples suggest that this pairing (is/is not) inevitable. For example, Yugoslavia is a (socialist/capitalist) country that relies heavily on (markets/planning) for the coordination of economic activity.

What difference does it make whether a country emphasizes markets or planning? We can keep score on the following five issues:

(4) 1. *What goods to produce.* Market economies respond to the preferences of _____,

and planned economies respond to the preferences of _____. Which option

one values depends, in part, on how much one values individual _____. A major shortcoming of planned economics is the lack of a feedback mechanism to correct any imbalance between the preferences of consumers and planners. In a market economy an imbalance of production and demand will result in shortages or surpluses which in turn lead to changes in prices as markets

adjust to equate demand and supply. It is the change in _____ that corrects imbalances and provides the incentive for firms and consumers to adjust their behavior.

2. *Production efficiency.* Here _____ economies have a clear advantage over

_____ economies. The _____ motive is a powerful device for promoting efficiency. Planned economies have not yet found an alternative incentive scheme that consistently works as well.

3. *The distribution of income.* When considering the distribution of labor income, market and planned economies show (a significantly different/about the same) degree of inequality. If planning is associated with socialism, there is apt to be (more/less) equality in the overall distribution of income. But remember planning need not be associated with socialism.

4. *Growth.* One can find examples of planned economies that have grown faster than market economies and vice versa. Different countries will probably continue to make different choices based on different political systems, value judgments, traditions, and aspirations.

5. *Business fluctuations.* Here _____ economies clearly have the better track record.

How one strikes the final balance on these five issues is a matter of trade-offs, the basic stuff of economics. Remember that one does not have to make all-or-nothing choices. While planning infringes on individual freedom, complete freedom does not exist anywhere. The experience of many countries indicates a wide variety of choices between markets and planning, socialism and capitalism, and the degree of individual freedom.

(5)   The Soviet Union has been an example of a (capitalist/socialist) economy with comprehensive, centralized planning. An understanding of how Soviet planning worked is important to an understanding of current pressures for change in the Soviet economy. The broad objectives of Soviet policy were set forth in

the (Five/One)-Year Plans while more detail for implementation was provided in _____.

Year Plans. Soviet planning relied extensively on targets and quotas. Because of the complexity of the Soviet economy it has been a problem to ensure that all the quantity targets are mutually consistent. The

Soviets refer to consistency as achieving _____ balance. Input–output analysis could be used here, but the enormity of the information requirements make it unfeasible for detailed planning.

A central planner needs to know the detailed production requirements of all goods as well as the capabilities of individual enterprises. She then needs to figure out how all these requirements interact to be sure that planned increases in production are mutually consistent. It is a virtue of a market economy that all this information need not be centralized in a single individual or agency. Production is efficiently coordinated as individual enterprises respond to changes in the prices of their inputs and their outputs.

The Soviet style of central planning, under which orders flow down from the top while information flows up from the bottom, places a tremendous burden on the transmission of information. The result is, almost of necessity, a considerable amount of inefficiency. Because rewards are based on achieving one's quota, **(6)** plant managers have an incentive to (be conservative/take risks). There is (little/strong) incentive for innovation. Compared with American experience, inventories of strategic materials are often excessively (high/low) and many consumer goods are of (high/low) quality.

Until the 1970s the Soviet economy reported high rates of economic growth. As described in Chapters 17 and 38, economic growth depends, in part, on growth in inputs and advances in technology. In the past the Soviet Union could borrow advanced technology from the West. An increased industrial labor force

(7) came from a reduced _____ labor force. A rapidly growing capital stock came from adjusting the composition of output to favor the production of (consumption/investment) goods over

_____ goods. These three factors are no longer able to contribute to Soviet economic growth. Declining economic growth and the growing inefficiencies of Soviet planning help to set the stage for the introduction of market oriented reforms during the last half of the 1980s. In early 1990 the Communist party endorsed individual ownership of the means of production. The transformation of the Soviet economy is still in progress and the final outcome is by no means clear.

(8) China is a (market/planned) economy with extensive (private/state) ownership. Chinese planning and economic growth have moved in fits and starts related to domestic ideological struggles. Chinese planning was patterned after Soviet planning, but the Chinese version was (less/more) centralized and placed less emphasis on (agricultural/industrial) development. During the 1980s the Chinese moved to increase the role of markets significantly. After June 1989 economic liberalization in China was put on hold.

The success of the Japanese economy has attracted a great deal of attention. Japanese experience has been characterized by export-led growth, under which business firms pay special attention to opportuni- **(9)** ties in (domestic/foreign) markets, and deliberate industrial policy that calls for close cooperation between

industry, banks, and the government. This cooperation represents a policy of _____

_____. The industrial structure of Japan is (less/more) concentrated than in the United States and labor–management relations have been (less/more) adversarial. A number of observers feel that some of the most important lessons we can learn from the Japanese relate to their ability to organize and motivate people.

DEFINITION QUIZ

Choose the letter that is the most appropriate definition for each of the following terms.

1. _____ Capitalism

2. _____ Socialism

3. _____ Consumer sovereignty

4. _____ Workers' management

5. _____ Export-led growth

6. _____ Material balance

7. _____ Industrial policy

a. Employees of an enterprise make most of the decisions concerning how the enterprise is run.
b. Cooperative planning for economic growth between government agencies and private firms.
c. Private individuals own the means of production.
d. Decisions about what goods are produced reflect consumer preferences.
e. Strategy of emphasizing production of goods for export.
f. The state owns the means of production.
g. Mutually consistent planning targets for all inputs.
h. Government regulation of firms that produce consumer goods.

SELF-TESTS FOR UNDERSTANDING

Test A

Circle the correct answer.

1. The form of economic organization in which the state owns the means of production is called
   a. capitalism.
   b. consumer sovereignty.
   c. socialism.
   d. laissez faire.
2. Market economies clearly do much worse than planned economies in which one of the following areas?
   a. Avoiding business fluctuations.
   b. Fostering a high rate of growth.
   c. Achieving efficiency in the production of goods and services.
   d. Achieving equality in the distribution of labor income.
3. Experience suggests that
   a. planning can only work in socialist economies.
   b. personal freedom tends to be greatest in economies that rely on markets and capitalism.
   c. it is easy for socialist economies to provide appropriate incentives for managerial efficiency and innovation.
   d. the distribution of labor income is typically more equal in socialist than in capitalist economies.
4. Match each of the following with the appropriate country

   _____ Material balance   a. China

   _____ Workers' management b. Japan

   _____ Export-led growth   c. Soviet Union

   _____ Great Leap Forward   d. Yugoslavia
5. The Soviet planning system
   a. makes extensive use of input–output analysis to ensure that each One-Year Plan has internal consistency.
   b. saves on information requirements by having plant managers maximize profits.
   c. is one of consumer sovereignty, since Soviet citizens are free to buy consumer goods of their own choosing.
   d. creates incentives for plant managers to play it safe by establishing easy quotas.
6. The record of the Soviet economy shows all but which one of the following?
   a. Low agricultural productivity.
   b. High levels of efficiency associated with centralized planning.
   c. Substantial amounts of low-quality consumer goods.
   d. Extensive use of wages, rather than quotas, in the allocation of labor.
7. The term "material balance" refers to
   a. inventories at the end of each planning period.
   b. consistency in plans so that the quantity demanded and the quantity supplied of each commodity are equal.
   c. the wealth of Kremlin leaders.
   d. the choices planners must make as they balance competing claims for consumption and investment goods.
8. In China, the record of the economy shows
   a. a consistent and unwavering commitment to highly centralized planning.
   b. extensive use of material incentives to motivate workers.
   c. a greater emphasis on agricultural development compared with the Soviet Union.
   d. a consistent emphasis on economic efficiency that protected the economy from domestic ideological struggles.
9. Compared with the United States, Japan shows
   a. a less concentrated industrial structure.
   b. a greater emphasis on internal as opposed to foreign markets.
   c. more adversarial labor–management relations.
   d. closer cooperation between government and industry.
10. When compared with the United States, which one of the following is not true of Japanese labor markets?
   a. Life-time employment guarantees.
   b. Greater loyalty to employers.
   c. Less worker resistance to the introduction of new production techniques.
   d. Large pay differentials between workers and managers.

Test B

Circle T or F for True or False as appropriate.

1. Socialism must be accompanied by central planning.   T F

2. Consumer sovereignty is the term used for the form of economic organization in which private individuals own the means of production.   T F

3. Planned economies have done a better job in terms of avoiding business cycles than have market economies.   **T F**

4. Market economies are clearly superior to planned economies in terms of the efficiency of production.   **T F**

5. A major problem with planned economies is devising an incentive mechanism for managers that works to promote efficiency.   **T F**

6. Under Soviet planning One-Year Plans set broad objectives while Five-Year Plans contain the details of implementation.   **T F**

7. Soviet planners have tried to use wage rates to equate demand and supply in later markets.   **T F**

8. The Chinese system of planning is a direct copy of Soviet planning.   **T F**

9. Average living standards in Japan now exceed those in the United States.   **T F**

10. Japan's emphasis on export-led growth is based on an abundance of natural resources.   **T F**

41

Dissenting Opinions: Conservative, Moderate, and Radical

LEARNING OBJECTIVES

After completing the material in this chapter you should be able to:

- define, understand, and use correctly the terms and concepts listed below.
- critically evaluate the libertarian dissent from mainstream economics and current public policy.
- critically evaluate Galbraith's criticisms of mainstream economic theory and the U.S. economy.
- critically evaluate radical economists' criticisms of mainstream economic theory and the U.S. economy.

- understand that critical evaluation does not imply that one must completely reject a particular viewpoint.

IMPORTANT TERMS AND CONCEPTS

Libertarianism
Economic power
Technostructure
Radical economics
Manipulation of the consumer
Alienation
Liberal versus radical views of the state

CHAPTER REVIEW

Not many would argue that mainstream economics is above criticism. Most economists, however, would argue for marginal changes, a shift of emphasis here or there. This chapter discusses three major dissenting views that call for more fundamental and far-reaching changes in analysis.

Libertarianism

(1)   Libertarianism is more a _____ than a system of economic thought. The

fundamental goal of libertarians is a maximum amount of individual _____ in both
economic and social relations. Libertarians think their goal is best achieved by (more/less) government
intervention.

       Among economists, Milton Friedman is perhaps the most effective spokesperson for the libertarian

(2)   viewpoint. Friedman argues that political freedom and _____-_____
economies go hand in hand. He also argues for a (larger/smaller) role for government. He sees a need for
government to fulfill three limited roles: to serve as umpire, that is, to enforce contracts, to control natural

_____, and to correct for market failure in the case of _____.
In Friedman's view these legitimate roles for government (are often/have never been) used to expand the
role of government into inappropriate areas.

The Liberal Viewpoint of John Kenneth Galbraith

According to Galbraith, mainstream economics is especially deficient in its failure to consider how the

(3)   use of economic _____ has subverted the idealized workings of market
processes as described in introductory economics textbooks. According to Galbraith, corporations (do/do not)
compete to meet the independent desires of consumers. Rather corporations use their power to manipulate

demand and control markets. Galbraith sees the economy as essentially a _____

system, run by _____ who are guided by _____

_____.

These technocrats work to maximize (profits/growth) which in turn maximizes _____

_____.

(4)   When looking at the U.S. economy, Galbraith is distressed by the relative abundance of (public/private)

goods and the relative scarcity of _____ goods. Galbraith also argues that the

U.S. economy shows a shocking disregard for the _____ of life.
       While many economists agree with some of Galbraith's personal evaluations of the U.S. economy, most
(5)   (agree/disagree) with Galbraith's analysis of the reasons why things have turned out this way. Galbraith argues
that profit maximization (is/is not) a useful way to understand business behavior. Mainstream economists
(agree/disagree). They see profit maximization as a workable approximation yielding useful results. Galbraith
argues that the volume of internally generated funds of large corporations gives them freedom to do as they
please and to avoid any market discipline. Others point out that even internally generated funds have a(n)

_____ _____, and any corporation that neglects its profits may be

vulnerable to a(n) _____.

Radical Economists of the Left

Radical economics is the most recent challenge to mainstream economics. The text discusses five major
radical criticisms of mainstream economics.

1. Radicals charge that modern economics is too narrow. Accepting institutions as given and immutable, it is

(6)   _____. As a result, mainstream economists end up, either implicitly or
explicitly, as apologists for the present system.

2. Radicals charge that mainstream economics accepts tastes and motivation as _____.
       Galbraith would agree with this charge. But the radical criticism is broader, extending beyond the modern

corporation to argue that social institutions, such as schools, only mold tastes and behavior to serve the

purposes of the _____ _____.

3. Radicals charge that mainstream economics is too heavily concerned with (efficiency/equality) and too

little concerned with _____. They argue that _____ rather
than marginal productivity is the better explanation of distribution of income.

4. Radicals argue that mainstream economics seems more concerned with quantity than with

_____. In the radical view, a larger GNP is apt to despoil the environment

and increase the _____ of workers.

5. Finally, radicals charge that many liberals have a (naive/sophisticated) theory of the state. Many liberals
think that the state can be made to serve the broad public interest. Radicals believe instead that the state

serves the _____ _____ by helping them to maintain their

_____.[1] Government policies that appear to advance the interests of lower-income

groups are either shams or attempts to _____ the working class.

Radical charges against mainstream economics have not gone unchallenged. As for the issue of
narrowness, mainstream economists argue that radicals are so broad in their approach that they tend to be

(7) superficial. Mainstream economists argue that narrowness (is/is not) necessary for scientific progress. Many
mainstream economists (agree/disagree) that modern economics seems overly concerned with efficiency. As
to the issue of power, many economists are concerned that due to a lack of precision, one runs the risk of

engaging in _____, not science. A similar concern arises in the use of concepts
like alienation and dehumanization.

Many radicals see themselves as the heirs of Marx. Like him, radicals have also concentrated on
detailed criticisms of capitalism. To date there is no agreed upon radical alternative. Two items that do seem

(8) to be elements of most radical alternatives are a _____ and _____
system rather than an authoritative, centralized system.

DEFINITION QUIZ

Choose the letter that is the most appropriate definition for each of the following terms.

1. _____ Libertarianism

2. _____ Economic power

3. _____ Technostructure

a. Present state of knowledge and technology.
b. School of thought emphasizing the importance of individual freedom.
c. Professionals who run large corporations and marketing firms.
d. Ability of a buyer or seller to influence the market price.

SELF-TESTS FOR UNDERSTANDING

Test A

Circle the correct answer.

1. Which of the following are likely to agree with the statements listed below?

Libertarians	_____
Galbraith	_____
Radical	_____
None	_____

a. Modern corporations are above the discipline of the marketplace.
b. There is an overabundance of private goods and a relative scarcity of public goods.

[1]A number of conservative economists also argue that liberals have a naive view of the state. These conservatives argue that rather than supporting a particular class, government bureaucrats work to advance their own interests in terms of bigger budgets and more influence, a viewpoint not unlike Galbraith's description of technocrats.

c. We would be better off with an expanded role for markets and a restricted scope for government.

d. Government actions are most likely to serve the purposes of the ruling classes rather than any broad social interest.

e. By the use of modern advertising, corporations are able to manipulate demand for their output.

f. Economic power is a more important determinant of prices than is supply and demand.

2. Milton Friedman would agree with which of the following government programs?

a. Government licensing of economists to protect the public from charlatans.

b. More extensive government regulation of important basic industries, such as steel.

c. The court system to enforce contracts.

d. Permanent wage–price controls.

3. Galbraith argues that

a. modern corporations are inherently inefficient because they are so big.

b. the technocrats that run corporations are primarily concerned with maximizing growth.

c. it would be best if the Federal Reserve increased the money supply at a fixed rate.

d. expansion of the federal government has meant an overabundance of public goods.

4. For each of the following indicate whether both Solow and Galbraith would agree or disagree.

	Solow	Galbraith
a. The modern corporation can safely ignore the market.	_____	_____
b. Profit maximization is useful as a description of firm behavior.	_____	_____
c. Modern advertising means that there is no effective consumer choice.	_____	_____

5. Which of the following is *not* a part of the radicals' charge that mainstream economics has too narrow a focus?

a. A preoccupation with marginal changes blinds one to important big changes.

b. Mainstream economics has spent too much time studying the evolution of modern institutions.

c. Mainstream economists have become apologists for the status quo.

d. Modern economics is ahistorical.

6. Which of the following is *not* a part of the radicals' critique of modern economics?

a. Mainstream economists are naive if they believe that the government is a consistent defender of the general public interest.

b. Alienation and dehumanization are fundamental defects of capitalism.

c. Most social institutions, such as schools, serve the purposes of capitalists.

d. Modern economics concentrates too much on equality while ignoring important questions of efficiency.

7. Most radical economists would prefer to see which one of the following?

a. Rigidly centralized government planning.

b. A participatory system for organizing firms and other institutions.

c. A larger reliance on unfettered and unlimited competition.

d. More government-industry cooperation, similar to the recent government guarantee of loans to Lockheed and Chrysler.

Test B

Circle T or F for True or False as appropriate.

1. Laissez faire means minimal government interference in economic matters.   T F

2. Libertarians argue that free markets, rather than the state, are the best bet for preserving freedom.   T F

3. According to Galbraith, the American economy is best described as a planning system rather than a market economy.   T F

4. Being concerned with profit maximization, the Galbraithian technocrat who runs the modern corporation is fundamentally different from the planners who ran the socialist economies of eastern Europe.   T F

5. Galbraith argues that the market economy places little emphasis on the quality of life. T F

6. Radical economists of the left view themselves as direct intellectual descendants of Adam Smith.   T F

7. According to radical economists, private ownership of capital and free markets are fundamental causes of much of what is wrong today.   T F

8. Radical economists accept the marginal productivity theory of income distribution of mainstream economics.   T F

9. In contrast to Marx, radical economists have offered a detailed description of alternatives to the existing market economy.   T F

10. The only way the government can expand aggregate demand to ensure full employment is by increased military spending.   T F

Answers

Page numbers under Self-Tests refer to *Economics: Principles and Policy.*

CHAPTER 1

Chapter Review

(1) information; value

Definition Quiz

1. f	5. m	9. d
2. b	6. a	10. l
3. e	7. c	11. k
4. h	8. j	

Self-Test

1. F	p. 9–10	4. T	p. 15
2. F	p. 15	5. F	p. 12–13
3. T	p. 6	6. F	p. 13

CHAPTER 2

Chapter Review

(1) horizontal; vertical; origin
(2) time series
(3) vertical; horizontal; constant; positive; up; negative; no
(4) ray; 45°
(5) tangent
(6) contour

Definition Quiz

1. f	6. q	11. c
2. g	7. l	12. k
3. d	8. r	13. e
4. n	9. m	14. i
5. h	10. b	15. p
		16. a

Basic Exercises

1. a. 300
   b. increased; 500
   c. decreased; 200
   d. −50
2. a. No, increases in aggregate income due to inflation or population do not increase individual purchasing power.

303

b. 14.3 times ($15,191 ÷ 1,066), column 3:
1,066; 1,687; 2,505; 5,291; 11,861;
15,191

c. 2.2 times ($11,685 ÷ $5,277); column 5:
5,277; 5,717; 7,037; 8,938; 10,628;
11,685

3. Graph in Figure 2–3 exaggerates the
decline as it omits the origin. It should also
be noted that housing starts show
significant month to month variation. For
calendar year 1988, housing starts totaled
1,488,000. For calendar year 1989, housing
starts totaled 1,376,000, for a year to year
decline of 112 thousand units or 7.5% as
compared with the 21.2% decline from
January 1989 to May 1989.

4. The trend line from 1968 to 1983 seems to
tell a similar story; but, just as in the
1960s, the trend line does not mean that
appropriate macroeconomic policy cannot
lower the rate of unemployment.

Self-Tests

Test A

1. (3), (1), (2), (4)   4. c   p. 21
p. 20   5. d   p. 23
2. A, E, C, B, D,   6. a   p. 23
none   p. 21   7. d   p. 23
3. d*   8. a**

*slope = (change in Y)/(change in X) = −6/3
= −2

**slope = (change in Y)/(change in X) = 2/5
= .4

Test B

1. F   p. 20   6. T   p. 23
2. T   p. 20   7. F   p. 23
3. T   p. 20   8. T   p. 23
4. F   p. 25   9. F   p. 23
5. T   p. 29   10. T   p. 27–28

Supplementary Exercise

1982 dollars:
Public $919; $1,084; $1,376
Private $3,846; $4,867; $6,608
Proportion of per capita real income:
Public   13.1%; 12.1%; 12.9%
Private   54.7%; 54.5%; 62.2%

CHAPTER 3

Chapter Review

(1) scarce
(2) opportunity cost
(3) scarce; specialized; less; more; more;
consumption
(4) slope
(5) increase; increasing; specialized
(6) inside; inefficient;
(7) will

Definition Quiz

1. g   7. a   13. e
2. i   8. s   14. l
3. n   9. f   15. h
4. r   10. q   16. d
5. m   11. p   17. o
6. j   12. b   18. k
                       19. t

Basic Exercise

1. a. 56,000; 4,000; rises; 12,000; continue to
rise; specialized
b. Point A is not feasible; point B is
feasible; point C is feasible; on and
inside
c. Point B is inefficient.

Self-Tests

Test A

1. c   p. 34
2. d   p. 43
3. c   p. 38–39
4. a   p. 37
5. b   p. 37
6. b   Position of PPF depends upon
resources available.
7. a   Producing corn is the alternative
foregone when production of
computers is increased.
8. b   Reflects economic growth. See p. 42
9. c   p. 39
10. c   p. 34

Test B

1. F   p. 39
2. F   p. 35

3. T   p. 38–39
4. T   p. 41–42
5. F   p. 33
6. F   p. 37–38
7. T   p. 43
8. T   p. 43
9. F   Any economic unit with limited resources will need to make choices.
10. F   p. 39

Supplementary Exercises

3. a. 300,000 cars; 1,000 tanks
   c. yes, it bows out.
   d. ½C^*, ½T^* should be on straight line connecting C^* and T^*. Combination is feasible, lies inside frontier; inefficient, not on frontier as frontier bows out.
   e. 6 cars; 30 cars; 120 cars
   f. opportunity cost = (0.6)T cars; yes, opportunity cost increases as the production of tanks increases.
   g. new frontier lies everywhere outside the old frontier.
4. a. When $I = 1,600$ the sustainable level of $C = 10,292$.
   b. C drops by 400 to 9,892 and then rises to its new sustainable level of 10,574.
   c. The increase in consumption, 10,574 to 10,761, is less than in question b. Additional machines add to output but at a decreasing rate. This increase at a decreasing rate is an example of declining marginal productivity, a concept that is discussed in Chapter 23.
   d. There can be too much of a good thing. Additional machines allow for an increase in total output, but additional machines also increase the amount of output that must be allocated to investment in order to maintain the new number of machines. With a large enough increase in the number of machines, the increase in investment needed to maintain machines swamps the increase in output available for consumption. Past this point, additional investment will actually lower the sustainable level of consumption. What is this critical point? In this problem, it depends upon the exponents on L and M in equation (1) and the rate of

depreciation, assumed to be 8 percent. Ask your instructor for more details.

CHAPTER 4

Chapter Review

(1) price; negative; more; movement along; shift in
(2) positive; more; shift in
(3) demand
(4) $200; 4000; less; 6000; 2000; surplus; reduction; shortage; demanded; supplied; increase
(5) intersection; equilibrium
(6) demand; supply; movement along; supply; demand; demand
(7) maximum; minimum
(8) hard; auxiliary restrictions
(9) high

Definition Quiz

1. k	6. q	11. h
2. e	7. o	12. m
3. g	8. p	13. d
4. c	9. n	14. j
5. i	10. f	15. b
		16. a

Basic Exercises

1. b. 40; 1100
   c. increased; 50; increased; 1200
   d. increase; decrease; 55; 1100
2. a. demand; right; rise; rise
   b. supply; right; fall; rise
   c. supply; left; rise; fall
   d. demand; left; fall; fall
3. a. 5; 5; neither, as ceiling exceeds equilibrium price
   b. 6; 3; shortage
   c. 4.5; 6; surplus
   d. 5; 5; neither, as floor is less than equilibrium price

Self-Tests

Test A

1. a   p. 59
2. a   p. 64

3. b The price of cotton cloth is the price of an important input. See p. 64.
4. a p. 59
5. c p. 57
6. b Steel is an important input.
7. b p. 61
8. a p. 70
9. d p. 66
10. b p. 56

Test B

1. F The law of supply and demand is an empirical regularity, not a Congressional statute.
2. T p. 53
3. T p. 55
4. F p. 59
5. F p. 55
6. T p. 56–57
7. T p. 56
8. F p. 59
9. F p. 64
10. T p. 66
11. F p. 70
12. T p. 66
13. F p. 68
14. F The increase in price and quantity comes from the movement along the supply curve following the shift in the demand curve.

Supplementary Exercises

1. a. domestic demand; 38; domestic supply; 31; imports; 7
   b. Quantity demanded would have declined to 34.8; domestic supply would have increased to 33.25; imports would have declined to 1.55.
   c. price = $13.75; quantity = 33.9
2. Price and quantity should approach $3 and 650.

CHAPTER 5

Chapter Review

(1) microeconomics; macroeconomics
(2) price; quantity; national product
(3) inflation; deflation; recessions; higher; higher; left; decrease; stagflation

(4) money; final; nominal; real; real; nominal; real; is not
(5) up; depends; rose; fell; risen
(6) inflation; stabilization; recession; inflation

Definition Quiz

1. q	6. p	11. d
2. h	7. r	12. j
3. e	8. l	13. g
4. i	9. b	14. k
5. m	10. o	15. c
		16. f

Basic Exercises

1. a. c; d
   b. b; yes, 1929–1933
   c. a
   d. c
2. a. shift aggregate demand curve to left
   b. shift aggregate demand curve to right
   c. Real GNP will fall as aggregate demand curve is shifted to the left; prices will rise as aggregate demand curve is shifted to the right.
3. a. col (3): $600; $300; $225; $1,125
      col (6): $868; $416; $297; $1,581
   b. 40.5%
   c. $620; $320; $247.50; $1,187.50
   d. 5.56%.
   e. The increase in real GNP is less than the increase in nominal GNP as the increase in nominal GNP includes both the increase in production and the increase in prices. The increase in real GNP is the better measure of the change in output. It is a weighted average of the increases in the output of hamburgers, shakes, and fries. The weights sum to one and reflect the relative importance of output in GNP for the base year, 1988 in this problem.

Self-Tests

Test A

1. a p. 76–77
2. d p. 81
3. b p. 83; d p. 79; a p. 79; c p. 87; f p. 88

4. a p. 80
5. c p. 80
6. a p. 82
7. b GNP is a measure of newly produced goods and services.
8. d Refer to Basic Exercise.
9. b p. 84
10. d The increase in nominal GNP could reflect increases in prices or real output.

Test B

1. F p. 76
2. T p. 77
3. F Not if the decrease comes from a decrease in prices.
4. T p. 80
5. F If aggregate demand curve shifts to the left, prices will fall.
6. F p. 84
7. F p. 83
8. T p. 87
9. T p. 88
10. F p. 88–89

CHAPTER 6

Chapter Review

(1) more; more
(2) cannot; partial; some
(3) potential; actual GNP
(4) is not; frictional; cyclical; structural
(5) discouraged; decrease; understate
(6) frictional
(7) real; the same; as; were unchanged
(8) different; less; more
(9) higher; nominal; real; inflation
(10) will; be unchanged; nominal
(11) usury; nominal; real; nominal; real
(12) creeping; galloping

Definition Quiz

1. b   6. g   11. n
2. d   7. a   12. j
3. f   8. q   13. c
4. h   9. p   14. i
5. l   10. k   15. o
                    16. e

Basic Exercise

1. a. $250,000; $5,250,000; $4,772,727; $5,750,000; $5,227,273. Borrowers gain at expense of lenders.
   b. $775,000; $5,775,000; $5,250,000; $5,225,000; $4,750,000. Both are treated equally.
   c. $1,000,000; $6,000,000; $5,454,545; $5,000,000; $4,545,455. Lenders gain at expense of borrowers.

Self-Tests

Test A

1. c p. 95   6. a p. 103
2. b, a, d, c   7. b p. 102–104
   p. 94–95   8. d p. 99–100
3. b p. 97–98   9. a p. 99–100
4. a p. 96   10. c p. 100
5. b p. 103

Test B

1. F Reduced hours, loss of overtime, and involuntary part-time reduce income for individuals counted as employed.
2. F p. 94
3. F p. 93
4. F p. 97
5. F p. 96
6. F p. 98
7. F p. 98
8. F p. 104
9. F p. 109–10
10. T p. 107

CHAPTER APPENDIX

Definition Quiz: Appendix

1. b   4. c
2. d   5. f
3. a

Basic Exercises: Appendix

1. a. 2500; 400
   b. $16,500 = 2500 × $2.36 + 400 × $26.50
   c. 110
   e. 10 percent
   f. $15,771 ($1990); 5.1 percent

2. 1990 index, using 1991 base, 91.1. 1991 base implies inflation of 9.8 percent. The slighly lower rate of inflation reflects a larger weight on more slowly rising clothing prices when using the 1991 expenditure pattern.

Supplementary Exercises: Appendix

1. a and b. Insufficient information; for example, the price index for Canada for 1985 shows how 1985 Canadian prices compare to Canadian prices in 1982–1984, not how Canadian prices compare to those in other countries.
   c. Italy; West Germany

CHAPTER 7

Chapter Review

(1) demand; consumption; investment; government; exports; imports; net exports
(2) before; after
(3) more; movement along; shift in
(4) C; I; G; X; IM; less; decrease
(5) increase; marginal; larger; more; smaller

Definition Quiz

1. g	5. k	9. n
2. d	6. l	10. i
3. h	7. b	11. e
4. c	8. a	12. m
		13. j

Basic Exercises

1. a. change in consumption: 2,400; 2,400; 2,400; 2,400; MPC: .6; .6; .6; .6
   b. .87; .80; .76; .73; .71
   c. APC and MPC differ.
   e. slope of the consumption function
   f. Rays become less steep; their slope declines.
2. a. $10,400; $20,000; $3,040,000
   b. .71; .87
   c. $12,800; $17,600; $3,040,000
   d. In the example, MPC is the same for rich and poor. The rich reduce their consumption by the same amount that the poor increase their consumption.
3. $C = 3200 + .6 \times DI$

Self-Tests

Test A

1. b   p. 117–18
2. d   p. 119
3. b   Circular flow diagram shows spending on newly produced goods and services.
4. c   p. 125–26
5. a   p. 127
6. c*   solve for ΔC
7. c*   solve for MPC
8. c*   solve for ΔDI through reduction in income taxes
9. a*   solve for MPC
10. d   p. 127
*For 6, 7, 8, and 9, remember: MPC = $\Delta C/\Delta DI$. Each question gives you two numbers; you must solve equation for the third.

Test B

1. F   p. 117
2. F   p. 121
3. T   p. 120–21
4. T   p. 125
5. T   p. 127–28
6. T   p. 127–28
7. F   p. 127
8. T   p. 129–30
9. T   p. 129–30
10. T   p. 123–24

APPENDIX A

Definition Quiz: Ch. 7 Appendix A

1. d   2. c   3. a

1. $1,600; $3,200; $4,800; $6,400; $8,000
2. change in savings: $1,600; $1,600; $1,600; $1,600; MPS: .4; .4; .4; .4
4. APS: .13; .20; .24; .27; .29
6. DI/DI = $C/DI + S/DI$ or 1 = APC + APS
   $\Delta DI/\Delta DI = \Delta C/\Delta DI + \Delta S/\Delta DI$ or 1 = MPC + MPS

APPENDIX B

Definition Quiz: Ch. 7 Appendix B

1. a   2. e   3. b   4. c

Appendix Review

(1) final; produced
(2) exports; imports; produced
(3) income; do not; net; depreciation
(4) value added

Basic Exercise: Appendix B

1. a. $2,200
   b. $1,700
   c. $1,700; wages = $1,200; profits = $500
   d. $500
   e. $1,200
   f. $1,700
   g. $1,700
   h. $1,700
2. a. $1,000; $2,100; $1,600; $4,700
   b. 0; $1,500; $3,200; $4,700

Self-Tests: Appendix B
Test A

1. a GNP includes only newly produced goods and services.
2. c p. 138
3. d p. 135–36
4. b The purchase of the Japanese computer is an import.
5. c p. 106
6. d p. 138
7. d p. 135
8. c p. 135
9. c p. 137
10. b p. 137

Test B

1. F p. 135
2. T p. 138
3. F p. 135
4. F No effect on GNP. Value added by GM up. Value added by suppliers down.
5. F p. 135
6. T p. 138
7. F p. 137
8. F p. 140
9. F p. 140
10. T These are alternative ways to measure national income.

Supplementary Exercises: Appendix B

1. Change in income: 905; 832; 844; 787; 1196; 1580; 1994; 3056; 3829
   Change in consumption: 531; 569; 625; 423; 773; 968; 1001; 1749; 1952
   MPC: .59; .68; .74; .54; .65; .61; .50; .57; .51
2. MPC $= 50/\sqrt{DI}$; MPC declines as income rises. Thus consumption spending rises following redistribution from rich to poor as increase in consumption by poor is greater than decline in consumption by rich. $S = DI - 100\sqrt{DI}$
   MPC + MPS = 1 and APC + APS = 1

CHAPTER 8

Chapter Review

(1) increase; increasing; decrease
(2) exports; imports
(3) intersection
(4) less; downward; lower; more; higher
(5) inflationary; recessionary

Definition Quiz

1. d	4. g	7. l
2. f	5. j	8. e
3. b	6. a	9. c

Basic Exercises

1. e. $4200
   f. 3900; 4000; 4100; 4200; 4300
   g. Spending would be greater than output, inventories would decline, firms would increase output.
   h. inflationary gap, $200; recessionary gap, $300
   i. Expenditure schedule shifts up; $4400; $3900; –$100
2. b. $4,000
   c. $4400
   d. aggregate demand curve
   e. negative
3. New aggregate demand curve should lie to the right of curve in question 2.

Self-Tests
Test A

1. c   p. 148
2. a   p. 149
3. c   p. 150
4. b   p. 149
5. b   p. 143
6. a   p. 155, assuming net exports equal zero.
7. b   p. 151–52
8. b   p. 152
9. c   The aggregate demand curve shows the impact of changes in prices on a given expenditure schedule. A shift in investment spending implies a new expenditure schedule and thus a new aggregate demand curve.
10. c   p. 152–54 assuming net exports = 0.

Test B

1. F   p. 143
2. T   p. 148
3. F   p. 154
4. F   p. 149
5. T   p. 151–52
6. F   p. 154
7. T   p. 153
8. F   p. 155
9. F   p. 152
10. T   p. 151–52

Appendix A

Basic Exercise: Appendix A

1. $100; $200; $300; $400; $500; $600
2. $4200; the same
3. $4400; the same
4. $S = I + (X - IM)$

Appendix B

Basic Exercises: Appendix B

1. $C + I + (X - IM) = Y$; $(1700 + 0.5Y) + 500 - 100 = Y$;
   $Y = 2100/(0.5) = 4200$
2. $Y = 2200/(0.5) = 4400$
3. $(1800 + 0.5Y) + 500 - 100 = Y$;
   $Y = 2200/(0.5) = 4400$

CHAPTER 9

Chapter Review

(1) more than; autonomous; induced
(2) MPC
(3) consumption spending
(4) income; MPC
(5) smaller; prices; taxes; financial; international trade
(6) do not; supply; autonomous; horizontal

Definition Quiz

1. d   2. a   3. e   4. b

Basic Exercises

1. a. 3850; 4000; 4150; 4300; 4450; 4600; 4750; equilibrium: 4000
   b. 4400
   c. 400
   d. 4; equilibrium level; income; autonomous spending
   e. .75
   f. $1/(1 - 0.75) = 1/(0.25) = 4$
2. a. Total Spending = 4050; 4200; 4350; 4500; 4650; 4800; 4950; equilibrium = 4800
   b. 400
   c. 4; it is the same as the investment spending multiplier.
3. less; autonomous
   a. 4600
   b. –200
   c. fall
   d. 200; 4
   e. the same
   f. It ignores effects of inflation, taxes, the financial system and international trade.

Self-Tests
Test A

1. c   p. 163
2. b   p. 169
3. c   p. 168
4. a   p. 168
5. b   p. 168
6. c   p. 168
7. c   p. 169
8. b   p. 171–72
9. b   p. 172
10. c   p. 171

Test B

1.	F	p. 163		6.	F	p. 171–72
2.	F	p. 163–64		7.	F	p. 169
3.	T	p. 172		8.	F	p. 170
4.	T	p. 168		9.	F	p. 171
5.	T	p. 169		10.	T	p. 173

Supplementary Exercises

1. It ignores the multiplier.
3. b. Model should show change in income of 400 for multiplier of 4 = 1/(1 − MPC).
   c. Autonomous change in saving is necessarily a change in intercept of consumption function. Review Appendix A to Chapter 7 if necessary.
   d. Larger MPC will mean larger multiplier; smaller MPC means smaller multiplier.

CHAPTER 10

Chapter Review

(1) increase; movement along; shift in
(2) steeper
(3) intersection; increases
(4) inflationary; is; inward; movement along; higher; lower
(5) less
(6) inflationary; supply

Definition Quiz

1. c   2. e   3. a   4. d

Basic Exercises

1. a. $4,200
   e. 95; $4,100
   f. Inflationary gap; increasing production costs would shift aggregate supply curve; 100 and $4,000
   g. no gaps
   h. recessionary gap; elimination of gap likely to be very slow; 90; $4,200
2. horizontal
   a. no
   b. At P^* aggregate demand would exceed aggregate supply. Prices would rise. The increase in prices would mean a

movement along the dashed aggregate demand curve to the equilibrium, (Y_2, P_2), given by the intersection of the dashed aggregate demand curve and the solid aggregate supply curve.

The increase in investment spending, which shifted the expenditure schedule and gave rise to the dashed aggregate demand curve, will lead to an increase in prices as part of the broader multiplier process, reducing the purchasing power of money fixed assets. The result is a reduction in autonomous consumption spending leading to a downward shift in the expenditure schedule (not drawn) that partially offsets the expansionary impact of the original increase in investment spending and reconciles equilibrium in the income-expenditure diagram with that of the aggregate demand-aggregate supply diagram. That is, to complete the analysis one would need to draw a third expenditure schedule between the solid and dashed ones already shown in Figure 10–4. We know from the equilibrium determined in the aggregate demand-aggregate supply diagram that this final expenditure schedule will intersect the 45-degree line at a real GNP level of Y_2.

3. s, m, −, −; m, s, −, +; s, m, +, +; m, s, +, −; s, m, +, +

Self-Tests

Test A

1.	b	p. 177		6.	d	p. 181
2.	b	p. 177–78		7.	d	p. 180
3.	a	p. 180		8.	c	p. 183–85
4.	a	p. 181		9.	a	p. 189
5.	c	p. 181–82		10.	d	p. 193–94

Test B

1.	T	p. 177
2.	T	p. 177–78
3.	T	p. 181
4.	F	p. 189
5.	T	p. 190–92

6. F while there is a tendency to move toward full employment or potential output, there is nothing that requires the aggregate demand and supply to always intersect there.
7. F p. 181
8. T p. 186
9. F p. 185–86
10. F p. 194

Supplementary Exercise

1. $C + I + (X - IM) = 1500 + .75Y - 5P$
2. $P = 300 - .05Y$ or $Y = 6000 - 20P$
3. $P = 95$; $Y = 4100$
4. $P = 90$; $Y = 4000$
   New expenditure schedule

   $C + I + (X - IM) = 1450 + .75Y - 5P$

   New aggregate demand schedule

   $$P = 290 - .05Y$$

CHAPTER 11

Chapter Review

(1) expenditure; demand; supply
(2) up; 1; 1; equal to
(3) are not; higher; increase; increase; 1; less; propensity; less; investment
(4) less; less
(5) income; consumption
(6) up; down; less; smaller
(7) smaller
(8) increase; decrease; decrease; increase
(9) supply; increase

Definition Quiz

1. c   3. g   5. f
2. e   4. d   6. a

Basic Exercise

1. $5,000
2. $4,500
3. 2.5
4. $5,000
5. 2.0

6. The multiplier for a change in taxes is less than the multiplier for a change in government purchases.
7. No. The $250 reduction in taxes raised the GNP from $4,500 to $5,000. The increase in GNP increased tax revenues by $125 for an overall decrease in tax revenues of $125.
8. $100; $125
9. $4,500; the multipliers are the same.
10. MPC = .8; tax rate = .25.
    G multiplier = 1/(1 −.8(1 − .25)) = 1/(1 −.6) = 2.5;
    Tax multiplier = .8/(1 − .8(1 − .25)) = .8/(1 − .6) = 2.0
11. Initial equilibrium = $5,000; G multiplier = 1/(1 − .8) = 4.0, which exceeds previous multiplier of 2.5. New equilibrium = $4,200.

Self-Tests

Test A

1. c p. 198
2. b p. 206
3. b p. 208
4. a a reduction in transfer payments will reduce disposable income and aggregate demand.
5. c p. 204–206
6. b income taxes lower the value of the multiplier. Lower tax rates increase the multiplier. See page 207.
7. b a change in any variable affecting demand except price will lead to a shift in the aggregate demand curve.
8. c p. 206
9. d p. 212
10. b p. 215

Test B

1. F see comment to question 6, Test A.
2. T p. 206–207
3. F multiplier applies to any change in autonomous spending.
4. F p. 202–204
5. F p. 206
6. F p. 206
7. F p. 210
8. T p. 206
9. F p. 214
10. F p. 214–16

Supplementary Exercises

1. Income taxes are the reason why Okun's multiplier is less than the oversimplified formula.
2. The tax multiplier is less than the multiplier for changes in autonomous spending.
3. The 1975 income tax rebate was a temporary tax change. The 1964 change was permanent.

Appendix

Basic Exercise: Appendix

1. $Y = 5,000$
2. No; Y declines by 25 to $4,975; tax and spending multipliers differ. Deficit increases from zero to 6.25.
3. Multipliers:
   $\Delta I = 2.5$
   $\Delta G = 2.5$
   $\Delta(X - IM) = 2.5$
   $\Delta T = 2.0$ (change in intercept)

CHAPTER 12

Chapter Review

(1) barter; harder
(2) money; commodity; fiat
(3) M1; M2
(4) 797.6; 3,217.0
(5) lending; 850; reserve requirement
(6) 1/(reserve requirement); less
(7) smaller; excess; smaller
(8) contraction; no

Definition Quiz

1. c	8. s	15. b
2. j	9. k	16. r
3. g	10. o	17. l
4. m	11. e	18. h
5. d	12. f	19. q
6. t	13. p	20. a
7. n	14. u	

Basic Exercise

1. $10,000; unchanged; col. 1: $1,000; $9,000
2. col. 2: $1,000; $9,000; $10,000; $1,000; 0
3. col. 3: $9,000; 0; $9,000; $900; $8,100; $19,000; $9,000
4. col. 4: $900; $8,100; $9,000; $900; 0
5. col. 5: $8,100; 0; $8,100; $810; $7,290; $27,100; $17,100
6. B: $9,000; C: $8,100; D: $7,290; E: $6,561; 0.1; $100,000; required reserve ratio.

Self-Tests

Test A

1. b   p. 225–26
2. c   p. 226–27
3. c   p. 233
4. d   p. 239
5. a   9000 net increase in money supply = deposit expansion – cash deposit.
6. a   p. 239
7. a   p. 241–42
8. d   p. 239
9. a   interbank claims lead to offsetting chains of deposit creation and destruction.
10. b   total reserves = required + excess = nonborrowed + borrowed.

Test B

1. T	p. 224–25	6. T	p. 233
2. F	p. 227	7. F	p. 241–42
3. T	p. 225–26	8. F	p. 240
4. F	p. 226	9. F	p. 234
5. F	p. 231	10. T	p. 234

Supplementary Exercises

1. 2500; 1500
2. Change in deposits = $(1/(M + E + C)) \times$ (change in reserves)

CHAPTER 13

Chapter Review

(1) 1914; central; 12; Board; Governors; Federal Open Market; fiscal; monetary
(2) excess
(3) increase; larger; expansionary; required; contractionary
(4) securities; buys; increase; reduction; destruction

(5) moral suasion; higher; higher
(6) more; fewer; more; larger
(7) right; demand
(8) decreases; increased; right; increased; left
(9) intersection; supply; right; increase; decrease; left; decrease; increase
(10) supply; demand; shift in; shift in; demand; supply

Definition Quiz

1. b
2. h
3. k
4. e

5. j
6. f
7. i
8. a

9. d
10. g

Basic Exercise

1. a. decrease; left; contractionary; fall; rise
   b. increase; creation; right; expansionary; rise; fall
   c. less; decline; decline; left; contractionary; fall; rise
2. a. The scatter of points has a positive slope suggesting that an increase in the difference between the federal funds rate and the discount rate is associated with a larger volume of bank borrowing from the Fed.
   b. Remember that borrowing is a privilege not a right. The Fed is likely to use moral suasion to limit bank borrowing when the economic incentive from interest rate differentials gets large.
3. Note that when the interest rate differential increases, the ratio of GNP to money gets larger. That is, individuals economize on the use of money as the opportunity cost of holding M2 balances increases.

Self-Tests

Test A

1. c p. 263
2. b p. 248–49
3. c p. 252
4. d p. 249
5. a p. 252
6. c p. 256
7. b p. 254

8. c multiplier is a function of income tax rate and MPC.
9. d p. 258
10. d p. 261

Test B

1. F p. 247–48
2. F p. 246
3. F p. 246
4. F p. 249–50
5. F reduction in reserve requirement shifts money supply schedule to the right, increasing M and decreasing R.
6. F p. 252
7. F p. 255
8. T p. 254
9. F Changes in monetary policy lead to shifts in the aggregate demand curve.
10. T p. 262

Supplementary Exercises

1. a. 2400; $C = 1525$; $I = 350$; $G = 425$; $X - IM = 100$
   b. increases to 2480
   c. In this model, equilibrium on the expenditure schedule depends on the rate of interest. The expenditure schedule is as follows:

   $$C + I + G + (X - IM) = 325 + .6(5/6)Y + 470 - 10r + 425 + 100.$$

   The 45 degree line is $C + I + G + (X - IM) = Y$. Solving these two equations for one expression in Y and r yields

   $$Y = 2640 - 20r.$$

   Setting the demand for money equal to supply of money yields a second expression in Y and r.

   $$Y = 20BR + 50r.$$

   When $BR = 90$ then $Y = 2400$, $r = 12$, and $M = 480$. The value of M can be found from either the demand for money equation or the supply of money equation.

d. Changing bank reserve shifts the second equation for Y and r. A little experimentation should show that bank reserves of 104 will yield an interest rate of 8 and a money stock of 540.

2. a. $1500; $600
   b. $1220.80; $698.87

CHAPTER 14

Chapter Review

(1) GNP; money
(2) nominal GNP; M; V; P; Y; velocity
(3) money; does not; nominal GNP; 100
(4) should not; opportunity cost
(5) velocity
(6) decline; increase; increase
(7) increase; higher
(8) monetary; fiscal
(9) higher; higher; left; right
(10) output; prices; steep; steep; flat;
(11) automatic
(12) judgmental; are not

Definition Quiz

1. e   4. b   6. f
2. c   5. a   7. d
3. h

Basic Exercise

1. V_1: 6.84; 7.17; 6.81; 6.82; 7.02; 6.85; 6.29; 6.12; 6.33; 6.59
   V_2: 1.74; 1.78; 1.66; 1.65; 1.66; 1.63; 1.57; 1.58; 1.63; 1.66
2. Col. 3: 2911.8; 3282.8; 3398.5; 3663.2; 4117.8; 4610.8; 4645.8; 4721.4; 5023.9
   Col. 5: 2983.4; 3338.5; 3440.1; 3745.2; 4088.2; 4376.1; 4501.1; 4728.6; 5131.3
3. Errors are largest when velocity changes.

Self-Tests

Test A

1. b   p. 267
2. c   p. 267
3. a   p. 267–68
4. d   quantity theory predicts nominal GNP, i.e., P times Q, but not P and Q separately.
5. b   p. 269–70
6. d   increase in taxes would lower GNP.
7. b   p. 275
8. b   p. 279
9. c   p. 284
10. c   p. 288

Test B

1. T   p. 267   6. F   p. 275
2. F   p. 267   7. F   p. 276–77
3. T   p. 271   8. T   p. 282
4. F   p. 271   9. F   p. 283–84
5. T   p. 275   10. T   p. 284

CHAPTER 15

Chapter Review

(1) spending; revenue; revenue; spending; deficit; surplus
(2) down; left; decline; decline; deficit; increase; decrease; accentuate
(3) will; will not
(4) small; without; small; large
(5) monetized
(6) foreigners
(7) investment; recession; war; crowding in; crowding out; high; out

Definition Quiz

1. c   4. i   7. f
2. g   5. e   8. d
3. b   6. h

Basic Exercise

1. 4640; 4760; 4880; 5000; 5120; equilibrium = 5000
2. 0
3. surplus; 50
4. 4800; deficit increased to 50; surplus; no change
5. raise; lower equilibrium level of income.
6. lower; lower equilibrium level of income.
7. 100; 4600
8. −133.33; 4,466.67

Self-Tests

Test A

1. d   p. 299–300
2. c   p. 302
3. c   p. 296
4. d   p. 300–301
5. c   p. 309
6. c   both actions shift the aggregate demand curve to the right.
7. a   p. 303–304
8. d   p. 313
9. b   p. 311
10. d   p. 311

Test B

1. F   p. 296
2. F   depending upon the strength of private demand, a deficit or surplus may be required to insure that aggregate demand and supply curves intersect at full employment.
3. F   p. 303–304
4. F   p. 314
5. T   p. 309
6. F   p. 300
7. F   p. 306
8. T   p. 311
9. T   p. 312
10. T   p. 312

Supplementary Exercises

1. It is important to distinguish between deficits during periods of recession and deficits from deliberate increases in G or reductions in T. All of the examples come from periods when the economy was falling into recession.
3. g. The ratio of debt to GNP should approach .7333.
   h. As long as g is greater than τ and λ is greater than R, the ratio of debt to GNP tends toward $(1 + \lambda)(g - \tau)/(\lambda - R)$. If g is less than τ, the government runs surpluses that eventually pay off the debt. If R is greater than λ, then interest payments on the debt are sufficient to make the national debt grow faster than GNP, and the ratio of debt to income grows without limit. If $R = \lambda$, the formula above will not work. Interest payments alone keep the ratio of debt to GNP constant. If in addition $G > \tau$, then the ratio of debt to income grows without limit.

   Is recent experience a case of adjusting to a lower value for τ and hence a larger, but stable, ratio of debt to GNP or is it a case of interest rates exceeding the growth of GNP, $(R > \lambda)$, in which case there may be no limit to the ratio of debt to GNP? Would spending and tax policies remain unchanged if the ratio of national debt to GNP appeared to be increasing without limit?

CHAPTER 16

Chapter Review

(1) higher; negatively; Phillips; negative
(2) incorrect; inflationary; natural; vertical
(3) smaller; larger; higher; steeper
(4) vertical
(5) expectations; is not
(6) indexing
(7) increase; nominal
(8) more

Definition Quiz

1. k	5. c	9. g
2. h	6. l	10. d
3. a	7. e	11. i
4. j	8. b	

Basic Exercise

1. purchase; decrease; decrease; increase; increase
2. 103
3. No; aggregate supply curve will shift up as long as output exceeds full-employment level of output; prices will tend to rise faster and faster.
4. a. 4800; 106
   b. expansionary; 109
   c. restrictive; 4600

Self-Tests
Test A

1. d   p. 326
2. d   p. 332
3. d   p. 340
4. b   p. 339
5. c   stabilization policy reduces unemployment more quickly as it moves the economy up the short run Phillips curve to the natural rate of unemployment.
6. d   p. 341
7. b   open market sales are monetary policy.
8. a   p. 343
9. c   p. 344
10. d   p. 345

Test B

1. F   p. 322
2. F   any shift in the aggregate demand curve, from whatever source, will affect prices.
3. T   p. 330
4. T   p. 332
5. T   p. 332
6. F   p. 340
7. T   p. 337
8. F   both monetary and fiscal policy would shift the aggregate demand curve along the aggregate supply curve with similar effects on prices.
9. F   p. 341
10. F   see comment to question 5, Test A.

Supplementary Exercise

1. 440,000; $2,200,000; $440,000; 10%; yes
2. 440,000; $2,200,000; $480,000; 7.5%; 20%; no, yes.
3. 440,000; $2,310,000; $462,000; both wages and profits increase by 15.5%.
4. What happens if inflation turns out to be different from the target rate?

CHAPTER 17

Chapter Review

(1) more; more; demand; supply; out; increase

(2) is; 200
(3) convergence; faster; slower; are not
(4) need not
(5) no

Definition Quiz

1. e   2. a   3. f   4. b   5. d

Basic Exercises

1. a. 2.7
   b. 7.2, more than twice.
   c. The concept of convergence suggests that major differences in the growth of labor productivity cannot be sustained for 100 years.
   d. 33 years
2. a. 23,643
   b. 34,450
   c. No, labor productivity still increases but at a slower rate. It more than doubled over the first 20 years and increased by less than 50 percent over the second. Numbers were chosen to illustrate American experience over the period 1950 to 1990.

Self-Tests
Test A

1. d	p. 353	6. c	p. 356
2. c	p. 353	7. c	p. 357
3. a	p. 354–55	8. b	p. 360–61
4. d	p. 365	9. b	p. 357–58
5. a	p. 362	10. a	p. 365

Test B

1. F	p. 356	6. T	p. 356–57
2. F	p. 353	7. F	p. 358
3. F	p. 361	8. F	p. 359
4. F	p. 359	9. F	p. 364
5. F	p. 360	10. F	p. 365

CHAPTER 18

Chapter Review

(1) comparative
(2) scale

(3) comparative
(4) A; B; 8000; wheat
(5) 2000; 1200; cars; wheat
(6) demand; supply; exporting; importing
(7) tariffs; quotas; subsidies; price; quantity
(8) government
(9) low; do not; can
(10) adjustment
(11) defense; infant

Definition Quiz

1. j   4. b   7. a
2. d   5. i   8. h
3. g   6. f   9. e

Basic Exercises

1. a. Japan; Japan
   b. ⅔; 1½; Canada; Japan; Canada; Japan
   c. Calculators; 1,000,000; 3,000,000; 4,000,000
      Backpacks: 1,500,000; 2,000,000; 3,500,000
   d. 300,000; 450,000
   e. 600,000 hours; 300,000 calculators; 200,000 backpacks
   f. increase; 250,000
   g. Calculators: 700,000; 3,450,000; 4,150,000
      Backpacks: 1,950,000; 1,700,000; 3,650,000
      The output of both calculators and backpacks has increased as compared to Question c.
   h. Canadian backpack output would fall to 1,050,000. Japan would need to reallocate 1,350,000 labor hours. Total calculator output would fall to 3,625,000. This reallocation is not in line with the principle of comparative advantage. The opportunity cost of backpacks in terms of calculators is greater in Japan than in Canada.
   i. There will be no change in total world output. Neither country has a comparative advantage. The opportunity cost of increased calculator or backpack production is the same in both countries.
2. a. India: $10,1000
      United States: $40,600
   b. $20; production in India increases to 1200; production in United States decreases to 400; India exports, United States imports 400 shirts.
   c. United States: price = $30, production = 500; imports = 200
      India: price = $15; production = 1100; exports = 200
      United States; India; United States; India; decreased
   d. Tariff of $15

Self-Tests

Test A

1. b   p. 376
2. b   p. 372
3. c   p. 379
4. a   p. 373
5. a   p. 373
6. a   export subsidies increase the volume of traded goods.
7. c   p. 379
8. c   p. 382
9. d   tariffs raise domestic prices allowing an increase in domestic production.
10. c   free trade keeps prices to consumers low.

Test B

1. F   p. 372
2. F   p. 370
3. F   trade should reflect comparative not absolute advantage.
4. T   p. 370
5. T   p. 376
6. F   as world exports must equal world imports, it is not possible for all countries to increase exports without increasing imports.
7. T   p. 381
8. F   p. 385
9. F   p. 388
10. F   p. 368

Supplementary Exercises

2. a. Baulmovia: 8,100; Bilandia: 17,150
   b. 12; Baulmovia; Bilandia; 100
   c. Baulmovia: price = 10;
      Bilandia: price = 14.5;
      Trade = 50.

d. 50

e. Tariff revenues accrue to the government. Tariffs do not protect high-cost foreign producers.

3. Production of 14.4 million bolts of cloth and 10.8 million barrels of wine allows Ricardia to choose from the outermost consumption possibilities line. Note that to be on the outermost consumption possibilities line Ricardia must choose to produce at the point where the slope of the production possibilities frontier equals the ratio of world prices.

CHAPTER 19

Chapter Review

(1) exchange; depreciated; appreciated
(2) demand; supply; exports; financial; physical; supply
(3) demand; increase; appreciation; supply; depreciation; appreciation
(4) purchasing power parity; depreciate; depreciating; appreciating
(5) Bretton
(6) deficit; demand; supply; surplus
(7) buy; increasing
(8) deficit; increase; decrease; contraction; reduction
(9) disliked
(10) speculators

Definition Quiz

1. e	8. r	14. d
2. b	9. o	15. m
3. n	10. h	16. a
4. s	11. q	17. j
5. k	12. l	18. p
6. t	13. i	19. f
7. c		

Basic Exercises

1. a. The demand curve may shift to the left if some Americans now find French investments less attractive. The supply curve shifts to the right as French investors are attracted by higher U.S. interest rates. With floating rates, the franc depreciates. With fixed rates, a deficit results.

b. The demand curve shifts to the right. There is no shift in the supply curve. With floating rates, the franc appreciates. With fixed rates, a surplus results.

c. The demand curve shifts to the left as Americans import less. The supply curve might shift to the right if a recession leads to lower dollar prices of U.S. exports. With floating rates, the franc depreciates. With fixed rates, a deficit results.

d. The demand curve shifts to the left. The supply curve might shift to the right if French citizens import more. With floating rates, the franc depreciates. With fixed rates, a deficit results.

2. 30

a. $6.40. Sales of French wine would increase. Sales of California wines would decrease. The U.S. balance of payments would show a deficit.

b. 18 cents; appreciation; depreciation

c. United States (50% vs. 33%)

d. deficit

e. depreciating

Self-Tests

Test A

1. b p. 394
2. b p. 394
3. b p. 398
4. c p. 401–402
5. c p. 408
6. d p. 397
7. c a 6 percent depreciation of the dollar is necessary to equalize the purchasing power of dollars and marks.
8. b p. 398
9. b higher inflation in the U.S. increases supply of dollars as Americans demand less expensive German goods resulting in U.S. deficit.
10. b exchange rates should adjust so that direct conversion between kronor and guilders costs no more or no less than first converting into dollars and then into kronor or guilders.

Test B

1. T a depreciating currency buys fewer units of foreign currency; an appreciating currency buys more units of foreign currency.
2. F a pure system of floating exchange rates involves no government intervention by definition.
3. T p. 396
4. T an increase in imports would mean an increase in the supply of dollars by Americans. The shift in the supply schedule for dollars would increase a deficit.
5. F p. 397
6. T p. 402
7. F p. 406–407
8. F p. 406
9. T p. 407
10. F p. 407

Supplementary Exercises

1. Col. 1: $28,000,000; £10,000,000
   Col. 2: $28,000,000; £10,769,231
   Col. 3: $28,000,000; £11,666,667
   If there is no devaluation, you are out only the transactions costs. If the pound is devalued, you stand to make a handsome profit. As the prospect of devaluation increases, there is a greater incentive to sell your pounds before their price falls. Your efforts to sell pounds, along with similar actions by others, will increase the pressure for devaluation.

CHAPTER 20

Chapter Review

(1) closed; open
(2) increase; are; less; increase; decrease; decrease; increase; decrease; increase
(3) shift in; decline; down; left
(4) less; downward; more; upward
(5) increase; appreciation
(6) decrease; up; right; increase; appreciation; left; down; offset; lower; increase; offset
(7) appreciation; enhance
(8) J

(9) expansionary; contractionary; contractionary; expansionary; exports; lower

Definition Quiz

1. a
2. e
3. h
4. f
5. c
6. g
7. d

Basic Exercise

1. Increase in G: Interest rate increases; exchange rate appreciates; GNP and price level down, which work to offset the initial impact of the increase in G.
   Decrease in G: Interest rate decreases; exchange rate depreciates; GNP and price level up, which work to offset the initial impact of the decrease in G.
   Open Market Sale: Interest rate increases; exchange rate appreciates; GNP and price level down, which work to enhance the initial impact of the open market sale.
   Open Market Purchase: Interest rate decreases; exchange rate depreciates; GNP and price level increase, which work to enhance the initial impact of the open market purchase.
2. The impact of monetary policy is enhanced. The impact of fiscal policy is diminished.

Self-Tests

Test A

1. d in an open economy $Y = C + I + G + (X - IM)$. $C + I + G$ can be greater, less, or equal to Y depending upon whether $(X - IM)$ is negative, positive, or zero.
2. c p. 417–18
3. c p. 417–18
4. b p. 424
5. c the decrease in exports following an appreciation of the dollar shifts the aggregate demand curve to the left.
6. c p. 425–26
7. b the reduction in interest rates from the move to expansionary monetary policy induces a depreciation of the dollar.
8. c p. 420–21

9. b   p. 429
10. a   p. 430

Test B

1. F   p. 417–18
2. F   a change in exports, whether from a change in foreign GNP or a change in the exchange rate, is modeled as an autonomous change in spending with multiplier effects similar to those of any other autonomous change.
3. F   autonomous shifts in investment spending affect interest rates, exchange rates, net exports, and the trade deficit in a manner analogous to changes in fiscal policy.
4. T   p. 423
5. T   p. 420–21
6. T   p. 425
7. F   p. 427
8. F   p. 425–26
9. T   p. 432
10. F   p. 431–32

Appendix

1. 4500; 4750; 5000; 5250; 5500
   The expenditure schedule is flatter when imports increase with income. The expenditure schedule shows how expenditures for domestic output vary with income. The increased spending on imports means a smaller increase in spending on domestic output and hence a flatter expenditure schedule.
2. 4750; 5000; 5250; 5500; 5750; equilibrium = 5500; multiplier = 2.0. The multiplier increase comes from the successive rounds of spending on domestic output. As some of the increased spending is directed at foreign goods, i.e., imports, there is a smaller cumulative impact on spending for domestic output.
3. $t = .25$; $b = .8$; $m = .1$; multiplier = $1/(1 - b[1 - t] + m) = 2.0$.

CHAPTER 21

Chapter Review

(1) marginal; will; decrease
(2) consumer's; consumer's surplus; price; greater; increase

(3) greater; marginal; more; up; negative
(4) shift in; utility; normal; inferior
(5) substitution; income; fewer; substitution; income; negative; substitution; income

Definition Quiz

1. d	4. i	7. a
2. h	5. b	8. c
3. e	6. g	

Basic Exercise

1. 110; 100; 80; 70; 50; 30; 20
2. 2; 4; 5
3. Col. 3: 20; 30; 20; 0; –40; –100; –170; 2
   Col. 5: 50; 90; 110; 120; 110; 80; 40; 4
   Col. 7: 70; 130; 170; 200; 210; 200; 180; 5
4. Consumer's; quantities are the same

Self-Tests

Test A

1. b   p. 461
2. a   p. 461
3. d   p. 462
4. c   p. 463
5. b   p. 466
6. d   p. 467
7. d   p. 469
8. c   p. 469
9. b   the demand curve for an inferior good may have a positive slope indicating that the quantity demanded increases with an increase in price.
10. a   p. 468

Test B

1. T   p. 466
2. F   p. 461
3. F   p. 467
4. T   p. 468
5. T   p. 468
6. T   p. 463
7. F   p. 468
8. T   p. 469
9. F   the label of inferior goods implies nothing about rationality. It refers to the impact of a change in income on the quantity demanded.
10. F   p. 466

Appendix

Appendix Review

(1) straight; negative; intercept; slope
(2) indifference; indifferent; are; never; negative
(3) in; more; substitution; decreases
(4) budget; indifference; highest; budget line
(5) budget line

Definition Quiz: Appendix

1. c   2. d   3. a   4. e

Basic Exercise: Appendix

2. b. 20; 10
   c. 3; 2
   e. equals the slope of the budget line
2. a. Z
   b. Y

Self-Tests: Appendix
Test A

1. c	p. 472		4. c	p. 474
2. d	p. 472		5. a	p. 473
3. b	p. 473		6. b	p. 474

Test B

1. F   p. 472
2. T   p. 473
3. F   p. 474
4. F   p. 474
5. T   p. 474
6. F   p. 476
7. T   p. 478
8. T   a doubling of money income and prices leaves the budget line unaffected.

Supplementary Exercise: Appendix

2. $F = (Y + 20P_C - 12P_F)/2P_F$
   $C = (Y - 20P_C + 12P_F)/2P_C$
   where P_F = price of food, P_C = price of clothing and Y = income. The demand curves come from solving the following two equations for F and C:
   Optimal purchases require that the

marginal rate of substitution equals the ratio of market prices, or

$$(F + 12)/(C = 20) = P_C/P_F$$

The budget constraint requires that:

$$F \bullet P_F + C \bullet P_C = Y$$

3. $F = 114$; $C = 43$
4. $F = 84$; $C = 44$
5. $F = 124$; $C = 48$; no

CHAPTER 22

Chapter Review

(1) horizontal
(2) negative; negative; law
(3) shift in
(4) elasticity; demand
(5) zero; infinite; changes
(6) elastic; inelastic; unit elastic
(7) will not; 1.0
(8) greater; increase; decrease
(9) cross
(10) complements; negative; substitutes; positives

Definition Quiz

1. c	5. f	8. e
2. j	6. b	9. k
3. h	7. i	10. a
4. g		

Basic Exercises

1. b. 1.0
   c. 1.0
   d. 1.0
2. straight
   a. 1.57; 1.0; .64; decreases
   b. $486,000; $540,000; $540,000; $486,000. Total revenue increases (decreases) as price declines if the elasticity of demand is greater (less) than 1.0. Total revenue increases (decreases) as price increases if the elasticity of demand is less (greater) than 1.0

Self-Tests

Test A

1. b   a and c—shift in demand curve; d— consistent with inelastic demand curve; b is exception as it implies positively sloped demand curve.
2. c   changes in own price lead to a movement along the demand curve.
3. b   changes in own price lead to a movement along the demand curve.
4. a $35/20 = 1.75$; curve is elastic.
5. a   p. 470
6. b   p. 465
7. b   b is an example of complements.
8. a   p. 474
9. c   p. 474
10. d   p. 474

Test B

1. T   p. 461
2. T   p. 460
3. F   p. 465
4. F   p. 469
5. T   p. 468
6. F   all negatively sloped demand curves show increase in quantity demanded following reduction in price whether they are elastic or inelastic.
7. T   p. 470
8. F   p. 473
9. T   p. 474
10. F   substitutes not complements.

Appendix

Basic Exercises: Appendix

1. Not much; plotting historical data is an inappropriate way to estimate a demand curve.
2. a. 1988: $P = 51.86$; $Q = 2,918.63$
   1989: $P = 59.73$; $Q = 2,997.33$
   1990: $P = 63.52$; $Q = 3,035.18$
   When only the demand curve shifts, the historical data on price and quantity trace out the supply curve. If you connect the three pairs of points, you should have a graph of the supply curve. Each point comes from the intersection of the demand curve for the specific year with the unchanging supply curve. In this case, the points of market equilibrium provide no information about the demand curve.
   b. 1988: $P = 51.86$; $Q = 2,918.63$
   1989: $P = 53.07$; $Q = 3,330.67$
   1990: $P = 50.19$; $Q = 3,701.85$
   With shifts in both demand and supply curves, the points of market equilibrium trace out neither curve. Try drawing the demand and supply curves for each year on the same diagram. As both curves shift, a line connecting the successive points of market equilibrium gives no information about either curve.

Supplementary Exercise: Appendix

1. $Q = 600 - 20P$
2. flatter
3. 3.0; equal
4. $Q = 300 - 8P$, $P > 30$; $Q = 600 - 18P$, $P \leq 30$; flatter; elasticity: Angela 3.0; Dan 1.50; market 2.08. Market elasticity is in between individual elasticities.

CHAPTER 23

Chapter Review

(1) increase; physical; revenue
(2) revenue; price
(3) reduce; less; more
(4) production; increasing; decreasing; constant
(5) short
(6) output; total
(7) long run; lower
(8) is unchanged; less; fall; more; rises

Definition Quiz

1. g	7. m	12. e
2. h	8. c	13. j
3. k	9. o	14. d
4. b	10. i	15. p
5. l	11. n	16. f
6. a		

Basic Exercise

1. 100 acres; increasing returns: 0 to 2 workers; decreasing returns: 2 to 4 workers; negative returns: 4 to 6 workers
2. 200 acres; increasing returns: 0 to 2 workers; decreasing returns: 2 to 5 workers; negative returns: 5 to 6 workers 300 acres; increasing returns: 0 to 2 workers; decreasing returns: 2 to 6 workers The output-labor curve shifts up as land increases.
3. 100: 1; 3; 2; 1; –1; –2
   200: 2; 4; 3.5; 2.5; 1; –1
   300: 3; 4.5; 3.5; 3; 2; 1
4. Marginal returns to land generally decline.
5. increasing; increasing; constant; increasing; decreasing
6. $10,000; $20,000; $17,500; $12,500; $5,000; –$5,000
   Hire 4 workers; $28,000 = (12,000 × $5) – ($8,000 × 4)

Self-Tests

Test A

1. d p. 486
2. b diminishing returns set in after second worker as MPP diminishes from 15 to 10.
3. b p. 486
4. c p. 487
5. d p. 501
6. c p. 501
7. d p. 503–504
8. b optimal choices need to consider additions to revenues and additions to cost. Technological considerations alone are insufficient.
9. a options b, c, and d all affect a firm's costs. Output prices help to determine revenue.
10. c p. 493

Test B

1. F	p. 503–504	6. F	p. 493
2. T	p. 483	7. F	p. 491
3. F	p. 486	8. F	p. 495
4. F	p. 503–504	9. T	p. 494
5. T	p. 502	10. F	p. 504

Appendix

Appendix Review

(1) production indifference; more
(2) negative; will; diminishing; marginal
(3) straight; horizontal
(4) lowest
(5) expansion

Definition Quiz: Appendix

1. c   2. d   3. a

Basic Exercise: Appendix

1. 200; 2; 100; 3. Total costs are constant along a single budget line. Total costs are greater along higher budget lines.
2. $80

Self-Tests: Appendix
Test A

1. b slope of indifference curve typically varies continuously and equals ratio of input prices at least-cost combination.
2. c p. 509–10
3. d production indifference curves represent technological relationships and do not shift with a change in input prices.

Test B

1. F p. 509
2. T p. 509
3. T p. 510
4. F an increase in the price of the input measured on vertical axis makes budget line flatter.
5. F a change in price of one input typically changes optimal use of all inputs.
6. F a change in output prices may induce a firm to move along its expansion path but does not shift the production indifference curves or the budget line.
7. T p. 510

Supplementary Exercise: Appendix

2. For labor: $MPP_L \cdot P_W = P_L$ or $(M/L)^{1/2}$ 50 = 12.

For machines: $MPP_M \cdot P_W = P_M$
or $(L/M)^{1/2} 50 = 48$.
Solving the two expressions for L in terms of M shows that when the price of labor hours is 12 and the price of machine hours is 48, then $L = 4M$.
From the production function
$$W = L^{1/2} M^{1/2}$$
Knowing that for the least-cost combination of inputs $L = 4M$, the equation can be rewritten as
$$500,000 = M^{1/2}(4M)^{1/2}$$
$$500,000 = (4M^2)^{1/2} = 2M$$
$$M = 250,000 \text{ machine hours}$$
$$L = 1,000,000 \text{ labor hours}$$

3. a. Total output $= 500\sqrt{L}$
   b. MPP of labor $= 250/\sqrt{L}$; the MPP of labor is the slope of the total product curve.
   c. For this production function, MPP of labor declines continuously, but is never negative.
   d. 1,085,069.45 labor hours; (Find the quantity of labor such that the MRP of labor is equal to the price of labor. $(250/\sqrt{L}) \times 50 = 12$.)
      Output $= 520,833.33$ widgets.
4. For this production function, the expansion path is a straight line.
5. Constant: $(2M)^{1/2}(2L)^{1/2} = 2M^{1/2}L^{1/2} = 2W$
   A doubling of inputs doubles output.

CHAPTER 24

Chapter Review

(1) average; marginal
(2) marginal; marginal; profits; revenue; cost
(3) total
(4) marginal; marginal; positive; zero; equals
(5) fixed; variable; variable; will not; will not

Definition Quiz

1. g
2. e
3. a
4. k

5. d
6. b
7. j
8. l

9. f
10. c
11. i

Basic Exercises

1. a. Marginal cost: $1,900; $1,800; $1,700; $1,600; $1,650; $1,950; $2,600; $2,800; $3,000
      Total revenue: $3,500; $6,800; $9,900; $12,800; $15,500; $18,000; $20,300; $22,400; $24,300; $26,000
      Marginal revenue: $3,300; $3,100; $2,900; $2,700; $2,500; $2,300; $2,100; $1,900; $1,700
   b. 7
   c. 7 widgets. Increasing output to 8 entails negative marginal profits as marginal cost exceeds marginal revenue.
   d. $7,700
   e. average cost: $2,000; $1,950; $1,900; $1,850; $1,800; $1,775; $1,800; $1,900; $2,000; $2,100
   f. profits; does not; does not
   g. marginal cost same as in a; average costs increase; 7; $6,700
2. is not, horizontal; vertical; horizontal

Self-Tests

Test A

1. b p. 488
2. b p. 518
3. d p. 518
4. a review problem 2 of the Basic Exercises to this chapter.
5. c p. 523
6. c p. 522
7. c p. 523
8. b p. 517
9. c average costs are increased at all levels of output.
10. a total profits increase by the decrease in fixed costs

Test B

1. F p. 515
2. F p. 516
3. F p. 518
4. F p. 488
5. F review problem 2 of the Basic Exercises to this chapter.
6. T p. 522
7. T p. 523
8. F p. 492

9. F a firm is making profits when AR exceeds AC but continuing to expand output beyond the point where MR = MC will result in a lower level of total profits.

10. F p. 527–28

Appendix

1. The marginal profit curve should equal zero where total profits are maximized.
2. The marginal cost curve should go through the minimum of the average cost curve.
4. Average cost declines as long as marginal cost is less than average cost. Average cost rises after six units of output when marginal cost exceeds average cost. Average revenue declines continuously as marginal revenue is less than average revenue.

Supplementary Exercises: Appendix

1. a. $16,000
   b. Average cost = $16,000/Q + 120 - .4Q + .002Q^2$
      Marginal cost = $120 - .8Q + .006Q^2$
   c. It should.
   d. Marginal revenue = $300 - .5Q$
   f. $Q = 200$
   g. Find the positive value of Q such that marginal cost = marginal revenue
      $120 - .8Q + .006Q^2 = 300 - .5Q$
      $Q = 200$
   h. Price = $250; total revenue = $50,000; total cost = $40,000; total profits = $10,000
   j. Average cost = $20,000/Q + 120 - .4Q + .002Q^2$
      No change in profit maximizing level of output; total profits = $6,000
2. Demand is elastic up to the point of 600 stereo sets and $150. Demand is inelastic beyond that point. The profit-maximizing level of output in Question 2, 200 sets and $250, is in the elastic portion of the demand curve.
3. a. Set marginal cost = marginal revenue.
      Marginal cost: From the supplementary exercise in Chapter 23, when $P_L = 12$ and $P_M = 48$, two hours of labor are used with a half hour of machine time to

produce each widget. As the production function exhibits constant returns to scale, average and marginal cost are equal at $48 per widget.

Marginal revenue = $100 - .00008W$

To find the profit maximizing level of output set marginal cost = marginal revenue.

$$48 = 100 - .00008W$$
$$W = 650,000$$
$$L = 1,300,000$$
$$M = 325,000$$
$$P_W = \$74.$$

b.   Output: $W = (200,000)^{1/2}L^{1/2}$
       Labor Input: $L = W^2/200,000$
       Total (labor) cost = $12W^2/200,000$
       Marginal (labor) cost = $24W/200,000$
       $= .00012W$
       Marginal revenue = $100 - .00008W$

   Set marginal cost = marginal revenue
   $$.00012W = 100 - .00008W$$
   $$.0002W = 100$$
   $$W = 500,000$$
   $$L = 1,250,000$$
   $$P_W = \$80.$$

CHAPTER 25

Chapter Review

(1) Many; Identical; Easy; Perfect; do not; zero
(2) horizontal; marginal
(3) marginal; losses; variable; sunk; marginal cost; variable
(4) horizontal; demand; supply
(5) loss; two; better; opportunity; economic; accounting
(6) profits; (shaded rectangle should go from the y axis to a quantity of 1450 and from 20 to 15.30, the difference between the market price and the firm's average cost when producing 1450 units of output); enter; right; fall; $15.00 (minimum average cost; see the Basic Exercise); long-run average

Definition Quiz

1. d   4. h   6. f
2. g   5. a   7. e
3. b

Basic Exercise

1. 1400; $5,544 = (P - AC)Q$; $5,310; $5,330
2. 1200; –$4,380 = $(P - AC)Q$; –$4,550; –$4,532; –$10,140 (fixed costs)
3. 0; price does not cover average variable cost.
4. Firm's short-run supply curve is the portion of its marginal cost curve above average variable cost.
5. While under perfect competition marginal revenue equals price, one also needs to consider how a change in output affects costs. That is, the relevant comparison is with marginal cost, not average cost.
6. $15.00; 1300 widgets

Self-Tests

Test A

1. b   p. 538
2. c   p. 537
3. d   p. 539, the firm's horizontal demand curve is perfectly elastic.
4. c   p. 544
5. b   p. 551
6. b   p. 550
7. c $P = MC$ is the condition for profit maximization in the short run and long run. Free entry and exit insures that $P = MC = AC$ in the long run.
8. c   p. 546–49
9. c   short-run profit maximization occurs where $P = MC$.
10. d   p. 551

Test B

1. F   p. 537
2. F   If $P > AC$, a firm can increase profits by expanding output as long as $P > MC$.
3. F   p. 551
4. F   p. 542
5. F   p. 546

6. F   If $P > AC$, a firm can increase profits by expanding output if $MC < P$.
7. F   p. 544
8. T   p. 551
9. F   p. 542
10. F   p. 538

Supplementary Exercise

1. a. Average Cost = $10,140/Q + .00001Q^2 - .02Q + 16.3$
   b. Average variable cost = $.00001Q^2 - .02Q + 16.3$
   c. Marginal cost = $.00003Q^2 - .04Q + 16.3$
3. To find the minimum of either average cost curve sets its derivative equal to zero. For AC, $Q = 1300$; AC = 15.00; at $Q = 1300$, MC = 15.00 For AVC, $Q = 1000$; AVC = 6.30; at $Q = 1000$, MC = 6.30
4. Supply = 0 if $P < 6.30$
   Supply =

$$\frac{.04 + \sqrt{-.0002 + .00012P}}{.00006} \text{ if } P > 6.30$$

CHAPTER 26

Chapter Review

(1) are not
(2) selection; planning; distribution
(3) was not; efficient
(4) efficient; decreasing
(5) utility; cost
(6) increase; cost; greater; is not; equals
(7) price; marginal cost; price; price
(8) utility; cost; equals
(9) input-output

Definition Quiz

1. c   3. a   5. g
2. f   4. e   6. b

Basic Exercise

1. 7; 5
2. 2; more
3. decrease; 2; fewer
4. 5

Self-Tests

Test A

1. d conditions for efficiency say nothing about necessities and luxuries. Prices will depend upon consumer preferences and production costs as explained on page 563.
2. b p. 564
3. b p. 568
4. a p. 568
5. b increased production typically increases marginal cost, while increased consumption typically lowers marginal utility.
6. c p. 556–57
7. b imposing Leon's preferences would be equivalent to imposing those of a central planner.
8. c p. 557
9. a p. 569
10. b p. 569

Test B

1. T	p. 563		6. F	p. 565–66
2. F	p. 557		7. T	p. 570
3. F	p. 565–67		8. T	p. 571–72
4. T	p. 568		9. F	p. 564–65
5. F	p. 567		10. T	p. 569–70

Appendix

Basic Exercises: Appendix

1. every consumer must have the same marginal utility for every commodity.
   a. No
   b. increase; 1; increase; 2; inefficient
   c. All consumers respond to the same set of prices and consume so that marginal utility equals price.
2. Ratio of marginal physical products for two inputs is the same in all alternative uses.
   a. 120; 1200; 160; 800; +40; +400
   Note that this reallocation of inputs should work to move the ratio of marginal physical products in the production of corn and tomatoes toward equality.
   c. In competitive markets, profit maximizing firms adjust the use of

inputs until the ratio of marginal physical products is equal to the ratio of input prices. By adjusting to common prices, the ratio of marginal physical products is equated across alternative uses.

CHAPTER 27

Chapter Review

(1) one; no
(2) natural; barriers; entry
(3) negative; lower
(4) marginal; marginal revenue; price; is not
(5) average; less; below; above
(6) demand; greater; less; less; will not; higher; lower
(7) price; price; marginal revenue; less; greater; greater
(8) down
(9) will not; does not; maker

Definition Quiz

1. e   2. a   3. d   4. b

Basic Exercise

1. a. Total revenue: $114,000; $120,900; $127,400; $133,500; $139,200
   Total cost: $84,816; $90,441; $96,516; $103,041; $110,016
   14
   b. Marginal revenue: $6,900; $6,500; $6,100; $5,700
   Marginal cost: $5,625; $6,075; $6,525; $6,975
   revenue; cost; 14
   c. 9,100
   d. 30,884
2. Total revenue: $114,000; $120,900; $127,400; $133,500; $139,200
   Marginal revenue: $6,900; $6,500; $6,100; $5,700
   Total cost: $96,816; $103,441; $110,516; $118,041; $126,016
   Marginal cost: $6,625; $7,075; $7,525; $7,975
   a. 13 widgets; $9,300; $13,000; $200
   b. $17,459
3. No change in output = 14 widgets; no change in price = $9,100; profits down

$13,000 to $17,884. No change in pollution as output is unchanged. The differences between Questions 2 and 3 reflect the differences between the effects of a change in marginal and fixed costs. Note that in Question 2 marginal cost changed as the tax was imposed on each widget produced. In Question 3 marginal cost is unchanged as the pollution charge is independent of the number of widgets produced.

Self-Tests

Test A

1. d   p. 578
2. c   p. 578
3. b   p. 579
4. c   p. 581–82
5. a   p. 583
6. c   p. 584
7. b   p. 584
8. b   profit maximizing level of output is determined where marginal cost equals marginal revenue. A change in fixed cost will not change marginal revenue or marginal cost and will not change the profit maximizing level of output.
9. b   profit maximizing level of output is determined where marginal cost equals marginal revenue. A change in fixed cost will not change marginal revenue or marginal cost and will not change the profit maximizing level of output.
10. a   see question 2 in the Supplementary Exercises.

Test B

1. F   p. 578
2. T   p. 579
3. F   p. 584
4. F   p. 581
5. T   p. 583
6. F   as compared to the competitive situation, price is up and quantity is down. See discussion on page 584.
7. T   p. 586
8. F   even if price exceeds average cost, profits will decline if marginal revenue is less than marginal cost.

9. F   p. 587–88
10. F   a per unit pollution tax would shift the industry supply curve as it affects marginal cost curves for all firms. The shift in the industry supply curve will increase market price. See also Chapter 34.

Supplementary Exercises

1. a. Total revenue $= 11,900Q - 200Q^2$
   Marginal revenue $= 11,900 - 400Q$
   Average cost $= 225Q + 52,416/Q$
   Marginal cost $= 450Q$
   c. $11,900 - 400Q = 450Q$; $850Q = 11,900$; $Q = 14$
   d. Per-unit charge:
   $TC = 52,416 + 225Q^2 + 1,000Q$
   $AC = 225Q + 52,416/Q + 1,000$
   $MC = 450Q + 1,000$
   Fixed charge:
   $TC = 65,416 + 225Q^2$
   $AC = 225Q + 65,416/Q$
   $MC = 450Q$
   Note that the addition of a fixed cost element does not change marginal cost.

2. If a monopolist is originally producing where demand is inelastic, then an increase in market price will increase profits. The increase in price reduces costs as quantity declines and increases revenue as the percentage decline in the quantity sold is more than offset by the percentage increase in price. Thus the initial point could not have been a point of profit maximization. Similar reasoning rules out b, the case of unit elastic demand, as a point of profit maximization. Again profits increase as the reduction in quantity from an increase in price reduces costs while revenue is unchanged from the assumption of unit elasticity of demand.

CHAPTER 28

Chapter Review

(1) monopolistic; negative; marginal revenue; marginal cost; zero; entry; average
(2) oligopoly; cartel; price leadership
(3) zero; lower; larger

(4) payoff; strategy
(5) will; will not; marginal; cost
(6) entry; exit; opportunity cost; capital

Definition Quiz

1. g   4. a   7. h
2. c   5. i   8. d
3. f   6. e

Basic Exercises

1. a. Profit-maximizing level of output = 100 meals
   b. Marginal revenue: $2,200; $1,400; $600; −$200
   Marginal cost: $998; $1,000; $996; $1,000
   Profit-maximizing level of output = 1000 meals
   MC is less than MR at less than 1000 meals
   MC exceeds MR at more than 1000 meals.
   See also the Supplementary Exercise to this chapter.
2. a. 1,000; $200; Marginal revenue exceeds marginal cost up to 1,000 sets and is less than marginal cost beyond 1,000 sets.
   b. No change in price or quantity. It is the kink in the demand curve that gives rise to the discontinuity in marginal revenue. Fluctuations of marginal cost within this discontinuity have no impact on the profit maximizing level of output or price.
   c. Marginal cost would have to rise above $150 a set.
   d. Marginal cost would have to fall below $50 a set.

Self-Tests
Test A

1. b   p. 592   6. c   p. 600
2. d   p. 594   7. b   p. 601
3. a   p. 593   8. c   p. 601–603
4. d   p. 596   9. c   p. 603–606
5. c   p. 598   10. b   p. 607

Test B

1. T   p. 597   6. T   p. 596
2. T   p. 592   7. F   p. 599
3. F   p. 593–94   8. F   p. 601
4. F   p. 595   9. T   p. 603
5. F   p. 596   10. F   p. 607–608

Supplementary Exercise

Total Revenue $= 25Q - Q^2/100$
Marginal Revenue $= 25 - Q/50$
Average Cost $= 10,000/Q + 5$
Marginal Cost $= 5$
Profit-maximizing level of output: $25 - Q/50 = 5$; $Q = 1000$

CHAPTER 29

Chapter Review

(1) opportunity
(2) marginal cost; marginal utility; on
(3) little
(4) externalities; detrimental; beneficial externalities
(5) higher; higher
(6) private; inefficient; much; less
(7) depletability; excludability; public
(8) difficult; rider
(9) zero; zero
(10) does not; less
(11) irreversible
(12) limited

Definition Quiz

1. q   7. l   13. o
2. h   8. p   14. g
3. e   9. f   15. m
4. b   10. k   16. c
5. h   11. i
6. j   12. d

Basic Exercise

1. Col. 1: 125; $2,640,000; $11; 100; $2,112,000; $10.56
2. Col. 2: 120; $2,640,000; $11; 100; $2,200,000; $11; cost of producing widgets unchanged; cost per hour of police service up 4.17 percent.

3. Col. 3: 80; $2,640,000; $11; 100;
   3,300,000; $16.50; cost of producing
   widgets unchanged; cost per hour of police
   service up 50 percent over 10 years.

Self-Tests
Test A

1. c Chapter 3 showed that production
       inside the PPF is inefficient.
2. d (possibly b) p. 613
3. b p. 613–14
4. a p. 613–15
5. a p. 617–18
6. b when you use gasoline, it is depleted
       and use can be excluded unless
       individuals pay.
7. b p. 617–18
8. d p. 624
9. b it is easier to introduce labor-saving
       innovations into the production of TVs
       than in the other examples which have
       more fixed labor requirements.
10. b the adjustment of nominal interest
        rates during periods of inflation is not
        an argument that private markets
        make inappropriate savings and
        investment decisions.

Test B

1. F	p. 610	6. F	p. 617
2. F	p. 614	7. T	p. 617–18
3. T	p. 613	8. T	p. 618
4. F	p. 614–15	9. T	p. 619
5. F	p. 617	10. F	p. 620

Supplementary Exercises

1. b. Widgets: MP(L) = 30.93 AP(L) = 61.86
      Recitals: MP(L) = 50   AP(L) = 50
   c. Widgets: MP(L) = 34.02 AP(L) = 68.04
      Recitals: MP(L) = 50   AP(L) = 50
   d. Opportunity cost of recitals has
      increased 10 percent from .619 widgets
      to .680 widgets;
      PPF: $M = 50[10,000 - W^2/(3600\ K)]$
   e. The new production possibilities frontier
      is never inside the original frontier.

CHAPTER 30

Chapter Review

(1) proprietorship; partnership; corporation;
    limited
(2) stocks; bonds; plowback
(3) are not; more; bonds; meet bond payments
(4) falls; loss; increase
(5) diversification; program; takeover
(6) are not; riskiness
(7) higher; lower; insurance
(8) random walk; today

Definition Quiz

1. e	6. o	11. g
2. i	7. k	12. h
3. l	8. m	13. c
4. n	9. j	14. a
5. b	10. d	15. p

Basic Exercises

1. 16%; 10%; 6.25%; 4%
2. $40; no; the price of the stock adjusts so
   that the dividend yield offers a competitive
   return.
3. Stock price will fall to $25; stock price will
   rise to $64.
4. At the previous price of $40; a dividend of
   $8 offers a 20 percent return, twice that
   available on corporate bonds. The
   increased demand for XYZ stock will
   increase its price now.
5. $80; $80 stock price and $8 dividend imply
   a 10 percent return.

Self-Tests
Test A

1. b p. 632
2. c p. 634
3. d p. 636
4. c p. 637
5. a p. 638–39
6. d p. 638–39
7. b changes in the price of outstanding
       shares mean gains or losses for
       current stockholders.
8. d p. 640

9. a   p. 644–45
10. b   speculators succeed when they buy low (excess supply) and sell high (excess demand).

Test B

1.	T	p. 631	6.	F	p. 644
2.	T	p. 631	7.	F	p. 644
3.	F	p. 634–35	8.	F	p. 644–45
4.	F	p. 638	9.	F	p. 648
5.	F	p. 642	10.	F	p. 647

Supplementary Exercises

1. The prices of bonds for all companies are likely to move together in response to changes in economy-wide interest rates. Stock prices are more heavily influenced by the fortunes and misfortunes of individual companies. As a result, changes in share prices are more likely to differ across companies.

2. The return on the diversified portfolio will be an average of the returns on individual stocks. The diversified portfolio misses the big gainers but minimizes the impact of the worst performers.

CHAPTER 31

Chapter Review

(1) regulate; nationalize
(2) scale; scope; is not; below; above; fixed; marginal
(3) high
(4) fully distributed; marginal; lower
(5) less; demand; marginal; stand alone
(6) less; performance
(7) inefficiency; efficiency

Definition Quiz

1. g		5. l		9. h
2. k		6. f		10. d
3. c		7. a		11. j
4. e		8. b		

Basic Exercise

1.
Output:	30	60	90	120
Average Cost:	27.5¢	16.25¢	12.5¢	10.625¢
Marginal Cost:	5.0¢	5.0¢	5.0¢	5.0¢

2. $6.75 million loss at all levels of output.
3. No; fixed costs are never covered.

Self-Tests

Test A

1. ICC = d
   FCC = c
   FERC = g
   Fed. Res. = a
   SEC = f
2. c   proponents argue that regulation is often necessary to protect consumers.
3. d   p. 657
4. c   p. 657
5. b   p. 660
6. c   p. 661
7. d   p. 663
8. b   p. 666–67
9. a   p. 666
10. a   p. 654

Test B

1.	F	p. 655	6.	T	p. 659
2.	F	p. 657	7.	T	p. 665
3.	F	p. 666	8.	F	p. 663
4.	F	p. 666–67	9.	T	p. 675
5.	T	p. 658	10.	F	p. 672–73

CHAPTER 32

Chapter Review

(1) Sherman; was not
(2) Clayton; price discrimination; tying; interlocking directorates
(3) reason; is not; conduct; was
(4) merger; vertical; horizontal; conglomerate
(5) less; innovation
(6) increasing; reduction; increase
(7) concentration; little

Definition Quiz

1. d	4. i	7. a
2. f	5. g	8. c
3. b	6. h	

Basic Exercise

1. Total Revenue: $2,400,000; $3,093,750; $3,675,000; $4,143,750; $4,500,000; $4,743,750; $4,875,000; $4,893,750
   Marginal Revenue: $37; $31; $25; $19; $13; $7; $1
   Price $33; Output 143,750; Profits $806,250
2. Centerville; Total Revenue: $480,000; $1,125,000; $1,680,000; $2,145,000; $2,520,000; $2,805,000; $3,000,000; $3,105,000
   Marginal Revenue: $43; $37; $31; $25; $19; $13; $7
   Price $30; Quantity 100,000
   Middletown: Total Revenue: $1,920,000; $1,968,750; $1,995,000; $1,998,750; $1,980,000; $1,938,750; $1,875,000; $1,788,750
   Marginal Revenue: $13, $7; $1; –$5; –$11; –$17; –$23
   Price $45; Quantity 43,750
   Profits: $1,031,250
3. Middletown; Centerville; yes

Self-Tests
Test A

1. c   p. 679
2. a   p. 679–80
3. d   p. 680
4. c   p. 681
5. a   p. 682
6. d   p. 682
7. b   p. 682
8. c   each firm produces 10 percent of industry output. Four firms produce 40 percent.
9. b   p. 686
10. d   p. 686

Test B

1. T	p. 676	6. F	p. 689
2. T	p. 679	7. F	p. 686
3. F	p. 680	8. F	p. 684
4. F	p. 682	9. F	p. 687
5. T	p. 684	10. F	p. 689

CHAPTER 33

Chapter Review

(1) direct; indirect; personal income; payroll; corporate
(2) average; marginal; progressive; proportional; regressive
(3) payroll; regressive; do not; zero
(4) sales; property; assessed; market; is not; federalism
(5) equity; horizontal equity; vertical equity; vertical; benefits; benefits
(6) burden; greater; excess burden; does not; smallest
(7) higher; lower; smaller
(8) incidence; flypaper; shifting
(9) demand; supply; inelastic; workers; firms

Definition Quiz

1. b	8. k	15. d
2. p	9. a	16. q
3. i	10. m	17. e
4. n	11. h	18. f
5. r	12. t	19. l
6. g	13. o	
7. s	14. c	

Basic Exercise

2. $42; 50 million
3. $46; 44 million
4. $4; it is less than increase in tax.
5. All are likely to decline.
7. The first demand curve.
8. $50; 48 million; Figure 33–3; Figure 33–3; consumers

Self-Tests
Test A

1. b   p. 695–96
2. c   p. 695–96
3. b   p. 694–95
4. d   p. 696
5. c   p. 696
6. b   p. 702
7. b   p. 702
8. c   p. 703
9. a   zero price elasticity of demand means a vertical demand curve. Any increase

in price from the sales tax induces no change in behavior.

10. d p. 706

Test B

1. F	p. 695	6. F	p. 703
2. F	p. 699	7. F	p. 704
3. T	p. 696	8. T	p. 705
4. T	p. 700	9. F	p. 710
5. T	p. 702	10. F	p. 710–11

Supplementary Exercise

Let s = statutory state marginal tax rate
 f = statutory federal marginal tax rate
 S = additional state taxes (effective marginal rate)
 F = additional federal taxes (effective marginal rate)
 T = total additional taxes (effective marginal rate)

$$T = F + S; F = f(1 - S); \text{ and } S = s(1 - F)$$

Solving for F and S as function of the statutory marginal rates yields $F = f(1 - s)/(1 - sf)$; $S = s(1 - f)/(1 - sf)$; and $T = (s + f - 2sf)/(1 - sf)$. Using these expressions yields the following effective marginal tax rates for Jules and Julia:

	State	Federal	Total
Jules	.0515	.1423	.1938
Julia	.0439	.2677	.3116

Note that Julia's total effective marginal tax rate increases by less than that of Jules.

CHAPTER 34

Chapter Review

(1) externally; decrease; taxes
(2) controls
(3) inefficient; efficient; marginal
(4) can never; price
(5) interest; increasing
(6) interest
(7) discourage; incentive; encourage; incentive; encouraging

Definition Quiz

1. d	4. e	6. a
2. f	5. h	7. g
3. b		

Basic Exercises

1. a. 15 cents; 10 million
   b. falls; rises; no change in short run, declines in long run; shifts up by 5 cents; short run—declines; long run—no change or falls to zero, i.e., some firms leave industry; declines as industry output declines in short- and long-run.
   c. Since the tax is per bag, not per unit of pollution, the pollution control equipment will not reduce a firm's pollution tax.
   d. No. Since the equipment is only 75 percent effective, the total cost of using the equipment (4 cents plus the 1.25-cent emission tax per bag) is greater than the tax of 5 cents per bag.
   e. less than 3.75 cents; more than 5.33 cents
   f. Price rises and industry output declines as at least some high-cost firms leave the industry.

2. Energy: 27.5; 27.3; 27.3; 27.1; 26.6; 26.2; 26.3; 25.8; 25.1; 24.7; 23.8; 22.8; 22.4; 21.5; 21.2; 20.4; 20.0; 19.9; 19.9; 19.6
   Energy use rose during the late 1960s as the relative price of energy fell. The rise in energy prices following 1973 led to a significant decline in energy consumption. Energy consumption per thousand dollars of GNP has continued to decline throughout the 1980s even as relative energy prices have fallen. Patterns of energy consumption per thousand dollars of GNP up to 1981 could be interpreted as a movement along a demand curve in response to changes in price, although the introduction of energy conservation practices, e.g., home insulation, energy-efficient machines and cars, are perhaps best seen as a shift in the demand curve to the left. These shifts mean that as energy prices decline, one would not expect energy consumption to return to earlier levels. The decline in energy consumption during the 1980s at the same

time that relative energy prices were declining reflects the continued introduction of energy-saving practices.

Self-Tests
Test A

1. b p. 719
2. b p. 722
3. a p. 722
4. b p. 725
5. d firms have an incentive to reduce pollution as long as it is cheaper to continue to reduce pollution than to pay the tax.
6. c p. 730
7. b p. 733
8. c p. 735
9. c p. 728
10. d p. 733–34

Test B

1. F p. 716
2. F p. 718
3. F p. 725
4. F as the example of the excise tax in Chapter 33 showed, an increase in price will reduce demand and hence the quantity of output and pollution.
5. F p. 719
6. F p. 735
7. F p. 732
8. F p. 730
9. T p. 733
10. T p. 735

Supplementary Exercises

2. a. MC = 15.
   MR = 65 − .05Q (P = 65 − .025Q; TR = 65Q − .025Q²).
   Set MC = MR to solve for profit maximizing output: 15 = 65 − .05Q; Q = 1000; P = 40¢; Profit = 25¢ on each of 1000 million bags or $250 million.

b. If price rises by 5¢, quantity demanded will decline to 800 million bags. At price of 45¢, profit is 25¢ a bag or $200 million.
   Set MC = MR to determine profit maximizing level of output: 20 = 65 − .05Q; Q = 900; P = 42.5¢; profits = 22.5¢ a bag or $202.5 million.

c. Long run equilibrium price equals minimum average cost = 15¢.
   Market quantity = 2000 million bags; 200 firms producing 10 million bags each.

d. Short run: For representative firm AC = .4(Q − 10)² + 20.
   TC = .4Q³ − 8Q² + 60Q.
   MC = 1.2Q² − 16Q + 60.
   As each firm supplies 1/200 of the market, we can find the short-run profit maximizing position of each firm by setting MC equal to price.

   MC = 65 − .025(Q × 200), or

   1.2Q² − 16Q + 60 = 65 − 5Q.

   The mathematics of solving this equation for Q are a bit cumbersome. Rounding off, firm output = 9.6 million bags; industry output = 1920 million bags; and price = 17¢. Note that price is now less than average cost.
   Long run: Some firms leave in response to short-run losses. Long-run equilibrium occurs where remaining firms produce at minimum average cost. Price = 20¢; market demand = 1800; each of 180 firms produce 10 million bags.

The conditions in this problem—marginal cost for the monopolist equal to the minimum average cost of competitive firms and the same demand curve under either market structure—imply the following: 1) by restricting output, the monopolist creates less pollution than the perfectly competitive industry; 2) the monopolist is unable to pass on the full extent of the pollution tax; and 3) in long-run equilibrium under perfect competition, consumers pay all of the pollution tax.

CHAPTER 35

Chapter Review

(1) productivity; revenue
(2) negative; more; positive; higher; below; intersection
(3) discounting; fewer; lower; negatively
(4) is not
(5) all; no
(6) most; part; is
(7) higher; equal; low
(8) increase; increase; more
(9) greater; greater; innovation; greater

Definition Quiz

1. g	6. o	11. i
2. c	7. e	12. a
3. j	8. f	13. n
4. m	9. l	14. h
5. d	10. k	

Basic Exercise

1. Economic profit = Total revenue – opportunity cost of labor – cost of other inputs; Economic profit = $400 – ($8 × 40) – $30 = $400 – $350 = $50.
2. $30; The rent for the sunny plot should reflect the difference in the cost of production as compared to the marginal plot.
3. If the owner of the sunny plot tried charging a rent that exceeded the $30 difference in production costs, Dionne would make a greater profit by growing her flowers on the marginal plot. With a rent of $30 for the sunny plot she would be indifferent about using either plot.

Self-Tests

Test A

1. c p. 742
2. c p. 741–42
3. b p. 746
4. d p. 744
5. a p. 751
6. b p. 751
7. c p. 753–54
8. b p. 755
9. b as seen in Chapter 6, nominal interest rates already include an estimate of future inflation. See also page 758.
10. a p. 759

Test B

1. F	p. 742	6. T	p. 755
2. T	p. 744	7. F	p. 751
3. T	p. 746	8. F	p. 751
4. F	p. 744	9. T	p. 755
5. F	p. 752	10. F	p. 757–59

Appendix

Definition Quiz: Appendix

1. b   2. a

Basic Exercise: Appendix

1. $4000; $1,818.18; $2,066.12; 3,884.30; –$115.70
2. cost; no
3. $4000; $1,904.76; $2,267.57; $4,172.33; $172.33
4. present value of returns; yes
5. 5 percent: $200; $4,200; $2,200; $110; $2,310
   10 percent: $400; $4,400; $2,400; $240; $2,640
6. 5 percent: $1800; $90; $4,390; $190
   10 percent: $1600; $160; $4,260; –$140

CHAPTER 36

Chapter Review

(1) leisure; more; decrease; income
(2) more; substitution; increases; offset; slope; position
(3) income; demand; higher
(4) does; do not
(5) minimum; higher; decrease; supply
(6) unskilled; unions; National Labor Relations; Taft-Hartley
(7) monopolist; demand; right
(8) monopsonist; wages; lower; higher; two; bilateral
(9) collective bargaining; mediation; arbitration; mediator; arbitrator

Definition Quiz

1. c	6. q	11. r
2. h	7. k	12. j
3. l	8. f	13. e
4. b	9. m	14. n
5. d	10. a	15. o
		16. i

Basic Exercise

1. 60; 55; 50; 45; 40; 35; 30; 25; 20; 15
2. $2400; $2200; $2000; $1800; $1600; $1400; $1200; $1000; $800; $600
3. 7
4. Total profits with 7 workers: $4,900
   (315 × $40) – (7 × $1100)
   Total profits with 6 workers: $4,800
   (285 × $40) – (6 × $1100)
   Total profits with 8 workers: $4,800
   (340 × $40) – (8 × $1100)
5. $1000; 800; 8; $5600; if 7 workers, profits = $5600 as MRP = wage for eighth worker.
6. a. $1800
   b. 900 workers
   c. $1400 and 600 workers, or $1200 and 700 workers

Self-Tests

Test A

1. d p. 766
2. b p. 769–70
3. a p. 769
4. b p. 767
5. b the marginal physical product of labor (MPP$_L$) derives from the production function for schmoos. An increase in employment that comes from an increase in the demand for schmoos will lead to a movement along the MPP$_L$ schedule, not a shift in the schedule.
6. c p. 771
7. c p. 775
8. a p. 776
9. d p. 774
10. d; a; e; f; b; c; f

Test B

1. T p. 768
2. T p. 768

3. F p. 766–67
4. F a change in wages leads to a movement along the supply curve.
5. F p. 773–74
6. F p. 781, a union is a monopolist, the sole supplier of labor. A monopsonist is the sole buyer of something.
7. F p. 781
8. F p. 778–79
9. F p. 780
10. T p. 783

Appendix

Definition Quiz: Appendix

1. b

Basic Exercise: Appendix

1. $1000; 8; no; Tony is a monopsonist. The marginal cost of labor is greater than average wages for a monopsonist when the supply of labor curve has a positive shape.
2. greater
   Total labor cost: $300; $800; $1500; $2,400; $3,500; $4,800; $6,300; $8,000; $9,900; $12,000
   Marginal labor cost: $300; $500; $700; $900; $1,100; $1,300; $1,500; $1,700; $1,900; $2,100
3. (no answer shown)
4. 6 workers
5. $800
6. $6,600 = $40 × 285 – 6 × $800. The competitive solution, hiring 8 workers at $1,000, would have produced profits of only $5,600 ($40 × 340 – 8 × $1,000).
7. Both wages and employment would increase. Tony would hire 7 workers at $1100 a month. The "high" minimum wage increases employment because Tony is a monopsonist. The minimum wage changes Tony's marginal cost of labor schedule.
8. No. If the union had more than 7 workers, it might want a lower wage to increase employment. If the union had 7 or fewer workers, it might be able to extract a higher wage by bargaining for some of Tony's profits.

CHAPTER 37

Chapter Review

(1) $12,700 absolute; relative
(2) Lorenz; zero; 45°; positive; below; very little
(3) 44; less than 5
(4) efficiency
(5) marginal; decrease
(6) decrease; break-even; negative; small
(7) different; are not; overstate; employers

Definition Quiz

1. a	4. g	7. e
2. c	5. b	8. j
3. i	6. f	9. h

Basic Exercise

1. 12,000; 12,339; 13,460; 13,524; 12,024; 12,959; 13,128; 14,824; 17,437; 18,408
3. Col. 4: 339; 1,121; 64; −1,500; 935; 169; 1,696; 2,613; 971
   Col. 5: 261; 4,779; 1,235; 1,501; 1,265; 81; 1,254; 3,537; 879
   Col. 6: 43.5; 81.0; 95.0; 150,100.0; 57.5; 32.5; 42.5; 57.5; 47.5
   The marginal tax rates in column 6 should be equivalent to the slopes of the line segments you graphed in Figure 37–1. In 1989 as income increased above $21,200, income plus social security taxes would have taken 22.51 percent of increases in income.

Self-Tests
Test A

1. b   p. 796
2. d   p. 799
3. a   p. 800
4. c   even in the absence of economic discrimination, incomes will differ. See pages 800–801.
5. c   p. 795
6. d   with a 50 percent tax rate, $4,000 in wages reduces benefits by $2,000 for total net income of $8,000.
7. a   reducing the tax rate raises costs which can only be offset by reducing the minimum guarantee.
8. d   p. 801–802
9. a   differences in schooling might reflect discrimination in access to schooling.
10. b   p. 803

Test B

1. T   in principle, growth can push all incomes past an absolute standard. Relative standards will increase with economic growth.
2. F   p. 795
3. F   p. 797
4. T   p. 799
5. T   p. 799
6. F   p. 802
7. T   p. 803
8. F   p. 797
9. T   p. 800
10. F   p. 811

CHAPTER 38

Chapter Review

(1) exponential
(2) inventiveness; entrepreneurship; work ethic; investment; research; development; embodied; disembodied
(3) opportunity; consumption; saving
(4) has not; increase; higher
(5) less (footnote: I; C; C; IM) difficult
(6) death; inexpensive; decrease
(7) brain drain; World

Definition Quiz

1. j	4. c	7. d
2. b	5. g	8. h
3. i	6. a	9. f

Basic Exercises

Brazil 286; 2,020
Canada 393; 15, 160
China 310; 290
Egypt 34; 680
Great Britain 593; 10,420

Indonesia 77; 450
Japan 1,924; 15,760
Kenya 7; 330
Korea 113; 2,690
Mexico 150; 1,830
Norway 72; 17,190
Poland 73; 1,930
West Germany 881; 14,400

Source: World Bank, World Development Report, 1989,
Table 1.

Self-Tests

Test A

1. d   p. 818
2. d   p. 820
3. c   p. 824
4. c   p. 824
5. a   p. 825
6. b   p. 830–31
7. b   p. 835
8. b   p. 832–33
9. c   although countries will want to be careful that there is mutual gain. See discussion on page 833.
10. b   as explained in Chapter 19, the International Monetary Fund helps developed and developing countries with exchange rates and balance of payments issues.

Test B

1. F   GNP per capita will decrease whenever the growth rate of population exceeds the growth rate of total GNP.
2. F   p. 821–22
3. F   p. 828
4. T   p. 823
5. T   p. 825
6. F   p. 826
7. F   p. 830
8. F   p. 830–31
9. T   p. 819
10. T   p. 835–36
11. F   p. 837
12. F   p. 837
13. F   p. 832–38
14. F   p. 839

Supplementary Exercises

3. 1,110 years, 4 days; 36 years, 267 days

CHAPTER 39

Chapter Review

(1) historical materialism; economic
(2) was not; was not
(3) labor time; is not; surplus value; labor
(4) adopted; the same; long
(5) labor; surplus value
(6) did not; alienation; alienation
(7) cycles; supply; demand; Say's

Definition Quiz

1. d   3. a   5. b
2. f   4. e   6. g

Self-Tests

Test A

1. c   p. 843   6. d   p. 847
2. b   p. 845   7. a   p. 850
3. d   p. 845   8. b   p. 850
4. c   p. 846   9. c   p. 849
5. d   p. 846   10. c   p. 852

Test B

1. F   p. 843   6. F   p. 849
2. F   p. 843   7. T   p. 849
3. T   p. 845   8. F   p. 847
4. T   p. 847   9. T   p. 847
5. F   p. 846   10. F   p. 852

CHAPTER 40

Chapter Review

(1) markets; planning
(2) capitalism; socialism
(3) is not; socialist; markets
(4) consumers; planners; freedom; prices; market; planned; profit; about the same; less; planned
(5) socialist; Five; One; material
(6) be conservative; little; high; low
(7) rural; investment; consumption
(8) planned; state; less; industrial
(9) foreign; industrial planning; more; less

Definition Quiz

1. c	4. a	6. g
2. f	5. e	7. b
3. d		

Self-Tests

Test A

1. c   p. 857
2. a   p. 860
3. b   p. 861
4. c   p. 865; d p. 867; b p. 871; a p. 868
5. d   p. 866
6. b   p. 865
7. b   p. 865
8. c   p. 869
9. d   p. 872-73
10. d   p. 872

Test B

1. F	p. 857	6. F	p. 863
2. F	p. 858	7. T	p. 864
3. T	p. 860	8. F	p. 868
4. T	p. 860	9. F	p. 870
5. T	p. 860	10. F	p. 871

CHAPTER 41

Chapter Review

(1) philosophy; freedom; less
(2) laissez-faire; smaller; monopolies; externalities; are often
(3) power; do not; planning; technocrats; their own self-interest; growth; opportunities for their own advancement
(4) private; public; quality
(5) disagree; is not; disagree; opportunity cost; takeover
(6) ahistorical; given; ruling (capitalist) classes; efficiency; equality; power; quality; alienation; naive; ruling classes; power; bribe
(7) is; agree; rhetoric
(8) participatory; decentralized

Definition Quiz

1. b   2. d   3. c

Self-Tests

Test A

1. libertarians: c; Galbraith: a, b, e, f; Radical: a, b, d, e, f   p. 877-89
2. c   p. 879
3. b   p. 883
4. Solow: disagree, agree, disagree; Galbraith: agree, disagree, agree   p. 883-88
5. b   p. 886
6. d   p. 887-88
7. b   p. 890-91

Test B

1. T   p. 878
2. T   p. 878
3. T   p. 882
4. F   p. 883
5. T   p. 883-84
6. F   p. 885
7. T   p. 890
8. F   p. 888
9. F   p. 890
10. F   an increase in military spending shifts the expenditure schedule and aggregate demand curve but so would increases in spending on schools, medical care and environmental clean up.